THE AMERICAN CLASS STRUCTURE
A new synthesis

The Dorsey Series in Sociology

Advisory Editor
Robin M. Williams, Jr.
Cornell University

Consulting Editor
Charles M. Bonjean
The University of Texas at Austin

THE AMERICAN CLASS STRUCTURE

A new synthesis

Dennis Gilbert
Hamilton College

Joseph A. Kahl
Cornell University

1982
THE DORSEY PRESS
Homewood, Illinois 60430

Japanese translation of first edition by Kunio Inamoto
(Tokyo: Jiji-Tsushinsha, 1958)

ISBN 0-256-02678-5
Library of Congress Catalog Card No. 81–70947
Printed in the United States of America

1 2 3 4 5 6 7 8 9 0 ML 9 8 7 6 5 4 3 2

Preface

The first edition of this book was published in 1957. The present revised edition is not merely an updated version of the original but rather a new book, rewritten from beginning to end, although it includes a few sections repeated from the original that analyze studies that are still relevant. Twenty-five years of hiatus requires more than some fresh statistics.

We have tried to keep certain features of the original book that proved popular with readers. *The American Class Structure* was never intended to be an encyclopedic survey of all stratification research, nor was it a creative exercise in stratification theory. Instead, it drew a simple organizing framework from classical theory and singled out the most essential empirical studies of social stratification in the contemporary United States for detailed critical examination. The book focused on two questions about those studies: what were the main conclusions? By what procedures were those conclusions reached? This thrust helped convey important factual information, a perspective for interpreting that information, and an understanding of the research process that underlies the conclusions of social scientists. By concentrating on a few studies of exemplary value, the book avoided intellectual indigestion and helped students gain a sense of participation in the search for knowledge. New questions and new answers are constantly arising, so the process of research is as important as are momentary con-

vii

clusions. The present edition keeps the same goals but brings theory and results forward into the 1980s.

Coherence is given to our interpretation of the American class system through a conceptual scheme that was chosen on utilitarian grounds: it starts with the main theorists of the field, Marx and Weber, and isolates nine "variables" that can be studied one by one and then combined to show major patterns. The "structure" in the title of the book refers to those patterns of convergence among the variables that create social classes. The patterns are tendencies, "ideal types," never fully realized in any one situation but discernable when one steps back from detail to think about underlying forces. We constantly emphasize the influence of economic forces on social and political consequences but do not neglect important points of feedback where social facts shape economic trends.

In contrast to some other approaches, we avoid the temptation to become theoretical imperialists: we do not try to use everything possible as a key variable of stratification, including differences among age, sex, and ethnic groups. Instead, we emphasize the core of socioeconomic stratification and then sometimes incorporate aspects of sex or ethnic influences when they intervene to affect the way stratification operates in practice.

We hope that we will serve the same two audiences that found the earlier version useful: undergraduate students studying the subject for the first time and more advanced students in research-oriented seminars who seek a quick review of the major literature on the United States as preparation for more careful study of selected themes, perhaps in a comparative perspective. For the benefit of both groups, we have kept the book as concise as possible so that other materials can be added by the instructor, either from one of the convenient readers that collects research articles or from monographic studies that pursue one or another aspect in depth.

Our approach to bibliography follows from our purposes: instead of being exhaustive, we are highly selective. We refer in the body of the text to the classic studies which have had major influence on the research tradition and then often add a recent article or two which in turn contains references to a wide range of contemporary investigation. The seminar student can use the latter as convenient guides to current work. At the end of each chapter, we suggest a few readings that explore big issues about the United States and occasionally a few more that allow pointed comparisons with other countries.

Among the many people who helped shape the first edition, two names deserve repetition here since their influence continues in the present text: Peter H. Rossi, who shared with Kahl the design and teaching of the first course in social stratification offered in Harvard College, which was the precursor to the first edition; and Kingsley

Davis, who contributed exceptional services as editor that clarified the construction of the text.

The present edition is privileged to have two godfathers who have read, criticized, and stimulated us at every turn: Robin M. Williams, Jr., the model of what a helpful colleague is imagined to be but rarely is, and Lee Rainwater, long-time friend whose commitment to practical knowledge inspires emulation.

Other friends, colleagues, and students who have given their time and help include Richard Alba, Charles M. Bonjean, Steven B. Caldwell, Denise DiGregorio, Ted Eismeier, Kenneth Hodges, Christopher Jencks, Marie Kaplan, Susan J. Mueller, and David Paris.

Typing, editorial, and bibliographic assistance was provided with grace and accuracy under pressure by Debbie Barnes, Mary Ann Beech, and Laurie Moses.

Dennis Gilbert
Joseph A. Kahl

Contents

Karl Marx. Max Weber. Nine variables. The variables as a system. What are social classes?

W. Lloyd Warner: Prestige classes in Yankee City. Prestige class as a concept. Are there six classes? Three methods of prestige placement. Coleman and Rainwater: Class structure of the metropolis. Is the American class structure changing? Prestige of occupations. International comparisons. Duncan's socioeconomic index for occupations. Occupations and social classes. The perception of rank and strata.

The Lynds: Middletown. Middletown revisited. Middletown's new classes. Industrialization and the transformation of the national class structure. The new upper class. The new working class. The new middle class. National occupational system. Recent occupational change and the class structure.

The income parade. Lessons from the parade. The distribution of income. Taxes and transfers: The government as Robin Hood? How many poor? Income distribution in international perspective. Trends in the distribution of income: 1929 to 2000. The distribution of wealth. Trends in the concentration of wealth. Sources of income inequality. Occupation and income. Marxist class categories and income. The dual labor market. Social class and life chances. Health and social class.

gan. Transfers in comparative perspective. Is there a permanent underclass? Conclusions: Poverty and inequality.

List of tables

List of figures

The dimensions of class

All communities divide themselves into the few and the many. The first are the rich and well-borne, the other the mass of the people. . . . The people are turbulent and changing; they seldom judge or determine right. . . . Give, therefore, to the first class a distinct, permanent share in the government. They will check the unsteadiness of the second, and, as they cannot receive any advantage by a change, they therefore will ever maintain good government.

Alexander Hamilton (1780)

1

Thoughtful observers have recognized the importance of social classes since the beginnings of Western philosophy. They knew that some individuals and families had more money or more influence or more prestige than their neighbors. And the philosophers realized that the differences were more than personal or even familial, for the pattern of inequalities tended to congeal into strata of families who shared similar positions. These social strata or classes divided society into a hierarchy; each stratum had interests or goals in common with equals but different from, and often conflicting with, those of groups above or below them. Finally, it was noted that many of the political activities of people in society flowed from their class interests. As Hamilton said, the rich sought social stability to preserve their advantages, but the poor worked for social change that would bring them a larger share of the world's rewards.

This book is an analysis of the class structure of the United States today. It examines the distribution of income, prestige, power, and other stratification variables among the different classes in the country. It will point out the ways in which the variables react upon one another; for instance, how a person's income affects beliefs about social policy or how one's job affects the choice of friends or spouse. And it will explore the question of movement from one class to another; for a society can have classes and still permit individuals to rise or fall among them.

In order to talk about a complex system and show how one part of it influences another, we must have a separate concept or word for each main aspect and a special method for estimating or measuring it. It is helpful to start the analysis by examining significant theories of stratification to identify the major facets of the subject as a guide to concept formation. We will look at the theories propounded by Karl Marx and Max Weber, whose work established the intellectual framework that has been used by most subsequent scholars. (See the Suggested Readings at the end of the chapter for other key theorists.)

KARL MARX

Although the discussion of stratification goes back to ancient philosophy, modern attempts to formulate a systematic theory of class differences began with the work of Karl Marx in the 19th century; most subsequent theorizing has represented an attempt either to reformulate or to refute his ideas. Marx, who was born in the wake of the French Revolution and lived in the midst of the Industrial Revolution, emphasized the study of social class as the key to an understanding of the turbulent events of his own day. His studies of economics, history, and philosophy convinced him that societies are mainly shaped by their economic organization and that social classes form the link between economic facts and social facts. He also concluded that fundamental social change is the product of conflict between classes. Thus, in Marx's view an understanding of classes is basic to comprehension of how societies function and also how they are transformed.[1]

In Marx's work, social classes are defined by their distinctive relationships to the means of production. Taking this approach, capitalists, or the bourgeoisie, are a class consisting of the owners of the means of production, such as mines or factories. Likewise, workers, or the proletariat, are a class consisting of those who must sell their labor power to the owners of the means of production in order to earn a wage and stay alive. Marx maintained that in modern, capitalist society, each of these two basic classes tends toward an internal homogeneity that obliterates differences within them. Minor businessmen lose out in competition with big ones, creating a smaller bourgeoisie of monopoly capitalists. In a parallel fashion, machines get more sophisticated and do the work that used to be done by skilled workers, so gradations within the proletariat fade in significance. But notice that these are statements about trends, about long-run tendencies. At any given moment, distinctions within each class that stem from historical residues—even from markedly different earlier epochs—may influence the situation in important ways that shape behavior. Sometimes Marx called these subdivisions *fractions* of a class, and sometimes he seemed to consider them as momentarily separate classes. Generally his descriptions of particular situations in his writings as a journalist and pamphleteer show more complexity in economic and political groupings than do his writings as a theorist of history analyzing long-term trends.

---

[1] This perspective stressed the notion that circumstances create ideas more than the other way around and was labeled "the materialist conception of history"; it was the opposite of the prevailing view of his epoch (especially in Germany) which assumed that the evolution of political, religious, and philosophical ideas was the force behind historical change.

Why did Marx look to production for the basis of social classes? In the most general sense, because he regarded production as the center of social life. He reasoned that people must produce in order to survive, and they must cooperate in order to produce. The individual's place in society, his relationships to others, and his outlook on life are shaped by his or her work experience. More specifically, those who occupy a similar role in production are likely to share economic and political interests which bring them into conflict with other participants in production. Capitalists, for instance, reap profit (in Marx's terms *expropriate surplus*) by paying their workers less than the resale value of what they produce. Therefore, capitalists share an interest in holding wages down and resisting legislation which would reinforce the power of unions to press their demands on employers.

From a Marxist perspective, the manner in which production takes place (that is, the application of technology to nature) and the class and property relationships which develop in the course of production are the most fundamental aspects of any society. Together they constitute what Marx called the *mode of production*. Societies with similar modes of production ought to be similar in other significant respects and should therefore be studied together. Marx's analysis of European history after the fall of Rome distinguished three modes of production which he saw as successive stages of societal development: *feudalism*, the locally based agrarian society of the Middle Ages, in which a small, land-owning aristocracy in each district exploited the labor of a peasant majority; *capitalism*, the emerging commercial and industrial order of Marx's own lifetime, already international in scope and characterized by the dominance of the owners of industry over the mass of industrial workers; and *socialism*, the technologically advanced, classless society of the future, in which all productive property would be held in common.

Unlike many later writers who believed that the level of technology by itself was the crucial determinant of social organization, Marx emphasized that modes of production entail patterns of both technology and social relations and that each can vary independently of the other. An agrarian society in which each producer cultivated land that he owned himself would not represent a feudal mode of production. Likewise, Marx viewed socialism as a new mode of production which could be built on the industrial technology already developed under the capitalist mode of production.

Marx regarded the mode of production as the main determinant of a society's *superstructure* of social and political institutions and ideas. He used the concept of superstructure to answer an old question: How do privileged minorities maintain their positions and contain the potential resistance of exploited majorities? His reply was that the class which controls the means of production typically controls the means of compulsion and persuasion, the superstructure. He observed that in feudal times, military and political power was monopolized by the landowners; with the rise of modern capitalism political power was captured by the bourgeoisie when they gained control of the national government. In each case, the privileged class could use the power of the state to protect its own interests. For instance, in Marx's own time the judicial, legislative, and police authority of European governments dominated by the bourgeoisie was employed to crush the early labor movement, a pattern that was repeated a little later in the United States. As Marx expressed it in the *Communist Manifesto* in 1848: "The executive of the modern State is but a committee for managing the common affairs of the whole bourgeoisie" (Marx 1979: 475).

But Marx did not believe that class systems rested on pure compulsion. He allowed for the persuasive influence of ideas. It was in this regard that Marx made one of his most significant contributions to social science, the concept of *ideology*. Marx argued that human consciousness is a social product. It develops out of our experience of cooperating with others to produce and to sustain social life. However, social experience is not homogeneous, especially in a society which is divided into classes. The peasant does not have the same experience as the landlord and therefore develops a distinct outlook. One important feature of this differentiation of class outlooks is the tendency for members of each group to regard their own particular class interests as the true interests of the whole society. What makes this significant is that one class has superior capacity to impose its self-serving ideas on other classes. The class which dominates production, Marx argued, also controls the institutions which produce and disseminate ideas, such as schools, mass media, churches, and courts. As a result, the viewpoint of the dominant class pervades thinking in areas as diverse as the laws of family life and property, theories of political democracy, notions of economic rationality, and even conceptions of the afterlife. In Marx's words, "the ideas of the ruling class are in every epoch the ruling ideas" (Marx 1979: 172). In extreme situations, ideology can convince slaves that they ought to be obedient to their masters, or poor workers that their true reward will eventually come to them in heaven.

Marx maintained, then, that the ruling class had powerful political and ideological means to support the established order. Nonetheless, he regarded class societies as intrinsically unstable. In a famous passage from the *Communist Manifesto* he observed in 1848 (Marx 1979: 473–74):

> The history of all hitherto existing society is the history of class struggles.
>
> Freeman and slave, patrician and plebeian, lord and serf, guild-master and journeyman, in a word, oppressor and oppressed stood in

constant opposition to one another, carried on an uninterrupted, now hidden, now open fight, a fight that each time ended either in a revolutionary reconstitution of society at large, or in the common ruin of the contending classes.

In the earlier epochs of history, we find almost everywhere a complicated arrangement of society into various orders, a manifold gradation of social rank. In ancient Rome, we have patricians, knights, plebeians, slaves; in the Middle Ages, feudal lords, vassals, guild-masters, journeymen, apprentices, serfs; in almost all of these classes, again, subordinate gradations. . . .

Our epoch, the epoch of the bourgeoisie, possesses, however, this distinctive feature: it has simplified the class antagonisms. Society as a whole is more and more splitting up into two great hostile camps, into two great classes directly facing each other: Bourgeoisie and Proletariat.

As these lines suggest, Marx saw class struggle as the basic source of social change. He coupled class conflict to economic change, arguing that the development of new means of production implied the emergence of new classes and class relationships. The most serious political conflicts develop when the interests of a rising class clash with those of an established ruling class. Class struggles of this sort can produce a "revolutionary reconstitution of society." Notice that each epoch creates within itself the growth of a new class that eventually seizes power and creates a new epoch; thus change is explained by an internal dynamic that Marx called *the dialectic*.

Two eras of transformation through class conflict held particular fascination for Marx. One was the transition from feudalism to modern capitalism in Europe, a process in which he assigned the bourgeoisie (the urban capitalist class) "a most revolutionary part" (Marx 1979: 475). Into a previously stable agrarian society, the bourgeoisie introduced a stream of technological innovations, an accelerating expansion of production and trade, and radically new forms of labor relations. These changes were resisted by the feudal landlords who felt their own interests threatened by those of the bourgeoisie. The result was a series of political conflicts (the French Revolution was the most dramatic instance) through which the European bourgeoisie wrested political power from the landed aristocracy.

Marx believed that a second, analogous era of transformation was beginning during his own lifetime. The capitalist mode of production had created a new social class, the urban working class, or proletariat, with interests directly opposed to those of the bourgeoisie. This conflict of interests arose, not simply from the struggle over wages between capital and labor, but from the essential character of capitalist production and society. The capitalist economy was inherently unstable and subject to periodic depressions with massive unemployment. These economic crises heightened awareness of long-term trends separating rich from poor. Furthermore, capitalism's blind dependence on market mechanisms built on individual greed created an alienated existence for most members of society. Marx was convinced that only under socialism, with the means of production communally controlled, could these conditions be overcome.

The situation of the proletarian majority made it capitalism's most deprived and alienated victim and therefore the potential spearhead of a socialist revolution. However, in Marx's view the objective situation of a class does not automatically cause its members to recognize their shared class interests and the need for militant class action—in short, to develop *class consciousness* leading toward political revolt. Some of Marx's most fruitful sociological work, to which we will return in Chapter 9, is devoted to precisely this problem. He asked: What intrinsic tendencies of capitalist society are most likely to produce a class-conscious proletariat? Among the factors he isolated were the stark simplification of the class order in the course of capitalist development, the concentration of large masses of workers in the new industrial towns, the deprivations of working-class people exacerbated by the inherent instability of the capitalist economy, and the sophistication gained by the proletariat through participation in working-class organizations such as labor unions and mass parties.

What, in sum, can be said of Marx's contribution to stratification theory? His recognition of the economic basis of class systems was a crucial insight. His theory of ideology and his conception of the connection between social classes and political processes, although oversimple as stated, proved a fruitful starting point for modern research. As for his conception of change, a series of 20th-century revolutions—including those in Mexico (1910), Russia (1917), and China (1949)—have established the significance of class conflict for radical social transformation. However, revolutions have typically occurred in peasant societies during early stages of industrialization under foreign influence and not in the advanced industrial countries where Marx anticipated them. In the industrial countries, the proletariat used labor unions and mass political parties to defend its interests, thus rechanneling the forces of class conflict into the legal procedures of parliamentary politics; it successfully resisted impoverishment. A century after his death, it is apparent that Marx was a better sociologist than he was a prophet: he identified many of the central processes of capitalist society, but he was unable to foresee all the consequences of their unfolding, and his own vision of a humane socialist future has yet to be actualized in the existing socialist countries.

MAX WEBER

The great German sociologist Max Weber, who wrote in the early years of the 20th century, was interested in many of the same problems that had fascinated Marx—among them, the origins of capitalism, the role of ideology, and the relationship between social structure and economic processes. Weber frequently benefited from Marx's work, even while reaching rather different conclusions. In the field of stratification, his special contributions were (1) to introduce a conceptual clarity which was often lacking in Marx's references to social classes, and (2) to highlight those situations where ideology, particularly religion, made an independent contribution to historical change.

Weber made a crucial distinction between two orders of stratification: *class* and *status*. The first term had roughly the same meaning for both Weber and Marx. It refers to groupings of people according to their economic position. Class situation or membership is defined by the economic opportunities an individual has in the labor, commodity, and credit markets. They determine *life chances*, a term Weber used to emphasize those fundamental aspects of an individual's future possibilities that are shaped by class membership, from the infant's chances for decent nutrition to the adult's opportunities for worldly success.

Following Marx, Weber observed that the most important class distinction is between those who own property and those who do not. However, he noted that many significant distinctions can be made within these two categories. Among the propertied elite, for example, those who support themselves with stocks, bonds, and other securities (rentiers) are in a different class situation from those who live by owning and operating businesses (entrepreneurs). The propertyless can be differentiated on the basis of the occupational skills which they bring to the marketplace: the life chances of an unskilled worker are vastly different from those of a trained engineer.

A class, then, becomes a group of people who share the same economically shaped life chances. Notice that this way of defining a class does not imply that the individuals in it are necessarily aware of their common situation. It simply defines a statistical category of people who are, from the point of view of the market, similar to each other. Only under certain circumstances do they become aware of their common fate, begin to think of each other as equals, and develop institutions of joint action to further their interests—in Weber's words, become a *community*.

By contrast, wrote Weber (1946:186–193):

> Status groups are normally communities. They are, however, often of an amorphous kind. In contrast to the purely economically determined "class situation," we wish to designate as "status situation" every typical component of the life fate of men that is determined by a specific, positive or negative, social estimation of honor. . . .
>
> In content, status honor is normally expressed by the fact that above all else a specific style of life can be expected from all those who wish to

belong to the circle. Linked with this expectation are restrictions on "social" intercourse (that is, intercourse which is not subservient to economic or any other of business's "functional" purposes). These restrictions may confine normal marriages to within the status circle and may lead to complete endogamous closure. . . .

Of course, material monopolies provide the most effective motives for the exclusiveness of a status group. . . . With an increased inclosure of the status group, the conventional preferential opportunities for special employment grow into a legal monopoly of special offices for the members. . . .

With some over-simplification, one might thus say that "classes" are stratified according to their relations to the production and acquisition of goods; whereas "status groups" are stratified according to the principles of their consumption of goods as represented by special "styles of life."

In those passages Weber specified many of the interrelations between class and status, between economy and society. Because of class position, a person earns a certain income. That income permits a certain lifestyle, and people soon make friends with others who live the same way. As they interact with one another, they begin to conceive of themselves as a special type of people. They restrict interaction with outsiders who seem too different (they may be too poor, too uneducated, too clumsy to live graciously enough for acceptance as worthy companions). Marriage partners are chosen from similar groups, for once people follow a certain style of life, they find it difficult to be comfortable with people who live differently. Thus the status group becomes an ingrown circle. It earns a position in the local community that entitles its members to social honor or prestige from inferiors.

Status groups develop the conventions or customs of the community. Through time they evolve appropriate ways of dressing, of eating, of living that are somewhat different from the ways of other groups and get expressed as moral judgments reflecting abstract principles of value which separate "good" from "bad." The application of these principles to individuals establishes rankings of social honor or prestige. These distinctions often react back on the market place; in order to preserve their advantages, high-status groups attempt to monopolize those goods which symbolize their style of life—they pass consumption laws prohibiting the lower orders from wearing lace, or they band together to keep Jews or blacks out of prestigious country clubs or universities. (Weber regarded invidious distinctions among ethnic groups as a type of status stratification.)

A status order tends to restrict the freedom of the market, not only by its monopolization of certain types of consumption goods, but also by its monopolization of the opportunities to earn money. If they can get the power, status groups often restrict entry into the more lucrative professions or trades, for example, giving the son of a bricklayer more chance of gaining a union card than the son of a farmer. And even without such formal restriction, birth into a high-status family gives children advantages of education and of personal contacts that eventually help careers. Weber indicates that in its pure form the class or economic order is universalistic and impersonal; it recognizes no status distinctions and operates solely on the basis of competitive skill. But the status order is exactly the opposite; it is based on particularistic distinctions among types of persons that make some "better" than others, and thus it tends to restrict freedom of competition in both production and consumption.

Weber did not view the status order as an automatic reflection of the class order, a superstructure. In fact, there are important ways in which class phenomena are subject to the influence of status phenomena. However, he said that in the long run the status order is created by the class order; consumption, after all, is based on production. For example, although elite society reacts against the status claims of newly rich social climbers, it readily accepts their descendants if they have properly cultivated the conventions of the higher-status group. On another level, the appearance of classes based on new sources of wealth—for instance, the emergence of an industrial bourgeoisie in Europe and America in the 19th century—signals a future restructuring of the status order as a whole.

Weber, like Marx, was interested in the relationship between class and status structures and political power. In fact, it would be accurate to say that for both men stratification was essentially a political topic. But Weber was highly skeptical of the implication in Marx's work that all political phenomena could be traced back directly to class. For instance, he suggested that the institutions of the modern, bureaucratic state exercise an influence on society that is not reducible to the control exercised by a single class. (In *The Eighteenth Brumaire*, Marx [1979: 594–617] himself reluctantly adopted this view for a special circumstance, but not Weber's corollary that a socialist state might be grimly similar to a capitalist state, reflecting bureaucratic domination of society.)

Weber opposed the "pseudo-scientific operation" of Marxist writers of his day who assumed an automatic link between class position and class consciousness (Weber 1946: 184). A common economic situation can and sometimes does lead to an awareness of shared class interests and a willingness to engage in militant class action, but it need not. Indeed, the very notion of class interest was highly ambiguous for Weber. Given his flexible conception of class, based on economic life chances, he realized that modern society has several classes rather than just two and that they are continually changing. Furthermore, individuals can perceive their own situation and its convergence with that of other persons in a variety of ways that cannot be neatly divided into an accurate or "true" versus an inaccurate or "false" consciousness of interest. He noted that the development of class consciousness is a complex process contingent on numerous factors (some of them already noted by Marx), including the "transparency" of the social arrangements which form the basis for divergent interests, the rate of social change, the dominant value system, the spread of radical interpretations of social reality that put dramatic labels on social experiences, and finally, the presence of leaders and associations, such as trade unions and political parties, capable of organizing class action into long-term conflict. Indeed, he investigated the different styles of party organization with such thoroughness that it almost seems he considered them to be a semiautonomous influence in the total process.

Implicit in Weber's approach to stratification is the idea that status considerations may undermine the development of class consciousness and class struggle. For example, the politics of the American South has long been shaped by the tendency of poor whites to identify with richer whites rather than with poor blacks who may share their economic position. Weber noted that political parties may be based on class, status, or other reasons for conflict over power. The major American political parties are amorphous coalitions that have never been as clearly oriented toward the pursuit of class interests as, say, the working-class parties of Western Europe.

In sum, Weber accepted Marx's idea of the underlying economic basis of stratification in the long run. However, he identified another order of stratification by differentiating between class and status. He argued that the two interact with each other and with the political process in complex ways not fully recognized by Marx.

NINE VARIABLES

The scientific study of social stratification in the United States began in the 1920s and 1930s with the pioneering investigations of small-town class systems we review in Chapter 2. Since that time, sociologists have collected a mass of empirical evidence about the character of the American stratification system, both local and national. Unfortunately, the facts are described from numerous points of view and frequently conveyed in a highly technical manner. Our purpose in this book is to present the best examples of the research in a coherent form; to do so, we need a standardized language but a minimum of technical jargon.

It is possible to combine the knowledge from the available empirical research by organizing it around a simple conceptual framework derived from our theorists, especially Weber, whose work suggests the difference between the economic, social, and political aspects of a stratification system. Under each of these rubrics, we can delineate a few basic variables which are significant for broad theories of stratification but still specific enough to be operationally defined and measured by the researcher. In the next few paragraphs we will define these basic variables and then in subsequent chapters examine each one in detail, both as a concept and as a body of verified information about the United States.

The economic variables we will consider are *occupation, income,* and *wealth.* The first may be defined as a social role which describes the major work that a person does to earn a living. Modern societies are characterized by an elaborate and stratified system of occupations, most of them related in some way to production or trade. *Income* refers to monetary gain received in the course of a given period of time (e.g., $10,000 per year). Income is closely related to, but must be carefully distinguished from, *wealth,* which refers to assets held at a given point in time. The principal categories of wealth are monetary savings; personal property, such as homes or automobiles; and business assets including real estate, equipment, inventory, and securities. Wealth can be viewed as an accumulation of past income. In certain forms, such as ownership of a business or of stocks and bonds, wealth becomes capital and is a source of new income. It is this possibility which makes wealth especially important for students of stratification.

Our consideration of the status aspect of the American class system will emphasize *personal prestige, association,* and *socialization.* The first is the most obvious of our stratification variables; if we study a local community, we notice immediately that some people have higher *personal prestige* than others.[2] People have high prestige when neighbors in general have an attitude of respect toward them. Another word that is used for this attitude is *deference,* or the granting of social honor. Prestige is a sentiment in the minds of men and women, although they do not always know that it is there. The shrewd observer can often notice deference behavior that is not recognized by the participants, such as imitation of ideas or lifestyles. Consequently, it is necessary to study prestige in two ways: by asking people about their attitudes of respect toward others and by watching their behavior.

People who share a given position in the class and status structures tend to have more personal contact or *association* with each other than with those in higher or lower positions. Such patterns of differential contact are significant because they promote similarities in behavior and opinion and a sense of community among the members of a stratum. Association (or interaction) is a variable which directs our

---

[2] The word *status* is often used as a synonym for *prestige,* but this usage is ambiguous and should be avoided since *status* has other uses in sociology.

attention to everyday social processes which can be studied scientifically. By counting its frequency, measuring its duration, classifying its quality, and watching who initiates and who follows, we can draw systematic conclusions about association and can judge its consequences.

Socialization is the process through which an individual learns the skills, attitudes, and customs needed to participate in the life of the community. Although socialization takes place throughout the life cycle of the individual, we shall be primarily interested in the socialization of children and teenagers. The early socialization experience of most members of a society is broadly similar; were it not, differences in expectations and behavior would be so great that social life would become impossible. However, social scientists have found significant variations in socialization among subgroupings within societies, especially complex societies. In the United States, research has uncovered class differences in socialization patterns which may reinforce differences in values, channeling the young toward interactions with others of similar background and eventually toward assuming the class positions of their parents.[3]

Two variables related to the political aspect of stratification systems will be of interest to us: *power* and *class consciousness*. Weber defined *power* as the potential of individuals or groups to carry out their will even over the opposition of others (Weber 1946: 180). This classic definition implies that power is a significant dimension in quite varied social settings, from the power of parents over children to the power of defense contractors over national security policy. We will restrict our use of the concept to broad political and economic contexts, dealing, for instance, with the power of corporations over national economic priorities or the power of the federal government to reduce inequalities in the distribution of income.

The degree to which people at a given level in the stratification system are aware of themselves as a distinctive group with shared political and economic interests is the measure of their *class consciousness*. In some circumstances, similar people do not have much contact with one another and think primarily in individualistic rather than in group terms. In other circumstances, they become highly group conscious, and then they are likely to organize political parties, trade unions, and other sorts of associations to advance their group interests. In general, Americans are thought to be less class conscious than Europeans; our traditions of equality lead many of us to deny that classes exist. But the traditions concern more what ought to be than what is.

---

[3] Formal education can be treated as part of the broad socialization process or as part of the direct preparation for occupational roles. We will deal with it both ways and thus do not list it as a separate variable.

In addition to considering the eight variables just outlined, we will examine a final variable, the dual concept of *succession and mobility*. When children inherit the class position of their parents, we speak of succession; when they move up or down relative to their parents, we refer to mobility. This variable stands apart from the others because it has a clearly implied time dimension, measured in generations, and because it cannot be assigned to the economic, social, or political aspect of stratification systems. In studying succession and mobility, we will be interested in measuring the degree of inheritance which prevails in American society today and in answering two questions: What factors shape the structure of opportunities which make mobility possible? and What characteristics of individuals account for differences in their ability to take advantage of mobility opportunities?

THE VARIABLES AS A SYSTEM

We have chosen these nine variables—occupation, income, wealth, personal prestige, association, socialization, power, class consciousness, and mobility—on pragmatic grounds. They constitute the set of variables that most efficiently organizes the existing empirical data on the American class system, and they are congruent with the thinking of the major theorists. Each variable, with the possible exception of power, can be measured by distinct and separate operations, and each can be used to stratify a given population. Thereafter, it is possible to study ways in which position on one dimension influences that on others.

The nine variables do not form a closed system, all on the same level of abstraction, in the strict sense of scientific theory. However, they do constitute a useful conceptual scheme. By gathering data on each of these variables—as we will do for the United States—we can develop a thorough description of our class system. Moreover, since all the variables are mutually dependent, they provide a framework for thinking about the dynamics of class systems. For instance, numerous studies have demonstrated a connection between the stratification of occupations and each of the remaining eight variables. There is also evidence that the occupational structure (that is, the relative proportions of individuals in different occupations) of the advanced industrial nations is gradually changing. An important question for students of stratification concerns the effect these changes are having on the other variables. Or, to pose a different sort of problem, we might look at our variables to help us understand how class systems—based, after all, on the unequal distribution of privilege—manage to persist. A few clues: The socialization of the less privileged appears to inculcate values supportive of the existing class order; mobility offers opportunities for dissatisfied individuals to change their class positions without changing the system; the privileged have disproportionate power over political and economic institutions.

There is much to be gained, then, by viewing these nine variables together. To say so, however, is not to imply that they are of equal importance. They are not. We are convinced that societies which are similar in their technology and economic institutions have broadly similar class systems, that classes develop out of relationships to the means of production, and that status communities emerge from stable distributions of economic privilege. In short, stratification systems are based on economic differences within societies. Therefore, among the variables defined here, those related to the economic aspect of stratification systems (occupation, income, and wealth) are of fundamental significance. Nonetheless, the effects of these variables on the behavior of men and women are mediated through the other variables, which often exercise an independent or autonomous influence, especially in the short run. Thus, while recognizing the primacy of the economic variables, we believe that they can most fruitfully be studied as part of a more complex system.

When we are thinking about the way the nine variables interrelate to form a complex system of stratification, it is crucial to make a distinction between the system as it is and the system as it changes. Much of the research in the United States tends to take the system or structure as it is—as given—and then seeks to understand the way individuals are placed in and influenced by that system. Thus, we concern ourselves with the influence of occupation on voting behavior, with the relation between income and health and longevity, or the prediction of a son's career chances from his father's social position. The main methodological procedure is to collect data on a sample of individuals and assign each person a numerical score or rank on each of two or more variables, then calculate the correlation coefficients among them.

The alternative approach is to concentrate on historical changes in the structure itself, paying more attention to its overall shape and dynamics than to the differences among individuals. This approach is exemplified in Chapter 3 by our discussion of the transformation of the American class structure brought about by industrialization at the end of the 19th century. Here various historical data are used to gain an understanding of the broad sweep of change in society as a whole.

Obviously, the two approaches are related, since the individuals we study are part of a structure that was determined by history and continues to change. Unfortunately, the languages used by the two approaches are less congruent than they appear to be, and much misunderstanding arises when people shift from one perspective to the other. Marx and Weber were more concerned with history than with description, yet they sometimes concerned themselves with the differential fate of individuals within a given system. American researchers are usually concerned with the differential fate of individuals, yet they cannot completely ignore historical trends. *Most theorists think historically; most empiricists think descriptively.* Let the reader be aware of this fundamental problem and notice which perspective dominates the discussion as we move from one research to another.

WHAT ARE SOCIAL CLASSES?

A stratified society is one marked by inequality, by differences among people that are evaluated by them as being higher or lower. The simplest form of inequality is based on the division of labor which always appears according to age and sex. Young children are everywhere subordinate to their elders; old people may have a high or a low position, depending upon cultural values; women are often ranked below men.

But there is another form of inequality that appears in every society (other than the very smallest and most primitive ones), which ranks families rather than individuals. A family shares many characteristics among its members that greatly affect their relationships with outsiders: the same house, the same income, the same values. If a large group of families are approximately equal in rank to each other and clearly differentiated from other families, we call them a *social class.*[4]

Logically, it is possible for a society to be stratified without having distinct classes, for there could be a continuous gradation between high and low without any sharp lines of division, but in reality this is most unlikely. The sources of a family's position are shared by many other similar families: there are only a limited number of types of occupations or of possible positions in the property system. One either works the soil, or uses his hands to manufacture things, or trades, or performs some function of intellectual, military, or political leadership that allows one to live from the productive labor of others. There is a tendency for the persons of each type to become similar to their fellows and distinct from the members of other types; the similarities are shared within families and often inherited by children. In other words, the various stratification variables tend to converge and jell; they form a pattern, and it is this pattern that creates social classes.

The pattern formed by the objective connections among the variables is heightened by the way people think about social matters, for

---

[4] Here we depart from the strict terminology used above that differentiates *class* from *status* in favor of ordinary English, which combines the two and uses *class level* or *social stratum* interchangeably.

popular thought creates stereotypes. Bankers are conceived of as a homogeneous group, and distinctions between big bankers and little ones are ignored. Similarly, poor people tend to lump together all bosses, and rich people overlook the many distinctions that exist among those who labor for an hourly wage.

It would not be true to go so far as to say that every family has an equal score on all nine variables. At least in our society, the stratification system is too vague and too fluid for that to occur with high regularity. But in the long run social life is such that a family *tends* to equalize its position on all of the variables. The forces toward convergence, toward the crystallization of the pattern, will be emphasized in this book despite the fact that many disturbing influences, mostly the results of rapid social change, keep the patterns from becoming as clear-cut in reality as in theory.

The classes that we talk about are ideal-type constructs. They are intellectual inventions, based on observation of reality, that describe how the classes would look if the system were freed of extraneous influences. Ideal types are complex models of the interrelations among variables; they are guides to research and frameworks for synthesizing the results of research. They seldom are phrased as specific propositions that can be completely proved or disproved. Consequently, it is not surprising that different authors use different sets of class divisions.

Comparing one society to another, we see that stratification systems differ in two ways: the distinctness of their strata and the amount of mobility that occurs between strata. These two characteristics are closely related but not identical. The type of stratification system that is most rigid on both characteristics is called a caste system. In caste systems each stratum is markedly different from the others; its members have a special occupation which is hereditary, they are endogamous (marry within the caste), and they have many special cultural characteristics, often including religious rites, that are unique to themselves. In law as well as fact, caste membership determines life. A caste system is composed of a number of quite separate social communities that live side by side in economic interdependence. The pure form of caste system was approached only in India, but many other societies have had castelike characteristics. Slaves are often a separate caste, but a caste system need not be an outgrowth of slavery.

At the other extreme is a modern, "open" class system. Here there are no legal recognitions of group inequality, and there are minimal differences between the cultural ways of life of the classes. Furthermore, there is much movement from one class to another, both during the lifetime of a person and from one generation to another. There are many societies with such open class systems, and they may vary in terms of the degree of differences between classes or in the amount of mobility that occurs among them, or both.

Having discussed the main strands of stratification theory, let us begin the detailed study of the American class structure. The next chapter starts with that aspect of it most immediately evident to every citizen: prestige in the local community.

SUGGESTED READINGS

Bendix, Reinhard, and Seymour Martin Lipset. 1966. *Class, Status and Power: Social Stratification in Comparative Perspective.* 2d ed. New York: Free Press.
A large collection of articles on important aspects of stratification in various countries. Part I covers basic theory.

Coser, Lewis. 1978. *Masters of Sociological Thought.* 2d ed. New York: Harcourt Brace Jovanovich.
Contains short personal and intellectual biographies of Marx and Weber which put them into the context of their times.

Giddens, Anthony. 1973. *The Class Structure of the Advanced Societies.* New York: Harper & Row.
Attempt to rethink the main ideas of Marx and his critics to arrive at an acceptable modern interpretation of class structure.

Lenski, Gerhard. 1966. *Power and Privilege: A Theory of Social Stratification.* New York: McGraw-Hill.
Ambitious attempt to explain the development of stratification in each of several evolutionary stages based on technology.

Marx, Karl. 1979. *The Marx-Engels Reader.* Edited by Robert C. Tucker. 2d ed. New York: W. W. Norton.
Convenient collection of the writings of Marx and his partner, Friedrich Engels. Particularly relevant are: The German Ideology, Part I; Wage Labour and Capital; Manifesto of the Communist Party; and Engels' Socialism: Utopian and Scientific.

Parkin, Frank. 1970. *Class, Inequality and Political Order: Social Stratification in Capitalist and Communist Countries.* New York: Praeger Publishers.
A comparative text focusing on relationships between dominant and subordinate classes.

Weber, Max. 1946. *From Max Weber: Essays in Sociology.* Edited by H. H. Gerth and C. Wright Mills. New York: Oxford University Press.
A selection of Weber's most important sociological writings (except for his book The Protestant Ethic and the Spirit of Capitalism). *Especially relevant are:* Class, Status, Party; Bureaucracy; The Protestant Sects and the Spirit of Capitalism.

Williams, Robin M., Jr. 1970. *American Society.* 3d ed. New York: Alfred A. Knopf.
Chapter 5 is a sophisticated view of social classes in the context of American institutions as a whole.

Position and prestige

Fame did not bring the social advancement which the Babbitts deserved. They were not asked to join the Tonawanda Country Club nor invited to the dances at the Union. Himself, Babbitt fretted, he "didn't care a fat hoot for all these highrollers, but the wife would kind of like to be among those present." He nervously awaited his university class-dinner and an evening of furious intimacy with such social leaders as Charles McKelvey the millionaire contractor, Max Kruger the banker, Irving Tate the tool-manufacturer, and Adelbert Dobson the fashionable interior decorator. Theoretically he was their friend, as he had been in college, and when he encountered them they still called him "Georgie," but he didn't seem to encounter them often. . . .

Sinclair Lewis (1922: 190)

2

In the small group, in the local community, in the society as a whole, we notice that some people are looked up to, respected, considered people of consequence, and others are thought of as ordinary, unimportant, even lowly. Everywhere we see notables and nobodies.

Prestige is a sentiment in the minds of people that is expressed in interpersonal interaction: deference behavior is expected by one party and granted by another. Obviously, it can occur only when there are values shared by both parties that define the criteria of superiority; deference at pistol point is not the result of prestige. But this does not necessarily mean that both parties agree about all aspects of the situation. For instance, the subordinate person may feel that the superordinate person *should not* have the right to deference and may try to foment a revolution to take it away; but so long as the subordinate recognizes that the superordinate *does* have the right to claim deference and feels constrained by group norms to grant it, then a prestige difference exists. The degree of consensus can range from a situation in which deference is given joyously as a recognition of moral worthiness that reflects the will of God, to one in which deference is given grudgingly, against part of one's own will which cries out against these claims to special privilege. However, stable situations are characterized by the development of legitimating ideologies which assure approval as well as acceptance for prestige inequalities.

The facts of institutionalized social life that are recognized in deference behavior usually include inequality in wealth and authority. Ideologies are reinforced by sanctions, and people of low prestige grant deference partly because they know that in the long run it is to their advantage to do so. Through symbolic submission to superiors, they gain favor in the eyes of those who are in a position to grant rewards—goods and services, promotion, protection, salvation, or perhaps just goodwill and a reassuring smile. The distinction between deference at pistol point and that from prestige is the distinction between usurpation of power by naked force and authority gained through control of legitimated institutions. In neither case is the will completely free.

The most direct way to study prestige is to go into a local community where everyone knows everyone else and observe how they treat one another. Part of that observation would include questions such as "What do you think of Jackson as compared to Albers?" If there were complete consensus among all the citizens, the observer could in a short time draw up a list of the inhabitants and rank them from top to bottom. If the community had more than just a few members, then it is likely that several persons would share equal ranks, and that there would be more people clustered in the lower than in the higher ranks. It is also likely, again assuming complete consensus, that this rank order would hold good in all situations: that whether one depended on direct verbal testimony of the inhabitants or watched them at work, at play, or at worship, the rank order would be the same.

Such a conceptual model assumes complete consensus among persons acting in a fully integrated social structure, and it is never exactly matched by reality. In the first place, prestige grows out of specific evaluated activities, and each person engages in many different activities. A man who gains high prestige as a banker may get low prestige as a golfer. In the second place, people may not agree on the relative worth of the different activities; granted that a man is a good banker and a bad golfer, which is more important? And in the third place, there are likely to be disagreements as to the relative merits of persons within the same activity: it is not always easy to get four bankers to agree on who is the town's top financial expert.

The first two problems involve the different social roles that we play; the last involves the question of performance within a role. In their more precise moods, sociologists say that the behavior of a person in a given role leads to *esteem* in the eyes of others, but the importance of the role itself is the source of the person's *prestige*. Thus a good garbage collector gets high esteem and low prestige, whereas a bad banker gets high prestige and low esteem. However, in ranking their friends, informants usually combine esteem and prestige into a single judgment of overall merit. When many people occupy roles of approximately equal prestige, we call them a *stratum*, such as the combination of bankers, accountants, and sales managers into the stratum of business executives. Sometimes the roles themselves are thought of as the stratum, regardless of the individuals in them.

In spite of the diversity of roles people play, and the differences in evaluation thereof made by different observers in the community, there is usually a trend toward consistency, for individuals carry with them some of their habits and reputation as they move from one role to another. Insofar as these roles are public and watched by the community at large, they tend to blend into an overall prestige reputation. For example, a man who is a successful banker gains the general respect of the community, but to keep it he should be a good family man, maintain the appearance of his house, and not curse too loudly when he muffs a shot on the golf course. Since his skill as a typist is not considered important, it neither adds to nor detracts from his general prestige reputation.

The prestige hierarchy of a local community represents the synthesis of all the other stratification variables. It is the result of the evaluation by the people of the totality of the class structure. Such exhaustive mutual evaluations are only possible in small communities whose members have detailed knowledge of one another's lives and backgrounds. In other social contexts, people must depend on more limited and superficial clues to assign prestige to others, and the sociologists who study them must invent indirect methods of ranking. Nevertheless, an understanding of such local prestige structures is an excellent beginning for the study of the dynamics of stratification, for if we can picture in detail the hierarchy of prestige, we can then look behind it for the factors that created it, in terms of both local circumstances and national conditions.

In this chapter we will examine some classic investigations of prestige structures in small towns, a related study conducted recently in two major cities, and a series of national surveys of the prestige associated with occupations. In each case we will want to answer two questions: *What* were the results? and *How* were they obtained? The answer to the second question allows us to assess the validity of the reply to the first.

W. LLOYD WARNER: PRESTIGE CLASSES IN YANKEE CITY

The concern of American sociologists with the prestige aspect of stratification can be traced back to a series of community studies conducted by W. Lloyd Warner and his students and colleagues. Their research began in the early 1930s. Warner had already completed a three-year study of Australian aborigines and wanted to employ the techniques of social anthropology—the study of the "whole man" in the complete context of his sociocultural life—in the United States. Although Warner and his associates realized that in many ways the metropolis was the typical social environment of modern society, they felt that the study of the great city "as a whole" from the viewpoint of social anthropology was too vast an undertaking for their techniques and resources. Furthermore, they believed that the big city was in many ways disorganized and did not represent a community life that was functionally integrated.

> If we were to compare easily the other societies of the world with one of our own civilization, and if we were readily to accommodate our techniques, developed by the study of primitive society, to modern

groups, it seemed wise to choose a community with a social organization which had developed over a long period of time under the domination of a single group with a coherent tradition. In the United States only two large sections, New England and the deep South, we believed were likely to possess such a community (Warner and Lunt 1941: 5; Warner et al. 1963).

Their first study, of a New England town of 17,000 called "Yankee City," was followed by studies of even smaller communities in the South and Middle West (Warner et al. 1949b contains references to all of them).

The decision to concentrate on small and homogeneous communities with a "coherent tradition" may have been practical for research purposes when using the techniques of social anthropology, but it was dangerous from a theoretical standpoint. These communities were not typical of all of America, in spite of the fact that a substantial part of our population still lives in places of less than 25,000 inhabitants. In many ways, the dominant forces in our society are found in the big cities and their suburbs, where many people with a diversity of cultural backgrounds live side by side. Some critics have said that instead of taking the techniques of anthropology as fundamental and searching for a community simple enough to use them, Warner should have started with the fact of urban heterogeneity and sought procedures that would help him to master its complexity.

But there is little point in wishing Warner had done otherwise than he did. If we recognize its proper sphere, we can accept his work as a great contribution to our understanding of prestige stratification in small communities and the methods that can be used to study it. And we can take his findings concerning stratification processes and use them as hypotheses to guide research in the metropolis.

Yankee City was once a famous seaport. It had a long history in New England commerce, having been a center of trade, fishing, and, more recently, manufacturing, especially of shoes and silverware. In many ways, its glory was in the past. In recent years it had become merely a small city not too far from Boston, and many of its young people left for the more exciting life to be found in Boston and New York. Ethnically the town was relatively homogeneous but not perfectly so. Some families had been there for 300 years. Half its inhabitants had been born in the community, and another quarter came from other parts of New England and the United States. But the remaining quarter were from French Canada, Ireland, Italy, and Eastern Europe.

When Warner began the research, he made explicit to his staff the hypothesis that

> the fundamental structure of our society, that which ultimately controls and dominates the thinking and actions of our people, is economic, and that the most vital and far-reaching value systems which motivate

Americans are to be ultimately traced to an economic order. Our first interviews tended to sustain this hypothesis. They were filled with references to "the big people with money" and to "the little people who are poor." They assigned people high status by referring to them as bankers, large property owners, people of high salary, and professional men, or they placed people in a low status by calling them laborers, ditchdiggers, and low-wage earners. Other similar economic terms were used, all designating superior and inferior positions (Warner and Lunt 1941: 81).

However, after the research team had been in Yankee City for a while, they began to doubt that social standing could so easily be equated with economic position, for they found that some people were placed higher or lower in the prestige scale than their incomes would warrant. Furthermore,

Other evidences began to accumulate which made it difficult to accept a simple economic hypothesis. Several men were doctors; and while some of them enjoyed the highest social status in the community and were so evaluated in the interviews, others were ranked beneath them although some of the latter were often admitted to be better physicians. Such ranking was frequently unconsciously done and for this reason was often more reliable than a conscious estimate of a man's status. . . .

We finally developed a class hypothesis which withstood the later test of a vast collection of data and of subsequent rigorous analysis. By class is meant two or more orders of people who are believed to be, and are accordingly ranked by the members of the community, in socially superior and inferior positions. Members of a class tend to marry within their own order, but the values of the society permit marriage up and down. A class system also provides that children are born into the same status as their parents. A class society distributes rights and privileges, duties and obligations, unequally among its inferior and superior grades. A system of classes, unlike a system of castes, provides by its own values for movement up and down the social ladder. In common parlance, this is social climbing, or in technical terms, social mobility. The social system of Yankee City, we found, was dominated by a class order.

In these interviews certain facts became clear which might be summarized by saying a person needed specific characteristics associated with his "station in life" and he needed to go with the "right kind" of people for the informants to be certain of his ranking. If a man's education, occupation, wealth, income, family, intimate friends, clubs and fraternities, as well as his manners, speech, and general outward behavior were known, it was not difficult for his fellow citizens to give a fairly exact estimate of his status. . . .

We noticed that certain geographical terms were used not only to locate people in the city's geographical space but also to evaluate their comparative place in the rank order. The first generalization of this kind which we noticed people using in interviews was the identification of a small percentage of the population as "Hill Streeters" or people who "live up on Hill Street," these expressions often being used as equivalent of "Brahmin," the rarer "aristocrat," or the less elegant "high mucky-muck," or "swell," or "snoot" (Warner and Lunt 1941: 82–84).

Warner concluded from his interviews and observations, in other words, that prestige rank was the result of a combination of variables that included wealth, income, and occupation but also differential patterns of interaction and associated distinctions in social behavior and lifestyle.

One of the most important of the interaction patterns was determined by kinship: not only did children get assigned the status of their parents, but certain families had a prestige position that was not entirely explainable by their current wealth or income and seemed to flow from their ancestry.

When an individual had an equivalent rank on all the variables, his townsmen had no difficulty in deciding how much prestige to give him.[1] But when he had somewhat different scores on the several variables, there was difficulty in knowing exactly how to place him. This usually meant that the person was mobile and was changing his position on one variable at a time; eventually he would be likely to get them all into line. Consequently, time was an important factor in stratification placement. For example, if a man who started as the son of a laborer became successful in business, he would be likely to move to a "better" neighborhood, join clubs of other business and professional men, and send his children to college. But if he himself did not have a college education and polished manners, he would never be fully accepted as a social equal by the businessmen who had Harvard degrees. His son, however, might well gain the full acceptance denied the father. In Warner's words: "Money must be translated into socially approved behavior and possessions, and they in turn must be translated into intimate participation with, and acceptance by, members of a superior class" (Warner et al. 1949b: 21).

After several years of study by more than a dozen researchers, during which time 99 percent of the families in town were classified, Warner declared that there were six groupings sharp enough to be called classes (Warner and Lunt 1941: 88):

1. Upper-upper, 1.4 percent of the total population. This group was the old-family elite, based on sufficient wealth to maintain a large house in the best neighborhood, but the wealth had to have been in the family for more than one generation. This generational continuity permitted proper training in basic values and established people as belonging to a lineage.

---

[1] We use the masculine pronoun, since at the time of the study most women did not work, and they usually were assigned the ranking of their husbands.

2.   Lower-upper, 1.6 percent. This group was, on the average, slightly richer than the upper-uppers, but their money was newer, their manners were thus not quite so polished, and their sense of lineage and security were less pronounced.
3.   Upper-middle, 10.2 percent. Business and professional men and their families who were moderately successful but less affluent than the lower-uppers. Some education and polish were necessary for membership, but lineage was unimportant.
4.   Lower-middle, 28.1 percent. The petty businessmen, the schoolteachers, the foremen in industry. This group tended to have morals that were close to those of Puritan Fundamentalism; they were churchgoers, lodge joiners, and flag wavers.
5.   Upper-lower, 32.6 percent. The solid, respectable laboring people, who kept their houses clean and stayed out of trouble.
6.   Lower-lower, 25.2 percent. The "lulus" or disrespectable and often slovenly people who dug for clams and waited for public relief.

This proportionate distribution among the classes represents not only a long New England history, but also the special conditions of the Great Depression of the 1930s, which, for example, probably inflated the size of the lower-lower class.

Once the general system became clear to him, Warner said, he used a man's clique and association memberships as a shorthand index of prestige position. Thus there were certain small social clubs that were open only to upper-uppers, while the Rotary was primarily upper-middle in membership, the fraternal lodges were lower-middle, and the craft unions were upper-lower. It seems that in cases of doubt intimate clique interactions were the crucial test: a repeated invitation home to dinner appears to be for Warner the best sign of prestige equality between persons who are not relatives.

PRESTIGE CLASS AS A CONCEPT

Warner maintained that the breaks between all these prestige classes were quite clear-cut, except for that between the lower-middle and the upper-lower. At that level there was a blurring of distinctions that made placement of borderline families quite difficult. Of course, the placement of mobile families at all levels was difficult.

When he said that the distinctions between the classes were clear-cut, he meant in the minds of the people of Yankee City. He saw his job of scientific observer as mainly one of staying around long enough to find out what the people "really" thought. But here he ran into difficulties. Since there are certain value traditions which maintain that social inequality is un-American, some people deny that it exists while at the same time behaving as though it does.

> In the bright glow and warm presence of the American Dream all men are born free and equal. Everyone in the American Dream has the right, and often the duty, to try to succeed and to do his best to reach the top. Its two fundamental themes and propositions, that all of us are equal and that each of us has the right to the chance of reaching the top, are mutually contradictory, for if all men are equal there can be no top level to aim for, no bottom one to get away from (Warner et al. 1949b: 3).

It is because he recognized this value conflict that Warner said in the passage quoted above that "ranking was frequently unconsciously done and . . . was often more reliable than a conscious estimate of a man's status. . . ."

The conceptual dilemma that Warner faced and that has plagued his readers is shown by the contrast between these two statements of his:

> These social levels [classes] are not categories invented by social scientists to help explain what they have to say; they are groups recognized by the people of the community as being higher or lower in the life of the city. The social scientist, when he hears that certain groups are superior or inferior, records what he hears and observes and tries to understand what it means. The designations of social levels are distinctions made by the people themselves in referring to each other (Warner et al. 1949a: xii–xiv).

> Naturally there were many borderline cases. . . . In order to make a complete study, it was necessary to locate all of them in one of the six classes, and this we did to the best of our ability on the basis of the entire range of phenomena covered by our data. . . . It must not be thought that all the people in Yankee City are aware of all the minute distinctions made in this book. The terms used to refer to such definitions as are made vary according to the class of the individual and his period of residence (Warner and Lunt 1941: 90–91).

In one breath Warner said that the class distinctions he made were simply descriptions of the distinctions that existed in the minds of his subjects, but in the next they became decisions made by him "on the basis of the entire range of phenomena covered by our data," and the subjects might not be fully aware of them. Are they descriptive summaries or abstract scientific constructs? Do they exist in the minds of the people or in the mind of Warner?

The answer can only be, both. The analyst has to create scientifically neat concepts or variables that approximate, as closely as possible, aspects of the real behavior of the subjects when they evaluate each other. Then the researcher has to formulate standard rules that show how to add up scores on each separate variable to arrive at the totality which will best predict the overall prestige judgment concerning a person that is made by others in the community. To be systematic and approach the goal of variables that make good statistics, the scientist is going to perform mental operations that are not identical to the automatic, half-conscious, and often contradictory thinking of the subjects. The aim of research is to predict, with reasonable accuracy, what most subjects will do in most circumstances. Furthermore, analysts must use variables that have theoretical meaning in other contexts, for only thus can they explain as well as describe.

Every variable in the mind of the analyst approximates a variable in the minds of the subjects. But each subject will not perceive that variable in exactly the same way as the other subjects; one may think that the possession of a Buick is a clear mark of top wealth, while another may settle for nothing less than a Cadillac. The different subjects will not all add up the variables in the same way to arrive at the identical total prestige judgment: some will emphasize wealth, others income, and still others family background. Consequently, one cannot claim that the analyst's mental operations are exact reflections of the ratiocinations of the subjects—if the community does not reach complete consensus, how can the analyst always know what to do?

In fact, concepts are *always* "categories invented by social scientists to help explain what they have to say," but they are not invented out of pure imagination. They are based on careful observation, plus scientific reasons for abstracting from those observations a few simple factors that are worth studying in detail. In his more cautious moods, Warner admitted the degree of scientific abstraction that lay behind his six classes: "Structural and status analysts construct scientific representations (or 'maps') which represent their knowledge of the structure and status interrelations which compose the community's social system" (Warner and Lunt 1941: 34). And a bit farther on, he admitted that some residents were more class-conscious than others and paid more attention to status distinctions (p. 69).

We can conclude that Warner's classes are ideal-type constructs which help him organize a vast amount of data on attitudes and behavior; they are not mere descriptions of the mental categories used by the inhabitants of Yankee City and other small towns. As such they stand as hypotheses, and other observers have a right to test them against the data. The only sense in which these classes can be called real is to claim that they organize the data more usefully than any alternative set of hypotheses.

ARE THERE SIX CLASSES?

How can Warner's scheme be tested? How can we find out whether his six classes make a better fit to reality than five, or seven, or six that are cut differently from his? Much of the rest of this book will deal with aspects of this question, for the full answer involves behavior in terms of values, interactions, class consciousness, and so on. Here we can give only a quick preview, emphasizing direct perception of prestige by local informants who rank people they know and live with.

In *Deep South*, by Warner's colleagues Allison Davis, Burleigh R. Gardner, and Mary R. Gardner, there appears an interesting chart showing the "social perspectives of the social classes," or the way the people at each level perceive the people at other levels; it is reproduced here as Figure 2–1. The chart suggests that the people at each level did not recognize six classes in Old City, a southern town of 10,000 inhabitants, but either four or five, though the scientists said that six classes existed in the white population. The people in the town made finer distinctions between persons close to themselves than between those who were far away. However, all the distinctions that were made coincided in spite of the fact that they might have had different names. Thus the lower-lowers made a distinction between "society" and the "way-high-ups but not society," but they did not subdivide "society." According to the authors, the line between society and the way-high-ups but not society was precisely the same as the line drawn by upper-uppers between "nice, respectable people" and "good people but nobody" (upper-middle and lower-middle). That is, when names of specific families were mentioned, both lower-lowers and upper-uppers placed them in the same one of these two groups. However, the upper-uppers made further subdivisions not recognized by the lower-lowers into "old aristocracy," "new aristocracy," and "nice, respectable people."

Davis and the Gardners wrote in *Deep South* (1941: 71–73):

> While members of all class groups recognize classes above and below them, or both, the greater the social distance from the other classes the less clearly are fine distinctions made. Although an individual recognizes most clearly the existence of groups immediately above and below his own, he is usually not aware of the social distance actually maintained between his own and these adjacent groups. Thus, in all cases except that of members of the upper-lower class the individual sees only a minimum of social distance between his class and the adjacent classes. This is illustrated by the dotted line in Figure [2–1]. Almost all other class divisions, however, are ·isualized as definite lines of cleavage in the society with a large amount of social distance between them.
>
> In general, too, individuals visualize class groups above them less clearly than those below them; they tend to minimize the social differentiations between themselves and those above. . . . In view of this situation it is not surprising that individuals in the two upper strata make the finest gradations in the stratification of the whole society and that class distinctions are made with decreasing precision as social position becomes lower.
>
> Not only does the perspective on social stratification vary for different class levels, but the bases of class distinction in the society are variously interpreted by the different groups. People tend to agree as to

FIGURE 2–1
The social perspectives of the social classes

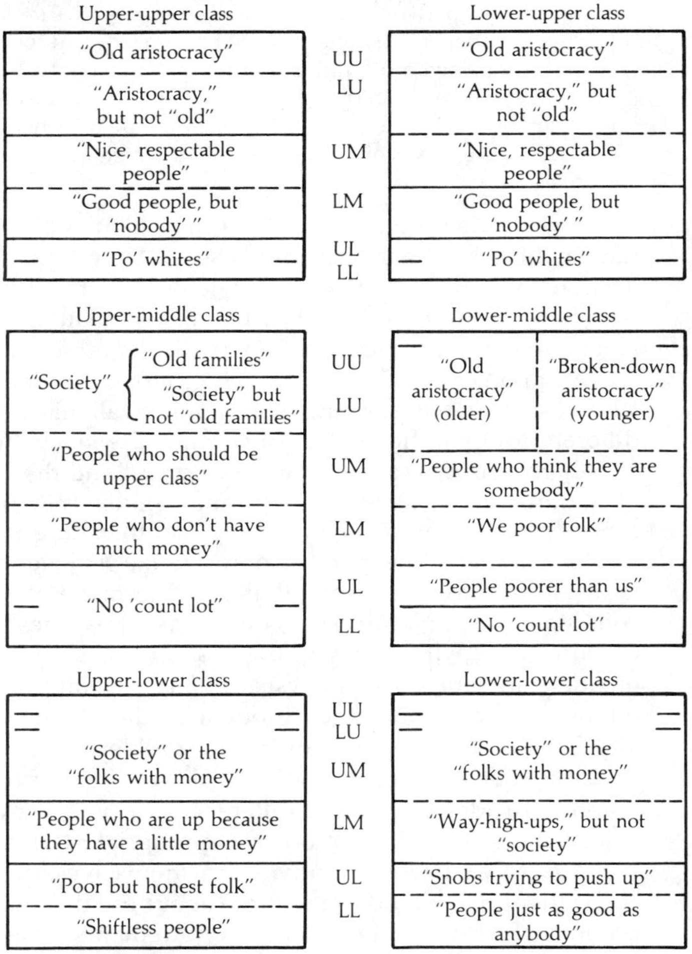

Upper-upper class		Lower-upper class
"Old aristocracy"	UU	"Old aristocracy"
"Aristocracy," but not "old"	LU	"Aristocracy," but not "old"
"Nice, respectable people"	UM	"Nice, respectable people"
"Good people, but 'nobody'"	LM	"Good people, but 'nobody'"
— "Po' whites" —	UL / LL	— "Po' whites" —

Upper-middle class		Lower-middle class
"Society" { "Old families" / "Society" but not "old families" }	UU / LU	"Old aristocracy" (older) | "Broken-down aristocracy" (younger)
"People who should be upper class"	UM	"People who think they are somebody"
"People who don't have much money"	LM	"We poor folk"
— "No 'count lot" —	UL / LL	"People poorer than us" / "No 'count lot"

Upper-lower class		Lower-lower class
UU / LU
"Society" or the "folks with money"	UM	"Society" or the "folks with money"
"People who are up because they have a little money"	LM	"Way-high-ups," but not "society"
"Poor but honest folk"	UL	"Snobs trying to push up"
"Shiftless people"	LL	"People just as good as anybody"

Source: Reprinted from page 65 of *Deep South: A Social-Anthropological Study of Caste and Class*, by Allison Davis, Burleigh B. Gardner, and Mary R. Gardner. This chart and accompanying text from pages 71–73 of the same work are reprinted by permission of The University of Chicago Press. Copyright 1941 by The University of Chicago.

where people are but not upon why they are there. Upper-class individuals, especially upper-uppers, think of class divisions largely in terms of time—one has a particular social position because his family has "always had" that position. Members of the middle class interpret their position in terms of wealth and time and tend to make moral evaluations of what "should be. . . ." Lower-class people, on the other hand, view the whole stratification of the society as a hierarchy of wealth. . . .

The identity of a social class does not depend on uniformity in any one or two, or a dozen, specific kinds of behavior but on a complex pattern or network of interrelated characteristics and attitudes. Among the members of any one class there is no strict uniformity in any specific type of behavior but rather a range and a "modal average." One finds a range in income, occupation, educational level, and types of social participation. The "ideal type" may be defined, however, for any given class—the class configuration—from which any given individual may vary in one or more particulars.

How do investigators discover these "modal averages" of behavior: how do they find the classes? They first observe differing patterns of general behavior or style of life—the high-society crowd who hang around the country club versus the little shopkeepers who belong to the Elks. Then they pay particular attention to the names of specific families who belong to each group. If different informants use labels with varying shades of moral evaluation to describe the different groups, the analyst can equate the labels by interpretation: the "high-society crowd" of one informant and the "old aristocracy" of another turn out to be identical, because *both* the behavior described and the individuals who are said to belong are the same.

The fact that all people do not recognize six levels is not so important, so long as the breaks that they do make all fit together in a consistent way. Naturally, people make the finest distinctions regarding those whom they know best and tend to merge others into broader categories. The analysts can take this into consideration and, if they wish, can subdivide a group according to the views of those in and immediately adjacent to it. The problem is like that of accommodating for perspective when making a map from aerial photographs. (Incidentally, these differences in perspective are not mere disturbances to be ironed out by appropriate techniques—they are social facts well worth studying in themselves. If we knew more about them, we would know more about the dynamics of social perception which underlie all prestige judgments.) The practical problems in social mapping reduce to two: Do all observers put Albers above Jackson in the hierarchy, and if they distinguish between their ranks at all, do they all divide Jackson's group from Alber's at the same place? These are the questions of *ranking consistency* and of *cutting consistency*.

THREE METHODS OF PRESTIGE PLACEMENT

The Warner group evolved its techniques for stratifying local communities out of its practical experience in the field and thus did not follow sharply explicit procedures in a consistent way throughout all the studies. Toward the end of the series of researches the group published a field manual to guide other researchers (Warner et al. 1949b). Their key method was called *Evaluated Participation*, which included various devices for matching the reputation of one family against another on the basis of what others said about them, along with their participation in the community through informal networks of association and formal memberships in organizations. These procedures produced the rank order of families. The final decisions about cutting the ranking into class levels were made by the investigators, using various symbols that were common in the language of the residents to divide their town into strata, as well as the clustering of network ties into groupings that tended to be mutually exclusive. To follow the method well, a team of researchers had to live for a while in the community and accumulate voluminous records on many (if not all) of the residents.

Simultaneously with the laborious procedures of Evaluated Participation, the Warner team developed a shortcut device for ranking local citizens, called the *Index of Status Characteristics*. Once the evaluated rankings were established, they discovered that they could accurately predict them by a numerical index composed of ratings on occupation, source of income (inherited income, wages and salaries, public relief, etc.), house type, and residential area. When the ratings on each of the four factors were pooled, weighted, and averaged, the resultant score came quite close to predicting the relative position of families on Evaluated Participation (for details, see Warner et al. 1949b). Not only is the index a useful device, but it suggests the main "causes" of prestige placement, which appear largely economic.

A simpler procedure for studying a community prestige hierarchy was developed by August B. Hollingshead, who did research in the same midwestern town the Warner group called "Jonesville"; Hollingshead called it "Elmtown." The Hollingshead method developed a control list of class-ranked families which could be employed as a measuring rod to place other families. The control list was constructed in the following way (Hollingshead 1949: 25–41).

After three months of field work, Hollingshead sifted through his interview notes and selected the names of 30 families who were frequently mentioned. These families were spread throughout the prestige range, and there seemed to be considerable agreement about their relative positions. Hollingshead placed the names of the husbands and wives on small cards and went back to 25 of the people who had been interviewed previously. They were asked to place the 30 families in different stations or classes by dividing the cards into stacks of equivalent rank. The informants could use as many stacks as they wished. Nineteen informants used five groups; 77 percent of the placements of specific families were in agreement.

In a second round of testing with a fresh group of subjects, Hollingshead improved these results by eliminating from the control list 10 families who had frequently received inconsistent ratings. He concluded that the level of agreement achieved was sufficient to sustain the judgment that the community had five classes and that residents could place their fellows fairly well into one or another of them.

Using the revised control list as a measuring rod, Hollingshead was able to place a sample of 535 Elmtown families in the class structure by asking a new group of informants to indicate which of the control-list families most approximated the social position of each additional family to be rated. When informants disagreed about the placement of a particular family, their judgments were averaged to produce a class rank. (Hollingshead noted that most of the disagreement centered on 74 families who were experiencing social mobility. This fact suggests more than the origin of some methodological headaches; it points to a significant source of ambiguity in perceptions of the class structure of modern societies.) Using his technique, Hollingshead proceeded to classify the families of all the students in the high school, where he was conducting his research.

Hollingshead's approach of asking informants to sort cards with the names of local families into stacks of equivalent prestige is a neat technique that establishes both ranking *and* cutting in one quick operation. The Warner Index of Status Characteristics is also easy to use, but its development assumes a previous and difficult operation of Evaluated Participation, unless one is willing to accept the guess that the index can be used in new communities without reevaluating it. In Jonesville-Elmtown, the methods produced roughly similar results: over 80 percent of the families were placed in equivalent categories by all three techniques. Both investigators ended up with five classes, since neither found the distinction between established wealthy families and those with new fortunes which subdivided the upper classes in Yankee City and Old City in the South; other than that, the class structures in all three towns were strikingly similar. (A general review of measurement techniques is Jackson and Curtis 1968; see also Rainwater 1974 and Nock and Rossi 1978.)

COLEMAN AND RAINWATER: CLASS STRUCTURE OF THE METROPOLIS

Although a few studies of small towns have been conducted in more recent years, they did not attempt to parallel the work of Warner and Hollingshead, and we do not know how much communities of the type they studied have changed since World War II. However, two former students of Warner have recently completed an urban study which clearly shows the mark of their mentor, to whose memory their book is dedicated.

The Warner group had earlier published a study of the black community in Chicago (Drake and Cayton 1945), but Coleman and Rainwater in *Social Standing in America* (1978) were more ambitious and described two metropolitan areas. In the early 1970s, they collected qualitative and quantitative data on public conceptions of social class through 600 interviews conducted in Boston and 300 in Kansas City. The procedures employed were designed to provide representative samples of adults in Greater Boston and Greater Kansas City—that is, of the respective Standard Metropolitan Statistical Areas (SMSAs) designated by the Bureau of the Census. The interviews were standardized and followed a fixed schedule of questions in the style of a social survey, but many were open-ended and allowed the respondents to choose their own words.

The hierarchy of prestige classes which Coleman and Rainwater stitched together from their analysis of the interviews is rather complex, and so we offer a simplified and schematic version in Table 2–1. (Note that the annual incomes were recorded in 1971 dollars. Doubling these amounts will give roughly equivalent values in inflated 1980 dollars.) Inspection of the table shows that the basic structure of the hierarchy is parallel to the one found by Warner in Yankee City. For instance, in both studies upper-upper and lower-upper classes correspond to a distinction between established families and "new money," although the distinction may be noticed only by those who are themselves close to the top. In Boston, the upper-class respondents spoke of the former as "the tip-top—as close to an aristocracy as you'll find in America . . . Yankee families that go way back; the WASPs who were here first . . . the bluebloods with inherited income—they live on stocks and bonds" (p. 150). The same respondents described the lower-uppers as "a mix of highly successful executives, doctors, and lawyers with incomes of $60,000 at least, many $100,000 and more. . . . They have help in the house, fancy cars, frequent and expensive vacations and at least two houses. . . . They're not considered top society because they don't have the right background—they're newer money, with less tradition in their lifestyle" (p. 151).

By contrast to those at the top, Coleman and Rainwater delineated a bottom class characterized by dependence on irregular, marginal employment or public relief, often shifting from one to the other. As in Yankee City, Boston and Kansas City families in this class were regarded as less than respectable and described in terms which implied that they were physically and morally "unclean." However, many of Coleman and Rainwater's informants made a distinction between families on the very bottom and a class of semipoor families

TABLE 2–1
Coleman and Rainwater's metropolitan class structure

Class	Typical occupations or source of income	Typical education	Annual income, 1971	Percentage of sample
I. Upper Americans				
Upper-upper Old rich; aristocratic family name	Inherited wealth	Ivy League college degree; often postgraduate	$60,000 and above	2%
Lower-upper Success elite	Top professionals; senior corporate executives	Good colleges; often postgraduate	$60,000 and above	
Upper-middle Professional and managerial	Middle professionals and managers	College degree; often post-graduate	$20,000 to $60,000	20
II. Middle Americans				
Middle class	Lower-level managers; small-business owners; lower-status professionals (pharmacists, teachers); sales and clerical	High school plus some college	$10,000 to $20,000	33
Working class	Higher blue-collar (craftsmen, truck drivers) lowest paid sales and clerical	High school diploma for younger persons	$7,500 to $15,000	37
III. Lower Americans				
Semipoor	Unskilled labor and service	Part high school	$4,500 to $6,000	
The bottom	Often unemployed; welfare	Primary school	Less than $4,500	8

Source: See text.

who worked more regularly and were slightly more orderly in their lifestyles. Apparently "lower Americans" were underrepresented in the Boston and Kansas City samples because of the reluctance of paid middle-class interviewers to deal with them; Coleman and Rainwater estimate, on the basis of census data, that the true proportion is not 8 percent but between 12 and 13 percent (p. 205).

As portrayed by Coleman and Rainwater, then, "upper America" and "lower America" neatly parallel corresponding prestige groupings in Yankee City. The same would appear to be true of "middle America," where Coleman and Rainwater's middle class and working class are equivalent to Warner's lower-middle and upper-lower classes. However, it was in the middle range of the class structure that they had the hardest time organizing the views of Kansas City and Boston respondents into prestige categories. In judging prestige, city respondents at this level gave almost exclusive emphasis to income and standard of living and paid relatively little attention to other stratification variables, such as occupation and association, that had seemed important to Warner.

Coleman and Rainwater reported that their middle American respondents recognized three levels among themselves, often called "people at the comfortable standard of living," "people just getting along," and "people who aren't lower class but are having a real hard time" (pp. 158–59). However, the two sociologists found these categories inadequate and insisted on the more traditional distinction between middle class and working class, which, they suggest, can each be subdivided along income lines. Their conclusion that the middle class/working class distinction is more fundamental than income differences is based on evidence which the survey collected on differences in lifestyles and patterns of association. For instance, among families at the same "comfortable" income level (approximately $11,000 to $20,000), they noted important differences in consumption patterns. The middle-class families were likely to spend more on living room and dining room furniture and less on television sets, stereos, and refrigerators and other appliances that were attractive to working-class families at these income levels. Working-class families own larger and more expensive automobiles and more trucks, campers, and vans. Moreover, income equality in middle America does not appear to produce social equality; patterns of friendship, organizational membership, and neighborhood location parallel lifestyle distinctions (pp. 182–83). Some respondents implicitly recognized these differences. A "comfortable" working-class man observed (p. 184):

> I'm working class because that's my business; I work with my hands. I make good money, so I am higher in the laboring force than many

people I know. But birds of a feather flock together. My friends are all hard-working people. . . . We would feel out of place with higher-ups.

The wife of a white-collar man was more explicit (p. 184):

> I consider myself middle class. My husband works for a construction company in the office. Many of the construction workers make a lot more than he does. But when we have parties at my husband's company, the ones with less education feel out of place and not at ease with the ones with more education. I think of them as working class.

The difficulties Coleman and Rainwater encountered in delineating the prestige hierarchy of middle America raise general, and by now familiar, questions about the methods by which the sociologist defines the structure of prestige classes in a community. They described their approach to prestige measurement as close to Warner's Evaluated Participation. However, the metropolitan context of their research imposed an important limit on their ability to replicate in a precise way Warner's methodology. Since the respondents in Boston and Kansas City did not know the same people in their communities, the technique of matched agreements comparing specific families (which Hollingshead had systematized with his control families) could not be employed. This made synthesizing individual judgments of the class system more difficult; the data consisted of verbal statements about general symbols and not details about particular others in the community.

Coleman and Rainwater were clear that their version of the prestige hierarchy was not a mirror image of the class structure as understood in the community but rather an ideal type defined by the researchers. "Ultimately, to number and name the American social classes is a task for the social scientists. The status structure is too complex to be comprehended fully by average persons from their inevitably narrow vantage point" (p. 120). They approached this "task" in two stages. First they attempted "to piece together hundreds of 'narrow' views on the subject and construct from them a single picture that is a summation of public impressions about the social class hierarchy" (p. 120). Subsequently this "image-based picture" was elaborated by combining it with data on behavior to produce "a picture that, in our view, is more nearly the truth about classes in America" (p. 120). As in Warner's work, the outcome is significantly dependent on the "clinical" judgment of the investigators.

The basic vehicle for the initial step was an open-ended question in the survey instrument: "How many classes would you say there are [in America], and what names would you give to them (or what names have you heard other people use)? What else could you say to describe each of the classes you've mentioned?" (p. 120). The most frequent answer to the first part of the question was three classes. However, this response was given by only one third of the informants. Other answers included two, four, five, six, seven, and nine classes or a flat refusal to say. One Bostonian replied, "You have too many classes for me to count and name. . . . Hell! There may be 15 or 30. Anyway, it doesn't matter a damn to me" (p. 121). Even respondents who suggested the same number of classes differed in the way they described and named the classes, especially when the number was greater than three.

The disparate character of responses to both parts of the question suggests, as Coleman and Rainwater admit, that there is no "clear public consensus as to the name and number of social classes in the United States" (p. 20), at least in large cities. However, the variations among images of the class system that emerged in Boston and Kansas City were in some ways systematic. As in the earlier studies by the Warner group, the researchers found that respondents tended to construct more class boundaries close to their own position in the prestige hierarchy and fewer at a distance from themselves. Furthermore, when they asked people for reactions to a series of hypothetical class names, they found that the names "were 'cheapened' in their assumed reference by respondents of successively lower-status" (p. 127). Thus, upper Americans understood middle-middle class to refer to those earning $15,000 or more a year, typically college graduates. But middle Americans associated the label with incomes of $12,000 to $13,000 and lower Americans assumed incomes of $9,000 to $10,000 (p. 127).

Coleman and Rainwater noted that the simplest division, that into a two-class model, emphasized the distinction between "us" and "them" and was usually offered by people slightly below average in their own position who expressed both "awe and animus" toward those above them in the hierarchy with more money (p. 121); this perception is linked to a conflict model of society. Citizens who thought in terms of a three-class model also generally used income as the basic criterion for dividing up the social system, but they added another class below themselves at the bottom—people who were poor, who lived in the slums on welfare—and gained some sense of pride by having someone to be above. Models that contained four or more classes usually used criteria other than money to make additional distinctions and often came from respondents in higher positions. They talked of education, the way people lived, family background, and other factors that modified the influence of money by itself. These respondents implicitly used an individualistic and competitive instead of a conflict model of society (for a theoretical elaboration of this difference, see Ossowski 1963; for a revealing study in England, see Bott 1954 and 1964).

Coleman and Rainwater imposed order on the many conceptions of the class system proposed by their respondents. As they viewed the problem, "All these seeming inconsistencies and variations should be thought of not as confusion but as a rich lode of imagery about the status system; represented therein are the best efforts of usually inarticulate people to express categorically and concretely the underlying continuum of status" (p. 123). The trick was to find the criteria for cutting points in the continuum, explicit or implicit in the comments of respondents, which indicate the class groupings which were most salient for them. This could be done without assuming that Bostonians and Kansas Citians agreed completely among themselves on the number of classes or the proper names for them. Approaching the matter in this way, Coleman and Rainwater located 13 logical dichotomies, of which only 6 "emerged with sufficient frequency and strength of supporting argument to be considered centrally significant" (p. 124). They were the following:

1. A source-of-income cut, placing those with inherited wealth socially above those with self-earned wealth.
2. A level-of-income cut, establishing "people who really have it made" financially above those who are "doing well but aren't really well-to-do."
3. A cut based on educational credentials and associated occupational accomplishments—"the degrees versus the non-degrees"—ranking the former above the latter.
4. A cut based on publicly perceived income level and associated standard of living—"people who have a comfortable salary and all the necessities plus a few luxuries" versus families who are "just getting along."
5. Another cut based on income and standard of living—"People getting by who have a decent house and the husband has a decent-paying job" versus "people who have to work at jobs that don't pay well. . . . Their housing is not slum, but it's undesirable."
6. A cut based on source of income, this time private earnings versus public charity—"the poor who are working and largely self-supporting" versus "the welfare class."

These six cuts combine to suggest a seven-class model close to the one outlined in Table 2–1. It is worth noting that, for the most part, the classes delineated by these cuts are not simply *quantitatively* distinguished from each other, as they might be on a single scale, such as income. The cuts imply *qualitative* differences among classes. For example, the first cut separates new money from old money; the third cut divides those with from those without college degrees. A full application of all the cuts allowed Coleman and Rainwater to further subdivide the seven classes shown in Table 2–1, but we need not follow them that far.

IS THE AMERICAN CLASS STRUCTURE CHANGING?

Can we assume from Coleman and Rainwater's results that the class structure of the United States has changed little since the Warner studies of the 1930s and 1940s? We might, but one intriguing finding from their surveys should make us cautious: people in Boston and Kansas City were convinced, and overwhelmingly so, that there have been very important changes since World War II. When asked, "Do you think social class is getting more important or less important in America these days than it used to be?" over two thirds of the respondents replied "less important" (p. 294). This response was connected to a series of perceived changes in the American stratification system. Bostonians and Kansas Citians believed the system had become more egalitarian through improvements in income distribution, reductions in ethnic and religious barriers, a wider availability of consumer goods, a decline in class consciousness, and, above all, rapid social mobility in recent decades. Americans, they argued, are not so bound to the class into which they are born as they once were, and therefore it makes less sense to speak of social classes: "We don't have social classes like that anymore" (p. 294). "Class distinctions are not what the people of my generation will base their lives on" (p. 298). The economic prosperity of the 1950s and 60s (which faded somewhat in the 70s) left its mark on the way Americans view their lives.

We will return to the question of change repeatedly in this book. In some areas, we will discover great transformations that most Americans are only faintly aware of, while in others we will find that change has not been nearly so sweeping as many imagine. In particular, we will see that, even though many Americans *believe* that class has become less important, they continue to *act* as if it were quite important. None of this, however, should lead us to deny that belief is itself a crucial aspect of the class system.

PRESTIGE OF OCCUPATIONS

Warner, Coleman, and Rainwater, and many other investigators have stressed the importance of occupation for the prestige evaluations Americans make of one another. Especially in metropolitan settings, where people do not have a detailed knowledge of one another's income, family background, lifestyle, associations, etc., they are forced to fall back on a few shorthand indicators of personal prestige, such as occupation. They know, of course, that occupation is a fair indicator of two other sources of prestige, income and education: physicians are typically affluent; not many janitors hold college degrees. They may also associate particular lifestyles and patterns of interaction with occupations, such as the general distinction between blue-collar and white-collar workers. These expectations account for the emphasis they place on occupation in making prestige assessments. For the sociologist engaged in a large-scale research operation, occupation is especially useful: it is more visible than income, and it can be studied with census data as well as direct social surveys and qualitative field studies. Furthermore, since census data are available for earlier periods, we can use occupation as an indicator in historical research.

There have been numerous studies of occupational prestige, going back at least 50 years, but the best known are national polls conducted under the auspices of the National Opinion Research Center (NORC), now located at the University of Chicago. The first of the NORC studies was conducted under the stimulus of professors Cecil C. North and Paul K. Hatt in 1947. It was based on the opinions of 2,920 persons, a representative sample of the entire adult population of the United States (NORC 1953). An exact replication of the original study was carried out in 1963 with a smaller national sample of 651 adults (Hodge et al. 1966).

The interviewing procedure in the two studies was straightforward; the respondent was handed a card printed as follows:

For each job mentioned, please pick out the statement that best gives *your own personal opinion* of the *general standing* that such a job has.

1. *Excellent* standing
2. *Good* standing
3. *Average* standing
4. *Somewhat below average* standing.
5. *Poor* standing
X. I don't know where to place that one.

Then a list of 90 occupations was read off, and the respondent was asked to give his or her opinion about each one. The technique seemed to bring forth real and stable opinions, a somewhat better result than is usual for polling operations of this type. Only seven occupations brought as many as 10 percent "don't know" answers. And for a check, in two instances two different titles were given to the same occupation, and the answers were almost identical.

The ratings given by individual respondents were combined by assigning numerical weights ranging from 100 for excellent to 20 for poor and then averaging the answers to produce a composite score. Table 2–2 presents a sampling of the findings from the 1963 survey. The results at the top and bottom of the scale are consistent with what we have seen in the Warner group's community and metropolitan studies (which, of course, are based on much more than occupation). The highest ranking occupations are professional (physician, chemist, accountant) and managerial (cabinet member, banker, building con-

TABLE 2–2
National opinion on prestige of occupations

Occupation	NORC score, 1963
U.S. Supreme Court justice	94
Physician	93
Nuclear physicist	92
Scientist	92
Cabinet member in the federal government	90
College professor	90
Chemist	89
Lawyer	89
Dentist	88
Member of the board of directors of a large corporation	87
Civil engineer	86
Banker	85
Accountant for a large business	81
Public school teacher	81
Owner of a factory that employs about 100 people	80
Building contractor	80
Railroad engineer	76
Electrician	76
Trained machinist	75
Farm owner and operator	74
Welfare worker for a city government	74
Policeman	72
Bookkeeper	70
Carpenter	68
Manager of a small store in a city	67
Mail carrier	66
Traveling salesman for a wholesale concern	66
Plumber	65
Automobile repairman	64
Barber	63
Machine operator in a factory	63
Owner-operator of a lunch stand	63
Truck driver	59
Clerk in a store	56
Dockworker	50
Night watchman	50
Farmhand	48
Janitor	48
Clothes presser in a laundry	45
Garbage collector	39

Source: Hodge et al. 1966: 324–25.

tractor), ordered by the level of expertise or administrative responsibility they entail.

The lowest are unskilled, manual jobs, such as garbage collector, janitor, or farmhand. Between these extremes are the less demanding office or sales positions (bookkeeper, traveling salesman, clerk in a store) and the more highly skilled manual jobs (electrician, carpenter, plumber, truck driver). But note that there is no clear distinction between white-collar and blue-collar jobs (in Warner's terms, lower-middle and upper-lower). The electrician ranks above the bookkeeper, the carpenter above the traveling salesman, and the truck driver above the store clerk. Obviously, when faced with this sort of task, respondents are interested in something more than just where someone works or the color of his shirt collar (Glenn and Alston 1968).

When interviewees were asked the main factor they had weighed in making their ratings, the most frequent replies were pay, service to humanity, education, and social prestige, but none of these criteria was volunteered by more than 18 percent of the sample (NORC 1953: 418). Whatever the bases of their judgments, the surveys demonstrate that respondents did have a scale in mind on which they could place occupations with a rough consensus. Although there were significant differences among individuals in their relative ratings of occupations, sociologists were more impressed with the great consistency of the average ratings given occupations by relevant subgroups of the population. The correlations between the ratings made by random pairs of individual raters ran about 0.6, but the correlations between the average ratings made by the prosperous and the poor, people in high- and low-prestige occupations, blacks and whites, men and women, residents of the Northeast and the South, and city and country dwellers were all 0.95 or above. Even those who proposed different criteria for judging occupations did not differ in the way they ranked occupations (Reiss 1961: 189, 193; Treiman 1977: 60–74).

What systematic differences there were can be summed up in two principles: (1) people tended to raise in rank their own and closely related occupations, and (2) people agreed with each other more concerning occupations that were well-known. For example, in 1947 many respondents did not know how to place "nuclear physicist" (answers in response to a question about this included "assistant to a physic" and "he's a spy"); yet they had no trouble deciding about a "scientist."

However, even in less esoteric fields brief occupational titles of the sort employed in the NORC surveys are somewhat ambiguous. Confronted by "banker," the respondent does not know if the reference is to the assistant manager of a small branch bank or the president of a major international bank. Of course, we can never capture with a survey the richness of detail that Warner reports from a community study since surveys force us to depend on few and simple categories. On the other hand, there is no substitute for the systematic knowledge a survey can provide. It is especially useful for making broad comparisons between different communities or different historical periods, but we must always remember that we are using social symbols about general types of jobs that leave out a lot of concrete detail.

The relative consistency of prestige ratings across the subgroups noted in the 1947 study led sociologists to wonder whether the ratings were stable over time. The second NORC study in 1963 offered an opportunity for a retest after 16 years. Despite a few changes in relative ratings (the nuclear physicist was better known in 1963 and more highly evaluated), the correlation between the two sets of scores was nearly perfect (0.97). In 1970 and 1971, Coleman and Rainwater surveyed occupational prestige in Boston and Kansas City, obtaining readings which correlated 0.87 with those of the second NORC study (this lower but still very high correlation apparently reflects differences in measurement procedure rather than real change) (1978: 57). Moreover, retrospective comparisons between the NORC studies and several earlier studies suggested that there had been virtually no changes in the rankings of occupational prestige since 1925 (Hodge et al. 1966).

INTERNATIONAL COMPARISONS

Occupational prestige is a convenient index for stratification studies because it transcends local communities. The consensus throughout the country found by the NORC confirms that statement. But the intriguing possibility arises that perhaps the meaning of occupation transcends national boundaries as well. A massive study by Donald Treiman dwarfs earlier attempts to deal with this question (Inkeles and Rossi 1956; Hodge et al. 1966; Treiman 1977). Treiman collected data from occupational prestige studies in 60 separate societies. From country to country, he correlated the relative prestige ratings given the same occupations. The average correlation between all pairs of countries was 0.8, slightly lower than found in earlier studies but remarkably high given the diversity of societies involved. Further analysis produced suggestive but by no means compelling evidence that countries at the same level of economic development have similar patterns of occupational prestige.

The consistency of occupational prestige judgments across societies and between subgroups of the same society suggests that the ratings correspond to some fundamental aspect of social structure which is quite widely perceived, even though, as we have seen, divergent explanations may be offered for it. Treimen argues that the tendency toward a common international system of ranking occupations is rooted in international similarities in the division of labor. A complex division of labor attaches quite specific social functions to each occupation. This occupational differentiation brings varying control over scarce resources (specifically skills, authority, and property). For example, a physician must have special skills and authority to carry out that job. But differential control of resources means occupational differences in power. Those with greater power can obtain greater privileges for themselves: the doctor claims high income. Finally, differential power and privilege are the sources of differential prestige: the physician's skill, authority, and high income become the bases of high prestige (for critiques of the occupational prestige literature see Goldthorpe and Hope 1972, and Coxon and Jones 1978).

DUNCAN'S SOCIOECONOMIC INDEX FOR OCCUPATIONS

The merits of applicability in different places, stability over time, and intergroup consensus have made occupational prestige rankings an attractive stratification measure for all sorts of sociological studies. But investigators who used the NORC ratings ran into one very serious difficulty: only 90 occupations were rated in the original NORC surveys. When researchers encountered occupations not listed, they were forced to assign approximate prestige scores on the basis of "similarity" to an NORC occupation.

Otis Dudley Duncan (1961) provided one solution to this problem that has been widely used by others. Duncan noted that both the average education and the average income of those who worked in various occupations were highly correlated with the prestige scores of the occupations. Taking advantage of this fact, he combined income and education in a simple regression formula designed to estimate how much education and income were required to produce the prestige of each occupation on the NORC list.

His income-plus-education formula turned out to be a very efficient predictor of occupational prestige: it correlated 0.91 with the combined percentages of "excellent" and "good" ratings received by the NORC occupations for which income and education data could be found. Duncan therefore felt confident in employing the same formula to estimate prestige scores for occupations *not* covered by the surveys, using census data to get typical incomes and educations for the people who worked in hundreds of different occupations.

Duncan was, in effect, using education and income as stand-ins for prestige (and the index is called SEI—Socio-Economic Index). His justification for doing so—beyond the obvious pragmatic argument that it seemed to work—was that education and income are both functionally and temporally related to occupation. Education is the necessary preparation for entering an occupation; income is the reward which flows from an occupation. We have, of course, already examined studies which point to close ties between prestige and income and education. If the NORC ratings do in fact provide an accurate prestige measure, Duncan's estimation formula confirms that income and education are strongly (and approximately equally) associated with the prestige of occupational titles.

OCCUPATIONS AND SOCIAL CLASSES

The NORC surveys reveal how the public places occupations on a continuum, but leave us in the dark as to how people might cut that continuum into occupational classes. The problem is obviously similar to the one we raised earlier concerning the grouping of families in Yankee City or Boston into prestige classes. Some evidence on this question was gathered in a national survey of approximately 2000 adults conducted by the University of Michigan's Survey Research Center in 1975 (Jackman 1979). The SRC questionnaire asked respondents to place a series of occupations into one of five class categories: poor, working class, middle class, upper-middle class, and upper class. This question and several others in the SRC study replicate items in a 1946 survey conducted by Richard Centers, whose influential work on class consciousness and political attitudes we will examine in Chapter 9 (Centers 1949). The results from the 1975 survey are presented in Table 2–3.

The data indicate that people do not have a difficult time associating occupations with social classes (there were few "don't knows") and that there is considerable popular agreement about where occupations should be placed in the five-class system that was suggested by the interviewer. In virtually all cases the most frequent class assignment (indicated in italics) accounted for over fifty percent of the responses.

As we can anticipate by now, class placement of occupations is easiest at the top and bottom of the scale. There is, for example, strong agreement that high ranking corporate officers are upper class and janitors and assembly-line workers are working class. The greatest ambiguity centers on the middle ranking occupations, especially skilled manual workers and foremen. Note also that the distinction between working class and middle class does not neatly correspond to the difference between blue collar and white collar jobs.

TABLE 2–3
Social class assignment of occupations

		Social class assigned (percent)					
Occupations	Poor	Working	Middle	Upper middle	Upper	Don't know	Total
Corporation directors & presidents	—*	1	3	22	72	2	100
Doctors & lawyers	—*	2	4	36	57	2	100
Executives & managers	—*	3	14	56	26	2	100
Supervisors in offices & stores	—*	17	56	23	3	1	100
Small businessmen......	2	18	61	18	1	1	100
Schoolteachers & social workers	—*	19	60	17	3	1	100
Foremen in factories	1	40	47	10	1	2	100
Plumbers & carpenters	1	44	40	12	2	1	100
Workers in offices & stores..............	2	60	33	3	1	1	100
Assembly-line factory workers	5	75	16	2	1	2	100
Janitors	25	67	6	1	—*	1	100
Migrant farm workers	73	22	2	1	1	2	100

Source: Jackman 1979:449.
* Less than 1. Totals may not add to 100 due to rounding. Numbers in italics represent modal category. Sample size = 1,850.

Here, as when ranking occupations in the NORC surveys, people are more discriminating than that. The majority place the lower white collar positions in offices and stores in the working class.

The 1975 data differ little from the original results that Centers obtained in the 1940s, except for minor variations which depend on the exact wording of the question. Both studies support the idea that the public perceives more than a rank order of occupational titles: it groups those titles into class categories that have widespread meaning, even though the agreement about the placement of particular occupations is less than perfect.

THE PERCEPTION OF RANK AND STRATA

Over the years, investigators have tried various devices to systematize the creation of groups or strata or classes out of an undifferentiated rank order. They generally find that the rank order is seen by the public with more clarity and consistency than are subdivisions into groups. Some people divide the world into conflicting groups of "us" versus "them," and they are likely to use labels like working class versus middle class. Others stress the openness of our society and the chance for people to keep climbing a notch or two, and they are likely to either deny sharp class divisions or use a lot of them with minor distinctions separating one from another. In other words, perception of classes is intimately linked with degrees and styles of class consciousness, which we will explore further in Chapter 9.

When a sociologist presents a subject with either a list of the families who are his neighbors in a small town or a list of occupations, and requests that the subject arrange them in categories of equivalent prestige, the stimulus presented is partly structured and partly ambiguous. During a total life experience, a subject will have run into a number of situations that indicate prestige differences, but these situations have not been so clear and so consistent that they completely determine the subject's perceptions. The very nature of our society is such that the worker in overalls can put on a business suit for special occasions. As he changes from one social role to another, his behavior changes somewhat—but not completely, for if he meets his boss on Sunday, he is deferential toward him, even if they both are wearing the same kind of suit. Consequently, the respondent in the survey will have a general idea of a prestige hierarchy but not a perfectly sharp one with fixed labels for each level plus standard status symbols to indicate who belongs where. The degree of existing ambiguity allows the subject to project some personal views into the data and shape them slightly to suit individual desires and values. Therefore, people at different levels give somewhat different answers for two reasons: their outer experience has been different, and their inner frames of reference are different.[2] Both stimuli and perceiver vary from one respondent to another.

There is no such thing as the "objective" status structure which can be viewed by the completely neutral observer. Prestige is embedded in attitudes about the relationships between persons, positions, and symbols, and it varies according to the perspective from which they are viewed. The neutral observer has to find a way of summarizing the agreements and disagreements but should not foolishly conclude that the result is a reality that is more "real" than the subjective perceptions of the respondents (and the behavior they determine).

From the many studies we have reviewed, three conclusions stand out and are confirmed by every one of them: (1) in American society there is a prestige hierarchy of both persons and occupations; (2) this hierarchy is not sharply divided in the minds of the citizens into discrete levels or strata; (3) there is more agreement about rank order

---

[2] There is, in fact, another cause of varied and inconsistent answers: people do not pay full attention to a task of this type, and a lot of random errors creep in.

than about the criteria used in making ranking decisions, and more agreement about ranks than about strata. There is enough consensus to allow us to arrange a rank order that permits further operations to seek the variables that correlate with it and to begin to study the causes of that covariation. We then find that the covariation between occupational prestige and personal prestige is higher than for most pairs of variables that sociologists are interested in. Either occupational prestige largely causes personal prestige, or else they both flow from the same underlying causes.

There are some tentative principles that seem to explain the differences in perceptions of both ranking and grouping, and these appear in a number of the different studies, though all the data are not completely consistent. The principles can be summarized as follows; they interact with and sometimes offset the effects of one another (for a recent appraisal of this synthesis of 1957, see Coxon and Jones 1978: 118–19):

1. People perceive a rank order.
2. People tend to enhance their own position:
   a. By raising their own position relative to others.
   b. By varying the size of their own group. Here the evidence is not consistent: apparently there is a tendency to narrow the group when thinking of individual persons about whom invidious distinctions can be made (especially those lower on the scale), and enlarge it when thinking of general categories of persons who are closely similar to one another.
   c. By perceiving separate but equal groups, thus accepting difference but denying hierarchy.
3. People agree more about the extremes than about the middle of the prestige range. This is probably a result both of clarity of stimulus and of aspects of perceptual organization. There are more people in the middle, and they are less publicized. Also errors at the extremes can be made only in one direction.
4. People agree more about the top of the range than the bottom and make more distinctions about the top than about the bottom. This probably reflects stimulus reality, for those at the top are more conspicuous and also more differentiated.
5. People lump together into large groups those who are furthest from them.
6. The better persons and occupations are known, the more agreement there is concerning them.
7. People have more consensus about the relative rank of persons or occupations that are closely related to each other in some functional way, such as the hierarchy of doctors, nurses, and orderlies.

8. People at the top are more consistent with one another, and make more divisions into groups, than those on the bottom.

9. People in the middle or at the bottom are more likely to conceive of class differences in financial terms, while those at the top are more conscious of prestige distinctions from lineage and style of life.

10. Mobility is a source of ambiguity in perception of the prestige order. People find it difficult to "place" mobile individuals. Perception of high rates of mobility leads to the conclusion that class boundaries are amorphous or nonexistent.

These 10 principles connecting social facts with the way people perceive those facts are sufficient to explain why there is no straightforward answer to the question that is asked so often: How many social classes are there in America? The moment we try to answer the question with data that come from the views of ordinary citizens, we are bound to come up with ambiguities that lead us to reply, "It all depends on how you view the situation." Only those theorists who have a scheme which allows them to stand above the system and decide for themselves what is important can arrive at a clear-cut answer to the question. And since the theorists disagree with one another, once more we end up saying, "It all depends on how you view the situation."

CONCLUSIONS

The studies of the Warner group found that personal prestige in small towns seems to reflect more directly than anything else the styles of life and clique memberships involved in consumption behavior. But in a modern society with a complex division of labor, consumption behavior reflects more than anything else the income derived from occupational roles. These roles are sufficiently standardized to permit a direct prestige ranking of occupational titles. That ranking has remained relatively constant in the United States for the last 50 years, and it bears striking similarity to the ranking in other industrial countries.

However, occupation implies more than just income. The full significance of work is best determined by those who understand it —a person's colleagues on the job. They use such criteria as the skill the job demands, the talent and training necessary to produce the skill, the responsibility and authority over others that the job entails, the pay it brings, and even the nature of the product. The pay has a double function: it is granted as a reward for skill, responsibility, and authority, but it soon becomes a symbol of them and a direct stimulus for effort—we say "he's a $50,000-a-year man." The product of work is judged by general social values; we believe that it is more important to save life than to beautify it (thus a doctor is ranked higher than a hairdresser), and we grant honor to those whose decisions have wide social impact (which puts justices of the Supreme Court at the top).

In a small community, people can be ranked on the totality of their roles—occupational, familial, and civic. In the larger cities, neighbors do not know so much about one another and tend to use shorthand symbols. Sometimes they judge in terms of income, sometimes they talk of styles of life which reflect both income and the education and values that shape the way income is spent, and sometimes they recognize that occupation may be the best index of all since it reflects education, skill, authority, and income (indeed, technical studies show that occupation is the best single indicator of general social position; see Kahl and Davis 1955).

The vitality of our materialistic and competitive culture requires a reasonably close relationship between these causes and consequences of occupational roles. People must believe that on the average fair rules apply so that those who have high skill and use discipline to train their skill will be rewarded with important jobs that pay well, and that money can buy a style of life which is admired in the community. Without such a chain of connections, motivation would suffer and legitimacy would weaken (Davis and Moore 1945; Tumin 1955 and 1966; Cullen and Novick 1979). We note tensions, for example, when those who spend lots of money seem to have gained it in ways that do not reflect proper occupational achievements—such as racketeers whose methods are suspect, or children of rich families who spend without earning. And those who turn their backs on conspicuous consumption may even withdraw from the rigors of occupational competition and go live in communes.

Many of the tensions derive from contradictions between principles of legitimacy and the actual operations of power. Salaries, for instance, are determined by people who have authority in organizations, and profits reflect decisions by owners of businesses, so it should not surprise us that people at the top receive lots of money and then assert that they deserve it and general prosperity requires it. Sometimes these determinations are considered fair and just by subordinates, but sometimes they are considered to be outrageous exploitation. Furthermore, the family system passes on property through the generations, which is usually considered to be more natural and appropriate by the rich than by the poor. Marx stressed that the rules of property are set by those with power; Weber emphasized the connection between occupational rewards and general values of legitimacy, rationality, and efficiency. When the ordinary facts of daily life are perceived by growing segments of the population to depart too far from the rules of fair play, the tensions produce conflict and change, as we shall see in subsequent chapters.

SUGGESTED READINGS

Coxon, Anthony P., and Charles L. Jones. 1978. *The Images of Occupational Prestige.* New York: St. Martin's Press.
Challenges the idea that occupational prestige ratings reflect a true social reality independent of perception.

Curtis, Richard, and Elton Jackson. 1977. *Inequality in American Communities.* New York: Academic Press.
Compares several communities on various indicators of stratification. Authors conceive stratification as a continuum rather than as a structure of classes.

Goode, William J. 1979. *The Celebration of Heroes: Prestige as a Social Control System.* Berkeley: University of California Press.
A recent reexamination of the uses of the concept of prestige.

Haug, Marie. 1977. "Measurement in Social Stratification." *Annual Review of Sociology* 3:51–77.
A technical discussion of recent research on measurement problems.

Okun, Arthur M. 1975. *Equality and Efficiency: The Big Tradeoff.* Washington, D.C.: The Brookings Institution.
An economist muses in stimulating prose about the minimum amount of income and status differentiation needed to promote competition and economic efficiency.

Veblen, Thorstein. 1934. *The Theory of the Leisure Class.* New York: Modern Library. (First published 1899.)
This book introduced the idea that "conspicuous consumption" was the way to buy prestige in competitive America.

Vidich, Arthur, and Joseph Bensman. 1960. *Small Town in Mass Society.* Garden City, N.Y.: Doubleday, Anchor.
Community study emphasizing what Warner left out: the small town in the national setting.

Warner, Lloyd, et al.1963. *Yankee City.* New Haven: Yale University Press.
Handy abridgement of the entire series of volumes on Yankee City.

Social class, occupation, and social change

A post-industrial society, being primarily a technical society, awards place less on the basis of inheritance or property . . . than on education and skills.

Daniel Bell (1976: xviii)

We may have created too many dumb jobs for the number of dumb people to fill them.

Quoted in Braverman (1974: 35)

3

Occupation is a crucial and convenient stratification variable. We have already found that it is closely tied to personal prestige, education, and income. In later chapters, we will see that occupation shapes social processes as disparate as the exercise of political power and the way that parents bring up their children. For the researcher, as we have noted, occupation is a convenient variable because it is not bound to the particular circumstances of a local community but has a national definition that is relatively stable over time. Stability makes occupation a useful measuring rod for historical change, especially since we have occupational data on both local and national levels which stretch back many decades. These data allow us to analyze shifts in the occupational structure (the proportional distribution of occupations in the labor force) which have important implications for the evolution of the class system in general.

THE LYNDS: MIDDLETOWN

There is one sociological community study which particularly emphasizes the occupational changes that have occurred in the past: the research on "Middletown" (for a recent reassessment of the study, see Caplow 1980). It began when Robert S. Lynd and Helen Merrell Lynd went to Indiana to describe a "typical" American community as it existed in 1924. At that time, Middletown (a pseudonym) had 35,000 inhabitants. In order to have a baseline for contrast, the Lynds reconstructed life in 1890 when the town had only 11,000 people and was going through the first stages of industrialization. They eventually returned to the city and wrote a second book about it, telling of its growth to 47,000 by 1935 and its reactions to the days of boom and bust which followed the first research. Thus we have three points of time to contrast: 1890, 1924, and 1935 (Lynd and Lynd, 1929 and 1937).

The Lynds lived in the town for over a year, meeting and talking to as many people as possible. They interviewed all the "important" people and many of the unimportant ones; they read newspapers, diaries, local histories; they went to various ritual gatherings of church and civic groups and luncheon clubs. Occasionally they passed out a questionnaire to get standardized information about such matters as budget behavior or attitudes of students in the high school, but the emphasis was more on qualitative than quantitative data.

In their first book, *Middletown,* the Lynds said this about life in 1924 (1929: 21–24):

> As the study progressed, it became more and more apparent that the money medium of exchange and the cluster of activities associated with its acquisition drastically condition the other activities of the people. Rivers begins his study of the Todas with an account of the ritual of the buffalo dairy, because "the ideas borrowed from the ritual of the dairy so pervade the whole of Toda ceremonial." A similar situation leads to the treatment of the activities of Middletown concerned with getting a living first among the six groups of activities to be described. . . .[1]
>
> At first glance it is difficult to see any semblance of pattern in the workaday life of a community exhibiting a crazy-quilt array of nearly 400 ways of getting its living. . . . On closer scrutiny, however, this welter may be resolved into two kinds of activities. The people who engage in them will be referred to throughout this report as the working class and the business class. Members of the first group, by and large, address their activities in getting their living primarily to *things,* utilizing material tools in the making of things and the performance of services, while the members of the second group address their activities predominantly to *people* in the selling or promotion of things, services, and ideas. . . . There are two and one-half times as many in the working class as in the business class—71 in each 100 as against 29. . . .
>
> While an effort will be made to make clear at certain points variant behavior within these two groups, it is after all this division into working class and business class that constitutes the outstanding cleavage in Middletown. The mere fact of being born upon one or the other side of the watershed roughly formed by these two groups is the most significant single cultural factor tending to influence what one does all day long throughout one's life; whom one marries; when one gets up in the morning; whether one belongs to the Holy Roller or Presbyterian church; or drives a Ford or a Buick; whether or not one's daughter makes the desirable high school Violet Club; or one's wife meets with the Sew We Do Club or with the Art Students' League; whether one belongs to the Odd Fellows or to the Masonic Shrine; whether one sits about evenings with one's necktie off; and so on indefinitely throughout the daily comings and goings of a Middletown man, woman, or child.

[1] The others are: making a home, training the young, using leisure, engaging in religious practices, engaging in community activities.

One of the central themes of the first Middletown volume was that, from 1890 to 1924, there were basic changes in the work pattern of both the business and working classes—changes, incidentally, that resulted in a wider gap between them. These changes flowed from three causes: larger population, more machinery, and increasing emphasis on money. The Lynds described in vivid detail a case study of the great transformation of modern life—industrialization.

Middletown in 1890 was a market town that was just beginning to turn to manufacturing. The work habits and values of its people were extensions of the traditions of their farmer parents. Those farmers were people who had conquered a wilderness: there had been land for all who would work it, and from such plenty, there emerged a society that lacked gradations of rank and privilege, a society that stressed individual initiative and progress, family solidarity, simplicity of manners and style of life, equality among neighbors. As trading and handicraft manufacturing succeeded farming as the base of livelihood, the old traditions could easily continue. A man earned whatever his own efforts deserved. True, there developed a gradation in income that extended from unskilled through skilled laborers to bosses (who were often ex-craftsmen) and a few professional men. But the gradation was not sharply divided into levels; a man often moved through several steps in a few years, and it was understood that the system was open to everybody in fair and equal competition. People started at the bottom of some line of endeavor and worked their way up. Income and prestige were direct outcomes of competence at work, and everybody could understand and agree that as competence increased with age and experience, it brought the right and necessity of teaching and directing the work of less-skillful men, and thereby it earned a higher income. But the machine began to change all this (1929: 31–32, 73–74):

> "When tradition is a matter of the spoken word, the advantage is all on the side of age. The elder is in the saddle" (Goldenweiser). Much the same condition holds when tradition is a matter of learned skills of hand and eye. But machine production is shifting traditional skills from the spoken word and the fingers of the master craftsman of the Middletown of the 90s to the cams and levers of the increasingly versatile machine. And in modern machine production it is speed and endurance that are at a premium. A boy of 19 may, after a few weeks of experience on a machine, turn out an amount of work greater than that of his father of 45. . . .
>
> The demands of the iron man for swiftness and endurance rather than training and skill have led to the gradual abandonment of the apprentice-master craftsman system; one of the chief characteristics of Middletown life in the 90s, this system is now virtually a thing of the past. . . . With the passing of apprenticeship the line between skilled and unskilled workers has become so blurred as to be in some shops almost non-existent.

There were basic changes among the business class as well. The old businessman was a small merchant or manufacturer, whose capital consisted mostly of his personal savings. He had started as a worker and had become a businessman. His relations with both employees and customers were personal, even intimate. But the new businessman operated in terms of bank credit, had too many employees and customers to know them personally, and had ties with other businessmen all over the country. True, the petty grocer and his kind still existed in 1924, but the major part of production and exchange in Middletown was passing into the hands of the new businessman (who was sometimes a branch manager of a national corporation).

Money had become the significant link between people. In the old days each family was more self-sufficient; they processed most of their own food and clothing (from purchased raw materials, of course); they entertained themselves at home and with the neighbors; when they did buy things, they paid cash. By 1924 "credit was coming rapidly to pervade and underlie more and more of the whole institutional structure within which Middletown earned its living" (1929: 45). Businessmen were much more dependent upon the banks and individuals upon the credit agencies and merchants who allowed them to buy on time. More articles of use were bought and fewer were homemade; more activities had changed from family and neighborhood affairs to commercial propositions. All of this was well symbolized by the automobile, and the Lynds devote some brilliant pages to the changes in life that centered around the family car. They sum up the transition to a money-centered life in these words (1929: 80–81):

> For both working and business class no other accompaniment of getting a living approaches in importance the money received for their work. It is more this future, instrumental aspect of work, rather than the intrinsic satisfactions involved, that keeps Middletown working so hard as more and more of the activities of living are coming to be strained through the bars of the dollar sign. Among the business group, such things as one's circle of friends, the kind of car one drives, playing golf, joining Rotary, the church to which one belongs, one's political principles, the social position of one's wife, apparently tend to be scrutinized somewhat more than formerly in Middletown for their instrumental bearing upon the main business of getting a living while conversely, one's status in these various other activities tends to be much influenced by one's financial position. As vicinage has decreased in its influence upon the ordinary social contacts of this group, there appears to be a constantly closer relation between the solitary factor of financial status and one's social status. A leading citizen presented this matter in a nutshell to a member of the research staff in discussing the almost universal local custom of "placing" newcomers in terms of where they live, how they live, the kind of car they drive, and similar

externals: "It's perfectly natural. You see, they know money, and they don't know you."

By 1924, Middletown was becoming too large and its productive system too complex and mechanized for community prestige to flow automatically from skill at work. People did not understand just what the activities of others were; a grocer knew little about glass blowing or automobile-parts manufacturing, and a glass blower knew little about financing a grocery store on credit. Concurrently, the money nexus was becoming increasingly important as more spheres of life became parts of the commercial market. The result was that people began to use money as a sign of accomplishment, a common denominator for prestige. The question "How much does he earn?" was heard more frequently than "How much skill does he have?"

The Lynds did not find it necessary to divide the population any further than business class and working class when they wrote about Middletown in 1924. True, they recognized some gradation within each group, but said that the working class was becoming more homogeneous through time as machines degraded skill, and the business class remained a small and basically undifferentiated group. They felt that no other distinction in Middletown was as important as this one.

The system could not work unless people believed that in a general way authority and income on the job and style of life and prestige off the job were automatic results of relatively free individualistic competition. This belief was brought to Middletown from the farms and villages; it was the American heritage of the frontier. Although some people were beginning to question this belief in 1924, the vast majority of both workers and businessmen clung to it. Free enterprise was not a mere theoretical discussion by economists of the workings of the market; it was a quasi-religious belief of the people.

MIDDLETOWN REVISITED

In 1935, the Lynds returned for a restudy. Both they and Middletown had changed. They had gone somewhat to the left in their political credo; as Robert Lynd wrote in the second book, *Middletown in Transition:* "Middletown believes that *laissez-faire* individualism is the best road to 'progress.' The present investigator holds the view, on the other hand, that our modern institutional world has become too big and too interdependent to rely indiscriminately upon the accidents of *laissez faire* . . ." (1937: xvii). Middletown had grown larger, reaching 47,000 people; its industrial plant was more mechanized, more centralized into larger units, more subservient to national corporations; it had gone through the boom of the late 1920s and the devastating crash of the early 1930s. Yet the interplay between the Lynds' assumptions and the reality of Middletown produced a report which stresses continuity in spite of change. The reader is surprised at how Middletown was able to take so much in its stride, to face such deep threats to its social structure, and yet come out with so many of the same beliefs—somewhat more tense and strained and defensive in their expression but basically unaltered. "The city's prevailing mood of optimism makes it view prosperity as normal, while each recurrent setback tends to come as a surprise which local sentiment views as 'merely temporary' " (1937: 13). In terms of this philosophy, Middletown never really admitted that it had a depression until it was all over.

The trend toward mechanization that was dominant from 1890 to 1924 continued on through 1935. It could be easily measured through occupational statistics. These showed that the city's increase in population went mostly into the service industries, for the machines were getting so efficient that a productive labor force only slightly increased could produce vastly more goods.

The details were these: Using the census figures for 1920 and 1930, the Lynds reported that the proportional increase of workers in the production industries was 26 percent, whereas the increase in the service industries was 66 percent. These service workers were becoming more professionalized through time; there were more school-teachers, more social workers, more dental hygienists. The new efficiency of the productive machinery could support more services of a "luxury" type.

Within the factories, there were changes in the composition of the work force. The trend toward semiskilled machine tenders continued —proportionally more men were in that category, fewer either unskilled or highly skilled. But a lot of half-trained men working on a complex production line needed a few very well-trained men to invent the machines and to direct and coordinate their work. These men were usually trained for supervision in school and college, rather than being promoted from the ranks. For an increase of only 10 percent in production workers who labored for an hourly wage, there was an increase of 31 percent in managers and officials, of 128 percent for technical engineers, and 900 percent for chemists, assayers, and metallurgists. At the same time the number of independent owner-manufacturers dropped 11 percent. (1937: 68). Thus we see the march of technology: a larger mass of machine tenders gathered into fewer but bigger factories directed by a tiny group of specialized technicians and executives. The gap between worker and manager had widened. And the manager had changed: he was not so often a self-made owner-businessman; he was more likely to be a member of "the new middle class" of technicians and administrators, trained in college, who worked for a salary. No longer could the complex system of

Middletown be adequately described by the simple division into business class and working class. (For Middletown's occupational system in 1970 see Caplow and Chadwick, 1979).

MIDDLETOWN'S NEW CLASSES

As a result of the changes they observed in Middletown, the Lynds described the class structure in 1935 as follows (1937: 458–60):

1. A very small top group of the "old" middle class is becoming an upper class, consisting of wealthy local manufacturers, bankers, the local head managers of one or two of the national corporations with units in Middletown, and a few well-to-do dependents of all the above, including one or two outstanding lawyers. . . .

2. Below this first group is to be found a larger but still relatively small group, consisting of established smaller manufacturers, merchants, and professional folk . . . and also most of the better-paid salaried dependents of the city's big-business interests. . . . These two elements in group 2 constitute socially a unity but, in their economic interests, often represent somewhat divergent elements. . . .

3. . . . Middletown's own middle class in purely locally relative terms: the minor employed professionals, the very small retailers and entrepreneurs, clerks, clerical workers, small salesmen, civil servants—the people who will never quite manage to be social peers of Group 2 and who lack the constant easy contact with Group 1 which characterizes Group 2.

4. Close to Group 3 might be discerned an aristocracy of local labor: trusted foremen, building trades craftsmen of long standing, and the pick of the city's experienced highly skilled machinists of the sort who send their children to the local college as a matter of course.

5. On a fifth level would stand the numerically overwhelmingly dominant group of the working class; these are the semiskilled or unskilled workers, including machine operatives, truckmen, laborers, the mass of wage earners.

6. Below group 5 one should indicate the ragged bottom margin, comprising some "poor whites" from the Kentucky, Tennessee, and West Virginia mountains, and in general the type of white worker who lives in the ramshackle, unpainted cottages on the outlying unpaved streets. These are the unskilled workers who cannot even boast of that last prop to the job status of the unskilled: regular employment when a given plant is operating. [Most of the city's few Negroes would also fit here.]

The Lynds add some general comments to the schematic outline just given (1937: 460–61):

Psychologically, groups 1, 2, and 3 cling together as businessfolk, over against groups 4, 5, and 6. . . . If the nascent "class" system of "Magic Middletown" appears to follow somewhat the above lines, Middletown itself will turn away from any such picture of the fissures and gullies across the surface of its social life. It is far more congenial to the mood of the city, proud of its traditions of democratic equality, to think of the lines of cleavage within its social system as based not upon class differences but rather upon the entirely spontaneous and completely individual and personal predilections of the 12,500 families who compose its population.

The Lynds offer us a scheme of six groups or classes emerging from "nascent" tendencies in the occupational system. Interestingly enough, this scheme based on occupational niches is almost the same as the Warner scheme based on prestige, consumption style, and interaction networks.

The processes by which occupation and income are transformed into style-of-life symbols, interaction networks, and personal prestige are sharply illustrated by the story of the emergence into prominence of the "X family." They were the leading group of businessmen in Middletown. They had founded their fortune before the turn of the century by starting a small glass-manufacturing plant on a capital of $7,000. There were five brothers, four who developed the business and one who practiced medicine. The legends of Middletown contain many tales of the simplicity and humbleness of these early business pioneers who took advantage of the natural gas that was the base for the city's early industrialization (1937: 75): "One of the city's veteran clothing dealers is fond of telling how one of the brothers borrowed a light-weight overcoat for a week-end party of young people in 1889. 'He didn't feel he could afford a new coat that year, as he was just starting in business.'" Then there is the newspaper editorial that appeared in 1925 when one of the brothers died: "He always worked on a level with his employees. He never asked a man to do something he would not do himself."

These men built up a great production machine that became world famous. They grew rich; they contributed vast sums to local charities and development projects; they became active community leaders. "In their conscientious and utterly unhypocritical combination of high profits, great philanthropy, and a low wage scale, they embody the hard-headed *ethos* of Protestant capitalism with its identification of Christianity with the doctrine of the goodness to all concerned of unrestricted business enterprise. In their modesty and personal rectitude, combined with their rise from comparative poverty to great wealth, they fit perfectly the American success dream" (1937: 75–76).

The brothers and their sons could not avoid becoming embroiled in all aspects of Middletown life. They became active in politics. They put up the money that kept the banks from collapsing in the depression, thereby gaining control. They were leaders in the fight against unionization. They took over the biggest department store in town when it failed in the early 30s. They opened a new residential subdivision for themselves and soon were surrounded by all the ambitious families in town who could afford to move. They contributed money to the local college (part of the state system), and one of them was elected president of the state university board of trustees. They bought a substantial interest in the local newspaper. They did not completely run the town, because there were other industries present, including manufacturing plants that were part of the General Motors empire. And the mass of the people still voted. But "the business class in Middletown runs the city. The nucleus of business-class control is the X family" (1937: 77).

It was not until the second generation that the X family gained leadership in consumption affairs (1937: 96):

> Around the families of the four now grown-up sons and two sons-in-law of the X clan, with their model farms, fine houses, riding clubs, and airplanes, has developed a younger set that is somewhat more coherent, exclusive, and self-consciously upper-class. The physical aggregation of so many of these families in the new X subdivisions in one part of town has helped to pinch off psychologically this upper economic sliver of the population from the mass of business folk. And the pattern of their leisure, symbolized by their riding clubs and annual horse show, tends to augment their difference. . . . Particularly as regards the male members of the older generation, there has always been a continuous preoccupation with business; and they did few of the things associated with a wealthy leisured class. It is the new note of a more self-conscious leisure built upon endowed wealth, and obviously expensive, that the younger generation is bringing to Middletown. They, too, work hard, but they play expensively and at their own sports, with somewhat more definitely their own social set.

Great wealth has to be used. Whether it is ploughed back into business, exchanged for elegance in leisure, used to patronize health, the arts, and education, or devoted to the training of a new generation who will be taught how to spend it gracefully, it enhances the power and prestige of those who own it. The second generation of owners is bound to be different: they cannot have the motives of ambitious men born in poverty. They will have the capital wealth that brings power, the income that brings luxury, and the values of those who have been reared to expect both; these values have been polished by attendance at national universities of high prestige, rather than the local college. Such people will be slightly different from first-generation businessmen of the same age—a difference that will be less important during the day at business than during the evening at play. They will be bound to seek the company of others like themselves. They will, in other words, create and become an upper class with links to the national elite.

INDUSTRIALIZATION AND THE TRANSFORMATION OF THE NATIONAL CLASS STRUCTURE

The changes which the Lynds chronicled in Middletown reflect the sweeping transformation of American society brought on by our conversion into an industrial nation. Although the process of industrialization was under way in the 1840s and 1850s, it was in the period after the Civil War that it was consolidated. Between 1870 and 1929, the population tripled, but the output of the American economy grew tenfold, largely as the result of the colossal gains in productivity made possible by new industrial technologies (Ross 1968). By 1900, the United States was the world's leading industrial nation (Hacker 1970: 192).

Closely associated with this achievement were other developments of critical significance for the American class system, most of which we have seen played out on a small scale in Middletown. For instance, Americans changed from predominently rural residents and farmers to city dwellers employed at urban occupations. In 1870, approximately three quarters of the population lived in rural places (under 2,500 inhabitants), and more than half the labor force was employed in farming. By 1930, most Americans lived in towns and cities, and nearly 80 percent of the labor force was engaged in non-farm occupations (Ross 1968: 26). Over the same period, occupational tasks were becoming increasingly subdivided and specialized. Thus, the steelworker and the metallurgist were among a multitude of successors to the blacksmith.

As the industrial economy expanded, the country's labor requirements grew faster than the native population. This labor deficit was met by encouraging immigration from abroad, a policy so successful that by 1920, 22 percent of the industrial labor force was foreign born.

Finally, the period saw a leap in the scale of economic organization. Large corporations emerged as the dominant force in the American economy. Industrial technology requires large enterprises, but it was the drive to control national markets and generate monopoly profits which produced such giants as Standard Oil, United States Steel, E. I. du Pont de Nemours, and General Electric, through a wave of corporate mergers at the turn of the century (Ross 1968: 40–41).

In the next few pages, we will try to show how the class structure was affected by these changes. First we will look at three broad class groupings (upper class, working class, and middle class) which were decisively transformed by industrialization. Then we will examine how the occupational structure was altered. In effect, we will be looking at the same phenomena from two different perspectives.

THE NEW UPPER CLASS

Our account of the upper class draws on the work of the late C. Wright Mills, whose classic study, *The Power Elite* (1956), is examined in greater detail in Chapter 8. Writing of the history of the upper class, Mills observed that the United States had never had a national aristocracy of the type known in Europe. In the absence of a feudal past or a single national center of wealth, power, and prestige like Paris or London, an enduring "pedigreed" class never developed. But at the time industrialization got under way, there were a series of relatively stable and compact regional upper classes across America:

> Up the Hudson, there were patroons, proud of their origins, and in Virginia, the planters. In every New England town, there were Puritan shipowners and early industrialists, and in St. Louis, fashionable descendants of French Creoles living off real estate. In Denver, Colorado, there were wealthy gold and silver miners. And in New York City, as Dixon Wecter has put it, there was a class made up of coupon-clippers, sportsmen living off their fathers' accumulation, and a stratum [of families] . . . trying to renounce their commercial origins as quickly as possible (Mills 1956: 48).

The prestige of these regional upper classes rested on old family fortunes, some on the eastern seaboard reaching back to colonial times. By gradually assimilating new moneyed families, the established families were able to keep prestige and wealth in close correspondence. But this system was overwhelmed in the post–Civil War era.

Mills noted that prior to the Civil War, there were very few millionaires. George Washington, among the richest men of this time, left an estate of $530,000 in 1799. In 1840, there were only 39 millionaires in New York City and the entire state of Massachusetts. However, the postwar expansion of the industrial economy created unprecedented opportunities for rapid accumulation of new wealth. By 1892, a survey revealed over 4,000 millionaires in the country (Mills 1956: 101–2). The wealth of the Lynds' "X" family and the fortunes associated with names like Rockefeller, Woolworth, Carnegie, Morgan, and Vanderbilt originated in this period.

The post–Civil War fortunes destroyed the neat coincidence which had obtained between family lineage, wealth, and prestige. The established families initially resisted the social pretensions of the new rich. But this was by no means easy since the size and national scope of the new wealth dwarfed the older family fortunes. Not by chance, this era produced one of the most famous attempts to define membership in upper-class society, Ward McAllister's list of the top 400. McAllister, who established himself as an arbiter of New York society on the basis of his close ties to the prestigious Mrs. John Jacob Astor, decided in the 1880s that there were " 'only about 400 people in fashionable New York Society. If you go outside that number, you strike people who are either not at ease in a ballroom or else make other people not at ease' " (Mills 1956: 54). The list was a defensive attempt to preserve the prestige of the old families against the pretensions of the social climbers. In 1892, McAllister finally published his list, which in fact contained only 300 names and was basically a directory of the best-known pre–Civil War families. Only nine of the richest men of the day (those with fortunes in excess of $30 million) were among the 300 (Mills 1956: 54).

McAllister's effort to specify the makeup of upper-class society was obsolete even before it was formulated. By 1883, Mrs. Astor has already overcome her disdain for Mrs. Vanderbilt's new railroad money and accepted an invitation from her to a fancy-dress ball. Gestures of this sort, Mills argued, have prevented the emergence of an American aristocracy. "Always in America, society based on descent has been either bypassed or bought-out by the new and vulgar rich" (Mills 1956: 52). In the late 19th and early 20th centuries, the family fortunes built after the Civil War were merged with the old society to create a new prestige class, national in scope like the new economy and centered in major cities such as New York, Philadelphia, Chicago, and San Francisco. (This class comprises the "upper-uppers" and some of the "lower-uppers" which Coleman and Rainwater identified in Kansas City and Boston.) The progress of this merger can be seen in the *Social Register,* an elite directory which first appeared during this era and proved to be the most successful and enduring effort to specify the socially elect. The first *Social Register,* published in New York in 1887, contained 881 families in a careful mix of new and old. Within a few years, registers were issued in other major cities. During the period 1890–1920, the rate of admissions to the *Social Register* was high, reflecting rapid assimilation of the new rich; since then, annual admissions have declined to more modest levels. By 1940, over three quarters of the families covered by Lundberg's study of America's great fortunes (most accumulated between the Civil War and World War I) were listed in the *Social Register* (Baltzell 1958: 20).

THE NEW WORKING CLASS

The economic transformation which forced a restructuring of the upper class also recast the bottom of the American class structure. Limited before the war to the mills of New England, factory production spread across the country and created a modern industrial working class. In 1860, there were 1.5 million industrial wage earners in the country; in 1900, there were 5.5 million (Brooks 1971: 39). By

1930, 17 million workers, constituting over a third of the work force, were employed (largely in manual occupations) in the three sectors most directly affected by industrialization: manufacturing, mining, and utilities and transportation.

Many of the new industrial workers were immigrants, actively recruited by business and government and drawn by the economic opportunities offered by an expanding economy. In the decades immediately after the Civil War, the immigrants were typically English, Irish, German, or Scandinavian, people historically and culturally similar to the native-born population. But after 1890, the character of immigration changed, and most of the immigrants of the late 19th and early 20th centuries came from southern and eastern Europe. These "new immigrants," as they have been called, were Italians, Jews, and Slavs, and by the time they arrived, the best jobs in the industrial economy were controlled by others. The new immigrants were therefore relegated to the least attractive manual-labor jobs, while native-born Americans and the offspring of the old immigrants dominated skilled occupations and supervisory positions (Link and Cotton 1973: 13–15; Hacker 1970: 88–92). Thus a close association grew up between stratification and ethnicity, with the highest positions being occupied by the members of the most culturally Americanized groups. This system was reinforced by active discrimination against many immigrants and their childen in schools and politics (Brooks 1971: 76–77).

The working conditions and wages offered America's expanding working class were dismal indeed, especially in the jobs available to recent immigrants. A contemporary who visited Italian and Jewish sweatshops in New York City described people crowded into rooms

> small as boat's cabins; crouched over their work in a fetid air which an iron stove made still more stifling and in what dirt; hunger hollowed faces; shoulders narrowed with consumption, girls of 15 as old as grandmothers, who had never eaten a bit of meat in their lives (Allen 1952: 52–53).

In Chicago, another observer described the early morning procession of industrial workers:

> . . . heavy brooding men, tired anxious women, thinly dressed, unkempt little girls, and frail, joyless lads passed along, half awake, not uttering a word as they hurried to the factories (Allen 1952: 52–53).

A Commission on Industrial Relations, appointed by President Wilson, concluded in 1915 that "a large part of our industrial population are . . . living in conditions of actual poverty . . . It is certain that at least one third and possibly one half of the families of wage earners employed in manufacturing and mining earn in the course of the year less than enough to support them in anything like a comfortable and decent condition" (Link and Cotton 1973: 38). The commission discovered that the children of the poor were dying at three times the rate of middle-class children and that 12 to 20 percent of all children in six major cities were underfed and undernourished. In 1897, the average workweek in industry was nearly 60 hours. Long hours and the indifference of employers to safety conditions produced an appalling record of industrial accidents. An incomplete survey showed that at least half a million workers were killed, crippled, or seriously injured on the job in 1907 (Link and Cotton 1973: 38).

In the early years of the new century, some improvement began in these conditions. State legislatures, over the determined opposition of upper-class employers, started to pass legislation controlling safety conditions, providing compensation for injured workers, prohibiting child labor, and regulating the labor of women. As industrial productivity increased, hours of work declined and wages went up. However, the life of the average worker remained unenviable. A survey of industrial accidents in 1913 (more reliable than the 1907 study) found that 25,000 persons had been killed and 700,000 seriously injured at work (Link and Cotton 1973: 38). Moreover, the benefits of increased pay and reduced hours were very unevenly distributed among workers; for the majority of workers who were unskilled and not unionized the gains were slight, especially relative to growing industrial productivity (Ross 1968: 37–40).

The contrast between the conditions of the working class and the opulent lifestyles of the new rich convinced many Americans that class divisions were becoming sharper in America. This impression was reinforced by the evidence of class conflict between the emerging industrial working class and its upper-class employers. The period from the Civil War to World War I saw the most violent labor confrontations in American history. For example, in 1877 when railroads cut the wages of their already overworked (15 to 18 hours per day) and underpaid workers, a wave of strikes hit the nation's rail system. State militia and federal troops (called out by officials sympathetic to the railroads to "maintain order") provoked bloody confrontations in which scores of people were killed or injured. Millions of dollars of damage was done to company property. In 1892 at Homestead, Pennsylvania, a private army of 300 Pinkerton detectives hired by management fired on striking employees of the Carnegie Steel Corporation (later United States Steel). In the ensuing battle, three Pinkertons and seven workers were killed. A few days later, the company prevailed upon the governor to send state militia to take over Homestead, which was under the (peaceful) control of a strike committee. Multiple indictments against strike leaders, charging crimes from murder to "treason against the state of Pennsylvania" broke the strike and the union itself by depleting the union treasury with legal expenses. However, not all strikes ended in management victories.

When textile workers in Lawrence, Massachusetts, struck in 1912, martial law was immediately declared, and three dozen strikers were arrested and summarily sentenced to prison. After several violent incidents, including an attack by police on a group of women and children from striking families, the strikers gained public sympathy and won concessions from employers (Brooks 1971: 50–55, 84–92, 118–21).

In the wake of the 1877 rail strikes, E. L. Godkin, the prestigious editor of *The Nation*, wrote: "We have had an uprising not against political oppression or unpopular government but against society itself." These events should serve to disabuse Americans of the illusion that "this was the one country in which there was no proletariat, no dangerous class." The problem, as Godkin saw it, was that the United States had been invaded by people of alien "blood" (immigrants, that is) who had no respect for "American ideals." The solution? Reinforcement of the army and militia and a reduction of loose talk "about the laborer and his rights" (Litwack 1962: 53–6).

If such violent incidents were exceptional, they were nonetheless symptomatic of the era. Workers who sought decent wages and working conditions had to contend with powerful companies which could generally count on the support of state and federal governments, the courts, and, as Godkin's remarks suggest, the press. Only gradually did the federal government begin to assume a more balanced attitude toward labor conflicts. As late as the 1930s, the legal right of workers to form unions was still in question.

In the late 19th and early 20th centuries, the United States came as close as it ever would to Marx's conception of a capitalist society. Readers of the *Communist Manifesto* would recognize the emergence of bourgeoisie and proletariat in an era of rapid industrial development, the creation of a political and ideological superstructure beholden to the bourgeoisie, and evidence of violent class conflict. But events did not take the course an orthodox Marxist might have anticipated. Despite Godkin's observaton about an "uprising against society," American workers proved to be more interested in earning reasonable wages than in creating a socialist society, and they used both their unions and their votes to help achieve their goals. In addition, two tendencies prevented stark polarization between two classes, a trend that Marx regarded as a prerequisite to proletarian revolution. One was differentiation *within* the working class among ethnic groups, among the races, and among workers at different skill and wage levels, which kept the entire working class from developing a homogeneous and combative class consciousness. The other was the expansion of the middle class (as we have seen in Middletown) in response to the special needs of a sophisticated industrial economy, which offered the chance of advancement to workers or their children. Added to this were long-term gains in the standard of living of most groups that appeared to absorb their attention more than did the differences between rich and poor. We will return to these themes in Chapter 9.

THE NEW MIDDLE CLASS

For an understanding of the transformation of the middle class in industrializing America, we turn again to the work of C. Wright Mills. In *White Collar* (1951), drawing on the earlier work of Lewis Corey (1935; 1953), Mills distinguished between two groupings he called "old middle class" and "new middle class." The former is composed of small entrepreneurs: farmers, shopkeepers, self-employed professionals, and the like. The hallmark of this class is its independence, based on the entrepreneur's ownership of the property with which he works. The new middle class is composed of salaried white-collar people, an exceedingly heterogeneous grouping of office workers, salespeople, and salaried professionals and managers. Early in the 19th century, the old middle class comprised as much as 80 percent of the total population, but as the country's industrial society matured, the working class became the majority, and at the same time there was a shift in the internal composition of the middle classes which Mills summarized with the labor force statistics shown in Table 3–1.

The changing balance within the middle class, Mills observed, represented the decline of property and the emergence of occupation as the principal basis of stratification. In the countryside, many small farmers were forced off the land or became tenants as agricultural prices fell relative to the prices of the urban products which farmers buy. Behind declining prices were the domination of national eco-

TABLE 3–1
The middle classes

	1870 (percent)	1940 (percent)
Old middle class:	85	44
Farmers	62	23
Businessmen	21	19
Free professionals	2	2
New middle class:	15	56
Managers	2	6
Salaried professionals	4	14
Salespeople	7	14
Office workers	2	22
Total	100	100

Source: C. Wright Mills, *White Collar* (New York: Oxford University Press, 1951), p. 65.

nomic policy by the new industrialists and financiers of the Northeast, intensified competition from foreign agriculture, and, ironically enough, significant advances in agricultural technology, which enabled fewer farmers to feed an expanding urban population.

In the cities, many businesspeople shared the financial plight of the small farmers. However, in this case the modest relative decline in the proportion of business owners in the labor force masked what was actually happening: each year millions of small business enterprises collapsed, only to be replaced by millions of new enterprises, most of them doomed to the same fate. In the developing post–Civil War economy, the small-business owner was relegated to the highly competitive retail sector of the economy, while much of the rest of the economy came under the domination of large corporations.

While the decline of the old middle class was evident in the fate of the farmer and small-business owner, the rise of the new middle class was tied to the triumph of the corporation. As the operations of corporations grew in productive efficiency, financial magnitude, and geographic scope, a decreasing proportion of the work force was required in the actual production of things, but an increasing proportion was needed to manage, design, sell, and keep account of production. Moreover the growth of the corporate economy imposed new tasks on government. The expansion of corporate and public bureaucracies meant rapid growth of the new middle class.

However, as the proportion of white-collar employees grew, their relative standing in the class system declined. Mills observed that, in the past, white-collar people had had strong claims on superior prestige. In contrast to blue-collar workers, they wore street clothes at work, engaged in occupational tasks which were more mental than muscular, and were likely to have direct contact with the entrepreneur, from whom they could, in effect, "borrow" prestige. White-collar workers typically had a high school education, and only a small proportion of the population stayed in school that long. Nearly all were white and native-born Americans who spoke good English. White-collar workers were paid substantially more than manual workers.

Virtually all of these traditional bases of white-collar prestige were weakened over time. The very growth of white-collar employment made white-collar status less special. As we will show later in this chapter, the character of work in the expanding white-collar bureaucracies increasingly approximated the experience of the assembly line. Contacts between most white-collar employees and ranking executives became infrequent. As the American-born sons and daughters of immigrants entered the labor market, the significance of nativity was reduced. The spread of education broke the new middle class's exclusive claim on the high school diploma. At the same time, the wage gap between blue-collar and white-collar workers began to close. In 1890, the average annual income of white-collar workers was approximately twice that of urban manual workers. By the mid-1930s, it was 1.6 times, and by the late 1940s, 1.2 times (Mills 1951: 72–73). Of course, well-paid professionals and managers, the top strata of the new middle class, earned salaries well above blue-collar wages. But the situation of the great mass of white-collar employees was approaching that of the working class, and the line between the two strata steadily grew more indistinct.

Another factor which produced change was the entry of a vast number of women into the labor force and especially into the jobs of the new middle class. By 1890, about 15 percent of the labor force was female; by the mid-1970s, that figure had grown to 40 percent. Women were disproportionately placed in a limited number of occupations that came to be regarded as "women's jobs"; in recent years, about half of the new middle-class workers have been female, and almost three quarters of the clerks and schoolteachers (Stromberg and Harkess 1978: 56, 294). For reasons we will consider in Chapter 7, women have been underpaid in relation to men, earning on an average 58 percent as much (U.S. Census 1980a: 244–46), and have been less likely to be promoted to supervisory positions. The concentration of women in the new middle class has tended to lower both the wages and the relative prestige attached to white-collar employment.

NATIONAL OCCUPATIONAL SYSTEM

The Lynds' chronicle of Middletown and the parallel national accounts by Mills and others suggest that the post–Civil War transformation of the American class system can be viewed as a result of a series of shifts in the distribution of occupations. We know, for instance, that there was a proportional decline in the number of farmers and a proportional increase in the number of factory workers and salespeople in the work force. Approaching social change this way has the advantage of being precise—we can count the number of people employed in different occupations at various points in time. It is also directly relevant to the technological and organizational shifts which have reshaped the economy. Fortunately, there is an excellent source of data on occupational change, the national census conducted by the federal government every 10 years. In 1820, the Bureau of the Census began to ask questions about occupations, although systematic and comparable series of statistics do not reach back further than 1870, and for some series, 1910. In the early 1940s, an official of the Census Bureau, Dr. Alba M. Edwards, delved into the bureau's dusty archives and reorganized and standardized the material on occupations, going back to 1870 (Edwards 1943).

In order to produce a series of comparable historical statistics, Edwards needed to find a way of classifying thousands of specific occupations into a few niches, each one with homogeneous "social-economic status." He decided against using a single indicator of social standing. Instead he lumped together factors such as the nature of the work, the skill and training involved in it, the income it brought, and common opinion about its prestige. He made his decisions on the basis of general knowledge at the time, without systematic tests.

The occupational hierarchy which Edwards proposed has been repeatedly modified in detail by the Census Bureau. But it is still recognizable in hundreds of government publications on occupations and on factors related to occupation, from fertility to income distribution. Moreover, versions of the Edwards schema have been adopted by many nongovernment researchers.

The major occupational categories in the schema, as currently employed by the Census Bureau, are given in Table 3–2, along with examples of specific occupations typical of each category. Since this system of classification is so widely used, it is worth studying the examples to get a sense of the range of each occupational grouping.

TABLE 3–2
The Edwards occupational classification,
as modified, with examples

Professional, technical, and kindred workers:
  Public school teachers
  Doctors
  Accountants
  Registered nurses
  Laboratory technicians
  Draftsmen

Managers and administrators:
  Sales managers
  Purchasing agents
  Bar managers
  Corporate executives
  Proprietors of small retail establishments

Sales workers:
  Retail-store clerks
  Insurance agents
  Manufacturers' sales representatives

Clerical workers:
  Bank tellers
  Bookkeepers
  Secretaries
  Cashiers
  Keypunch operators

Craftsmen:
  Carpenters
  Masons
  Foremen in construction or manufacturing

TABLE 3– 2 (*continued*)

Machinists
Telephone repair workers

Operatives:
Assembly line workers in manufacturing
Butchers
Gas station attendants
Truck drivers*

Laborers except farm:
Unskilled construction workers
Freight and stock handlers
Garbage collectors

Farm workers†
Farmers (owner-operator)
Farm managers
Unpaid farm-family laborers
Migrant farm laborers

* Frequently listed in separate category as "transport equipment operatives"
† Category sometimes split into "farmers and farm managers" and "farm laborers"
Source: U.S. Census, *Statistical Abstract of the United States*, 1980.

Edwards maintained that his classification was the most practical means for making a *scale* of occupations that would increase in prestige, education, and income as one ascended step-by-step. We can test this claim using current government data on income and education, together with occupational prestige scores drawn from the

TABLE 3–3
Occupational groups: Earnings, education, and prestige

Occupational group	Median income employed workers (1978)	Median years education (1979)	Median prestige score
Professional and technical workers	$14,424	16.5	82
Managers and administrators	16,451	13.7	75
Sales workers	8,360	12.9	67
Clerical workers	8,099	12.7	65
Craftsmen	14,151	12.4	68
Operatives	9,846	12.1	58
Laborers, except farm	7,085	12.1	46
Service workers	4,880	12.2	47
Farm workers	6,138	12.1	61/50*
All workers	10,142	12.7	

* First figure refers to farmers, second to farm laborers.
Source: U.S. Bureau of the Census, *Money Income of Families and Persons in the United States: 1978 Current Population Reports*, P-60, no. 123, 1980, pp. 244–45; U.S. Department of Labor, *Educational Attainment of Workers, March 1979*, Special Labor Force Report 240, 1981, p. A-19; Albert Reiss, *Occupations and Social Status* (Glencoe, Ill.: Free Press, 1961), p. 68.

NORC survey. These statistics are presented in Table 3–3 for the Edwards categories, plus the new group of service workers.

The major occupational groupings do form a rough scale on the three dimensions. When the categories are arranged as they are in the table, the prestige and education rankings are fairly consistent, but the rankings on earnings do not always coincide with the other two dimensions. For instance, managers earn more than professionals; workers in the blue-collar categories of crafts and operatives outearn some white-collar workers.

Another problem is disguised by the median statistics employed in the table. In practice, some of the categories are quite broad and include specific occupations that are not very similar. This creates particular problems for stratification analysis, especially in regard to the upper strata. For example, the professional grouping includes doctors and lawyers, who rank high on all three dimensions. However, the most numerous professionals by far are public school teachers, who are characterized by modest earnings and prestige. Another example is the managerial category, which is large enough to encompass both the owner of a small hamburger stand and the president of a multinational corporation.

The Edwards schema, then, is less than perfect as a stratification measure. However, it is doubtful that Edwards or his successors at the Census Bureau could have done much better given the difficulty of reducing the multitude of occupations represented in the work force (the government's *Dictionary of Occupational Titles* lists over 20,000 of them) to a simple set of categories (Reynolds 1979). The original purpose of Edwards' scheme was to organize occupational data in order to make broad historical comparisons, and it serves well for that purpose.

Table 3–4, which is based on Edward's compilation and more recent census data, reveals massive changes in the American occupational structure since 1870. The largest change by far is also the most predictable: farm occupations have declined from over half the labor force in 1870 to under 3 percent in recent years. As the percentage of agricultural workers declined, the proportion of operatives, the grouping which includes most factory workers, expanded until it became the single largest occupational category. However, there is a small but significant surprise here. After 1950, the proportion of operatives also began to decline. This happened in spite of the fact that manufacturing production was expanding steadily. The other two major blue-collar categories, craftsmen and nonfarm laborers, have followed a similar curved trajectory, although the proportional decrease in laborers began much earlier.

While the agricultural categories have continuously contracted and the blue-collar groupings first expanded and then contracted, white-

TABLE 3–4
Occupational structure of the United States: 1870–1980

Occupation:	Percent of the labor force				
	1870	1900	1930	1950	1980
Professionals and technicians	3	4.2	6.8	8.6	16.0
Managers, officials, and proprietors	6	5.8	7.4	8.8	11.2
Sales workers .... }	4	4.5	6.3	7.0	6.3
Clerical workers .... }		3.0	8.9	12.3	18.6
Craftsmen and foremen	9	10.5	12.8	14.2	12.9
Operatives	10	12.8	15.8	20.4	14.2
Laborers, except farm	9	12.5	10.9	6.6	4.6
Service workers	6	9.0	9.8	10.4	13.3
Farmers and farm laborers	53	37.5	21.0	11.8	2.8
Total (rounded)	100	100	100	100	100
Number in labor force (millions)	12.9	29.0	48.7	59.0	97.3
Percent of labor force female	15	18	22	28	42.4

Source: 1900–1950 from U.S. Bureau of the Census, *Historical Statistics of the United States* (Washington, D.C.: U.S. Government Printing Office, 1975), Pt. I: 139; 1870 estimated from Alba M. Edwards and U.S. Bureau of the Census, *U.S. Census of Population, 1940: Comparative Occupational Statistics, 1870–1940* (Washington, D.C.: U.S. Government Printing Office, 1943), p. 101, and from C. Wright Mills, *White Collar* (New York: Oxford University Press, 1951), pp. 63–65; 1980 from U.S. Department of Labor, *Employment and Earnings*, January 1981, pp. 180–81.

collar employment has grown steadily, as shown in Figure 3–1. By 1980 white-collar workers constituted over half the labor force. Two classifications within that group have grown especially rapidly in recent decades, professional/technical and clerical, both having increased their proportion by about fivefold.

The relatively modest growth of a third white-collar grouping, the managerial occupations, obscures a continuing evolution. The decline of the independent entrepreneur and complementary increase of salaried managers, noted by Mills in the period 1870–1940, has not abated. The proportion of managers who were self-employed dropped from 57 per cent to 27 per cent between 1957 and 1970 (Levitan 1976: 67). The United States has truly become a nation of employees.

The service worker category has also changed in composition as it has grown. At the beginning of the century, most of the workers falling under this rubric were domestic servants (or in the more neutral current language of the Census Bureau, "private household workers"). Today the largest and most rapidly expanding service occupations include hospital attendants, waitresses, janitors, and security guards. While making a hospital bed or washing windows in an office building may be no more satisfying than performing similar tasks in a private home, the change does imply a more democratic set of class relationships. Of course, there are still some privileged American households where domestic chores are done by hired ser-

FIGURE 3–1
Occupational distribution of the labor force

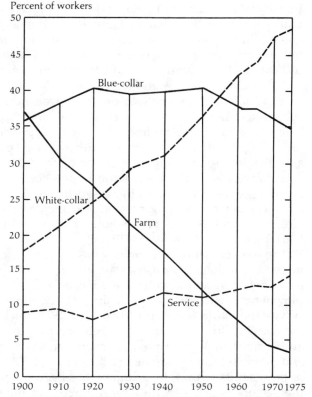

Percent of workers

Source: U.S. Bureau of the Census, *Bicentennial Statistics, Pocket Data Book, U.S.A.*, 1976, p. 387.

vants. In 1977 the Census Bureau found 1.2 million private household workers, enough people to fill a good-sized city (U.S. Census 1978: 421).

There are several keys to these long-term patterns of occupational change. Earlier we noted the growth of large bureaucratic organizations associated with the modern corporation and the expansion of government. This tendency increases the demand for managers; certain professionals, such as accountants; and, above all, clerical workers. The phenomenal expansion of clerical employment is also linked to the increasing participation of women in the labor force, as noted above.

However, the fundamental cause of changes in the occupational structure since 1870 has been the transformation of the United States from an agricultural to an industrial and finally to a postindustrial society. In 1870, agriculture was still the mainstay of the economy, and most working Americans were farmers. By 1930, the United States was a mature industrial society, in which employment in manufacturing exceeded that in agriculture. But as early as 1950, the United States could be described as a postindustrial society[2]—that is, one in which most workers are *not* employed in the goods-producing industries of agriculture, manufacturing, mining, and construction.

Both shifts were conditioned by technological change. The transition to industrial society was predicated on new technology which substituted machine power for animal and human muscle. The emergence of a postindustrial society depended on continuing technological advances which steadily increased productive efficiency and enabled a shrinking proportion of the labor force to meet the material needs of the rest of the population. This dependence on technology, of course, has increased the demand for scientific and technical personnel. Engineering, for instance, is now among the largest of professional occupations, exceeded in numbers only by teaching (U.S. Census 1978: 419–20).

The workers whom technology has been freeing from employment in goods-producing industries are absorbed into other sectors of the economy. In recent decades there has been a rapid expansion of employment in such areas as retailing, government, and the so-called service industries (Levitan 1976: 63). By 1975, the last category, which includes health care, education, legal services, and hospitality (hotels and restaurants), accounted for more employment than agriculture and manufacturing combined (U.S. Census 1978: 407). The net result of these shifts within the economy has been to move workers out of the sectors which require large numbers of blue-collar production workers into those which depend more on white-collar or service workers. (For an analysis of trends in the male labor force, see Featherman and Hauser 1978, chapter 2.)

RECENT OCCUPATIONAL CHANGE AND THE CLASS STRUCTURE

How are these economic and occupational changes affecting the American class structure? We have already shown how industrialization restructured the upper class and created an urban working class and a bureaucratized middle class of salaried white-collar workers. Many social scientists expect to find changes of similar magnitude associated with the emergence of a postindustrial society. The most optimistic of them see evidence of a more egalitarian class system

---

[2] On the origins of this term see Daniel Bell, *The Coming of the Post-Industrial Society* (New York: Basic Books, 1976), pp. 13–40.

taking form in recent occupational trends. Focusing on the growth of the professional, managerial, and clerical groupings and the shrinkage of the farm and nonfarm laborer categories, they anticipate the further decline of menial work and an overall upgrading of occupational skills and prestige. Thus, one writer celebrates the "white collarization" of America (Wattenberg 1974: 26), while another detects a "status upheaval" (Bell 1976: 134). It might be inferred from such descriptions that the class structure is being reshaped to resemble an inverted pyramid, narrow at the bottom and broad at the top. Unfortunately this image finds little support in a closer examination of occupational trends.

The expansion of the professional-technical category, for example, does not indicate as large a proliferation of opportunities at the top of the class structure as some writers have assumed. As Table 3–5 demonstrates, the most significant growth in this occupational grouping has been among technicians and so-called semiprofessionals, such as librarians, social workers, and nurses rather than doctors, lawyers, and other high-status professionals.[3] The income and education associated with these positions are typically well below the averages for "professional and technical" workers. Moreover, the findings of the NORC occupational prestige surveys and Coleman and Rainwater's study of social standing in Boston and Kansas City rank semiprofessionals and technicians below people in the established professions and higher managerial posts (see Tables 2–1 and 2–2). Coleman and Rainwater place both groups among their middle Americans.

The less dramatic expansion of the managerial category may also leave a misleading impression of growth at the top. Available data on income, education, and prestige suggest that many of the new managerial opportunities are middle-ranking within the class structure (U.S. Census 1980a: 248; Tables 2–1 and 2–2). This conception would certainly fit the managers of small retail establishments or the relatively low-level government officials who are counted in this occupational grouping. Unfortunately the Census Bureau's detailed classification of occupations within the managerial category is insufficient for a finer stratification analysis.

At the bottom of the occupational structure, the declining proportion of "laborers" in the work force has been taken by some as an indication of a shrinking lower class. The most recent data are not

---

[3] There is no generally accepted definition of a "semiprofession," although it is widely acknowledged that some occupations, such as those cited here, constitute a distinct and marginal category of professionals, lacking in the independence, training, power, prestige and income typical of the established professions (Etzioni 1969; Ritzer 1977: 178–198). See Table 3–5 for a list of the occupations we have classified as semiprofessional.

TABLE 3–5
Professional and technical workers

Occupation	As percent of all "professional, technical and kindred workers"		As percent of labor force	
	1950	1980	1950	1980
Semiprofessionals*	44.7	45.4	3.7	7.3
Technicians†	7.6	11.5	0.6	1.8
Other professionals	47.7	43.1	4.3	6.9
Total	100.0	100.0	8.6	16.0

* Accountants, librarians, social and recreation workers, teachers except college and university, nurses, dieticians, therapists, pharmacists, computer specialists, and personnel and labor relations workers.
† Health, science, engineering, and other technicians, except pilots. This category does not include engineers.
Source: U.S. Bureau of the Census, *Historical Statistics of the United States* (Washington, D.C.: U.S. Government Printing Office, 1975), Pt. I: 140; U.S. Department of Labor, *Employment and Earnings*, January 1981, p. 180.

consistent with this view. It is true that both the number and proportion of laborers, both on the farms and in the cities, has declined. But at the same time, a new category of people who do similar unskilled work for low pay and uncertain employment has been growing, namely cleaning workers and some others within the "service" category. If we grouped together all farm and nonfarm laborers, cleaning workers, private household workers, and hospital attendants, and considered them as persons doing menial labor, we would find that the number of such workers held about steady from 1950 to 1970 and then began to increase. The details are given in Table 3–6. The *proportion* of menial workers in the labor force, which was declining up to 1970, is likely to increase in the future since some of the larger service categories are growing rapidly, while the proportions of agricultural

TABLE 3–6
Menial laborers

Year	Number	As percent of labor force
1950	8,580,000	14
1960	8,783,000	13
1970	8,458,000	11
1980	10,223,000	11

Source: U.S. Bureau of the Census, *Historical Statistics of the United States* (Washington, D.C.: U.S. Government Printing Office, 1975), Pt. I: 140; U.S. Bureau of the Census, *Statistical Abstract of the United States, 1978* (U.S. Government Printing Office, 1978), p. 421; U.S. Department of Labor, *Employment and Earnings*, January, 1981, p. 181.

workers and private household workers have already fallen to such low levels that further declines can have little effect on the overall pattern.

We have scrutinized trends at the top and the bottom of the occupational structure. What can we say about developments in the middle? On the blue-collar side, we have noted a significant contraction of craft and operative positions since 1950 (Table 3–4). (The latter category is more diverse than the former and includes some well-paying factory jobs in unionized corporate enterprises.) On the white-collar side, sales opportunities are contracting in recent years. Clerical employment, of course, is expanding at a vigorous rate. But even as this happens, the long-term erosion of the economic and social status of lower white-collar workers continues. The average earnings of clerical workers are now below those of all other occupational categories except service workers and farm workers. In the prestige surveys, sales and clerical workers rank just behind craftsmen (Table 3–3). A slight drop in the scores received by occupations in these lower white-collar categories was noticeable between the 1947 and 1963 surveys (Hodge et al., 1966: 331). Perhaps more important in the long run is the fact that a white collar in itself counted for less in 1963 than in 1947. Glenn estimated the independent influence of white-collar status on the NORC prestige scores, once the influences of education and income had been statistically controlled, and concluded that a white collar "made a modest unique contribution to occupational prestige in 1947 but . . . its contribution had largely disappeared by 1963" (Glenn 1975: 187).

As we noted earlier, the very expansion of office employment is contributing to the decline of clerical prestige. In a labor force which is already over half nonmanual, a white collar becomes less distinctive and finally less valued. At the same time, the character of office labor is changing, and this also contributes to its declining status. Office work is being subject to the same process of routinization for mass production purposes that marked the advance of the modern factory. Again occupational skills are being fractured into simple, monotonous operations which can be quickly mastered by untrained workers. The introduction of computerized operations has furthered this development in the office just as the assembly line did in manufacturing (Braverman 1974: 293–358). For example, when a multi-branched bank computerized its accounting procedures, it reduced a relatively highly skilled bookkeeping staff of 600 to 150 and expanded its data-processing staff to 122. The vast majority of data-processing jobs involve low-paid, minimal-skill work such as encoding, which requires nothing more than the simple ability to operate a 10-button keyboard (Braverman 1974: 338).

The essence of this process in both factory and office is the separation of execution from conception. Initiative is transferred from factory operatives or clerical workers to administrative and technical personnel, who plan each work task in fine detail. Thus the expansion of the high white-collar categories is directly related to the creation of low skilled white-collar and blue-collar jobs.

The occupational trends associated with postindustrial society do not, then, prove that we are moving toward the more egalitarian class system illustrated by the image of the inverted pyramid. Nor do they support the notion of a consistent upgrading of occupational skills. Americans are certainly better educated on the average than they have been in the past, but that is not to say that they are always able to use their education on the job. Many are caught in the trap described by a job-design consultant who observed, "We may have created too many dumb jobs for the number of dumb people to fill them" (Braverman 1974: 35).

The implications of current occupational trends for the class structure are too complex to be conveyed by a single graphic image. But we can characterize the tendencies we have examined in this section in terms of the class model proposed by Coleman and Rainwater (Table 2–1):

1. Upper America. Slow expansion representing new high-level professionals and managers.
2. Middle America. Expansion at the top through increasing employment of semiprofessionals, technicians, and low-level managers. Below this level, the growth of clerical employment is offset by declining opportunities for sales workers, craftsmen, and operatives. Moreover, the prestige value of lower white-collar positions is falling.
3. Lower America. Stabilization or incipient expansion in the employment of menial labor.

This version of the system suggests certain tendencies toward sharper boundaries between strata rather than reinforcement of a single gradation from top to bottom. Those who are in the positions of upper America train for them in college and professional school: it has become exceedingly difficult to achieve such jobs through experience alone. Thus many see the college degree as a sorting device of special importance, which Weber predicted from his analysis of increasing bureaucratization of all spheres of life. Those in the middle represent the least clearly defined group: within it are technicians, semiprofessionals, most clerical and sales workers, and stable blue-collar workers. The gap between them and those below them appears to be growing as high unemployment becomes a more permanent feature of the economy and an increasingly isolated underclass appears, whose members are employed at unstable menial jobs or wholly divorced from the labor market.

CONCLUSIONS

This chapter has been devoted to tracing the evolution of the occupational structure and drawing out its implications for the class system. We have seen the country transformed from an agricultural to an industrial and finally to a postindustrial society. In the first stage of this process, the farm population dropped precipitously, while in the cities an industrial proletariat grew and a stratum of white-collar workers appeared. In the second stage, the farm sector was reduced to numerical insignificance, the industrial proletariat began to contract, the white-collar sector swelled and became internally differentiated, and a new stratum of service-oriented menial workers developed. Both stages saw the decline of independent entrepreneurs and their replacement by salaried employees. The new class structure which took form as a result of these shifts might be described as follows: a national *capitalist class* built on corporate wealth; an *upper-middle class* of college-educated professionals and managers; a *lower-middle class* of blue-collar workers and routine white-collar workers; and a *lower class* of people engaged in menial jobs or simply unemployed.

Our assessment of recent occupational trends finds little support for claims that an egalitarian class order is evolving out of these processes of change. Such notions are contradicted by the incipient contraction of blue-collar employment in industry, by the declining quality of white-collar work and the relative rewards attached to it, by the expansion of menial positions, and by the implications of permanent high levels of unemployment in the American economy. Further, we see signs of a hardening of class lines both above and below the lower-middle class as just defined.

There is, of course, more to a class system than the distribution of positions in an occupational hierarchy. The material we have presented here needs to be supplemented with other information—in particular, data on trends in the distribution of wealth and income and on patterns of mobility—before we can draw final conclusions about the direction of change in the class structure.

Before closing this chapter, it is appropriate to add a few observations on the political implications of the developments we have outlined. Since Marx, observers of Western society have been keenly aware of the importance of the political role of the industrial working class. As we will observe in greater detail in Chapter 9, this class has provided the social basis for the emergence of socialist movements in many European countries and for liberal politics in the United States.

However, the weight of the traditional blue-collar categories within the labor force is declining. Does this tendency foreshadow a shift to the right in the politics of postindustrial societies? The answer to this question will largely depend on the political behavior of those who work in the occupations which are growing as blue-collar employment contracts. Service and clerical workers could conceivably provide the basis for a new "working-class" political block. Professionals and managers could join the established propertied class in a new conservative alliance. Nothing is certain but the fact that occupational change will be one of the major forces reshaping American politics in the coming years.

SUGGESTED READINGS

Bell, Daniel. 1976. *The Coming of Post-Industrial Society.* New York: Basic Books.

> *Broad and optimistic interpretation of postindustrial society, emphasizing changes in technology, economic organization, and occupational structure.*

Braverman, Harry. 1974. *Labor and Monopoly Capital.* New York: Monthly Review Press.

> *Key work on the division of labor and the transformation of work in capitalist industrial societies. Challenge to Bell.*

Ritzer, George. 1977. *Working: Conflict and Change.* 2d ed. Englewood Cliffs, N.J.: Prentice-Hall.

> *Synthesis of the sociological literature on work and occupations.*

Stromberg, Ann H., and Shirley Harkess, eds. 1978. *Women Working.* Palo Alto, Calif.: Mayfield.

> *Useful collection of articles on the social impact of women in the labor force.*

Terkel, Studs. 1974. *Working: People Talk about What They Do All Day and How They Feel about It.* New York: Avon.

> *A provocative series of interviews with people from ranking executives to unskilled laborers.*

Income, wealth, and life chances

Let me tell you about the rich. They are different from you and me.

F. Scott Fitzgerald (1926)

Yes, they have more money.

Ernest Hemingway (1936)

4

Procrustes, the giant of Greek mythology, was in the habit of altering the stature of his guests to fit the length of the available bed by either stretching them or chopping off their legs. In the next few pages we will apply Procrustes's approach to the study of income. We have put together an imaginary parade in which the heights of the marchers are made proportional to their incomes (Pen 1971: 48–59). The parade is a convenient way of gaining an overview of the distribution of income—who gets how much?—our first concern in this chapter. Later we will take up the distribution of wealth, the causes of income inequality, and finally the personal effects of economic class position.

THE INCOME PARADE

The income procession is organized as follows: the marchers will include all people over 18 who fall in the Census Bureau's "families and unrelated individuals" category, which is to say, nearly the entire adult population of the country, and they will be placed in position in the ranks according to their total pretax money income from all sources. Each family that pools income and lives together is counted as a single unit or household, as is each person who lives alone. Those units which receive the average (mean) income (about $17,000 in 1978) will be of average height. Those who receive more or less than the average will, in good Procrustean fashion, be stretched or shrunk proportionally, so that those getting $34,000 will be over 11 feet tall and those earning $8,500 will be slightly under 3 feet (the parade is based on data from U.S. Census 1980a, U.S. Internal Revenue Service 1981, and Rose and Livingston, n.d.).

We will have a special rule for families in which both husband and wife work. The men will carry their wives standing on their shoulders, unless, of course, the wife makes more (a rare circumstance), in which case the taller woman will carry her shorter husband. Either way, their total height will represent their combined income and determine their place in line. Househusbands and housewives who are not in the labor force will be of the same height as their working spouses and walk inconspicuously by their sides. In all cases, husbands and wives will count as single marching units, and children will be left home.

One last thing: since we want a quick impression of the distribution of income, we will make the entire procession, about 100 million people, pass by our reviewing stand at a uniform pace, in exactly one hour. This will be rough on the marchers, but it has a particular advantage for us. At any moment, we will be able to tell how much of the parade has gone and how much is to come just by looking at our watches. Let's begin the parade with the shortest marchers, the income pygmies, and work up to the giants.

The procession opens on an odd note. In the first few seconds we see nothing except a few wisps of hair moving across the horizon. It seems that the first people are marching in a deep ditch. They do not appear above ground because they are business people who have suffered income losses during the past year and have had to borrow from the bank or use up their own capital to cover them. Given the high failure rate of small businesses, which was noted in Chapter 3, we should not be surprised at this sight, however peculiar.

Five minutes. After they pass, we see tiny people, the size of a match or a cigarette. Five minutes into the parade, the marchers are still only a foot tall, since they receive around $3,000 a year. All who have gone thus far (and many who are to come, depending on the size of their families) are "poor" by the federal government's official poverty standard. Some of these dwarfs are single working people or students living independently of their families. About every seventh tiny marcher is a woman, single, divorced, widowed, or separated, with children at home. But the largest group consists of older people, couples or more frequently widows, living alone and subsisting on social security or other meager sources of support. Many of these elderly and their fellow dwarfs are hungry, since their nutritional needs were not reduced when we had them shrunk to their present size. Most could get government food stamps (which, by the way, are not counted by government statisticians as part of money income), but about half of those who qualify do not receive stamps, either because they are too proud to accept them or because they are ignorant of their rights. The same can be said of public assistance payments (which *are* included in income since they are distributed in cash).

Blacks and Hispanics tend to show up early in the parade, but nevertheless the majority of early marchers are white and "Anglo." Actually, the single most encompassing characteristic of the dwarf marchers is that they are not employed, because they are old or disabled, temporarily out of work, studying, or home with children. Yet there is a substantial minority that does work, and among them are many people who work full-time, all year long, without exceeding dwarf height; they simply do not get paid much for their labor.

Twenty-five minutes. As the procession moves on, the marchers get taller but only very gradually, in spite of the breakneck pace we have imposed. After 25 minutes, we are still seeing 3½-foot midgets who earn just over $11,000 a year.

What sort of lifestyle do these midgets buy with their money? The answer depends in part on household size, since the same income will provide more comfort for a few people than for many. A family of four at this level could afford a "lower budget" living standard, the slimmest of three basic standards devised by Labor Department experts (Table 4–1). The "lower budget" would provide our midgets an austere lifestyle befitting people of small stature. It assumes that families are required by their incomes to rent modest homes or apartments rather than own them, and drive old cars which they purchased used or depend on public transportation. The budget includes a food allowance which is theoretically adequate for a healthful diet if the homemaker is clever at using low-cost, high-nutrition foods, such as dry beans and peas, but only about a quarter of the families spending the amount specified for food actually achieve proper nutrition (U.S. Labor 1969: 9).

Most of the households represented by these 3½-foot marchers, in contrast to those represented by the 1-foot people, have at least one member in the labor force. Sometimes we see people who have attained this income level by carrying their spouses on their shoulders, but such two-earner families are still infrequent in the parade. Most three-foot people work at low-paying, low-skilled, blue-collar and clerical jobs. But occasionally we see semiprofessionals, low-ranking managers, and struggling proprietors of small businesses.

By half past the hour, we are seeing little people, about 4 feet 10 inches. They represent the median income of $14,000. Not until 35 minutes after the hour do we notice marchers whom we can look in the eyes (assuming, of course, that we ourselves receive the mean income of $17,000 and are therefore of average height).

Thirty-six minutes. Shortly thereafter, we catch sight of 6 foot 6 inch people with incomes around $18,500. A family of four represented at this point in the parade would be able to afford the Labor Department's "intermediate budget," which provides a living standard somewhere between the austerity of the lower budget and the comfort of the department's higher budget (Table 4–1). At 6½ feet, they may look like prospective basketball players, but many will never make the team since they can only play mounted on someone

TABLE 4–1
Three budget standards for an urban family of four persons

	Lower budget	Intermediate budget	Higher budget
Food	Emphasis on low-cost/nutritious foods, such as potatoes, dry beans and peas, flour and cereal. Smaller quantities of meat, poultry, fish, fruits and vegetables other than potatoes. Diet nutritionally complete, but estimated that only 25 percent of families spending this amount actually achieve adequate nutrition.	Assumed "suitable for average U.S. family." More generous allowances of milk, eggs, meat, fruits, and vegetables than lower budget. Some higher priced meats, out-of-season foods, and convenience foods.	More variety, more meats, fruits and vegetables than other plans. More expensive choices within all food categories.
Housing	A low-cost, five-room rental unit with full bath and properly equipped kitchen. Household items cheaper, fewer, and less frequently replaced than higher budgets. For example, new sofa every 50 years, new vacuum cleaner every 20 years. No purchase or energy allowance for air conditioning as in higher budgets.	Assumes ownership of moderately priced house. Allowance for household items approximately twice lower budget.	Assumes ownership of house in top third of market. Allowance for household items approximately twice intermediate budget. Includes allowances for lodging away from home, dry cleaning, and domestic help in home (approximately five full days per year) not included in lower budgets.
Transportation	Half families own car approximately eight years old. Others use public transportation. Total transportation costs 50 percent of intermediate standard. No allowance for car repairs; assumed that car must be junked if it develops serious mechanical problems.	Most families own car. Assumes purchase of two-year-old used car, replaced every seven years.	All families own car: 55 percent will purchase new. Total transportation costs 130 percent of intermediate budget.

	Lower budget	Intermediate budget	Higher budget
Clothing and personal care	30 percent less than intermediate budget.	Difference in clothing costs based on differences in quality of items purchased. At higher standards, wife's clothing increases and husband's and boy's clothing decreases as proportion of total costs. Higher budgets have successively greater allowances for wife's beauty care, including some services not included in lower budget.	50 percent higher than intermediate budget.
Medical care	Assumes same as intermediate standard, although actual expenditures are lower because the families often defer needed care or use free clinics.	Group hospital and surgical insurance coverage. Other items based on national averages for age-sex categories of utilization of dental and eye care, drugs, etc.	Same as intermediate standard plus major medical insurance coverage.
Other family consumption	Includes daily newspaper and small allowance for other reading matter. TV and radio but no phonograph or recordings. Minimal education allowance. Eight adult and 24 children's movie tickets per year. Assumes considerable dependence on free public recreational facilities. No allowance for cigarettes in this or higher budgets. Alcoholic beverages: nine (12 ounce) bottles of beer every two weeks (no liquor).	Nearly twice lower standard. Includes allowances for items such as recordings, sports, pets and pet supplies, hobbies not included in lower budget. Alcoholic beverages: less beer than lower budget but 3½ fifths of a "blend" whiskey (86–90 proof) and 6 fifths of a sweet domestic wine per year.	Over three times lower standard. Alcoholic beverages: less beer than intermediate budget standard; 5½ fifths straight bourbon whiskey (100 proof) per year.
Total cost, 1978*	$11,546	$18,622	$27,420

* Includes items not described above, such as personal and social security taxes.

Source: U.S. Bureau of the Census, *Statistical Abstract of the United States, 1980* (Washington, D.C.: U.S. Government Printing Office, 1980); and U.S. Department of Labor, *Three Standards of Living for an Urban Family of Four Persons, Spring 1967* (Washington, D.C.: U.S. Government Printing Office, 1969), and *Supplement*, 1972.

else's shoulders. About half of the people marching in this part of the procession got here by combining two incomes. The proportion of two-worker families is highest among blacks and Hispanics, who are, by the way, represented here in approximately their proportion in the general population. At this point in the parade, we see many more skilled workers than we spotted earlier. There are also increasing numbers of managers and semiprofessionals. However, blue-collar workers still outnumber those in higher-prestige occupations.

Fifty minutes.   Only after 50 minutes of patient watching—the parade is almost over—are we confronted by the 9½-foot giants who can afford to maintain a family of four on the Labor Department's "higher budget." This budget carries signs of relative affluence: a house in the top third of the market, a new car, a small allotment for hourly domestic help, and a generous allowance for family recreation.

More than half of the giants earn their place in the procession by riding on their spouse's shoulders. And for the first time in the procession, professionals and managers are edging out blue-collar workers in total numbers. We still see significant numbers of black marchers here, but their representation has been waning since the 6 foot 6 inch people passed.

The final minutes.   The procession has only 10 minutes to run. Yet some of the most extraordinary moments lie ahead. It took nearly 25 minutes before we saw 3½-foot midgets and another 25 minutes before the 9½-foot giants appeared, but about 9 minutes from now we will see 50-foot Goliaths, seconds after that, 200-foot King Kongs, and a split second later towering leviathans, thousands of feet tall. In fact, if we look down the line at the people who have yet to pass, it appears as if a steep mountain peak is advancing on our reviewing stand.

In these last minutes of the procession, the character of the marchers is changing rapidly. The giants reached the fringes of affluence through better-paying professional, managerial or highly skilled blue-collar positions, or by combining two incomes from lesser jobs. But among the Goliaths, dependence on dual incomes is insignificant, and blue-collar workers are nowhere to be seen. The Goliaths, for whom $100,000 to $250,000 is a respectable income, are generally highly successful professionals (most often lawyers and doctors), corporate executives, or the owners of prosperous small enterprises. Another shift comes with the arrival of the King Kongs, who would consider $500,000 a modest living. There are several thousand couples and individuals with incomes in excess of this amount. Many of these people hold important positions; for instance, the earnings of the top officers of the biggest corporations place them in the ranks of these monsters. However, the greater part of income at these levels does not come from jobs, but rather from income-producing assets. It is return on wealth and not salaries from employment which accounts for their colossal incomes and overpowering stature.

The final instant. Within the last microsecond of the parade, the leviathans we spotted earlier flit by. There are a couple of hundred people in this category whose incomes in excess of $10 million make the smallest of them over one-half mile tall. Who are these monsters? About half are people who have inherited great wealth. They include such familiar names as Rockefeller, Ford, Mellon, and Du Pont. Others built their fortunes on modest inheritances or even started with nothing and achieved leviathan status through activities ranging from the marketing of innovative products or services to real estate or financial speculation, or the discovery of oil.

The Labor Department does not publish household budgets for those who earn millions or even for those who earn hundreds of thousands. But let's take a concrete case—Ray Kroc, who put together a fortune of several hundred million dollars raising McDonald's golden arches across America. This is what Big Macs bought: "a 210-acre spread in Southern California, a stadium-sized apartment on Chicago's Lake Shore Drive, a 90-foot yacht, four helicopters, and a luxurious Florida beach house whose doorbell chimes familiarly: 'You deserve a break today' to all callers" (Greene 1978: 211).

While multiple residences are fairly common among the wealthy, other elements of Kroc's lifestyle might be a bit ostentatious for the current tastes of the established rich. But consider this: the minimum feasible staff for a proper New York City town house, according to one of Manhattan's better domestic employment agencies, consists of a live-in "cook-houseman," a "come-in" maid, and an hourly worker to do the heavy cleaning. The total annual cost of these services in 1978 was something in excess of $40,000, well over the price of the Labor Department's higher budget for a family of four (Greene 1978: 94–95).

LESSONS FROM THE PARADE

This chapter will elaborate some of the themes introduced by the procession. But before going on, we should pause briefly to list the general lessons that can be drawn from what we have just seen.

1. Our most general impression is one of extremely gradual increase in income levels until a break point very late in the procession. At half past the hour, we were still looking at 4 foot 10 inch runts. The

slow climb continued until the final minutes of the parade when heights rose precipitously as the small numbers of Americans with very high incomes, and finally colossal incomes, strode by.

2. The parade tells us something about the relative welfare of different segments of the population. It took about 25 minutes to reach the income levels which could maintain a family of four on the Labor Department's stingy "lower budget" and another 10 minutes to reach the point where the family could afford the modest "intermediate budget."

About the budgets: the Labor Department developed the three standards as a way of estimating annual living costs for a "typical" American family.[1] The items in the budgets were determined through a combination of surveys of actual consumer preferences at different income levels and expert opinion about basic needs in such areas as health and housing. The budgets are intended to cover all family expenditures, including taxes and such items as gifts and entertainment. Although the contents of the budgets have not been altered since they were devised in the 1960s, every year the Labor Department reestimates the current total cost of each budget. The price tags for 1978 are indicated in Table 4–1.

Of course these costs are applicable only to four-person families. If we want to use budgets to gauge the living standards of the entire population, we need to adjust them upward or downward for larger or smaller households, assuming, for example, that a two-person family could save on certain budget items (food) but not on others (a washing machine). Table 4–2 is based on such adjustments and shows how Americans stack up against the three living standards. According to our estimates, about 30 percent of families and individuals cannot afford the lower budget standard, an equal proportion live above the higher standard, and the remaining 40 percent are more or less evenly distributed in between. (Note that here as later in this chapter "Individuals" refers to people who do not live with relatives, typically single adults living alone.)

3. The degree of participation of income units in the labor force turned out to be a critical determinant of their place in line. At the very beginning of the parade, there was a high proportion of families and individuals without any wage or salary income. Later in the parade, we noted that many of the families with relatively high incomes were dependent on the earnings of two working spouses to maintain their standard of living. This generalization applied with particular force to black families and working-class families.

---

[1] We will treat the "poverty line," the best-known federal income standard, separately.

TABLE 4–2
Families and unrelated individuals by living standard, 1978

	Percent		
Adjusted income level*	_Families_	_Individuals_	_Families and individuals_
Below lower budget	22%	44%	29%
Between lower and intermediate budgets	21	20	21
Between intermediate and higher budgets	22	17	20
Above higher budget	35	20	30
Total†	100	100	100
Number (thousands)	57,804	24,585	82,389

* Based on Labor Department's urban United States, four-person family budgets. Income levels adjusted for family size using ratios employed by Census Bureau in estimating poverty population. Budget levels for different size households relative to the four-person standard are as follows: 1 person = 0.50; 2 persons = 0.64; 3 persons = 0.78; 5 persons = 1.18; 6 persons = 1.33; 7 or more persons = 1.65.
† May not add to 100 due to rounding.
Source: U.S. Bureau of the Census, _Money Income of Families and Persons in the United States: 1978 Current Population Reports_, P-60, no. 123, 1980, p. 3; and U.S. Bureau of the Census, _Statistical Abstact of the United States 1978_ (U.S. Government Printing Office, 1978), p. 465.

4.   Wages and salaries are virtually the only source of income for most people. However, in the course of the parade, we noted shifts in the relative importance of different income sources. For many of the early marchers, government transfer payments, such as social security and public assistance (welfare), are crucial. Most of the remaining marchers depend on wage or salary income from their jobs or entrepreneurial income from small businesses and professional practices. However, in the final moments of the procession, we saw marchers who are supported by wealth in the form of income-producing assets, such as stocks, bonds, and rental property. The succession of income sources toward the end of the parade is evident in Table 4–3, which is based on data on taxable income supplied by the Internal Revenue Service. Note that wages and salaries produce less than half of all income for those with incomes above $200,000 and are all but insignificant for those with incomes over $1 million. In the range $50,000 to $500,000, small business income assumes significant proportions, reflecting the affluence of some professionals and private entrepreneurs. For those who receive over $500,000, most income is from capitalist sources, largely dividends and capital gains.

5.   Occupational category, the marchers show us, is an important determinant of income but not the overpowering cause that we might have anticipated. From the reviewing stand, we saw occupational representation in the parade gradually shift from lower- to higher-

TABLE 4–3
Sources of income, 1978

Size of taxable income*	Percent				
	Wage and salary	Small business†	Capitalist‡	Other§	Total‖
Less than $20,000	88	8	2	2	100
$ 20,000–$50,000	87	10	3	0	100
$ 50,000–$100,000	64	25	12	0	100
$100,000–$200,000	56	24	21	0	100
$200,000–$500,000	44	20	35	2	100
$500,000–$1,000,000	30	16	52	3	100
Over $1 million	16	16	65	4	100

* Adjusted gross income.
† Small businesses, professional practices, farms, partnerships, interest, and rent.
‡ Dividends, capital gains, trusts and estates, small business corporations. Excludes a significant proportion of capital gains not subject to taxation.
§ Includes pensions and annuities.
‖ May not add to 100 due to rounding.
Source: Calculated from U.S. Internal Revenue Service, *Statistics of Income, 1978: Individual Income Tax Returns* (Washington D.C.: U.S. Government Printing Office, 1981), pp. 16–23. See also Frank Ackerman et al., "Income Distribution in the United States," *Review of Radical Political Economics* 3 (1971): 20–34.

prestige categories. But there was considerable overlapping of occupational groupings. For example, managers and professionals appeared in substantial numbers early in the parade, even before we hit intermediate budget incomes, while some blue-collar workers were seen among the marchers as late as the higher budget standard. (Of course, this is not to say that a high proportion of blue-collar families live at that standard.)

6. Women were at a special disadvantage in the income parade. At the very beginning, when the marchers were 1-foot dwarfs, we saw many older women living alone. Women supporting a family by themselves were a common sight among low-income marchers. In general, women make less than men even in the high-income sectors of the parade, where they typically were part of two-income families.

7. Blacks and Hispanics were also at a disadvantage in the parade. They were overrepresented among the early marchers, often by female heads of households. On the other hand, given their traditional position in American society, we were not prepared for the substantial number of them who marched among middle-income people.

8. The relationship between the distribution of income and the structure of prestige classes is clear at the extremes but somewhat blurred in the middle. We can think of the problem in terms of Coleman and Rainwater's model of the class structure (see Table 2–1). The little people at the beginning of the parade who have no employment

income or work at very low-wage jobs correspond to Coleman and Rainwater's lower Americans. The high-prestige professionals or managers and people with major income from assets at the end of the procession correspond to their upper Americans. The ambiguity appears in the middle, where occupational prestige and family income do not necessarily agree with one another. They do not agree in part because there is significant overlap in earnings from occupations at different prestige levels but even more because a second income can substantially shift a family's place in line. Thus a semiskilled worker and his secretary wife may earn more than a small-businessowner whose wife stays home. Such phenomena account for many of the difficulties Coleman and Rainwater experienced in formulating class categories among middle Americans.

THE DISTRIBUTION OF INCOME

Although a symbolic parade of the adult population may seem like an excellent means of expressing the national distribution of income, the data are usually published in more prosaic forms. The most common are (a) the distribution of the population among statistical income classes and (b) the distribution of aggregate or total income among various fractions of the population. The first, which was the basic source of data for our income parade, is illustrated in Table 4–4. The second, which we will examine presently, conceives of income as something akin to a national pie which has been sliced into portions, ranging in size from stingy to generous, for distribution among segments of the population.

TABLE 4–4
Families and unrelated individuals by income, 1978

	Percent		
Income	Families and individuals	Families	Individuals
Under $5,000	17.2%	8.2%	38.6%
$ 5,000–9,999	19.6	15.8	28.2
$10,000–14,999	16.8	16.6	16.6
15,000–19,999	14.6	16.9	9.1
$20,000–24,999	11.3	14.5	3.8
$25,000–49,999	18.0	24.3	3.2
$50,000 and over	2.7	3.6	0.6
Total	100.0*	100.0*	100.0*
Number (thousands)	82,389	57,804	24,585
Median income	$13,815	$17,640	$6,705

* Percentages may not add to 100 due to rounding.
Source: U.S. Bureau of the Census, *Money Income of Families and Persons in the United States: 1978 Current Population Reports*, P-60, no. 123, 1980, p. 3.

Table 4–4 confirms our basic impression of the income parade: a large chunk of the population has very low incomes, below $5,000; most people fall below $25,000; and an affluent few have high incomes, exceeding $50,000 (in 1978 dollars).

Four "economic minorities" (Thurow 1980: 184) present significant variants on this basic pattern: blacks, Hispanics, Native Americans, and female-headed families. No recent data are available on the incomes of Native Americans, although their living standards are known to be well below those enjoyed by the majority of Americans. Table 4–5 presents income statistics for the other three groups. The plight of the female-headed families is especially striking. Although substantial numbers of black and Hispanic families with male heads have attained the relative comfort of incomes over $15,000, female-headed families of all ethnic groups (and whites) remain highly concentrated at the low end of the income scale.

The slices-of-pie approach to income distribution assumes that we have divided the parade into, say, five equal intervals. We want to see what part of the total income pie goes to those in each interval. Figure 4–1 shows that marchers in the first (poorest) fifth of the parade

FIGURE 4–1
Shares of aggregate income received by fifths of families and unrelated individuals in 1978

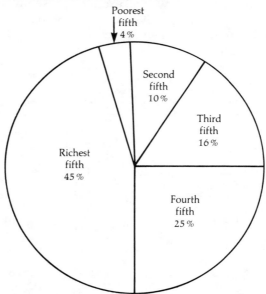

Source: U.S. Bureau of the Census, *Money Income of Families and Persons in the United States: 1978 Current Population Reports*, P-60, no. 123, 1980, p. 62.

TABLE 4–5
Income of economic minorities, 1978

Family income:	White		Black		Hispanic	
	Male head	Female head	Male head	Female head	Male head	Female head
Less than $5,000	4.3%	22.4%	8.1%	42.6%	6.5%	44.3%
$ 5,000–9,999	13.1	28.0	18.2	31.7	21.2	31.3
$10,000–14,999	15.9	21.3	19.9	13.7	23.3	13.2
$15,000–19,999	17.9	13.1	19.2	6.6	19.4	6.1
$20,000–24,999	16.3	7.8	13.2	2.9	12.9	2.9
$25,000–49,999	28.1	6.9	20.5	2.5	15.4	2.0
$50,000 and over	4.4	0.4	1.0	*	1.3	0.2
Total†	100.0	100.0	100.0	100.0	100.0	100.0
Number (thousands)	43,636	5,918	3,244	2,390	2,089	542

* Less than 0.05 percent.
† May not add to 100 due to rounding.
Source: U.S. Bureau of the Census, *Money Income of Families and Persons in the United States: 1978 Current Population Reports*, P-60, no. 123, 1980, pp. 107–9.

would receive less than a 4 percent portion of such a pie. Had the pie been cut into portions of equal size, each income fifth would have received 20 percent.

The income pie illustrates the heavy concentration of income at the high end of the scale. The portion of aggregate income received by the richest fifth is about 12 times that obtained by the poorest fifth. In fact, more detailed data indicate that the top 5 percent alone receives almost five times the aggregate income of the lowest 20 percent. Such comparisons belie the common notion that most income is received by the middle class. Indeed, a modern Robin Hood could transform the lives of the poor and near-poor by transferring income from the richest 5 percent of families to the poorest 20 percent until he had equalized the incomes of the two groups. This tactic would raise the average income of the bottom group from roughly $5,000 to $17,000.

TAXES AND TRANSFERS: THE GOVERNMENT AS ROBIN HOOD?

But isn't the government Robin Hood? Doesn't the government use progressive taxation to collect more money from the rich than from the poor, leaving us more equal after taxes than before them? The income distributions we have presented so far are all based on pretax data. What would they look like if we took taxes into consideration? The answer is, not very different.

We do have a national personal income tax which is somewhat progressive in its overall effect. That is, people with higher incomes pay a greater *proportion* of their total income to the Internal Revenue Service than those with lower incomes. However, there are other taxes which operate in the opposite direction. Chief among these regressive taxes are the sales taxes, which are levied by states and localities. A sales tax imposes the same tax rate on a pair of children's shoes whether the purchasing parent is a welfare mother or a millionaire. But since a welfare mother spends a much higher proportion of her income on taxable consumer items than the millionaire, she loses a higher percentage of her income to the sales tax.

Table 4–6 presents one estimate of the combined impact of all taxes on people at various income levels. These figures show that the personal income taxes do operate in a somewhat progressive fashion. However, for two reasons, the effective or actual rate of taxation on big incomes is less than many people think: (1) the higher rates (which go up to 70 percent) only apply to marginal or incremental income above the cutoff point where the rate begins to apply and not to all the income received; and (2) there are many deductions or tax breaks which the rich can use, aided by the advice of specialists in the complex rules. As a result, the redistributive effect of income taxes is

TABLE 4–6
Effective tax rates by annual income, 1966 (in percent except family income figures)

Adjusted family income ($1,000)	Individual income tax	Corporation income tax	Property tax	Sales and excise taxes	Payroll taxes	Personal property and motor vehicle taxes	Total taxes
0–3	1.4	2.1	2.5	9.4	2.9	0.4	18.7
3–5	3.1	2.2	2.7	7.4	4.6	0.4	20.4
5–10	5.8	1.8	2.0	6.5	6.1	0.4	22.6
10–15	7.6	1.6	1.7	5.8	5.8	0.3	22.8
15–20	8.7	2.0	2.0	5.2	5.0	0.3	23.2
20–25	9.2	3.0	2.6	4.6	4.3	0.2	24.0
25–30	9.3	4.6	3.7	4.0	3.3	0.2	25.1
30–50	10.4	5.8	4.5	3.4	2.2	0.1	26.4
50–100	13.4	8.8	6.2	2.4	0.7	0.1	31.5
100–500	15.3	16.5	8.2	1.5	0.3	0.1	41.8
500–1,000	14.1	23.0	9.6	1.1	0.1	0.2	48.0
1,000 and over	12.4	25.7	10.1	1.0	*	0.1	49.3
All classes	8.5	3.9	3.0	5.1	4.4	0.3	25.2

* Less than 0.5 percent.
    Source: Joseph A. Pechman and Benjamin A. Okner, *Who Bears the Tax Burden?* (Washington, D.C.: Brookings Institution, 1974).

limited, and it is countered by the regressive taxes. The combined incidence of all taxes is virtually the same at every level, except for very large incomes.

The estimate in Table 4–6 is based on the reasonable assumption that a substantial share of corporate and property taxes are passed along to consumers through higher prices. If this assumption is abandoned, a more progressive picture emerges, particularly at the income extremes. However, even when tax incidence is estimated according to the assumptions most favorable to progressivity, the redistributive effect of overall taxation is slight: in no case is the share of aggregate income received by any fifth of the families in our slices-of-pie distribution changed by more than 2 percent through taxation (calculated from Pechman and Okner 1974: 56).

The government has one other way of playing Robin Hood with income, and that is through transfer payments, such as social security payments, veterans' benefits, and public assistance. Since transfer payments are counted as part of cash income, they are, unlike taxes, already reflected in the income data we saw in the last section. (Noncash benefits, such as food stamps and medicare, are treated in Chapter 10). Although government expenditures for transfers have increased substantially in recent years, they involve only about 11 percent of GNP, a figure below that for most other industrial countries (U.S. Census 1977: 140). Moreover, by early 1981, a newly elected conservative administration was making plans to cut levels of transfer spending.

The effect of transfer payments on incomes is generally progressive. Over half of such payments go to the elderly, who tend to be at the low end of the income scale. Approximately two thirds of the money goes to the poorest 40 percent of families. The most significant redistributive impact is to shift about 3.5 percent of the income pie from the top fifth to the bottom fifth of families. Although this involves a substantial contribution to the well-being of many low-income families, the net effect of cash transfer payments on the distribution of income is modest (Fried et al., 1973: 50).

HOW MANY POOR?

Our discussion of income distribution and redistribution has skirted an important issue: How many people have such low incomes that they can be considered poor? The easiest answer is based on official government statistics, which recorded 24 million poor Americans in 1978, about 11 percent of the population (U.S. Census 1980b: 491). However, any count of the poor is dependent on the standard or definition of poverty used by the counters. Some researchers would want to adjust these figures upward or downward because they are skeptical of the standard employed by government statisticians. We will take up the problem of defining poverty in Chapter 10 so that readers will be able to draw their own conclusions.

INCOME DISTRIBUTION IN INTERNATIONAL PERSPECTIVE

Would Robin Hood's job be easier in some other country? Most Americans would be inclined to say no, since they are accustomed to thinking of their country as democratic and egalitarian. The distribution of income in the United States does compare favorably with the distributions in most underdeveloped countries, but comparisons with other developed, capitalist countries are less flattering. Among the 10 major industrial countries in Table 4–7, the United States has the dubious distinction of providing the smallest share of income to the bottom fifth. In general, the American distribution is slightly less egalitarian than those of most of the countries represented in the table, although no country deviates far from the general pattern characteristic of advanced capitalist societies.

TRENDS IN THE DISTRIBUTION OF INCOME: 1929 TO 2000

Only since the end of World War II has the government maintained a consistent series of personal income statistics; data collected prior to that time are less dependable. However, the existing evidence does

TABLE 4–7
International distribution of household income by income fifths (percent share)

Country and year		Poorest fifth	Second fifth	Third fifth	Fourth fifth	Richest fifth	Total*
Australia, 1966–1967	Pretax	6.6%	13.5%	17.8%	23.4%	38.9%	100%
	Posttax	6.6	13.5	17.8	23.4	38.8	100
Canada, 1969	Pretax	4.3	10.9	17.3	24.2	43.3	100
	Posttax	5.0	11.8	17.9	24.3	41.0	100
France, 1970	Pretax	4.3	9.9	15.8	23.0	47.0	100
	Posttax	4.3	9.8	16.3	22.7	46.9	100
Germany (Fed. Republic)	Pretax	5.9	10.1	15.1	22.1	46.8	100
	Posttax	6.5	10.3	15.0	21.9	46.1	100
Japan, 1969	Pretax	7.6	12.6	16.3	21.0	42.5	100
	Posttax	7.9	13.1	16.8	21.2	41.0	100
Netherlands, 1967	Pretax	5.9	10.9	15.8	21.6	45.8	100
	Posttax	6.5	11.6	16.4	22.7	42.9	100
Norway, 1970	Pretax	4.9	11.6	18.0	24.6	40.9	100
	Posttax	6.3	12.9	18.8	24.7	37.3	100
Sweden, 1972, ...	Pretax	6.0	11.4	17.4	24.3	40.5	100
	Posttax	6.6	13.1	18.5	24.8	37.0	100
United Kingdom, 1973	Pretax	5.4	12.0	18.1	24.2	40.3	100
	Posttax	6.3	12.6	18.4	23.9	38.7	100
United States, 1972	Pretax	3.8	10.0	16.8	24.5	44.8	100
	Posttax	4.5	10.7	17.3	24.7	42.9	100

* May not add to 100 due to rounding.
Source: U.S. Bureau of the Census, *Social Indicators, 1976* (Washington, D.C.: U.S. Government Printing Office, 1977), p. 477.

allow the following generalizations about trends in the distribution of income over the last half century (Miller 1971: 36–52; Solow 1960; Thurow and Lucas 1972; Thurow 1980: 160):

1. Income inequality, which was probably at a peak on the eve of the Great Depression, declined significantly in the 1930s and early 1940s as a result of (*a*) declining returns to investors during the depression and (*b*) government intervention in the economy designed initially to promote economic recovery and later to regulate wartime production.

2. Since the war, the distribution of family income has been relatively stable. No income fifth has gained or lost as much as 3 percent of aggregate income. However, family size and composition have changed: there are more households with a single individual; older people and younger people split off and form their own households more frequently, reducing the average size per household; married couples have fewer children. If the distribution of the pie is recalculated to reflect those trends by counting per capita household income, then each of the lowest four fifths in the income distribution has gained a little in the last three decades at the expense of the top fifth.

3. During the postwar period, incomes have risen for people at most levels in step with the growth of the gross national product. In other words, the income pie is getting bigger, and most people have more pie to eat, even though the relative sizes of the portions served remain unchanged. Since 1947, average family buying power has doubled, and as Table 4–8 demonstrates, this growth is reflected in the average incomes of those in all income fifths. (Note that the 1947 figures have been adjusted to reflect real purchasing power in inflated 1978 dollars.)

The most striking feature of the last three decades has been the stability of income distribution, especially among families. But some hints of change suggest an alteration in that picture in the future. Recently, wage and salary differences among individual workers have actually increased, but the trend toward inequality has been offset for families because poorer wives have tended to work more often than richer ones and because transfer payments to poor families have been going up (Henle 1972; Thurow 1980: 157). But there is considerable political resistance to further expansion of income transfers and furthermore, the wives of upper-income men are rapidly entering the labor force and closing the gap in participation rates. If such women earn more than the wives of lower-income men, which seems likely, female participation in the labor force will cease to favor family-income equality and instead will reinforce the trend toward inequality. A recent article in *Fortune* magazine comments on the long-term significance of this change (Ehrbar 1980: 127–28):

> The young executive whose wife stayed home and joined the Junior League was getting along on a family income not much different from that of a two-income family in a nearby blue-collar suburb. Now that the Junior Leaguers are joining the work force, entering with the for-

TABLE 4–8
Mean income received by each fifth of families, 1947 and 1978

	Mean income (1978 dollars)	
	1947	1978
Poorest fifth	$ 2,589	$ 5,224
Second fifth	6,161	11,653
Third fifth	8,801	17,580
Fourth fifth	11,959	24,210
Richest fifth	22,261	41,689
All families	10,354	20,901

Source: Calculated from U.S. Bureau of the Census, *Money Income of Families and Persons in the United States: 1978 Current Population Reports*, P-60, no. 123, 1980.

midable advantages of connections, intelligence, and education, they may create a kind of "superclass" that is already emerging in Washington, where real estate dealers in affluent suburbs speak of the "typical" customer as a GS-15 ($40,000) married to a GS-13 ($30,000).

Thus, the most recent trends in salary and wage inequality, female labor force participation, and the restriction of income transfer systems all point toward greater income inequality in the closing decades of this century. We are on the verge of changing the way we cut up the income pie by reducing the relative sizes of the slices going to the lower fifths. These shifts are likely to have important implications for American politics.

THE DISTRIBUTION OF WEALTH

Dependable data on wealth holding are considerably harder to come by than equivalent income statistics, which are published at regular intervals in various forms by the government. Wealth data are technically more difficult to compile, and there also appears to be considerable bureaucratic resistance to gathering them or providing relevant material to independent researchers. This state of affairs is a tribute to both the political sensitivity of the topic of wealth concentration and to the political power of the wealthy themselves.

The last thorough survey of wealth holding was done in 1962 by the Federal Reserve Board (Projector and Weiss 1966). Subsequent research suggests that the distribution of wealth has changed little since that study (Smith 1974; U.S. Internal Revenue Service 1973).

The major conclusion that can be drawn from the 1962 survey is that wealth is extraordinarily concentrated in the United States, even in comparison with the distribution of income. The slices-of-pie distribution of wealth presented in Figure 4–2 can be compared with the similar distribution for income of families and individuals in Figure 4–1. The wealthiest fifth of consumer units holds over three quarters of total assets, more than the proportion of aggregate income received by the upper two fifths of income recipients. Were Robin Hood to transfer the holdings of the top 6 percent to the bottom 60 percent, he would multiply the holdings of the lower group seven times over.

In a sense, these general statistics underestimate the concentration of wealth by mixing together widely held consumption-oriented assets, such as automobiles and homes, with investment assets, such as corporate stocks and rental property. A more detailed analysis of asset holding demonstrates that assets in the latter category are much more highly concentrated. As Table 4–9 suggests, we may think in terms of three broad classes of wealth holders:

1. A virtually propertyless mass, constituting nearly half the popu-

106

FIGURE 4–2
Shares of total wealth held by fifths of consumer
units, 1962

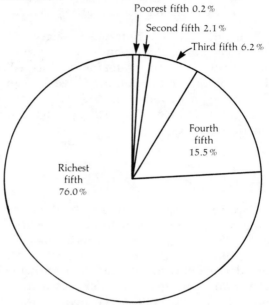

Poorest fifth 0.2%

Second fifth 2.1%

Third fifth 6.2%

Fourth
fifth
15.5%

Richest
fifth
76.0%

Source: United States Office of Management and Budget,
Social Indicators, 1973 (Washington, D.C.: U.S. Government
Printing Office, 1973), p. 182.

lation and holding no significant proportion of any asset type
except automobiles.

2. A slightly larger class of households which have built up small
nest eggs of holdings in automobiles, homes, and savings, and
equity in owner-managed businesses and professional practices.

3. A small capitalist class, 6 percent of the population, which owns
more than half of total wealth and virtually monopolizes all
income-producing assets held by individuals.[2]

The close tie between very high incomes and wealth which we
noted in our discussion of income distribution is confirmed in the
Federal Reserve survey. For example, the data, adjusted to 1977 dollar
values, showed that 93 percent of those with incomes over $200,000
had net worths (gross assets minus debts) in excess of $1 million
(Projector and Weiss 1966: 96). The researchers were curious about

---

[2] It should be remembered that a significant proportion of stocks, bonds, and commercial real estate mortgages are owned by *fiduciaries*—institutions that invest the
savings of millions of people that are grouped in life insurance and pension funds.

TABLE 4–9
Distribution of equity in different assets, by wealth class (percent shares of total), 1962

Wealth class	Household units	Total wealth	Home	Auto	Own business, farm, professional practice	Business managed by others	Liquid assets	Stocks	Other securities	Mortgage assets	Real estate	Miscellaneous, mostly trusts
Capitalist...........	6%	57%	24%	19%	69%	79%	38%	89%	91%	72%	63%	90%
Nest egg	50	41	72	64	30	20	55	11	10	27	36	9
Propertyless	45	2	4	17	1	1	6	*	*	2	1	1
All units†	100	100	100	100	100	100	100	100	100	100	100	100

* Less than .05 percent.
† Columns may not add up to 100 due to rounding.
Source: Jonathan H. Turner and Charles E. Starnes, *Inequality: Privilege and Poverty in America* (Pacific Palisades, Calif.: Goodyear Publishing, 1976), p. 34.

the sources of such large fortunes. They found that the majority of those with $1 million–plus net worths reported some inheritance, and 34 percent had inherited a "substantial" proportion of their net worth (Projector and Weiss 1966: 148; Thurow 1975: chapter 6).

The largest concentrations of private wealth are not held by single households, the units of analysis for the Federal Reserve survey, but by extended families, sometimes encompassing dozens of households. Such family fortunes are generally inherited and administered jointly through holding companies and trust funds. The value of the largest holdings of this sort must be measured in the billions of dollars (Lundberg 1968: 132–247). The implications of this concentration of wealth for the exercise of political power will be examined in Chapter 8.

TRENDS IN THE CONCENTRATION OF WEALTH

The history of the distribution of personal wealth roughly parallels that of the distribution of income, although the paucity of data makes a detailed account impossible. The best available estimate of trends is based on estate-tax records and for that reason focuses on the top of the distribution. Figure 4–3 traces the shares of the top 0.5 percent of wealthholders. As with income, wealth became less concentrated in the period which included the Great Depression and World War II. Since the war, concentration has remained stable.

SOURCES OF INCOME INEQUALITY

So far our efforts in this chapter have been largely devoted to describing the way income is distributed among families and individuals. Now we want to shift perspectives and ask how we might account for the existing distribution. We have already encountered some elements of the answer. For instance, we have observed that the concentration of wealth is the key to explaining extremely high incomes. We know that the number of workers in a family is crucial to

FIGURE 4–3
Share of personal wealth held by richest 0.5 percent, 1922–1969

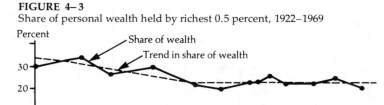

Source: James D. Smith and Stephen D. Franklin, "New Dimensions of Economic Inequality: The Concentration of Personal Wealth, 1922–1969," *American Economic Review* 64 (1974): 162–67.

its standing in the overall distribution and that female-headed
families have especially low incomes. We have seen that the government is shaping the distribution when it conducts transfer programs
and imposes taxes. By logical extension, all the political activity which
aims to influence these policies forms part of the income-distribution
system.

As these disparate observations suggest, it is no simple matter to
account for the distribution of income. In fact, there is no comprehensive and viable theory of how the whole system works; what we do
have are partial views of certain key aspects of the situation, usually
divided into structural and individualistic approaches. The relative
importance of the two approaches must be inferred by indirect
analysis; what we observe and measure are the combined results as
shown in the income parade. Unseen factors influence both the shape
of the curve of heights in the parade and the selection of persons for
the earlier or later parts of the march.

There are underlying *structural*, or institutional, factors that stem
from the economic system itself and influence the opportunities that
exist for earning money; they create positions or slots which individuals compete to enter. The capitalistic system which concentrates
assets into the hands of a few is an obvious example; it permits some
to collect enormous incomes without working and forces most of us to
look for jobs. Furthermore, long-term trends in technology and management change the mix of different types of jobs, as shown in Chapter 3. Those who seek work do so in a preexisting labor market. The
reasons why some jobs in that market provide 5 or 10 or 20 times
more earnings than others are not at all obvious; neither theories of
supply and demand, nor "return on human capital," nor administrative power fully explain the differences. Some combination of theories
will be needed.

The trends in the labor market create and maintain a certain proportion of low-paying and unstable jobs, and the people who have
those jobs will be poor regardless of personal skills or ambitions;
indeed, even if every worker had a college degree, some would be
poor as long as the job structure remained the same. Similarly, owners of successful businesses will get rich even if they failed to graduate
from high school.

Yet, *individual characteristics* obviously have some influence on the
way young people get sorted into various career paths that lead them
to higher or lower incomes. The structure may be the result of past
history, but personal careers reflect talent, education, ambition, and a
certain amount of luck. The relative weight of those characteristics
will be carefully examined in Chapter 7.

Here we will deal with only one issue: the relation between occupations and the salaries they provide. We postpone all discussion of
why some people get the good jobs and others get the bad ones. That

means we will postpone analysis of income differences among the educated compared to the uneducated, whites compared to blacks, men compared to women.

OCCUPATION AND INCOME

Occupation is the main key to the distribution of income for most people; occupational title predicts income better than any other single variable we have. However, even among people employed in the same general occupation, there is considerable variation in income. For example, in 1978 the top fifth of operatives employed full time in manufacturing earned over $18,500, while the bottom fifth earned under $8,250. Among accountants, the figures were $32,000 and $14,250 (U.S. Census 1980a: 250–251). Thus, many operatives earned more than many accountants. These are not unusual examples. As they suggest, the correlation between occupational prestige ratings and earnings is rather modest, about 0.40 for white males employed in the nonfarm labor force; thus only 16 percent of the variation in income can be directly connected with occupational category.

The effect of occupation on the overall distribution of income depends not simply on the wages paid to particular occupations, but also on the distribution of occupations in the economy. For example, the incomes of farm workers are quite low, but this fact has little importance for the distribution of income since the proportion of the labor force employed in agriculture is now so small. The broad changes in the economy in past decades which altered the occupational structure shifted the distribution of income. As was shown in the preceding chapter, the expansion of new urban jobs for skilled blue-collar workers, coupled with the even faster growth of white-collar jobs, increased the proportion of citizens who belong to middle-income categories.

MARXIST CLASS CATEGORIES AND INCOME

In their research on income determination and related work on social mobility, American sociologists generally use occupational status or prestige as their basic class variable—indeed, the Duncan Socioeconomic Index, or SEI, is one of the most widely used indicators in all such research. But recently, its monopoly has begun to be challenged, particularly by researchers of a Marxist orientation who remind us that occupational title is an incomplete stratification measure because it sidesteps the basic distinction made by Marx concerning the social relations of production. Erik Olin Wright expanded the Marxist logic and applied it to the more complex situation of contemporary industry that grew up after the epoch of Marx and, with Luca Perrone, attempted an empirical demonstration of the power of this logic to go beyond a prestige ranking of occupations in predicting income. They wrote:

> The term "occupation" designates positions within the *technical* division of labor, i.e., an occupation represents a set of activities filling certain technically defined functions. Class, on the other hand, designates positions within the *social* relations of production, i.e., it designates the social relationship between actors. (Wright and Perrone 1977: 35)

Knowing that a man is a carpenter, Wright argued, tells us that he turns lumber into buildings but leaves us in the dark about his class position. He may be a worker, but he can easily be an independent contractor who employs others. Wright did not argue that class in this sense could supplant occupation as an analytical concept, but rather that it should be recognized as a distinct aspect of the stratification system. (To avoid confusion with our other uses of *class* we will refer to Wright's notion as *structural class*.)

Wright suggested a system of four structural class categories: (1) *capitalists,* who own enterprises and employ others; (2) *managers,* who sell their labor but also exercise authority over other employees; (3) *workers,* who simply sell their labor; and (4) *petty bourgeoisie,* who own enterprises but do not employ others. The managerial group represents an addition to the traditional Marxist class categories. Wright recognized that ownership and authority are not so consistently bound together as they were in Marx's day; a large nonowning managerial class has grown up in capitalist societies.

Wright and Perrone modified this schema slightly for their income research. They dropped the petty bourgeoisie category, apparently to simplify the empirical analysis, and relabeled capitalists *employers,* admitting that most of those in the national surveys they used who fell into this category did not merit so grand a title as capitalist. In fact, 78 percent of the employers had fewer than 10 people working for them.

The objective of the income research was to demonstrate that an individual's structural class position exercises an influence on income which is independent of occupation. Wright and Perrone applied the modified class schema to data from two earlier national surveys of employed adults (1969 and 1973), each covering about 1,500 individuals. Their major findings were consistent with Wright's general argument. First, they discovered that structural class position could account for about as much of the variation in individual incomes as occupational status (measured by Duncan's index): all other things being constant, the two variables were about equal in explaining income.[3] In general, managers earned about 50 percent more than workers, and employers took home double or more the pay of workers, depending on the size of their business.

The second major finding refers to the influence of education on income. Wright and Perrone wondered whether those in higher structural class positions would find it easier to "cash in" on their education—that is, to get more return in dollars for each increment in education. The results showed that they did. Wage workers seemed to be limited in chances for advancement—to face a ceiling on income that neither education nor experience could fully penetrate.

What do we learn from this research? At the very least, that the social relations of production which separate people into such categories as owners, managers, and workers goes beyond the technical aspects of the division of labor that define specific work operations and that both have independent influences on income. There may be three factors involved that are easy to separate analytically but difficult to measure empirically: (1) profits from business enterprises, even smaller ones, are still important parts of income for many people; (2) various skills, both technical and social, are useful in obtaining advancement in a management hierarchy (but have somewhat less impact on the shop floor), and these skills and attitudes are to some extent learned in school; (3) managers and owners have more power in setting salaries than do workers, and they naturally tend to favor themselves.

However, the relationship of Wright and Perrone's study to Marx's understanding of class society is problematic. Managers do not fit neatly into Marxist theory, and many Marxists would not agree with Wright's effort to accommodate them. The employers in Wright and Perrone's sample are generally very small business owners of the sort that Marx would probably have labeled petty bourgeoisie. They are not the bosses of most Americans who would fall in their worker category. Workers in the bigger corporations are subject to the direct authority of managers, and yet they produce profits that flow to those who own assets. This crucial ambiguity is yet to be fully reflected in most empirical research.

THE DUAL LABOR MARKET

The dual labor market perspective emerged in the late 1960s from the efforts of researchers to understand the persistence of poverty in

---

[3] Technically speaking, a combination of education, age, occupational status, and structural class accounted for 27 percent of the variance in income. By themselves, occupation and class each partially accounted for 14 percent. Others studies have demonstrated the additional impact of industrial sector (Beck et al. 1978) and firm size (Stolzenberg 1978). Guidance to these issues can be found in McClendon (1980) and Jencks (1980).

the United States. The particular question that intrigued them was this: Why is it that in a generally prosperous economy, many people work full time without rising above the federal poverty line? The answer given by the dual labor market theorists centers on the idea that the labor market is split into two sectors, primary and secondary, and that the working poor fall on the wrong side of the divide. The sectors are distinguished by the type of jobs they offer. Primary sector jobs are typically characterized by

> several of the following traits: high wages, good working conditions, employment stability and job security, equity and due process in the administration of work rules, and chances for advancement. . . . [The] secondary sector has jobs which, relative to those in the primary sector, are decidedly less attractive. They tend to involve low wages, poor working conditions, considerable variability in employment, harsh and often arbitrary discipline, and little opportunity to advance. (Piore 1977: 93).

To understand why the working poor find themselves in the low-wage, secondary sector, we must think in terms of two separate phenomena: (1) the structure of job opportunities offered by the economy and (2) the relative standing of workers in a hypothetical "job queue" which expresses the preferences of employers among potential employees (Thurow and Lucas 1972).

A study by Barry Bluestone provides some important insights into the first aspect. Bluestone looked at the distribution of the working poor in the national economy in the mid-1960s (a period of low unemployment), when nearly a third of the families below the poverty line were headed by people who worked full time, 50 to 52 weeks a year (Bluestone 1974: 140–141). He found that the working poor were disproportionately concentrated in the South and were most likely to be employed by firms in certain sectors of the economy—for example, manufacturers of cotton textiles, southern sawmills and planing mills, laundries, restaurants, and limited-price variety stores. Bluestone's "character sketch" of low-wage industries emphasizes low productivity, limited capital investment, low profit margins, highly competitive markets, and product demand which is volatile with respect to price. This combination of economic characteristics makes it difficult for firms in such industries to offer their workers stable employment and a decent wage. Their inclination to pay low wages is reinforced by the absence or weakness of labor unions in these industries and federal legislation which exempts workers in some sectors from minimum wage legislation.

It should be noted that the secondary labor market is not limited to jobs in these industries. In other areas of the economy, firms which share some of their general features are also likely to be employers of low-wage labor. Even economically secure firms may depend on such labor for certain phases of their operations, either directly or by subcontracting work to secondary sector firms. Bluestone's analysis, then, suggests that a certain amount of poverty is built into the wage structure and that it continues to exist even in times when the economy approaches full employment. For this reason, prosperity does not trickle down to those on the bottom of the wage hierarchy.

Job seekers get channeled into primary or secondary sector jobs on the basis of their position in the figurative labor queue from which employers recruit workers. Sometimes trained and experienced workers match closely the needs of the available jobs, and they get hired first. But particularly for new entrants to the labor force, the employer has to do a lot of guessing about which persons in the queue might best suit the needs of the jobs. And much of the guessing concerns such qualities as punctuality, responsibility, and ability to learn simple tasks that are taught on the job. Some writers on the dual labor market believe that the significance of formal education and job skills has been overestimated. Bluestone notes that occupation-by-occupation comparisons between workers in low-wage industries and those in other industries show only slight educational differences. He argues that there is no real difference in skill levels between operatives in a low-wage sawmill and those in the automobile industry. Other writers stress that most skills are acquired through on-the-job training. In fact, many skilled positions are not filled from competitive labor markets accessible to all but from the restricted "internal markets" of individual firms (Doeringer and Piore 1971). For example, skilled jobs in manufacturing are typically filled through promotion, often on the basis of seniority, from the low-skilled, entry-level positions. One of the main differences between primary and secondary sectors of the labor market is that the secondary sector offers only dead-end positions, unconnected to promotion ladders.

Behavioral expectations may be a more crucial barrier to primary sector jobs than job-related skills. Primary sector employers demand greater labor discipline and are less tolerant, for example, of lateness or absenteeism. In the secondary sector, more lax employer expectations, frequent layoffs, and the absence of promotion incentives all tend to erode the work attitudes which would make an employee more attractive to primary sector firms. Nonetheless, dual labor market researchers note that many perfectly dependable workers are trapped in the secondary labor market. Some may be victims of geography; they live in areas where better jobs are rare. Others may be excluded from more attractive positions because employers in the primary market are practicing "statistical discrimination" or stereotyping as an inexpensive screening method (Piore 1977: 94). Since it is difficult to measure the abilities and work attitudes of potential employees, they discriminate among job applicants on the basis of

superficial resemblance to the least desirable secondary sector employees. Thus, a high school diploma may be largely irrelevant to
work on an assembly line, but an employer hiring for such a position
may require one on the assumption that high school graduates are on
average more disciplined than nongraduates. Among the bases for
such discrimination are race, sex (blacks and women are greatly overrepresented in the secondary sector), accent, demeanor, and scores
on various sorts of tests.

Two national income studies (Wachtel and Betsy 1972; Müller 1978)
have compared the effects of personal characteristics (including education, work experience, job training, race, and sex) and aspects of
economic structure (including industry, region, and union membership) on workers' incomes. Both indicate that economic structure has
a substantial impact on wages *independent* of personal characteristics.
In other words, two workers with precisely the same occupational
abilities and backgrounds may earn different wages because of
differences between the firms that employ them.

From the dual labor market perspective, neither an upgrading of
the personal characteristics of secondary sector workers nor the
elimination of discrimination would substantially change the current
situation. Their effect would be to rearrange the rank ordering of
workers in the job queue or perhaps simply cause them to "bunch
up" in line as they become more equal to one another. As long as a
proportion of the existing opportunities in the labor market involve
insecure, low-paying jobs, *somebody* will get them, and the working
poor will continue to be among us. Having examined the distributions of wealth and income and considered some of the structural
causes of economic differences among individuals, we can turn to our
final section: the *effect* of economic differences on people's lives.

SOCIAL CLASS AND LIFE CHANCES

On the night in 1912 when the *Titanic* sank on her maiden voyage
across the Atlantic, social class proved to be a key determinant of who
survived and who perished. Among the females on the ship, 3 percent of the first-class passengers drowned, compared to 16 percent of
the second-class and 45 percent of the third-class passengers. Of the
victims in first class, all but one had refused to abandon ship when
given the opportunity. On the other hand, third-class passengers had
been ordered to stay below deck, some of them at the point of a gun
(Lord 1955: 107, cited in Hollingshead and Redlich 1958: 6).

The differential fate of the *Titanic*'s passengers presents a grim
illustration of the association between class structure and *life chances*.
We owe the latter term to Max Weber who, it will be recalled, meant it
to encompass a range of experiences from the child's opportunity for

adequate nutrition to the adult's prospects for occupational success as they are shaped by class position in an economic sense. When we add differences in social prestige and power, then it becomes clear that the implications of class position for a wide variety of outcomes during the course of a single human life are manifold. A number of contingencies will be examined in following chapters: chances of getting a good education; likelihood of selecting a certain type of spouse; opportunities of having a successful career; probability of voting Democratic or Republican.

The literature is full of other examples that we do not have space to study; indeed, social class or status position is so important a determinant of human thought and behavior that an index of it is included as a control variable in almost every social research design. Table 4–10 gives a few examples of influence of social class on life chances: people at the bottom of the class structure have higher death rates, are more likely to suffer from chronic diseases, and are more frequently the victims of violent crime. Those at the top live longer, have more stable marriages, are less likely to be obese, and are more likely to attend college. It is no wonder that they more frequently report

TABLE 4–10
Life chances by income class

	Lower class	Middle class	Upper middle and upper class
Mortality ratio			
White males 45–54 (mean, all classes = 1)[a]	2.12	1.01	.074
Victims of heart disease			
Prevalence per 1,000 persons[b]	114	40	35
Obesity in native-born women[c]	52%	43%	9%
Marital instability			
White males, 25–34, ever divorced[d]	23%	10%	6%
Victims of violent crime			
Per 1,000 population[e]	52	30	27
Children who attend college[f]	23%	35%	60%
Describe selves as "very happy"[g]	29	38	56
Political conservatives[h]	30%	38%	38%

[a] By wage income of taxfilers approximately five years before death. Steven Caldwell and Theodore Diamond, "Income Differentials in Mortality: Preliminary Results Based on IRS-SSA Linked Data," in *Statistical Uses of Administrative Records*, edited by Linda Del Bene and Fritz Scheuren (Washington, D.C.: U.S. Social Security Administration, 1979), p. 58.

[b] U.S. Bureau of the Census, *Social Indicators, III* (Washington, D.C.: U.S. Government Printing Office, 1980), p. 101.

[c] Robert G. Burnight and Parker G. Marden, "Social Correlates of Weight in an Aging Population," *Milbank Memorial Fund Quarterly* 45 (1967): 81.

[d] Richard S. Udry, "Marital Instability by Race and Income, Based on 1960 Census Data," *American Journal of Sociology* 72 (1967): 673.

[e] U.S. Law Enforcement Assistance Administration, *Criminal Victimization in the United States, 1975* (Washington, D.C.: U.S. Government Printing Office, 1976).

[f] United States Bureau of the Census, *Statistical Abstract of the United States* (Washington, D.C.: U.S. Government Printing Office, 1980).

[g] George Gallup, *The Gallup Poll: Public Opinion 1935–1971* (New York: Random House, 1972).

[h] Ted G. Goertzel, *Political Society* (Chicago: Rand McNally, 1976), p. 146.

themselves very happy and politically conservative. They have a lot to be happy about and much to conserve. (Attitudes such as happiness and conservatism are not, strictly speaking, in the realm of life chances, but they are clearly influenced by them.)

HEALTH AND SOCIAL CLASS

Health is affected by such varied aspects of daily experience that it is a convenient summary measure of the quality of life. As the mortality and morbidity data cited above suggest, health is related to social class (for alternative approaches, see Kadushin 1966; Antonovsky 1967). For example, in health interviews conducted in 1975 by the U.S. Public Health Service, those with incomes under $5,000 were five times more likely to report themselves in poor or fair health than those with incomes over $25,000. Lower income is also associated with more "restricted activity days," greater health-related work-time losses, and more frequent treatment for "severe conditions" requiring medical care (U.S. Public Health Service 1977: 18).

The relationship between health and social class is not limited to physical condition but also encompasses psychological health. Two pioneering studies conducted in the 1960s established a link between class structure and the distribution of mental illness. The first was conducted in New Haven, Connecticut, by a sociologist-psychiatrist team consisting of August Hollingshead, whose work on Elmtown we reviewed earlier, and Frederick Redlich, both of Yale University (1958). By contacting practitioners in public and private facilities in New Haven and elsewhere, Hollingshead and Redlich compiled a virtually exhaustive list of all residents of greater New Haven who had been under psychiatric care during a specified six-month period. A systematic household survey was conducted in the New Haven area to enable the researchers to compare psychiatric patients with the general population. (Nonresident college students in New Haven were excluded.) Both groups were stratified into class levels using Hollingshead's Index of Social Position (occupation and education).

The most significant finding of the New Haven study was that the prevalence of treated mental illness varied inversely with social class. The data indicated very low rates of mental illness among members of the upper class (266 per 100,000 persons) and extremely high rates within the lower-lower class (1,659 per 100,000). Hollingshead and Redlich also found that the types of disorders for which people were treated and the therapies employed varied with class. Neuroses became more prevalent toward the top of the class structure, while the more serious psychoses were more prevalent toward the bottom. For obvious reasons, higher-class patients were more likely to be treated in private hospitals and lower-class patients in state and veterans' hospitals. But even among patients treated in the same type of facility for the same disorder, there were class distinctions in therapy. Lower-class patients had less contact with their therapists; they were less likely to be treated with individually oriented psychotherapies and more likely to be subject to organic therapies, such as shock treatments, drugs, and lobotomies.

The second study, conducted by a five-member interdisciplinary team (Srole et al. 1962) in Midtown Manhattan, confirmed the relationship between class and mental health detected in New Haven. Instead of studying mental patients, the Midtown researchers assessed the psychological condition of a randomly selected sample of 1,660 New Yorkers through interviews which placed particular emphasis on symptom formation. Thus their estimates are free of the potential bias introduced by class differences in willingness or ability to obtain professional care.

The class measure employed in the Midtown study precluded direct comparisons with the New Haven results, but the two studies both demonstrate an inverse relationship between class and pathology and a sharp rise in the prevalence of mental illness in the bottom class. The two psychiatrists who participated in the research diagnosed 47 percent of those in the lowest of six classes as "psychologically impaired" compared with 13 percent of those in the top class. The study also uncovered a relationship between social mobility and mental health. Pathological symptoms were most prevalent among the downwardly mobile and least prevalent among the upwardly mobile. However, their data allowed the Midtown researchers to reject the "drift hypothesis" which argues that the high rates of mental illness toward the bottom are the result of the tendency of the mentally ill to move downward in the class structure. Like Hollingshead and Redlich, they found that the slight differential in mobility patterns associated with mental status could account for only a small part of the class gradient in the prevalence of psychopathology.

While the existing research has shown a strong association between lower-class position and mental illness, the cause of the relationship has never been clearly established. The most commonly proposed explanations revolve around the notion that life at the bottom of the class structure subjects people with meager material resources to enormous stress. Certainly the class differences in life chances which we have noted suggest that the distribution of stress is as inequitable as the distribution of income. However, a reformulation of the problem by Melvin Kohn in an article on class and schizophrenia throws so simple an explanation into doubt. Kohn cites evidence from the Midtown study indicating that "at any given level of stress, people of lower social class position are more likely to become mentally disturbed than are people of higher social class position" (1976: 179). Therefore, he argues, the more stressful life circumstances at the bottom of the class structure cannot fully explain the association between class and schizophrenia. Those in lower-class positions are not only subject to more stress, they appear to be more vulnerable to it.

Kohn points to two additional influences which may explain the class differential. One is genetic inheritance, which research has linked to the etiology of schizophrenia. If schizophrenics are more likely to be downwardly mobile, a disproportionate concentration of genetically susceptible people could accumulate in the lower classes over a number of generations. But Kohn places less emphasis on such multigenerational genetic drift than on the second factor, which relates more directly to class structure. Lower-class position, research has shown, promotes more rigid, fatalistic, authoritarian conceptions of social reality. Kohn's own work, which we examine in the next chapter, indicates that these attitudes represent an adaptation by those at the bottom of the class structure to their life circumstances, in particular to the experience of low-ranking, menial, repetitive jobs. He suggests that such attitudes may undermine the capacity of lower-class individuals to confront potentially stressful situations which are (for them) novel and difficult. Drawing the strands of his reasoning together, Kohn offered the following hypothesis about the connection between social class and schizophrenia:

> The conditions of life experienced by people of lower social class position tend to impair their ability to deal resourcefully with problematic and stressful situations. This impairment, occurring in conjunction with a genetic vulnerability to schizophrenia and the experience of great stress, could be disabling. Since both genetic vulnerability and stress appear to occur disproportionately at lower social class levels, people in these segments of society may be in triple jeopardy. (1976: 180)

CONCLUSIONS

This chapter has been built around the image of an income parade. First we looked at the shape of the parade and found that, as the minutes on the clock ticked by, a lot of short, poor, and almost-poor people had to pass our reviewing stand before we began to see people tall enough to live at the Labor Department's modest intermediate standard of living. After that the situation improved more rapidly; toward the end of the parade, the people passing by were much more affluent with every minute until finally we saw the supergiants with incomes so large that most observers could not really grasp their implications.

There were not many of these supergiants, but they were extraordinarily tall. That led the imagination to the idea that some demigod, whether Procrustes or Robin Hood, might cut them down to size and share their incomes with the short people. Such an act of redistribution could, in theory, much improve the levels of living of the poorer folk. But then someone suggested that perhaps the government was already acting like Robin Hood and was producing such a redistribution. Careful examination of the data indicated that the lives of the poor were indeed being improved by government transfer payments, but most of the benefits came, not from cutting the giants down very much through progressive taxation, but by other forms of redistribution, particularly social security, which takes money from workers and gives it to those who have retired. After the government has both taxed and transferred, the very poor are less poor, but most other people's relative incomes have not been greatly altered.

After observing the income parade, we began to look at a few of the reasons why some people pass by the reviewing stand early and some arrive late. The first explanation is the ownership of wealth: the tallest people at the end of the parade get most of their money from return on assets in the form of interest and dividends, whether they work or not. The people in the middle of the parade get almost all their money from wages and salaries, and so the type of job they hold and the number of people in the family who have jobs determine family income and level of living. The working wife is a particularly important element. The shorter and poorer people at the beginning of the parade either do not work or have jobs that pay no more than the minimum wage; indeed, most of them are disabled and cannot work, or old and retired, or single women with small children to care for.

Then we begin to raise questions about access to jobs: Why does it happen that, among those who work, some people have good jobs that pay well and others have jobs that pay poorly? And at this point we began to hedge the answers. We noted that the question really is double-edged: (1) Why do good and bad jobs exist in the economy? and (2) What selects people for the various types of jobs that do exist? The answer to the first question involves economic history, technological change, and administrative structures within a capitalist system constantly adjusting to world trends—and this book cannot delve deeply into such issues. The second question is less structural or institutional and more individualistic, since it concerns the characteristics of individuals that give them advantages or disadvantages in competing in the existing labor market, as it is defined by institutional features. Some aspects of the selection process are obvious: people with more education tend to get better jobs which tend to pay more money. But the details of how that works in practice turn out to be far from obvious. To take but one illustration: people with the same type of job do not always receive the same income, especially if some are women. That paradox will be explored later, particularly in Chapter 7.

Finally, we looked at a few of the consequences of differential income, various aspects of life chances which ranged from the probability of living or dying during a shipwreck, or even during routine lives without such dramatic events, to the chances of being fat or getting robbed (further paradoxes, since those with the most possessions eat less and get robbed less often).

In the next chapter, we take up another aspect of life chances; what type of person are you likely to meet and become friendly with in school, and maybe even marry?

SUGGESTED READINGS

Atkinson, A. B. 1975. *The Economics of Inequality*. Oxford, Eng.: Clarendon.
   A lucid introduction.

Edwards, Richard. 1979. *Contested Terrain: The Transformation of the Workplace in the Twentieth Century*. New York: Basic Books.
   Development of segmented labor markets in historical perspective.

Rainwater, Lee. 1974. *What Money Buys*. New York: Basic Books.
   The social meaning of income and how to measure it.

Sanota, Gian Singh. 1978. *Theories of Personal Income Distribution: A Survey. Journal of Economic Literature* 16:1–55.
   Convenient review of the relevant work in economics.

Smith, James. 1975. *The Personal Distribution of Income and Wealth*. New York: Columbia University Press.
   Smith has done some of the most important recent work on wealth.

Thurow, Lester. 1980. *The Zero-Sum Society: Distribution and the Possibilities for Economic Change*. New York: Basic Books.
   Problem of distribution in the context of a lively treatment of national economic problems.

Turner, Jonathan H., and Charles E. Starnes. 1976. *Inequality: Privilege and Poverty in America*. Pacific Palisades, Calif.: Goodyear Publishing.
   An introductory text with strong emphasis on wealth and income. Interesting historical data.

Socialization, association, lifestyles, and values

A lawyer won his case for a heavy income tax deduction by proving that his country-club activities had a direct effect on his income. Furthermore, he hated playing golf. . . . The best approach is the indirect one in which the young executive never talks shop, never seems to be selling anything. Instead, he lets things take their natural course, picks up a game in the occasional two-some or threesome, makes polite conversation, may later offer to buy a drink, play a hand of cards, swap a story or two. Meanwhile, his wife is getting to know the other wives, his children are busy making friends in the club swimming pool. . . . Eventually, it pays off in dozens of direct and indirect ways.

Time (August 8, 1955)

5

Since Weber, many students of stratification have thought of prestige classes as "communities" characterized by more or less distinctive lifestyles and values. Sociological research has examined differences among classes in areas as diverse as consumption patterns, role relationships in marriage, sexual behavior, and language usage. Two of the variables outlined in Chapter 1 are critical for the emergence and maintenance of such differences: socialization and association. When people of similar prestige associate more often with one another than with persons of lower or higher prestige, they create identifiable strata that generate their own special subcultures. Since people tend to inherit the class position of their parents, the socialization of successive generations of the community into the patterns of thought and behavior characteristic of their elders contributes to the solidification of these subcultures.

Although this chapter will treat association and socialization as processes played out within social communities, we will find that both are shaped by occupational life and may in turn react upon it. Patterns of association through friendship, marriage, residence, and membership in formal organizations are structured by occupation. "I'm a carpenter," comments one of Coleman and Rainwater's Kansas City informants, "and I won't fit with doctors and lawyers or in country club society" (1978: 81). The professionals and business executives who do fit, as the quotation at the head of this chapter suggests, may be able to enhance their careers through informal contacts made in country club society. Furthermore, research which we will examine demonstrates that occupational position influences the way that parents socialize their children, and conversely, we will show that childhood socialization cultivates attitudes and abilities which affect subsequent occupational achievement.

CHILDREN'S CONCEPTION OF SOCIAL CLASS

Socialization is a social learning process which prepares new members of a society for adult life. The knowledge imparted ranges from

123

how to hold a fork to conceptions of appropriate male or female behavior. The child also absorbs adult notions about class differences. An early study of grammar school students in a New England town of 15,000 showed that by the sixth grade children had a fairly sophisticated awareness of the class significance of items such as an English riding habit, an elegantly furnished room, tattered clothing, and different occupational activities, all presented to them in pictures. And when they were asked to place their peers in one of three classes, the sixth graders agreed 70 percent of the time with adults who rated parents from the same households (Stendler 1949). In Jonesville, one of Warner's co-researchers found that fifth- and sixth-grade students associated desirable qualities, such as popular, good looking, plays fair, with children from higher-class families and negative qualities, such as dirty, unpopular, and bad manners, with children from lower-class position (Neugarten 1949). More recently, Simmons and Rosenberg (1971) demonstrated that young children have a clear conception of occupational prestige differences. Even the third graders in their sample from the Baltimore city schools ordered 15 occupations from the NORC list in a way which correlated almost perfectly with the rankings in the 1963 national survey of adults. (The children did tend to raise the relative position of their fathers' occupations, much as adults inflated the standing of their own occupations.) These investigations suggest, then, that even young children develop a reasonably accurate conception of the class system.

KOHN: CLASS AND SOCIALIZATION

While studies such as those just reviewed approach socialization through the child's developing conception of the world, a separate research tradition focuses on the parent. For several decades, studies of the latter type have recorded class differences in the way people raise their children (Bronfenbrenner 1966; Gecas 1979). The most intriguing recent work along these lines is that of Melvin Kohn and his associates at the National Institute of Mental Health in Washington, D.C. What makes Kohn's work special is his effort to isolate the particular characteristics of the lives of adults which could explain the class variation in styles of parenting. In brief, Kohn was able to show that the values which parents attempt to inculcate in their children reflect the character of parents' occupational experience. His findings suggest, moreover, that the transmission of these values plays an important role in the perpetuation of the existing class order.

Kohn directed three studies of parental values between 1956 and 1964: a survey of 421 white parents of fifth graders in Washington, D.C., a comparative survey of 861 parents in Turin, Italy, and a national survey of 3,101 men representative of all men engaged in civilian occupations in the United States (Kohn 1969: 9). In each study he asked parents to select from a list of characteristics those which they considered most desirable for a child of the same age and sex as their own child. Here are a few examples (Kohn 1969: 218):

That he is a good student.

That he is popular with other children.

That he has good manners.

That he is curious about things.

That he is happy.

Although the studies found considerable consensus across class levels about the importance of many values, others varied among levels. For example, an emphasis on consideration of other people, curiosity, responsibility, and self-control increased at successively higher class levels, while emphasis on good manners, neatness, obedience, honesty, and being a good student increased at lower class levels (Kohn 1969: 54). Table 5–1 presents class differences in mothers' responses for selected values in the Washington, D.C., study (a smaller sample of fathers produced similar results). In this case parents had been asked to choose the 3 most important values from a list of 17. Households were stratified by father's class position as measured by Hollingshead's Index of Social Position, which uses education and occupation as indicators (class I is the highest). The table should be read to indicate, for example, that 61 percent of upper class mothers considered happiness an important value. (Since mothers were permitted more than one choice, the figures in the table do not add to 100.) Although the table suggests that there are few sharp breaks between classes on parental value orientations (the breaks between classes I and II on curiosity and happiness are interesting exceptions), a clear class gradient is evident for most of the characteristics in the table.

TABLE 5–1
Mothers' choices of "most desirable" characteristics in child, by class (percent), Washington, D.C.

	Class				
Characteristic	I (upper)	II (upper-middle)	III (lower-middle)	IV (upper-lower)	V (lower-lower)
Obedience	14	19	25	35	27
Neatness, cleanliness	6	7	16	18	27
Consideration	41	37	39	25	32
Curiosity	37	12	9	7	3
Self-control	24	30	18	13	14
Happiness	61	40	40	38	30
Honesty	37	49	46	50	65

Source: Melvin L. Kohn, *Class and Conformity: A Study in Values* (Homewood, Ill.: Dorsey Press, 1969), p. 30.

The pattern becomes even more prominent when the occupations of employed mothers are taken into account. Kohn found that among wives of working-class men, those with white-collar jobs were closer to middle-class mothers in their responses, while those with manual jobs presented the sharpest contrast with middle-class orientations.

Kohn's interpretation of this class pattern in parental values is based on the idea that the middle-class parents who stress self-control, curiosity, and consideration are cultivating capacities for self-direction and empathetic understanding in their children, while working-class parents who focus on obedience, neatness, and good manners are instilling behavioral conformity. The middle-class pattern, particularly in the emphasis laid on happiness, curiosity, and consideration, is oriented toward the *internal* dynamics of the person—both the child and others. The working-class pattern, on the other hand, assumes fixed *external* standards of behavior. This general difference is neatly illustrated by the contrasts between having curiosity versus being a good student, or showing consideration versus good manners—in each pair of contrasts, the first choice shows internal development, and the second shows conformity to rules.

An additional finding substantiates this interpretation. Parents were asked about the specific sorts of misbehavior for which they would discipline their children. Their responses revealed that middle-class parents were more likely to punish a child for the *intent* of his or her behavior, in contrast to working-class mothers, who were more likely to discipline for the *consequences* of behavior. For example, a middle-class mother might penalize her child for throwing a temper tantrum, while a working-class mother penalizes for boisterous play. The first suggests a loss of internal control, the second a violation of external standards.

Kohn noted that working-class and middle-class mothers also differ in their attitude toward sex-role socialization. The surveys indicate that working-class mothers are more likely to choose separate "masculine" values (dependability, ambition, school performance) for boys and "feminine" values (cleanliness, happiness, good manners) for girls. Middle-class mothers are less inclined to make such gender distinctions. Kohn argued that this difference is also related to the distinction between internal dynamics and external standards, since the working-class emphasis on traditional sex roles implies an external focus; however, this connection is certainly not so intuitively obvious as the one regarding occasions for punishment.

Kohn labeled the two underlying patterns *self-direction* and *conformity*. He demonstrated a consistent relationship between the class position of parents and the values they chose for their children. At successively higher class levels, parents value self-direction more and conformity to external standards less. But what are the roots of these differences? Kohn suggested that they reflect generalized value orientations which develop out of a specific aspect of social class: occupational experience. He reasoned, for example, that people who hold professional and managerial jobs which are relatively unsupervised and require the considerable exercise of individual judgment and initiative are more likely to value self-direction than those who work at highly routinized blue-collar jobs. In brief, self-direction at work should produce self-direction in values.

Evidence from both the U.S. national survey and the Italian study in Turin supports this interpretation. General value orientations in two key areas—attitudes toward authority and judgments about work—were shown to vary with social class in both countries. Authoritarian attitudes stressing "conformance to the dictates of authority and intolerance of nonconformity" (Kohn 1969: 79) became more frequent at lower-class levels. The same is true of judgments about work which focus on the *extrinsic* qualities of a job (pay, hours, etc.), while judgments emphasizing *intrinsic* qualities (how interesting the work is, the amount of freedom it has, the chance it affords to use abilities, etc.) are more likely at higher-class levels. Moreover, these value orientations are systematically related to the character of respondents' occupational experience. Men whose work is (*a*) closely supervised, (*b*) repetitive, and (*c*) oriented toward things rather than people or data are the most likely to subscribe to authoritarian values, to judge jobs on their extrinsic qualities and, finally, to favor the conformity value pattern for children. The opposite holds for those whose work is unsupervised, unrepetitive, and oriented toward people or data.

These findings fit the causal chain which Kohn had anticipated to explain the relationship between social class and socialization patterns: occupational experience gives rise to general value orientations which in turn shape parental value preferences for children. Further scrutiny of the data showed that a second aspect of social class, level of education, also correlates with value orientations and parental value preferences and that this reinforces the class patterning of socialization. Kohn observed that education appears to "provide the intellectual flexibility and breadth of perspective that are essential for self-directed values . . ." (1969: 186). Education, of course, is closely related to occupation. It does not, however, "explain" the correlation between occupational experience and values. Kohn found that education and occupational conditions have independent impacts on parental values, although the effect of occupational conditions is substantially stronger.

Kohn's work has important implications for our understanding of the class system as a whole. Since Marx, sociologists have been aware that life experience, especially occupational experience, shapes social values. Kohn observed that "the essence of higher class position is the expectation that one's decisions and actions can be consequential; the essence of lower class position is the belief that one is at the mercy of forces and people beyond one's control, often, beyond one's understanding" (1969: 189). If this is true, we should expect people in top positions to learn to value self-direction and those at the bottom to learn to value conformity to authority. We might also anticipate that they will teach these values to their children. It is at this point that the larger significance of Kohn's work becomes clear. When parents inculcate values which reflect their experience of the class system, they are preparing their children to assume a class position similar to their own and, by so doing, are contributing to the long-term maintenance of the class system. But notice that these socialization values are not on the level of Marx's class consciousness. They concern the appropriate behavior of children. The connection between that behavior and the world of work is seldom recognized by the parents.

ADOLESCENT CLIQUES

The family is only one of several important socialization influences on children in American society. Some researchers believe that the impact of other forces, especially the schools, television, and the child's peers, has been increasing relative to that of parents. The significance of peer influence is well appreciated by every parent who has heard, "Billy and Tommy do it, why can't I?" To the extent that the children's peer associations follow class lines, we can expect them to reinforce the tendency toward the development of distinct class subcultures which is evident in the child-rearing practices of parents.

Warner, Hollingshead, and others have used the concept of *clique* to study the informal association patterns of both children and adults. Warner defines the clique as "an intimate nonkin group." Such groups are typically small, 2 to 30 members. They do not have formal procedures or rules of membership, but relationships among members are guided by "very exacting rules of custom," and members have a strong sense of the distinction between themselves and "outsiders" (Warner and Lunt 1941: 110–11).

There are characteristic clique patterns for each age group. The first clique relationship is likely to be with the boy or the girl next door: mother doesn't permit her four- or five-year-old child to play very far from home. At this age, children are not too discriminating; they do not ask whether their potential friends share the same interests concerning all aspects of life. The desire for companionship is paramount, and interests emerge from shared activity. But there is a selective factor at work; the ecological patterning of the city usually means that the children next door are of roughly the same socioeconomic level. This is so important a sorting device that it is often the major motivation behind a family's choice of residence: they want to control the influences of peers on their children by living in an "appropriate" neighborhood. The interactions of the children often bring the mothers together as friends. There are common interests (children) to talk about and common problems to solve (Who started the fight?). Occasionally the fathers also become friends, but less often.

When the children start grammar school, they have a much larger group of age mates to play with, yet for the first few years they are more likely to stay with those friends they already know in their immediate neighborhood, partly because mother wants them to come home directly after school and not wander far away. But as the children grow older, the physical area they are permitted to cover in their play activities grows, and so does the number of people from whom they choose intimate friends. Some new principles of choice must take the place of mere proximity.

By the time of junior high school, several definite patterns of adolescent clique relationships usually emerge. Some boys and girls will remain isolates, but most will have a close buddy or two and also will belong to a larger circle of friends. Some of these cliques will remain based on neighborhood proximity, especially those boys' gangs that are mainly concerned with sports. But others will have grown out of school contacts and be centered around specialized activities that would not have enough supporters in the local neighborhood, such as music or hunting. These cliques are characterized by the activity that most interests the members; adolescents do not just sit and "interact," they do things together. But the cliques do not draw their memberships from everyone in the school interested in the central activity, for they are composed of boys and girls from a similar class background. In fact, the activities themselves become class related, partly because the amount of available spending money has a lot of influence on the activity. Thus, upper-class boys play golf, tennis, and racquetball and go sailing, while those of the lower class play basketball and football and learn to box—activities that can be pursued on the streets or on vacant lots.

The typical American public high school is a large and comprehensive one which teaches all things to all boys and girls. A small town has only one high school, and there is a common idea that it is completely democratic because "everybody" is mixed together. The facts are quite different. First, some adolescents quit school before receiving a diploma, and these come almost entirely from the lower classes. Once they have withdrawn, they have very little contact with those who stay in school. Second, most of the upper- and some of the middle-class children are sent to private schools and many of the

Catholics to parochial institutions. Third, there is separation within the public school through "tracking," which distinguishes among students on the basis of ability or postgraduation aspirations (for instance, college preparatory, commercial, or trade). There is a substantial correlation between prestige class and academic track, and this separation carries over into recreational cliques. Fourth, even within tracks, boys and girls separate according to family background.

It is true that the mere presence of all sorts of adolescents in a school makes it possible for a person to make contacts with others who come from a class different from one's own—and in fact, most upwardly mobile students make a specific effort to do just that. But evidence indicates that students are more likely to separate themselves into cliques that are relatively homogeneous in their prestige-class composition. Moreover, many high schools, especially in large metropolitan areas, serve neighborhoods which are themselves quite homogeneous and thus limit the opportunities to form cliques which are varied in class makeup.

In the course of his Elmtown (Jonesville) study, Hollingshead carried out what remains the most thorough study of adolescent cliques. In Chapter 2, we discussed his procedures in placing the families of the town into five prestige classes. Here we turn to his substantive findings about adolescent behavior.

Hollingshead found that just under half of the 735 adolescents of high school age had withdrawn from the one public high school in Elmtown and that they had very little contact with those who stayed on. Most of those who quit school were from lower-class families: 89 percent of the class V adolescents, 41 percent of the class IV, 8 percent of the class III, but none of the class II or class I boys and girls had left school.

Hollingshead then studied the clique patterns of those who remained in school. He watched them in the hallways, he observed who went home with whom after school, he interviewed and questionnaired the students to find out "who they hung around with." He discovered 106 cliques of about five members each that were mostly based on associations in the school during and after classroom hours. He found 120 recreational cliques that gathered away from the school; they were slightly smaller in size and often had many of the same members as the school cliques. There were 33 cliques based on church or other institutional ties.

The students tended to associate with others of the same family-prestige class. Indeed, 63 percent of interpersonal relationships with cliquemates were with persons of the same class, 33 percent crossed one class line, and only 4 percent crossed more than one class line. Most relationships were among students in the same year of school.

When asked to name their best friend, over 70 percent of the students named someone of their own prestige class, and it was always someone who belonged to a common clique. Dating patterns were similar, except that boys tended to date girls a year younger than themselves and occasionally dated one from a prestige class lower than their own (but seldom from a higher one).

The details of the clique memberships of the high school students are shown in Table 5–2, which represents 1,258 clique ties among some 390 adolescents. In every instance, each class cliqued more among itself than with outsiders. This is all the more remarkable at the extremes when it is remembered that there were only 35 class I and class II students and only 26 class V students in school, so they had a very restricted choice at their own level. Yet it can be noted, for example, that of all the clique ties maintained by boys of classes I and II, 49 percent were with persons of the same class, 38 percent with class III students, 13 percent with class IV students, and none with class V students.

Hollingshead picked a few students from different prestige levels and asked them to rate the reputations of their fellow students in a manner similar to the way in which he had derived the prestige classes of families. The students agreed with each other in their rankings to the extent of a mean coefficient of correlation of 0.76, and they divided their fellows into three broad groups (with some subdivisions ignored by Hollingshead), which were described as follows (Hollingshead 1949: 221):

1. The Elite. The elite is composed of leaders in extracurricular student activities, as well as in church work, in the youth groups, and in social affairs. . . .

TABLE 5–2
Elmtown High School: Percentage of clique relations within and between prestige classes

Class	I and II (high)	III	IV	V (low)	Total
Boys:					
I and II	49	38	13	0	100
III	11	61	27	1	100
IV	5	33	60	2	100
V	0	13	31	56	100
Girls:					
I and II	56	26	18	0	100
III	7	64	28	1	100
IV	4	21	70	5	100
V	0	4	36	60	100

Source: August B. Hollingshead, *Elmtown's Youth* (New York: John Wiley & Sons, 1949), p. 214.

2. The Good Kids. In adolescent language the good kids are "never this or that." They come to school, do their work, but do not distinguish themselves with glory or notoriety. Some two thirds of the students are in this category.
3. The Grubby Gang. Grubbies are set off from the other students for many reasons—unfortunate family connections, personality traits, lack of cooperation with teachers, living in the wrong part of town. Boys and girls identified as grubbies are "nobody" in the eyes of the nongrubbies. To be rated a grubby is comparable to being blacklisted. According to student beliefs, grubbies have no interest in school affairs; besides, they are troublemakers. . . .

Among these high school students, as among the fifth and sixth graders in the same town who were tested by the Warner group, reputation proved to be a function of family-prestige class; there was a corrected coefficient of contingency of 0.77 between the two variables. Seventy-seven percent of the class I and class II students were put into the elite; 78 percent of the class III and 73 percent of the class IV students were considered good kids; and 85 percent of the class V students were rated as grubbies. Thus clique relationships, dating patterns, and personal reputation among peers were explained to an extraordinary degree as flowing from class membership of families. Hollingshead added that those adolescents who spent their time with members of a clique whose class standing was higher than their own were usually persons of considerable charm and talent who were on the path of upward mobility.

A class-based system of adolescent cliques such as Hollingshead described provides a crucial medium for maintaining the stratification system. It reinforces the attempts of most families to shape their children in their own images. The cultures of the various types of cliques adapt to the specific activities of teenagers the general values typical of the class levels of their parents and thereby teach those values more effectively than can the preachments of the parents. A boy who goes around with a group of adolescents who all take the college-preparatory courses in high school and expect to go to college absorbs a way of life that keeps up his motivation for the minimum requirements of bookwork in high school and subtly prepares him for the years ahead. He learns to behave in school in a way that does not alienate the teachers; he learns the manners and the poise that will get him into a college fraternity; he learns that dependence on parents for an allowance, although often inhibiting, is a small price to pay for the long-run rewards of an occupation that will bring leadership and community prestige.

By contrast, lower-class youths learn to value other behaviors. Athletic prowess (especially for boys) is more important than success with books; early sexual activity is the mark of maturity; a constant though subdued war with authority figures—be they parents or teachers—is the mark of self-respect, for the rewards the authorities can offer are not worth the price of subservience. The clash between these values and the ones emphasized by the teachers motivates many adolescent boys to quit school, to go to work early, and to end up with low-skill jobs, and many girls to become pregnant at an early age.

There is no recent equivalent of the Elmtown study. However, some later investigations did collect data on adolescent friendship choices, typically by asking each respondent to name his or her best friend. By comparing the family backgrounds of those who named each other as friends, researchers could measure the extent of class segregation in association patterns. Cohen (1979) reanalyzed data of this sort which had been gathered in Elmtown in 1958 (15 years after the original study). Comparisons with roughly similar material reported by Hollingshead (1949: 216) indicated a decline in the class homogeneity of friendship pairs. The shift was greatest among girls. Among boys its main effect was to reduce the relative isolation of class V, Hollingshead's bottom class. Cohen attributed the reduction to population growth, economic expansion, and occupational differentiation in Elmtown during the period between the two studies. Such conditions of change can blur established prestige-class distinctions by promoting social mobility and introducing new families into the community.

Two other studies include findings on the class patterning of adolescent friendships. Duncan, Haller, and Portes (1968) studied 300 17-year-old boys in a semirural county in Wisconsin. They found a relatively modest correlation (0.27) between the occupational prestige of respondent's father and that of friend's father. A much more substantial correlation (approximately 0.50) was reported by Rhodes, Reiss, and Duncan (1965) for a systematic sample of white boys, ages 11 through 16, attending public and private schools in metropolitan Nashville. The authors of the study, having determined that friendship choices were largely limited to students attending the same school, manipulated their data to determine how much of the observed pattern of association could be attributed to class segregation among schools. Although they found that residence patterns had produced considerable class differentiation in the school system, they concluded that the class bias in friendships was primarily the result of choices made among schoolmates.

These studies show that the extent of class homogeneity in adolescent cliques may vary with the setting and over time. However, all report *some* class structuring of association which tends to reinforce direct parental influences on children.

CLASS ENDOGAMY

Out of adolescent life grow marriages. Many studies indicate that marriage choices tend to occur among prestige-class equals or similars (Hollingshead 1950; Dinitz, Banks, and Pasamanick 1960; Laumann 1966; Rubin 1968). Part of this may be due to the sheer factor of propinquity, for residential areas sort people into class levels, and a young man is likely to meet (and perhaps to propose to) a young woman in his own neighborhood or school. But many other factors put class equals in contact, such as adolescent cliques, clubs and associations, college fraternities, and the like.

As an example, we can cite findings from Laumann's Massachusetts study (1966) which is examined in greater detail in the next section. Laumann asked married men the occupations of their father and father-in-law at the time of the respondent's marriage. The responses, organized by five occupational prestige categories, showed that 44 percent of the respondents had married women drawn from the same stratum. Seventy-one percent had married women from the same or an immediately adjacent stratum. The inclination toward class endogamy (in-group marriage) was especially notable in the "top professional and business" grouping. Although this category constitutes a small proportion of the population surveyed, creating relatively few opportunities for endogamous marriages, 60 percent of the sons of top professionals and businessmen married women who shared their class background (Laumann 1966: 74–81). A couple of quotations from Laumann's informants neatly reveal the attitudes which underlie this phenomenon (1966: 29):

> What sort of husband would a carpenter be? What sort of education would he have? My viewpoint would not jibe with a carpenter. Marriage is based on equals. I would want my daughter to marry in her own class. She would go to college and would want her husband to be educated. I would want to be able to mix with in-laws and converse with them.

> I was born into a family of great privilege—but I think I have a responsibility. Family responsibilities will be better held if the background of the members are similar. My own interests are not manual. Our family relations are very close. It would be very demanding to have an unskilled or factory worker in the family. The tradition in our family is the professions or landowning. I would not turn out a daughter who married a machinist but—a machine operator is bound to have a modest education—probably not interested in intellectual things. Even with the best will in the world, a family relationship would be very difficult to accomplish.

The pattern of class endogamy observed by Laumann and others has an important implication for class biases in childhood socialization. It means that similar class influences are likely to be transmitted through both parents to the child.

MARRIAGE STYLES

Rainwater has studied class differences in marital patterns by looking at the role relationships of husbands and wives, "their typical ways of organizing the performance of tasks, their reciprocal expectations, their characteristic ways of communicating, and the kind of solidarity that exists between them" (1965: 28). His conclusions are based on interviews with approximately 400 husbands and wives, most living in Chicago but some living in Cincinnati and Oklahoma City.

Following Bott's (1964) earlier work on English couples, Rainwater distinguished three types of role relationships on a continuum: "jointly organized," "intermediate," and "segregated." Joint relationships focus on companionship and deemphasize the sexual division of labor. Husbands and wives with joint role relationships share the planning of family affairs, carry out many household duties interchangeably, and value common leisure activities. Even when responsibilities are parceled out by gender (wife-homemaker, husband-breadwinner), each partner is expected to take a sympathetic interest in the concerns of the other. In the segregated relationship, there is clear differentiation of concerns and responsibilities which minimizes the husband's involvement with household matters and the wife's with the world of (the husband's) work. Husband and wife are likely to have distinct leisure pursuits and separate sets of friends. Intermediate relationships fall between these two poles.

On the basis of questions about family decision making, duties of husbands and wives, interests and activities of the partners, and the general character of the relationship, the couples surveyed were classified into one of the three categories. Of course, all couples were in some sense "intermediate"; there were no pure types. Classification was based on the preponderant tendency in each marriage. A glance at Table 5–3 will show that joint relationships predominate in the upper-middle class and segregated relationships in the lower-lower class, while the classes between them exhibit a neat gradient. Data by race for the bottom two classes (financial limitations precluded interviews with middle-class blacks) suggest a subcultural pull toward segregated relationships among blacks. However, it is not clear how precisely the black and white samples were matched, and the apparent divergence in marital role patterns may simply represent intraclass economic and educational differences between the races. In any event, the racial variance is relatively small, especially in comparison with the class differences among both blacks and whites.

TABLE 5–3
Social class and conjugal role relationships

Class	Number	Role relationships (percent)			
		Joint	Intermediate	Segregated	Total
Upper-middle class	(32)	88	12	—	100
Lower-middle class	(31)	42	58	—	100
Upper-lower class					
Whites	(26)	19	58	23	100
Negroes	(25)	12	52	36	100
Lower-lower class					
Whites	(25)	4	24	72	100
Negroes	(29)	—	28	72	100

Source: Lee Rainwater, *Family Design: Marital Sexuality, Family Size, and Contraception* (Chicago: Aldine Publishing, 1965), p. 32.

The relationship between social class and marital role types is more than a matter of idle curiosity. Reported marital happiness increases with class level, especially for women (Bradburn 1969: 156), and this phenomenon is tied to the character of the organization of marital roles. In Rainwater's study, middle-class couples reported greater sexual satisfaction than lower-class couples, but the difference was largely a function of the level of role segregation. For example, most lower-class wives in segregated relationships evaluated their sexual experience in marriage negatively (68 percent), while those in intermediate relationships were positive (68 percent) (Rainwater 1965: 28). In national surveys, companionship in marriage (which would appear to be similar to joint organization) is positively correlated with social class and with marital happiness (Bradburn 1969: 163).

Let's take a closer look at conjugal role types by examining how they function in upper-middle-class and working-class families. In important ways, the very character of upper-middle-class life lends itself to the joint role relationship, since the wife's social activities are often linked to the husband's career advancement (especially if she does not have an independent career). Joint role relationships are also reinforced by the high rates of social and geographic mobility typical of this class. Isolated from kin and removed from successive sets of friends as they move from community to community and up the corporate hierarchy, husbands and wives must look to each other for support and companionship.

Among blue-collar couples, wives have no significant role to play in regard to the husband's work. Since blue-collar careers are less likely to require geographic mobility, it's easier for working-class spouses to maintain ties with kin and friends from adolescence and early adult years. Dependency on the couple's parents is intensified by the economic insecurity which is especially typical of young working-class families (Rubin 1976: 69–92). These social ties tend to draw husband and wife to separate sources of support and companionship outside the marriage. Bott's (1964) work in England showed that couples who come to a marriage with tight-knit networks of friends and kin (that is, the people each spouse knows tend to know one another) and maintain these ties are the most likely to develop segregated marital relationships. Her data suggest that social networks of that sort are least typical of professionals and most typical of manual workers. A variant on this theme can be seen in the work of Stack (1974), who found that lower-lower-class black women in the United States develop extensive networks of kin and friends as a shield against economic vicissitudes. Such networks provide security that the erratically employed black men of this class cannot give, but they also maintain an insistent claim on the loyalties of their members which undermines strong relationships between women and their lovers or husbands.

We have dealt with the origins of joint and segregated role relationships at the top and at the bottom of the class order. What can we say about the mix of marriage types in the middle? Two social processes seem relevant. One is social mobility: people moving up or down in the class structure may carry with them lifestyles acquired in their class of origin. Thus the upper-middle-class origins of many lower-middle-class couples may help explain the predominance of joint relationships among them. An analogous argument can be made for the spread of segregated relationships upward. The second process, which is discussed in more detail below, is the tendency of upper-middle-class lifestyles to become generally fashionable models and filter downward. Through these processes, couples are exposed to conflicting influences which may be resolved by the compromise implied in intermediate role relationships.

Working-class sex-role socialization is another source of differences in marital-role organization. As we noted in our discussion of Kohn's work, working-class parents are more likely than middle-class parents to hold separate sets of expectations for boys and girls. Vanfossen (1977) found that college-age daughters of working-class fathers are more likely than their middle-class peers to subscribe to traditional sex-role values as expressed in questionnaire items such as "A woman should not expect to go to exactly the same places or have the same freedom as a man." Such women are the most likely to find the segregated marital role acceptable. On the other hand, boys of all classes are taught to be more controlled, more instrumental, less emotional, and less empathetic than their sisters, but the distinction is made much more emphatically in blue-collar families (Rubin 1976: 116–17, 125–26). Rubin, who conducted lengthy interviews with working-class and upper-middle-class couples, reported:

Not once in a professional middle-class home did I see a young boy shake his father's hand in a well-taught "manly" gesture as he bid him good night. Not once did I hear a middle-class parent scornfully—or even sympathetically—call a crying boy a sissy or in any way reprimand him for his tears. Yet, these were not uncommon observations in the working-class homes I visited. Indeed, I was impressed with the fact that, even as young as six or seven, the working-class boys seemed more emotionally controlled—more like miniature men—than those in the middle-class families. (1976: 126)

Boys who are taught to be "manly" in this way are less likely as adults to feel comfortable with joint role relationships in marriage.

RUBIN AND LEMASTERS: NEW STRAINS IN BLUE-COLLAR MARRIAGES

Rubin's study and another recent book by E. E. LeMasters (1975) provide an intriguing postscript to Rainwater's earlier work. Despite important differences in setting, method, and the populations studied, Rubin and LeMasters reached very similar conclusions about contemporary blue-collar marriages. Rubin (1976) conducted intensive, wide-ranging interviews with 50 blue-collar couples and a smaller control group of 25 upper-middle-class couples in their homes in the San Francisco Bay Area. In all cases, the wife was under 40 and the couple had at least one child under 12. LeMasters spent five years in a participant observation study of approximately 50 men and women, regular patrons of a "family-type," working-class tavern (The Oasis) in Wisconsin. Virtually all the men in LeMasters's study were skilled construction workers; on average they seem to have been older and more prosperous (he calls them "blue-collar Aristocrats") than Rubin's respondents. However, both Rubin and LeMasters concluded that marital norms filtering down from the upper-middle class are creating enormous strains in working-class marriages.

Studies of working-class family life from the period of Rainwater's research (for example, Komarovsky 1962) depicted unmistakably segregated marital relationships. One of LeMaster's informants, a woman married for 30 years, bitterly described the traditional pattern:

The men go to work while the wife stays home with the kids—it's a long day with no other adult to talk to. That's what drives mothers to the soap operas—stupid as they are.

Then the husband stops at some tavern to have a few with his buddies from the job—not having seen them since they left to drive home 10 minutes ago. The poor guy is lonely and thirsty and needs to relax before the rigors of another evening before the television set. Meanwhile the little woman has supper ready and is trying to hold the kids off "until Daddy gets home so we can all eat together." After a while, she gives up this little dream and eats with the kids while the food is still eatable. About seven o'clock, Daddy rolls in, feeling no pain, eats a few bites of the overcooked food, sits down in front of the TV set, and falls asleep.

This little drama is repeated several thousand times until they have their 25th wedding anniversary and then everybody tells them how happy they have been. And you know what? By now they are both so damn punch drunk neither one of them knows whether their marriage has been a success or not (LeMasters 1975: 42).

Now this pattern is being challenged by notions of intimacy, companionship, sharing, and equality which are received from above. The problem is that these ideals do not appeal equally to wives and husbands. Women have been prepared for them by their socialization and in many cases by contact with a middle-class world through white-collar employment. They are exposed to the new thinking through women's magazines and television soap operas. Men, on the other hand, are quite satisfied with traditional role relationships, which they regard as part of the natural order of things:

I couldn't stand being home every day, taking care of the home, or sick kids, or stuff like that. But that's because I'm a man. Men aren't supposed to do things like that, but it's what women are supposed to be doing. It's natural for them so they don't mind it (Rubin 1976: 105).

Men sense, of course, that many women do "mind it," but they are inclined to think that women's complaints are groundless. From The Oasis:

What in the hell are they complaining about? My wife has an automatic washer in the kitchen, a dryer, a dishwasher, a garbage disposal, a car of her own—hell, I even bought her a portable TV so she can watch the goddamn soap operas right in the kitchen. What more can she want? (LeMasters 1975: 85)

But behind the bluff there is fear. From the less "macho" setting of his living room, one of Rubin's informants phrased the problem differently:

I swear I don't know what she wants. She keeps saying that we have to talk, and when we do, it always turns out I'm saying the wrong thing. I get scared sometimes. I always thought I had to think things to myself; you know, not tell her about it. Now she says that's not good. But it's hard. You know, I think it comes down to that I like things the way they are, and I'm afraid I'll say or do something that'll really shake things up. So I get worried about it, and I don't say anything (Rubin 1976: 121).

For their part, working-class women in these studies are very dissatisfied but also frightened and confused and occasionally given to wondering whether asking a man to be more than a conscientious provider is indeed asking too much.

> I'm not sure what I want. I keep talking to him about communication, and he says, "Okay, so we're talking; now what do you want?" And I don't know what to say then, but I know it's not what I mean. I sometimes get worried because I think maybe I want too much. He's a good husband; he works hard; he takes care of me and the kids. He could go out and find another woman who would be very happy to have a man like that and who wouldn't be all the time complaining at him because he doesn't feel things and get close (Rubin 1976: 120).

There is a second aspect of blue-collar marriage which is being subject to strain as middle-class norms filter down: sexual adjustment. Problems in this area are not new. For instance, husbands and wives have long clashed over the desirable frequency of sexual intercourse. LeMasters heard this complaint among patrons of The Oasis (1975: 101). However, difficulties of more recent origin, deriving from the sexual revolution of the 1960s and 1970s, are evident in the comments of the younger couples interviewed by Rubin.

Comparative evidence from the 1940s and 1970s, including Rubin's own research, suggests that working-class sexual behavior is moving closer to middle-class norms. For example, working-class couples have nearly caught up with middle-class couples in their willingness to engage in once exotic sexual variants such as cunnilingus and fellatio; working-class men have become similar to middle-class men in their concern for their wives' sexual satisfaction (Rubin 1976: 134–35, 137–48). But change is not without psychological costs. Again, differential receptivity to new standards—in this case husbands are the more open—creates stress for working-class marriages. The blue-collar men whom Rubin interviewed wanted freer, more expressive, more mutually satisfying sexual relationships with their wives, as their remarks show:

> I think sex should be that you enjoy each other's bodies. Judy doesn't care for touching and feeling each other, though.
>
> She thinks there's just one right position and one right way—in the dark with her eyes closed tight. Anything that varies from that makes her upset.
>
> It's just not enjoyable if she doesn't have a climax, too. She says she doesn't mind, but I do (Rubin 1976: 136).

But their wives respond warily. This comment from a woman married 12 years is typical:

> He says I'm old fashioned about sex and maybe I am. But I was brought up that there's just one way you're supposed to do it. I still believe that way, even though he keeps trying to convince me of his way. How can I change when I wasn't brought up that way; [*with a painful sigh*] I wish I could make him understand (Rubin 1976: 138).

The emphasis here is on "how I was brought up." Working-class women have been socialized to fear or deny their own sexuality and to expect men to divide womanhood into "bad girls" whom they use and "good girls" whom they marry. Thus, even married women pressed by their husbands for freer sexual expression are inhibited by the fear voiced by this woman after 10 years of marriage: "How do I know in the end he won't think I'm cheap?" (Rubin 1976: 141). If working-class men find change easier to assimilate, it is because they have less at stake. Nonetheless, Rubin finds that some of the husbands are, in fact, still ambivalent in their own attitudes toward female sexuality and probably convey that ambivalence to their wives.

Rubin reports a different situation among her upper-middle-class couples. While the working-class woman had typically remained at home until they were married, the middle-class women had the more open atmosphere of their college experience (typically in the 1960s) to free themselves psychologically from traditional sexual constraints. Nearly all the couples in both groups had had premarital intercourse, but the middle-class wives expressed less guilt about having done so (1976: 60, 62). The distinct character of the upper-middle subculture in sexual matters is reflected in two of Rubin's observations. The middle-class men were less likely than their working-class counterparts to issue ambivalent messages in sexual matters and less given to "good girl" versus "bad girl" conceptions. And the middle-class women were more likely to feel guilty about their sexual inhibitions than about their sexual behavior.

INFORMAL ASSOCIATION AMONG ADULTS

What about the non-marital association patterns of adults? Warner (1941: 350–55) conducted an elaborate study of adult clique memberships in Yankee City. Unfortunately his findings are not strictly comparable with Hollingshead's adolescent clique data, but we can draw some broad conclusions. In both cases the lower-middle class interacts more down than up, and the upper-lowers interact more up than down—indicating a blurred line between those two groups and their relative isolation from the upper-middle and lower-lower groups. In fact, Warner sometimes lumps the two classes together as the "common man" class. In general, most clique memberships in Yankee City joined people of the same or adjacent classes, but the adults had a looser clique system than the Elmtown high school students, perhaps reflecting certain adult activities, such as politics, which draw from all levels. There was certainly enough variation around the trend of cliquing within a class level to make it dangerous to define a prestige class as those people who associate exclusively with one another, as Warner occasionally did (see Chapter 2).

Warner tried to accumulate data on every family in Yankee City. Such thoroughness is impossible in a larger urban setting, but sampling methods can be used. Laumann has conducted two surveys of adult association patterns in metropolitan areas. We have already referred to the initial study, published in 1966, which was based on a poll of 422 white male residents of Cambridge and Belmont, Massachusetts, both part of the greater Boston metropolitan area. (Areas of Cambridge close to Harvard, MIT, and Radcliffe were not included in the survey because of their large student populations.) The second survey conducted three years later covered approximately 1,000 white male residents of greater Detroit (Laumann 1973). The two studies reached similar conclusions, but we will focus on the Cambridge-Belmont results, which are reported in a more accessible form.

In both studies respondents were asked the occupations of their three closest friends. The distribution of respondents from the Cambridge-Belmont survey is given in Table 5–4. In the percentage distribution (the middle part of the table) it is evident that men at all levels are most likely to choose intimate friends from among the members of their own, or an adjacent, occupationally defined class. The tendency is strongest at the extremes. For instance, unskilled and semiskilled workers found more than three quarters of their friends close to their own group and relatively few within any of the white-collar categories. Members of the top professional and business class drew approximately three quarters of their friends from their own grouping. This tendency toward self-selection appears weakest in the middle-status categories, particularly clerical–small business. Nonetheless, the pattern does not indicate the disappearance of the distinction between middle class and working class. Most clerical–small business friends are drawn from the white-collar categories (65 percent), and most friends of skilled workers are themselves manual workers (62 percent). Overall, fewer than one quarter of all friendships reported cross the manual-nonmanual line.

Again, it is worth quoting Laumann's informants for the attitudes behind associational choices. The following remarks are in response to questions eliciting subjective reactions to association with people in occupations ranging from janitor to physician (Laumann 1966: 28–29). Unfortunately, Laumann does not indicate the speaker's own occupation, though it can usually be inferred.

> I am not a snob, but it is a fact of life that in most of these occupations we would have nothing in common. There must be an intellectual ground for my associations.
> I have had experiences with factory workers as a class of people and they're rough. They tend to go on the rough side of living—"hurray for me and the hell with the other guy" is their attitude. . . . Top executives

TABLE 5–4
Cambridge-Belmont study: "Best friends' " occupations by respondent's occupation

Friends' occupations	Respondents' occupation					
	Top professional, business	Semi-professional, middle business	Clerical, small business	Skilled	Semi-and unskilled	Total
	Frequency distribution					
Top professional, business	178	54	34	19	14	299
Semiprofessional, middle business	41	113	47	34	40	275
Clerical, small business	6	31	35	28	44	144
Skilled	9	21	39	73	82	224
Semiskilled, unskilled	6	17	24	56	180	283
Total	240	236	179	210	360	1225
	Percent distribution					
Top professional, business	74.2	22.9	19.0	9.0	3.9	24.4
Semiprofessional, middle business	17.1	47.9	26.3	16.2	11.1	22.4
Clerical, small business	2.5	13.1	19.6	13.1	12.2	11.8
Skilled	3.8	8.9	21.8	34.8	22.8	18.3
Semiskilled, unskilled ..	2.5	7.2	13.4	26.7	50.0	23.1
Total	100.0	100.0	100.0	100.0	100.0	100.0
	Ratio of observed to expected frequencies					
Top professional, business	3.0	0.9	0.8	0.4	0.2	
Semiprofessional, middle business	0.8	2.1	1.2	0.7	0.7	
Clerical, small business	0.2	1.1	1.7	1.1	1.0	
Skilled	0.2	0.5	1.2	1.9	1.2	
Semiskilled, unskilled	0.1	0.3	0.6	1.2	2.2	

Source: Edward O. Laumann, *Prestige and Association in an Urban Community* (Indianapolis, Ind.: Bobbs-Merrill, 1966), p. 65.

tend to, when that high up, to get standoffish and independent, and I can't afford to have independent friends.

The doctor has his trade; the machine operator also has his trade. As long as a man puts his mind into his trade, it is OK. A tradesman is not much of a big man compared to a top executive. The top executive would try to be uppity—would try to lord it over me. I have a little bit of this in the family already. This guy (my relative) is too big for his own family. His wife is not good enough for him any more. Just because you are a top executive does not mean that you can act uppity.

Not all informants accepted class segregation in friendships as desirable. One man commented:

I just don't believe it is possible to know anything about a man just by knowing his occupation. If he is a good guy, I don't care what he does. . . . The job isn't important—it's what he's like himself.

Laumann's analysis deals systematically with a problem which appears to be ignored by Warner (Warner and Lunt 1941: 350–55) and is only alluded to by Hollingshead (1949: 214) in their discussions of cliques. Classes, by most definitions, vary in size. Thus, the statistical opportunities that an individual has to associate with members of his or her own class vary with the size of the class. If there are more low-skilled, blue-collar workers than clerical workers in the local population, it will be easier for the blue-collar workers than for the clerical workers to develop friendships with peers. There is a related "ceiling" and "floor" problem which is especially significant in the top and bottom categories. Members of the top class cannot choose superiors as friends but have a broad opportunity to select status inferiors. The reverse holds true for those in the lowest class. These tendencies in the data reflect a structured social reality, but they may also derive from the system of categories chosen by the investigator to present the data. Fewer and broader categories will tend to exaggerate the degree to which peers associate by masking selection upward and downward within categories.

The bottom part of Laumann's table measures the extent to which the tendency toward differential association goes beyond statistical or random opportunities. It is based on the assumption that, if men selected their friends without regard to class, then we would expect the distribution of friendships reported by the respondents in each occupational grouping to be roughly the same as for the sample as a whole. Thus, since 23.1 percent of all friends reported were low-skilled workers, we would expect the same proportion of low-skilled workers among the friends of top professionals and businessmen. The actual figure (from the second part of the table) is 2.5 percent, approximately one 10th that amount. Ratios between the expected and actual frequencies are given in the corresponding cells of the third section of the table; a ratio equal to the random probability is indicated by 1.0. Thus top professionals and businessmen were 3 times more likely than chance to choose friends from their own class, and 10 times less likely to choose unskilled workers.

These ratios confirm the impression given by the percent distribution that friendship choices are structured by social class. For most categories the probability of self-selection is approximately twice chance. Moreover the probabilities fall off in a regular pattern with increasing prestige distance. In both senses the self-isolation of the top professional and business elite is greater than for any other grouping including the bottom blue-collar category. On the other hand the friendship patterns of clerical workers and small-business owners show a weaker class bias than other groups.

FORMAL ASSOCIATIONS

Studies of formal associations—large groups or organizations with explicit purposes and rules of membership—show the same class patterning that we have observed for cliques and friendships. In Jonesville, Warner and his associate Marcia Meeker (Warner 1949a: chapter 9) found that most associations draw their membership from only one or two strata, and the prestige of the association matches that of its members. Furthermore, each stratum favors different types of organization. The general pattern they observed would seem to fit most American communities (Hodges 1964: 105–15), with the exception that larger cities typically have special upper-class men's clubs such as New York's Links or Boston's Sommerset (Domhoff 1967: 19). (In Chapter 8 we will treat the political and economic significance of these organizations.)

Jonesville's upper class patronized the country club, three exclusive women's clubs, and certain professional and business groups. The women's groups were partly social, partly charitable in function. Actually these organizations had as many upper-middle- as upper-class members, but the latter dominated them and set the tone. This tone was well described for the women's clubs:

> The members of the upper class profess an interest in travel, a knowledge of foreign lands; they value objects associated with tradition and antiquity; they are preoccupied with leisure-time pursuits, with activities which have dubious economic value, but which are considered worthy, noble, and honorable. The upper-class woman who has both sufficient money and sufficient leisure time (with servants to take care of her home) is expected to become a patron of the arts.
>
> Through these associations, the members of the upper class not only express their common interests, but also perform activities of high value to the total society. They preserve relics and other symbols of prestige which are valued by the community. They patronize and sponsor the arts, through lectures and discussions of books, music, and the theater. They perform charitable activities by contributing to needy individuals and institutions. (Warner 1949a: 133)

Many upper-middle-class people belonged to the upper-class organizations but stood somewhat aside in deference to their superiors (the small size of the upper class in Jonesville forced them to mix with those of slightly lower rank). The upper-middle class also belonged to many groups that reached far below them in status, such as lodges. But their major energy and leadership aspirations went into civic clubs—the Rotary, the women's clubs, educational and health groups. Instead of emphasizing graceful leisure pursuits, the civic clubs were busy promoting community improvement. Most characteristic, probably, were the male luncheon clubs, which featured conviviality and ritual expressions of community solidarity, guest speakers with messages of uplift, and committees that promoted betterment projects of various sorts.

> There is, in general, a sharp break between the upper-middle and lower-middle classes with respect to the kind and amount of participation in associations. While the members of the upper and upper-middle classes participate together, there is little participation between the upper-middle and the lower-middle classes. . . . While the differences between the upper-middle and the lower-middle classes are quite clear, it is difficult to distinguish between associational behavior of the lower-middle class and that of the upper-lower. (Warner 1949a: 138)

This gap in participation above the lower-middle group, and the continuity between that group and the upper-lower, parallel their behavior in informal cliques, as discussed above. But Warner and Meeker reported that this vast "common-man" group displayed two different types of activity: the fifth who were white-collar workers tended to participate either in the civic clubs already mentioned or in others that were modeled after them but catered to the "little fellows." Thus they were either quiet members of Rotary or more active members of Lions. They also belonged to the more ritualized lodges like the Masons and the Eastern Star. Their wives participated in the ladies' auxiliaries of the lodges, emphasizing a more rigid sex separation than was the case with higher-status families. These white-collar families were usually very active church members (probably more so than any other group) and participated extensively in the clubs sponsored by their churches.

The four fifths of the common-man group who were foremen and skilled workers and steady semiskilled operatives were much less active in formal organizations. They might belong to a church or a lodge or a labor union, but in general they preferred to stay at home.

The organizations of the common man stressed inclusiveness—they said they were friendly folk and anybody could belong. Thus their clubs had a wider spread of rank within them than did the exclusive groups of the top people in town. Warner and Meeker added:

> The ideologies of the lower-middle and the upper-lower associations express the ideologies of the people—patriotism, brotherhood, democracy, equality—and the symbols are those which provoke common interest on the part of the "common man." This preoccupation with equality gives satisfaction to individuals of low status, for it minimizes, or overlooks, status distinctions and gives them a sense of similarity with other individuals regardless of their position in the community. It reflects the attitudes of those people who are reluctant to accept an inferior status and declare, "We haven't any classes here, we're all equal." (Warner 1949a: 142).

Members of the lower-lower class, feeling hostile and suspicious toward the "snotty" folk above them, seldom join anything, and attempt to reduce interaction with people outside their own level to an absolute minimum. They withdraw to escape being snubbed.

Even churches—institutions supposedly rejoicing in the common brotherhood of a common Father—are class typed. In most American towns, the people of higher status belong to those Protestant denominations that feature services of quiet dignity and restrained emotion, such as the Episcopal or Unitarian groups. The common men are more often seen at the Methodist and Baptist churches, where the services are more vigorous, or in Catholic churches (reflecting their origins as part of the "new" immigration from southern and eastern Europe). Those lower-class individuals who go to church at all are most likely to join revivalistic and fundamentalist sects (Demerath 1965; Laumann 1966: 55). Some authors believe that the higher-status groups are expressing in ritual and dogma attitudes of conformity and support for the good life within the current social system, whereas the religions of the lower-status people are offering a palliative for failure in this life through salvation in the next (Weber 1946: 267–302).

CLASS SEGREGATION IN RESIDENTIAL AREAS

The patterns of informal association which we have examined in this chapter are, in part, shaped by the residential geography of class. Both professional and casual observers have noted the tendency of neighborhoods to take on a more-or-less-uniform class character. In many communities, the names of particular neighborhoods become a shorthand designation for social classes. Warner, Hollingshead, and other researchers have taken advantage of this phenomenon by using areas of residence as formal indicators of class position.

The best systematic analysis of class segregation in housing comes from a series of studies of 10 metropolitan areas based on the 1950, 1960, and 1970 censuses (Duncan and Duncan 1955; Wilkins 1956; Uyeki 1964; Simkus 1978). The areas covered (Hartford, Syracuse, Chicago-Gary, Cleveland, Columbus, Indianapolis, Fort Worth, Atlanta, Memphis, and Richmond) provided a wide size and geographic range. The studies measured the segregation of major occupational groups among census tracts (units of 1,000 to 1,500 residents). Results for 1970, averaged across the 10 urban areas, are given in Table 5–5. Here the degree of mutual segregation of any pair of occupations is given by an Index of Dissimilarity, which is simply the percentage of people in one group or the other who would have to be moved to different census tracts in order for both groups to have the same geographic distribution. A very low index figure, such as that for professionals and managers (16), indicates that the two groups tend to live together within the metropolitan areas; a high figure, such as

TABLE 5–5

Indexes of residential dissimilarity among employed males in major occupational groups, ten metropolitan areas, 1970

Major occupational group	Major occupational group							
	Professional	Manager	Sales	Clerical	Craft	Operative	Service	Laborer
Professionals		16	16	28	36	45	40	46
Managers			14	30	36	46	42	48
Sales workers				27	34	44	39	45
Clerical workers					20	25	22	29
Craft workers						20	25	29
Operatives							19	19
Service workers								19
Laborers								

Source: Albert Simkus, "Residential Segregation by Occupation and Race," *American Sociological Review* 43 (1978): 84.

that for managers and laborers (48), indicates that the two groups are quite segregated from one another. A figure of 100 would indicate that no census tract contains representatives of both groups.

In general the findings are as might be anticipated (with some intriguing exceptions); the relative prestige differential between occupations is reflected in their relative physical isolation from one another on the city map. This can be seen quite easily by reading across the "professional" row at the top of the table or down the "laborer" column at the end. In each case the index changes in a fairly regular pattern with increasing social distance. Note that the top three white-collar categories are quite close to one another, forming a "residential elite" clearly set apart from all other groupings. But the traditional blue-collar–white-collar distinction is blurred: clerical workers are somewhat closer to the manual categories than to workers in the white-collar categories above them.

Two anomalies in the table are worth examining. One is the inclusion of sales workers in the residential elite, in spite of a substantial prestige and income gap separating them from professionals and managers. The other is the inversion of the usual ranking of service workers and operatives, placing service workers relatively closer to the top categories. In their analysis of the 1950 data, Duncan and Duncan (1955) demonstrated that the unanticipated situation of these two groups was at least partly related to the class origins of their members. The authors found that the occupational distribution of fathers of service workers placed them closer than operatives to the higher groups. Similarly, the origins of sales workers situated them relatively close to professionals and managers. (More recent mobility data show similar tendencies [Featherman and Hauser 1978: 537.]) It may well be that many of those included in these categories are young workers drawn from higher prestige backgrounds who will move up in the course of their careers. Duncan and Duncan determined that, overall, the residential distribution of occupational groups is more closely related to class origins (parents' position) than to present income or education. "One may suppose," they conclude, "that preferences and aspirations concerning housing are largely formed by childhood and adolescent experiences in a milieu of which the father's occupation is an important aspect" (1955: 503).

Two other conclusions from these studies are worth reporting, one related to race and the other to change. As regards race, the data show that racial segregation vastly exceeds occupational segregation. When Simkus (1978) divided occupational groups by race for 1960 and 1970, he obtained interracial Indexes of Dissimilarity which were extraordinarily high, even for similar occupations. White managers and black professionals, for instance, had an index of 86 in 1970, which exceeds *any* intraracial index. On the other hand, the analysis showed that blacks and whites have very similar intraracial patterns of occupational segregation.

Comparing the global results from 1950 through 1970 and the interracial results from 1960 and 1970, the clearest generalization that emerges is that there has been no significant change in either interoccupational or interracial residential segregation (Simkus 1978). This is a remarkable conclusion given the enormous transformations of our urban areas in the two decades after 1950 and the upheaval in white-black relationships during the course of the 1960s.

CLASS DIFFERENCES IN SOCIAL PARTICIPATION

We have demonstrated a strong tendency for people to associate with class equals in their friendships, marriages, organizational memberships, and residential choices. To this generalization we can add a second observation about the relationship between social participation and class: the *amount* of formal and informal association in which people engage is directly related to their class level. For example, a study of the friendships of 199 men in Cambridge, Massachusetts, conducted by Kahl and Davis found that the percentage of people who live without close friends (defined as those with whom one exchanges house visits once a month or more) increases continuously as one descends the occupational hierarchy. The proportion of such social isolates ranged from 10 percent among top professionals and managers to 30 percent among unskilled workers (Kahl 1957: 138). These findings were supported by Hodges (1964) for the San Francisco area. Curtis and Jackson (1977: 169) studied six communities, varying in population from 5,000 to 700,000, and found in each a significant correlation between higher class position and the frequency of men's visits to friends.

The patterns of participation in formal organizations parallel those for informal association: people of higher prestige status belong to more voluntary formal associations than people of lower status—this despite the fact that many organizations are especially designed for lower-status people. For instance, Warner and Meeker reported that in Jonesville the distribution of memberships in formal organizations ranged from an average of 3.6 memberships per upper-class family to 0.7 per lower-lower class family (Warner 1949b: chapter 9).

Comparable data from Yankee City (Warner and Lunt 1941: chapter 16), New York City (Komarovsky 1946), Evanston, Illinois (Reissman 1954), the six communities surveyed by Curtis and Jackson (1977: chapter 8), and three national surveys conducted by NORC all show the same tendency: middle- and upper-class people are much more active in formal organizations than members of the working and lower classes. Furthermore, when an organization has members of various prestige backgrounds, the higher-status persons are much more likely to be the leaders—with the exception of some instances where upper-class people stay in the background and use upper-middle-class representatives as their agents.

CONTRASTING LIFESTYLES

Let's explore a little further the contrast suggested above between a socially active upper-middle class and the relatively inactive working class. Many middle-class people combine their social and business lives. In a crude sense we may say that they use social opportunities to make contacts that have a business or professional function in that they provide new customers or clients or opportunities for bureaucratic advancement. But in a broader sense it is better to say that these people simply merge the two spheres and do not see them as separate compartments of living. The husband meets people through his business life, entertains them, and they become friends; or his wife meets people in the community who become business contacts. It is a basic part of the job of most businessmen to be at ease in their contacts with new people; they come to value sociability as an end in itself, and it cannot be expected that they will suddenly reverse themselves at 5 P.M.

Business people live in neighborhoods filled with others like themselves, who share the values of sociability. Their homes are not overcrowded, and they can entertain without strain. They become activists in club work and are likely to run into the same townspeople at the parent-teacher association, the Rotary Club, or the country club. Particularly in small towns, the number of such active business families is small enough for them all to become acquainted. Even their children form a single, extensive web of contacts.

In the past, business connections were primarily based on buying and selling: the insurance man, the doctor, the owners of the retail stores and the small factories all were tied together in a mutual exchange of goods and services. But the more recent tendency is for these men and women to turn into executives in large corporations, for the local stores and factories have often become branches of national chains. This change means that the executives are less-permanent members of their local communities, for their companies shift them around from one part of the country to another. And it means that the relationships among them have changed flavor somewhat, for instead of independent entrepreneurs who both cooperate and compete with each other in the open market, they have become incumbents within hierarchies who are more likely to seek personal esteem and advancement than a sale.

William H. Whyte, Jr., of *Fortune* magazine, wrote a penetrating account of the clique behavior of the male executive of 1952 in *Is Anybody Listening?* He got most of his information from their wives but also interviewed many junior executives as well as some of their bosses. The senior men told him, "with a remarkable uniformity of phrasing," that the social activities of junior executives and their wives were extremely important for business success, and that the good wife is "(1). . . highly adaptable, (2) highly gregarious, (3) realizes her husband belongs to the corporation" (Whyte 1952: 146) Here are a few examples of descriptions of the ideal wife:

Executive: She should do enough reading to be a good conversationalist. . . . Even if she doesn't like opera she should know something about it, so if the conversation goes that way she can hold her own. . . .

Executive: The hallmark of the good wife is the ability to put people at their ease.

Wife: The most important thing for an executive's wife is to know everybody's name and something about their famliy so you can talk to them—also, you've got to be able to put people at their ease. (Whyte 1952: 152–54)

There are patterns of behavior that are appropriate for each level of the hierarchy, and no ambitious junior executive dares to get far out of line. He cannot drive a Cadillac before he has passed through the Buick stage or he will be thought "pushy." On the other hand, he must not drive an old Ford, or he will look like a failure. One wife, speaking of this pattern, told Whyte:

It makes me laugh. If we were the kind to follow The Pattern, I'll tell you just what we would do. First, in a couple of years, we'd move out of Ferncrest Village (it's really pretty tacky there, you know). We wouldn't go straight to Eastmere Hills—that would look pushy at this stage of the game; we'd go to the hilly section of Scrubbs Mill Pike. About that time, we'd start going to the Fortnightly's—it would be a different group entirely. Then about 10 years later, we'd finally build in Eastmere Hills. (Whyte 1952: 154–55)

Whyte (who wrote in a time when almost all business executives were male) emphasized that the rule was to keep up with the Joneses but never to get far ahead of them. The timing of each shift had to be carefully calculated. Similarly, one must not have odd personal tastes that made him too "different." An "intellectual" or "aesthete" was mistrusted because he was different, and different people could not be understood; thus their actions could not be anticipated. It was because competition within corporate hierarchies depended so much on the interpersonal relations among executives (equals and immediate superiors) that their total way of life, which included their wives and children, became important. If you dealt with a man in a market situation, you dealt primarily with the quality of his goods or services. But if you had to work with him every day, his total personality was relevant. Therefore, corporations thought of themselves as "one big happy family," and most families are intolerant of too much "difference" among members which might threaten the smooth operation of joint living.

A similar picture emerges from Rosabeth Kanter's more recent *Men and Women of the Corporation* (1977), a study of a single multinational corporation which she calls "Idsco." The similarity is ironic because Idsco, in contrast to at least one of its competitors, maintained a "libertarian" policy which officially denied any claim on the private lives of its employees and avoided involving spouses in company-related activities. Nevertheless, the social lives of the company's executives and their families were inextricably bound to corporate concerns. Although a few wives with serious careers of their own insisted on their total independence of Idsco, the kind of complaint Kanter heard most frequently from the wives of Idsco executives revolved around the contradiction between the company's official denial of their existence and the "strong demands to be gracious, charming hostesses and social creatures, supporting their husband's careers and motivating their achievements, with the boundaries of their own life choices set by the company . . ." (Kanter 1977: 108). By the time Idsco men reached middle-management positions their wives, like the women Whyte interviewed,

> realized that friendships were no longer a personal matter but had business implications. Social professionalism set in. The political implications of what had formerly been personal or sentimental choices became clear. Old friendships might have to be put aside because the organizational system makes them inappropriate. . . . The public consequences of relationships made it difficult for some wives to have anything but a superficial friendship with anyone in the corporate social network. Yet since so much of their time was consumed by company-related entertainment, they had little chance for other friendships and reported considerable loneliness. A few wives complained about other costs to instrumentalism in relationships; having to entertain in their homes people they did not like and would not otherwise have invited, the need to be consistently cheerful and ready to be on display. Duplicity in relationships was one result. (Kanter 1977: 116)

These examples have been stressing the clique life of executives working for the same company, but of course in most communities the executives from many companies might mix together. There is rather rigid age grading, for the promising young men interact in their own set where they feel comfortable; only rarely are they invited to the homes of the older and more senior men. Such occasions require "company manners," and the younger men must always be on guard, for they are being watched and evaluated by their boss or his friends.

Junior executives gain many advantages from ties with young men from other companies. Such contacts give them a chance for a social circle in which it is possible to relax, in which the competition among men in the same company can be avoided. But this interaction also provides useful contacts, for it is much easier to do business with another company through people who are friends. And sometimes the contacts turn into opportunities; junior executives are relatively interchangeable and often move from one company to another when there is a good opening and a chance for promotion. To take advantage of such an opening, a man has to know about it. Where top executives are concerned, social contacts with people outside the corporation serve "diplomatic" functions, providing an informal basis for the company's relations with other organizations, both private and public.

There is a sharp contrast between this merged recreational and business life and the separated work and family spheres of the average male factory worker. He seldom brings his workmates home; he never entertains the foreman, and the foreman certainly gives no thought to a worker's wife before promoting him.

A study that illuminates this difference was done by Floyd Dotson in New Haven, Connecticut, in 1948. He interviewed 50 working-class couples in their homes. They no longer lived in the ethnic districts of their parents and were typical of the "new" working class who were reared in American cities and not on farms or in Europe. Most of the husbands held semiskilled jobs in the factories. Most of the wives stayed home and did not work for pay (Dotson 1950; 1951).

Dotson found that in some respects the way of life of these people approximated middle-class norms: they emphasized the importance of the nuclear (as compared to the extended) family and preferred not to live with relatives nor to depend upon them much for exchange of such services as baby-sitting. The notion of "permissiveness" in child rearing was widespread. It appeared to Dotson that, as these young couples had learned American ways different from those of their parents, they had learned family patterns that were not far divergent from middle-class standards.

However, there were two striking differences: (1) these working-class people had very few intimate friends other than kinfolk; (2) they interacted frequently with siblings. It must be remembered that because they came from working-class homes, they tended to come from large families and had many brothers and sisters available. Furthermore, a sizable proportion of their siblings lived in or near New Haven, as working-class people tend to stay put if employment opportunities are available. About two fifths of the families had no intimate friends other than kin; an almost equal number belonged to loose friendship groups that included husbands and wives, but exchange of visits was not frequent. In only 2 instances (out of 50!) did the husband and wife participate in a tight clique of the middle-class style. In six instances, the wife continued to interact with a group growing out of her school contacts, and in five the husband continued to spend much time with his boyhood friends (usually via an athletic club). Rarely did a man interact in evening hours with friends from work.

Why did these people not participate in much clique activity? The sheer availability of siblings was one reason, for they offered all the companionship many of the couples desired. Furthermore, they were easy to interact with—they all understood one another, lived in the same way, did the same things. It was simple to bundle up the kids, take them to sister Jane's house, put them to sleep on any available bed, and then play cards and talk and drink beer. In those few instances where the respondents had a sibling who had climbed into the middle class, visits were rare. Several couples reported receiving invitations to Christmas dinner from successful siblings which they declined because they would not feel natural and relaxed in the more opulent homes.

Similarly, a few of the respondents found it easy to maintain contact with some old school chums. But as the number of small children in the house multiplied, interaction rates went down. Money was one reason: it was expensive to hire a baby-sitter, and they felt less free in taking infants on visits with nonrelatives. Furthermore, the emphasis on family life led many people to prefer the company of their children: "Sure, kids are a hell of a lot of expense and trouble, but what would a home be without them? If you want the honest-to-God lowdown on me, you can say that my real life is right here with my family. We're family people; we find most of our fun in life right here at home" (Dotson 1950: 122).

Through the years these factors (plus movement from one part of town to another) broke up most of the adolescent cliques that these people once had had. Dotson expected new friendships formed from the immediate neighborhood or from work to replace them and was surprised to find so little interaction. Although the informants verbalized about the ideal of neighborliness, mostly they meant only that it was proper to smile and say hello. Many were quite reluctant to form close ties with neighbors. One man said: "I've found out you can't really be friends with most people because pretty soon they'll do you dirt" (Dotson 1950: 161). Nonetheless, some women did have one or two close friends among immediate neighbors (about two fifths of the respondents). And interestingly enough, most of the couples remembered with pleasant nostalgia the more intimate atmosphere that existed in the ethnic neighborhoods of their youth and regretted that their current area was "colder." Yet they made it cold by their own behavior.

No recent study gives as systematic a picture of working-class association patterns as Dotson's work, but its general outlines are confirmed by later research. Curtis and Jackson's survey of six communities, although it does not deal separately with working-class people, shows that lower-prestige individuals are more likely to value visits with relatives over those with friends, are more likely to have relatives in the same community, and, largely for that reason, visit their relatives more frequently (1977: 161–78). Lillian Rubin, whose study of working-class families in the San Francisco Bay Area we examined above, found that the extended family is still "at the heart of working-class social life" (1976: 197). Visits with parents and siblings are frequent. Holidays are typically celebrated with large family dinners, which may include aunts, uncles, and cousins. Most important, kin are those "whose lives are shared both emotionally and socially . . . with whom intimacies are maintained, who can be trusted with the care of young children on the rare occasion when a couple takes an evening out alone . . ." (Rubin 1976: 197).

Rubin believes that working-class couples are more likely to exchange visits with nonkin than they were in the past, but the practice is still infrequent. The dinner party, "that backbone of middle-class social life" (Rubin 1976: 195) is virtually unknown. Couples with young children are the most likely to invite friends to the house—typically late Saturday night, when the kids are asleep, for dancing or cards:

> We don't have money to go out hardly at all, but I get lonely to see some friends without the kids around sometimes. So once in a while, we invite them over, and we play some cards and have a little beer and a snack. (Rubin 1976: 196)

Women who are not in the labor force may see old friends during the day and develop casual relationships with female neighbors. Employed men and women find new friends at work, and men often "stop off for a beer with the guys" after work (a custom much resented by their wives). But the guys are seldom invited home, and the neighbor has her well-defined place in the housewife's daily routine; so these new relationships do not change the essentially kin-oriented character of the working-class pattern of informal association.

The Lynds remarked about Middletown that working-class people were taught to use their hands and middle-class people their personalities—that the one group sold physical labor, the other social skill. It may well be that social skill is a trait of personality that, on the average, gets people into middle-class occupations. Or it may be that the cultural traditions of urban working-class life do not teach people to make friends easily or to trust them too fully. At any rate, the evidence indicates a marked quantitative and qualitative difference between the two classes in social behavior.

CONCLUSIONS

This chapter has moved back and forth between the economic circumstances of people and certain aspects of their values and lifestyles. We noted that parents are influenced by the characteristics of their jobs and the sizes of their incomes; they learn to adjust attitudes and behaviors to economic reality. Oversimplifying, we can say that most working-class parents tend to see their lives as limited to routine and subordination, and they train themselves and their children to conform. By contrast, most middle-class people see the world as more open to control, and they encourage themselves and their children to develop active personalities that seek to shape the environment rather than adjust to it.

These characteristics of personality are linked during adolescence to behaviors at school and interactions among school friends. Attitudes toward books, sports, sex, work, and authority all reflect these class-related perspectives. Young people sort themselves out so as to associate with others like themselves; this facilitates friendships and shared activities, but it also tends to reinforce and sharpen the original subcultural perspectives by reducing contact with people who are different and might teach new ideas. The residential segregation of large cities adds to the separation; people with the same incomes live near one another and send their children to local schools. The net result is to close the circle: ideas that seem appropriate to the types of jobs parents have and to their ways of handling given amounts of money for family consumption—ideas, in other words, that stem from material or economic circumstances—shape the thinking and behavior of children in ways that lead them to re-create the same economic circumstances when they are adults. Material facts and human feelings about those facts influence each other in a reciprocal fashion.

However, in a society like that of the United States, all of these statements are no more than loose trends. The trends are real, as shown by statistical comparisons of attitudes studied in opinion polls, in counts of who interacts with whom, and more dramatically revealed in the conversations of men and women when they are talking freely about their lives. Some aspects of the reciprocity between circumstances and ideas they see clearly and can articulate; other aspects are more subtle and less conscious and must be inferred by the observer. But our social classes are not sharply defined groups completely segregated from one another, and our society does not stand still long enough for subcultural patterns to grow entirely consistent within themselves and then be passed on from one generation to the next with little change. The economy keeps transforming itself—from farming to small business to corporate enterprise; large numbers of people move from one part of the country to another; immigrant groups get assimilated and lose much of their ethnic tradition; individuals climb or fall from one social level to another in their own lifetimes, or experience such mobility between generations. Consequently, there are always people at any social level who show values and behaviors that are typical of another level—from which they came or toward which they aim. And people of all levels learn standardized ideas and lifestyles from the pervasive mass media, even if they lack the jobs or the money to allow them to fully play out the appropriate roles.

This constant state of flux brings tensions. People are not always sure how they want to behave, or they lack the economic means to live as they desire. Husbands, wives, and children in the same family may have different goals. To some degree, an open society allows people to reorganize their lives: children move away from the world of their parents; spouses separate and seek new partners who are more appropriate to changing lifestyles; people change careers in midlife, especially housewives who go to work outside the home. The tensions from change bring more change, which sometimes solves problems. But for many people, life remains, as so often portrayed in contemporary literature, a matter of accepting quiet desperation. The novelist tends to heighten individual idiosyncrasy; the sociologist looks for the common patterns—especially those linked to the facts of life shared within each prestige class—that help explain why so many lives are indeed similar to one another. These similarities in private lives get projected through formal organizations into public influences; each prestige class formulates goals and policies and creates appropriate organizations to promote its interests or solve its problems, and these differing policies become the battlegrounds of political action, as we shall see in more detail in a later chapter on class consciousness and ideology.

But first, let us study in more detail the issue of social mobility: What proportion of the population moves up or down? Are the rates changing through time? What factors cause mobility? The next two chapters examine these questions.

SUGGESTED READINGS

Gans, Herbert. 1962. *The Urban Villagers: Group and Class in the Life of Italian Americans.* New York: Free Press.

_____. 1972. *The Levittowners: Ways of Life and Politics in a New Suburban Community.* New York: Pantheon Books.

Two rewarding studies of class subcultures in residential settings—the first of a working-class/lower-class Italian-American neighborhood in Boston, the other of an ethnically varied, working-class/lower-middle-class suburb of Philadelphia.

Gecas, Victor. 1979. "The Influence of Social Class on Socialization." In *Contemporary Theories about the Family,* edited by W. R. Burr. New York: Free Press.
Systematic critical review of the literature.

Kanter, Rosabeth. 1977. *Men and Women of the Corporation.* New York: Basic Books.
Like the books by LeMasters and Rubin below, a rich ethnographic work whose full range we were only able to sample in this chapter.

LeMasters, E. E. 1975. *Blue-Collar Aristocrats: Life Styles at a Working-Class Tavern.* Madison: University of Wisconsin Press.

Maccoby, Michael. 1976. *The Gamesmen.* New York: Simon & Schuster.
The career games of corporate executives.

Miller, S. M., and Frank Reissman. 1961. "The Working Class Sub-Culture: A New View." *Social Problems* 9:86–97.
Excellent synthesis.

Rubin, Lillian Breslow. 1976. *Worlds of Pain: Life in the Working-Class Family.* New York: Basic Books.

Succession and mobility: Structural opportunities

I don't think that the management picks its successors: I think that the successors just rise by their own ability and the force of their own personalities. It's perfectly obvious who is coming to the top.

An Executive

What's the use of trying to get someplace around here—the boss is training his son to take over.

A Worker
(from interview files)

6

As each generation succeeds its predecessor, there occurs a vast sifting process that places individuals into class levels. If a society were completely "open," the forces of pure competition would sort people according to their native talents and the efforts with which they used their talents. Individuals would get neither help nor hindrance from parents in the competition for worldly success; the correlation coefficient between the class positions of parents and those of adult sons and daughters would be low (reflecting purely genetic influences).

Reality does not match the abstract model of the completely open society. Not only is talent partly inherited in the genes, but in addition, families greatly influence the motivations of children through both deliberate and unnoticed patterns of socialization that shape ambitions and the drive for success. And parents teach skills of personality, verbal fluency, and technical adroitness in various tasks that affect later life chances.

Furthermore, there are sharp limits on the free play of competition in the market which bias the distribution of rewards. Education is necessary before talent can be properly exploited, and it is expensive in tuition and in the less obvious but often higher costs of supporting students during the years of study and of replacing the income that might otherwise be earned during the same years. And once out of school, a young person gains advantages from parents with lots of money or good connections or even a distinguished name in the community. There are limits on free competition because the stratification variables reinforce one another: because occupation, money, connections, and values are interdependent and through the family are partly passed on from one generation to the next. This is sufficient reason, even if there were no other, to speak of a class system instead of a collection of separate stratification variables.

No society is completely open. In order even to imagine a high degree of openness in his ideal republic, Plato had to suggest that children be separated from parents, sorted into homogeneous groups by potential talent, and then reared by the state in ways that would maximize the development of talent; some were trained for war, others for politics, others for labor. But neither is it possible to have a society that is completely closed, with a system in which all children inherit their parents' positions and no movement up or down the scale ever occurs. The latter type is most closely approached in caste systems, where occupation is normally inherited and marriage is usually confined to caste equals, but even in traditional India some mobility existed. The correlation coefficient between the positions of parents and children is never equal to 1.0.

In order to understand the degree of openness that exists in the United States today, we must approach the problem in stages. Our first task is to measure the amount of inheritance of class position that occurs from one generation to the next. Inheritance of position will be called *succession*, and movement to a different level will be called *mobility*. The total amount of mobility that occurs in our society is a complex result of many past influences on our occupational structure. Once we understand the structure itself and its changes through time, we can focus attention on the sorting of particular types of individuals into their different careers, which is called the *process of status attainment*.

PROBLEMS OF PERSPECTIVE AND MEASUREMENT

The distinction made above suggests two perspectives that can be applied to the overall question of succession and mobility, and it is important to keep them separate in both theory and measurement. The first concerns the shape of the stratification structure and the trends that influence it; here we are concerned with the relative proportions of positions at high, middle, and low levels of the system, and also tendencies that are changing those proportions. For instance, an aristocratic society that is made up of a mass of peasants dominated by a handful of large landowners and their administrators will show a shape like a pyramid that is distorted by a very high peak and a narrow middle. When such a society industrializes, the landed aristocrats are replaced by industrial and commercial capitalists at the top, probably in greater numbers than the landlords they push aside, and the middle sectors grow with new engineers, teachers, and skilled workers who are needed in profusion to make the system function with efficiency. The pyramid gets more squat in shape. A hierarchy with few positions at the top allows few people to move up regardless of how fair the system is, but a hierarchy with many positions at the top is likely to generate movement. Particularly during the period of transition from the one type of society to the other, the very expansion of new positions which are disproportionately placed in the middle and upper levels creates mobility. That is, many sons and daughters of peasants have a chance to climb into newly created jobs and thus raise themselves above their parents. In such a situation, it is possible to have a lot of upward mobility without much downward slippage. Thus, changes in the structure can increase opportunities for everybody or, to phrase it another way, can enhance life chances throughout the system: children of people near the top can stay there, and at the same time, many children from below get a chance to improve their position.

Once we have described the structure and its trends, we can turn our attention to the second perspective on succession and mobility, that of the particular factors that influence the careers of individuals. Within a given structure, we still might wonder why particular individuals manage to take advantage of the existing opportunities and others do not. Here we pay attention to the many stages of careers and try to understand what is happening at each decisive step, and overall, to determine the relative weight of factors that combine to cause final status placement as adults. For instance, how much difference does a father's occupation make for a son's career, once we control for the son's education? Or, does an intelligent son have a good chance to become successful even if his parents are poor? Or, do the careers of daughters follow the same model as those of sons? Or, do black people suffer from discrimination to the point where they cannot get good jobs even if they have a good education?

In order to simplify our story, we start with a discussion of the gross amounts of succession and mobility in the United States and of the structural facts and trends which explain them. Furthermore, we will begin by comparing the careers of fathers and sons. Since women have only entered the labor force in massive proportions in recent years, the basic patterns of careers, especially in the past, have been mainly studied by concentrating on men. Once male patterns are understood, we will ask questions about women. And we will first concentrate on structure, then turn to the process of individual status attainment in the next chapter.

It would be useful to compare a large sample of fathers and sons on their overall status placement, their scores on some standard SES (socioeconomic status) index. But in practice, that is impossible because we never have enough data on both the fathers and the sons to compute a good composite index for each generation. To get a large sample, we must start with sons and ask about their fathers, but many of the fathers are retired or dead, and the most reliable information the sons can give about them concerns occupation. Thus, it is useful to begin with a simple comparison of just the occupations of fathers and sons, and most large-scale studies have done so.

Whenever we work with occupational data, we must decide how to group the hundreds of specific occupational titles used by our respondents into some form of ranking that approximates the hierarchy of socioeconomic status. Many different schemes are used, but in essence they reflect only two options: (1) discrete categories taken directly from or somewhat adapted from those used by the U.S. Census or (2) a continuous scale that assigns to each occupational title a numerical value that has been shown to approximate its prestige value in the minds of the public; both procedures have been explained above in Chapters 2 and 3. Many researchers have shown that the relative prestige ranks of occupations change slowly; so for practical purposes we can compare fathers and sons by assuming similar ranks in each generation.

When using the census categories, two facts should be remembered. First, the classification is a crude one and obscures many shades of meaning. For instance, in the category of proprietors, managers, and officials, the scheme puts all sorts of men together, ranging from the president of General Motors to the man who runs a peanut stand. The occupational classification treats these two gentlemen as equals, which they may be before God and the law but are not in the stratification system. Second, it should be noted that the smaller the size and the larger the number of categories, the more the mobility, assuming mobility is defined as the number of men born in one category who ended up in another. By creating more categories, one creates more places to move and thus more mobility.

HOW MUCH MOBILITY EXISTS?

How much movement is there in the United States from one generation of men to the next? A survey conducted in 1962 that asked sons to compare themselves with their fathers has become the model for all others; it was reported by Peter M. Blau and Otis Dudley Duncan in *The American Occupational Structure* (1967). Eleven years later, their study was replicated by David L. Featherman and Robert M. Hauser, as reported in *Opportunity and Change* (1978). Some small shifts in pattern were discovered, but for the most part the two surveys gave similar results, and that allows us to use them interchangeably in our discussion. (Hauser and Featherman [1977] also present reanalyses of the original 1962 data, along with some subsequent trends.)

The researchers arranged with the Bureau of the Census to insert two extra pages of questions concerning career history and parental background into the regular monthly survey of employment and un-

employment. In 1962, there were 20,700 useable cases with information on both sons and their fathers; in 1973, there were 33,600 cases.
These serve as exceptionally good representative samples of sons
aged 20 to 64 in the total population but are not very good samples of
the generations of fathers, since about a third of all fathers in any
given generation have no sons at all and thus could not show up in
the sample, and some fathers had more than one son and could have
shown up more than once. Nevertheless, for some limited purposes,
we can use the fathers as acceptable samples of their generations.

The raw data were first organized in the form of a mobility table
which cross-classified the occupational levels of fathers and sons,
using 17 categories. The fathers were grouped in terms of the occupations they held when their sons were 16 years old and about to enter
the labor force, thus determining the sons' point of "origin" in the
system. The 17 categories are subdivisions of the ones first used by
Alba M. Edwards of the Census Bureau, as described in Chapter 3. In
most instances, there was a steady decrease in average education and
income for each step down the occupational prestige ladder from
professionals to laborers, although a few discrepancies existed; a bit
of disorder is always present in social data, and we must learn to live
with it.

The mobility table was organized by listing the categories of
fathers' occupations down the left-hand column and identical
categories of sons' occupations across the top row, producing 289
cells. The original table of raw data looked like Table 6–1 except that
numbers of persons who fell in each cell were given instead of percentages. However, the numbers shown were not those actually in
the sample but projections from the sample to the total labor force,
which facilitated comparisons with census data (the table is given in
Blau and Duncan 1967: 496 and unfortunately was not exactly replicated in Featherman and Hauser).

The original table of raw data from 1962 permitted observations
such as the following: Of the 45 million men between the ages of 20
and 64 in the United States in 1962, 39,969,000 were represented in
the sample and shown in the table. About 3,172,000 were managers.
Among the fathers of the men sampled only 1,414,000 were managers. The growth is something we would expect from our earlier
discussion of the relative expansion of the upper-middle levels of the
occupational hierarchy, plus some general population growth. There
were 275,000 men in the cell in the table where manager fathers and
manager sons crossed—that is, manager sons with manager fathers.

At this point, simple description stops, and we must make some
decisions growing out of theoretical interests before we can decide
how to interpret the numbers. The first way to proceed might be to
concentrate on career life chances and calculate the probable destina-

TABLE 6–1
Outflow from father's occupation to son's occupation: 1973

Father's occupation	Son's occupation (in percent)																	Total
	(1)	(2)	(3)	(4)	(5)	(6)	(7)	(8)	(9)	(10)	(11)	(12)	(13)	(14)	(15)	(16)	(17)	
1. Professionals, self-employed	12.6	32.5	18.0	5.9	3.4	3.4	2.5	3.3	4.9	3.3	3.2	3.3	1.4	0.7	1.0	0.5	0.3	100%
2. Professionals, salaried	3.6	34.6	15.1	4.5	1.4	7.3	2.2	4.7	6.0	3.0	4.3	4.1	5.3	1.0	2.0	0.7	0.2	100
3. Managers	3.4	23.0	24.9	7.9	3.2	5.3	3.7	4.2	5.7	2.4	4.9	4.2	3.8	0.5	2.0	0.4	0.4	100
4. Salesmen, other	3.7	21.2	21.0	12.5	2.5	6.1	2.9	4.2	6.1	2.5	5.2	4.1	4.4	0.5	2.3	0.2	0.6	100
5. Proprietors	2.7	16.6	19.9	7.9	8.0	5.9	2.9	5.7	5.4	5.1	3.8	5.6	5.5	1.0	2.1	1.2	0.5	100
6. Clerks	1.4	22.3	16.4	4.2	2.0	10.5	2.0	6.4	5.7	4.5	5.4	6.0	7.6	1.3	3.4	0.5	0.4	100
7. Salesmen, retail	4.2	13.6	15.8	8.2	6.6	8.7	4.6	5.7	7.9	2.7	5.5	5.4	6.6	1.4	2.2	0.6	0.0	100
8. Craftsmen, manufacturing	1.1	16.4	11.1	4.6	2.5	7.3	1.8	13.4	8.7	4.1	5.2	6.4	12.5	1.5	2.7	0.5	0.2	100
9. Craftsmen, other	0.8	15.1	11.7	4.0	2.9	7.6	2.3	8.6	12.7	5.1	5.8	7.9	9.6	1.4	3.4	0.8	0.3	100
10. Craftsmen, construction	0.7	11.6	12.1	3.1	4.2	6.1	1.7	6.4	9.2	15.2	5.1	7.4	9.1	1.0	4.4	0.8	0.9	100
11. Service	1.3	12.3	10.5	3.1	3.3	8.3	2.1	6.4	8.8	4.9	10.8	8.8	11.6	2.0	5.1	0.2	0.4	100
12. Operatives, other	0.6	10.0	9.3	2.6	2.7	8.1	1.6	8.6	10.5	5.5	6.1	14.3	12.0	1.5	5.1	0.6	0.8	100
13. Operatives, manufacturing	0.9	11.2	8.8	2.7	2.6	7.5	1.9	12.5	8.0	4.8	5.9	7.4	19.5	3.0	2.8	0.5	0.2	100
14. Laborers, manufacturing	0.9	7.0	7.9	2.5	2.6	5.6	1.8	10.4	8.2	7.6	5.0	10.2	18.7	5.8	4.6	0.4	0.7	100
15. Laborers, other	0.8	7.0	8.7	2.1	2.8	6.5	1.4	8.5	8.7	6.5	8.2	11.3	15.8	2.0	8.3	0.4	0.9	100
16. Farmers	0.7	7.0	8.2	2.1	3.4	4.0	1.7	7.0	8.0	7.2	6.0	8.4	12.9	2.4	5.2	12.4	3.3	100
17. Farm laborers	0.4	4.4	4.4	1.5	2.4	4.8	1.3	10.1	8.7	6.5	7.1	11.2	16.1	3.5	7.4	4.2	6.2	100

Source: David Featherman and Robert M. Hauser, *Opportunity and Change* (New York: Academic Press, 1978), p. 535.

tions of the sons of managers, starting with sons who had the same occupation as their fathers. Thus we determine the chance that the son of a manager father will also become a manager, or 275,000 divided by 1,414,000, which equals 19 percent. The second procedure reverses our direction in time, and calculates the chance of a manager son having had a manager for a father, or 275,000 divided by 3,172,000, which equals 9 percent. The difference in percentages obviously comes from changing the denominator: there was a larger number of managers in the later generation.

Which is the "correct" way to calculate percentages? It all depends on your purposes, and you can choose those for yourself. However, it is always important to keep in mind the direction in which you, or someone else, computes the percentages; otherwise grand confusion ensues. If one thinks of a flow from fathers to sons, one is asking questions about the life chances or destinations of men from known origins in the form of an "outflow," and the percentages will be calculated across rows in the table, following the procedures of the first example in the preceding paragraph. If one thinks in the opposite direction, one is asking questions about the earlier backgrounds of men in currently known positions; one seeks the origins of the "inflow," and the percentages will be calculated down the columns in the table. In the first case, the sons of each category of fathers add up to 100 percent; in the second case, the fathers of each category of sons add up to 100 percent.

For most purposes, people prefer the outflow form of the table, and we give an example from the 1973 survey in Table 6–1. This allows us to observe the career chances of men reared at any given level of society. For example, the data show that 25 percent of the sons of managers ended up in the same category as their fathers (a larger percentage than we calculated from the first survey). And 26 percent ended up in one of the professional groups. Adding these high-level sons together, we can conclude that one-half of the sons of managers succeeded to top positions, and since many others are young and still climbing, the percentage will increase a little. As one moves the eye to the right in the same row, one notes that there is a fair percentage of salesmen, but every other cell contains less than 6 percent; all the 10 blue-collar or manual cells combined only add up to 29 percent. This reflects a double influence: the hierarchy itself, which tends to keep sons fairly close to fathers, and the dividing line between nonmanual and manual occupations, which tends to be hard to cross in the downward direction (Blau and Duncan 1967: 58–59).

Taking another row in the table, we find that 20 percent of the sons of operatives in manufacturing (factory workers) followed exactly in their fathers' footsteps, while 38 percent rose to higher levels in the blue-collar world, 35 percent achieved white-collar positions, and only 7 percent slipped below their fathers to the level of laborers. Somewhat similar proportions of succession and upward and downward mobility were found for other men in the middle levels of the hierarchy, with a lot of upward movement, a fair amount of direct succession, and a small amount of downward movement.

Now we are close to a more general answer to the question we started with: how much succession and mobility is there in the United States? It would be possible to calculate for each row in the table the proportion of sons who rose above, equaled, or fell below the positions of their fathers, but for summary purposes that would be too complex. Indeed, most discussions of mobility in the class system are concerned with broader strata that condense the 17 occupational levels into a few large groups, and Featherman has conveniently done so, as shown in Table 6–2. Notice that in both years the sons of upper white-collar workers were at the same level as their fathers more often than they were in any other category, with slightly more than a 50-50 chance of staying at the top. The next highest probability of succession was in the group of lower manual workers. There was much more movement in the middle of the distribution than at the extremes.

We can summarize the various rows in the table and arrive at a very simple view of mobility in the United States in 1973:

49 percent of sons moved up.

32 percent were stationary.

19 percent moved down.

TABLE 6–2
Outflow from father's occupation to son's occupation, 1962 and 1973

| Year and father's occupation | Son's occupation (in percent) | | | | | | Row percentage |
	Upper white-collar	Lower white-collar	Upper manual	Lower manual	Farm	Total	
1962:							
Upper white-collar	54	17	13	15	1	100%	17
Lower white-collar	46	20	14	18	2	100	8
Upper manual	28	13	28	30	1	100	19
Lower manual	20	12	22	44	2	100	27
Farm	16	7	19	36	22	100	29
Total	28	12	20	32	8	100	100%
1973:							
Upper white-collar	52	16	14	17	1	100%	18
Lower white-collar	42	20	15	22	1	100	9
Upper manual	30	13	27	29	1	100	21
Lower manual	23	12	24	40	1	100	29
Farm	18	8	23	36	15	100	23
Total	30	13	22	31	4	100	100%

Source: David Featherman, "Opportunities Are Expanding," *Society* 13 (1979): 7.

In other words, despite the fact that about one third of all sons ended up in the same broad stratum as their fathers, there was still opportunity for almost half of all sons to climb into a higher stratum. There was considerable succession, but even more mobility, especially in the upward direction.

In 1962, the percent of upward mobility was the same, but 2 percent more were stationary and 2 percent fewer moved down—a small difference. (Remember, all of these percentages depend on the number of cells in the table; if we counted the movement in Table 6–1 with 17 occupational categories producing more cells of smaller size, then the amount of succession would be less and the amount of mobility more.)

In order to compare their 1962 results with still-earlier studies, Blau and Duncan found it convenient to compress their tables even more, separating white-collar from urban blue-collar from farm occupations. They were able to find appropriate studies for comparison going back to 1947 and reported these relatively small trends:

> (1) a decreasing proportion of men with farm origins remained on farms, whereas an increasing proportion achieved manual status; (2) an increasing proportion from manual origins moved up into white-collar positions; (3) yet there was no compensatory increase in downward mobility from white-collar origins; on the contrary, increasing proportions of those originating at this level remained there (p. 103).

They added the comment that these changes all reflected shifts in the underlying occupational structure that occurred "in such a way as to provide greater opportunity for upward mobility for everybody." But they reminded us that farmers had already become such a small part of the work force that their further decline could not change that structure much more.

Simplified mobility tables permit comparisons between studies done in different countries. We have many of them that compute the proportions of men moving up and down across the line that divides white-collar from blue-collar occupations, and some that use strata similar to those in Table 6–2. They show rather similar (though not identical) rates for most of the advanced industrial countries, which contradicts the myth that the United States has a society much more open than others (Lipset and Bendix 1959; Miller 1960; Fox and Miller 1966; Cutright 1968; Tyree, Semyonov, and Hodge 1979).

Still another way to analyze mobility tables is to compute the mobility in each cell as a ratio of the observed mobility to that which would be "expected" on the assumption of the type of open society in which chance rules and there is complete statistical independence between origin and destination. (This turns out to be more complicated than it first appears, for one must correct for differences in the occupational distributions in the two generations; see Featherman and Hauser 1978: chapter 4.) Some people consider that such a society is a completely fair one, although they put aside genetics and family socialization in doing so. Mobility ratios show that there is a lot of succession—far more than chance would bring about—at the top and bottom of the hierarchy, and a lot of mobility—rather close to what chance would produce—in the middle of the hierarchy.

CHANGING CAUSES OF MOBILITY

In this section we study two questions: (1) What are the main causes of mobility in the occupational structure from one generation to the next? (2) What are the trends in those causes? Obviously, if we are to sum up the recent past and attempt to foresee the near future, we must disaggregate the causes and look at each one by itself, for some may be tending toward increasing rigidity and others toward increasing fluidity.

If one starts with a mental image of a completely closed society in which all sons replicate the positions of their fathers and then seeks reasons that would open it up to some movement, one can find four basic causes:

1. *Circulation or exchange mobility.* Some sons slip down the scale and thereby make room for others to climb up. In this instance, mobility is a two-way street: there must be some who lose for others to gain.
2. *Occupational or structural mobility.* If technological and organizational changes are occurring in an asymmetric way that creates jobs at a faster rate in the middle and upper levels of the hierarchy than in the lower levels, then some sons will have the chance to climb into the new positions without displacing anybody. In this instances, mobility is a one-way street, and everybody gains.
3. *Reproductive mobility.* If men in upper levels of the system have fewer children than those in lower levels, then the system will reproduce itself in an asymmetric way that allows some sons from the bottom to climb into higher positions without forcing anybody to decline. This is another one-way street.
4. *Immigration mobility.* If many immigrants enter the system at the lower levels, they make it possible for the system as a whole to grow in ways that give native-born sons more chance to move into higher positions than they would otherwise have.

Complexities of data and measurement make it impossible to give precise answers on exactly how much mobility at any given moment comes from each of the four causes, but some partial estimates can be made and some rough trend lines drawn (Duncan 1966). One of the most obstinate complexities could be called the *multiplier effect:* if a new job is created near the top of the hierarchy, it is likely to be filled by someone from the middle, and that person's job in turn is taken by someone from below. Thus, one new opening can create two or more moves in a step-by-step progression. Another problem is caused by the fact that many men change jobs during their careers; therefore intergenerational and intragenerational mobility get confounded.

Of course, a man who has advanced in the world as compared to his father has no idea which of the causes made it possible for him to get ahead, and he probably would not care if he were told. Thus analyses of these separate factors cannot be used in a direct way to explain class consciousness or other subjective phenomena. But a student who looks at the system as a whole to measure the amount of mobility that exists wants to understand the main causes of that mobility and current tendencies among them.

Let us begin with occupational or structural change. We have already discussed the trends in Chapter 3, where it was shown how the middle and upper levels of the occupational hierarchy have been expanding at rates that exceed those for the lower levels, particularly farming. For example, in the three decades from 1940 to 1970, professional and technical jobs for men increased 192 percent, whereas jobs for farm laborers decreased by 75 percent. The average growth for the whole male labor force was 20 percent, as shown in Table 6–3 (remember that in earlier discussions we dealt with the full labor force, including women, but at the moment are focusing on fathers and sons).

Concentrating on the nonmanual jobs, most of which put men into the middle and upper classes of society, we note that the categories of professional and technical, managers and proprietors, and clerical and sales have expanded in absolute numbers from 10,434,000 to

TABLE 6–3
Male occupational distributions, 1940 and 1970

	1940	1970	Percent change
Total	39,169,000	46,970,000	20
Professional and technical	2,271,000	6,621,000	192
Managers and proprietors	3,356,000	5,189,000	55
Clerical and sales	4,807,000	6,883,000	43
Craftsmen and foremen	6,069,000	9,911,000	63
Operatives	7,067,000	9,183,000	30
Nonfarm laborers	4,742,000	3,221,000	−32
Service workers	2,370,000	3,839,000	62
Farm owners and managers	5,205,000	1,288,000	−75
Farm laborers	3,282,000	835,000	−75

Source: U.S. Bureau of the Census, *Historical Statistics of the United States* (Washington, D.C.: U.S. Government Printing Office, 1975), Pt. I: 139. To preserve comparability, figures for males 14 years and older are used.

18,693,000 positions in three decades, or a growth of 79 percent. If those positions had expanded at the same rate as the average for the labor force as a whole, then there would only be 12,521,000 men in those jobs in 1970. The difference of the actual over the "expected" growth is 6,172,000 positions, and that many men had a chance to move up in the system to fill the newly created jobs. Those men constituted 13 percent of the male labor force in 1970. And this estimate is an absolute minimum, since we have no way of adding in those men who moved up as a result of the multiplier effect described above. Also, we are not counting here the sizeable expansion in jobs at the craftsman and foreman level, which is often called the "aristocracy" of manual labor.

Similar calculations for the three decades preceding 1940 show that the average growth for the male labor force was 31 percent, but the growth of the nonmanual jobs was 73 percent. The relatively faster growth of the better jobs allowed at least 9 percent of the labor force to experience upward mobility, a somewhat smaller percentage than occurred in more-recent decades. Consequently, the rate of mobility caused by occupational or structural change appears to have speeded up during the middle years of the century.

We have only limited information about the relative reproduction rates of men at different levels of the occupational hierarchy, but do know that before World War II the families of white-collar workers were much smaller than those of blue-collar workers, especially farmers. To take a specific example to illustrate the difference: it was estimated that 1,000 professional men had 870 sons, whereas 1,000 farmers had 1,520 sons (Kahl, 1957: 257). Thus the sons of professionals were too few in number to take over their fathers' occupational positions, to say nothing of filling the expanding number of professional jobs in the system. It was calculated that if fathers at all status levels had generated families of equal size, then the mobility of blue-collar sons would have been reduced by some 7 percent in the decades before the war. Since then the differences in reproduction rates among the strata have declined markedly, thus reducing the mobility opportunities arising from this particular cause.

Until recent decades, the natural growth of the American population produced by an excess of births over deaths was not sufficient to meet the needs for labor in an expanding economy. In the 18th and 19th centuries, we had a wilderness to conquer, and millions of farmers were enticed or forced to come from Europe and Africa to clear and cultivate the land. Around the beginning of the 20th century, the farm population began to stabilize, and the new demand for workers was in the mines and urban factories. "In 1907, the peak year of the pre–World War I immigrant inflow, one third of the nearly 1 million immigrants who reported an occupation upon arrival were classified as farm laborers and nearly three fourths of the total were classified as either farm or nonfarm laborers, as domestics, or as other service workers" (Wool 1976: 63). In fact, most of those who arrived as farmers took jobs in the cities. In other words, the expanding needs for unskilled and semiskilled labor were still being partly met by immigrants. Their presence was essential for economic growth and permitted native-born citizens (including the sons of foreign-born parents) to climb into the ranks of skilled manual and nonmanual workers.

The First World War was a major turning point. After it was over, modern methods of farming increasingly replaced men with machines, and the farm population began to decline, both relative to the total and also in absolute numbers: sons of farmers moved to the city seeking work. In 1910 there were 10.4 million male farm owners and laborers; in 1940 there were 8.5 million, and by 1970, only 2.2 million. These "internal migrants" were somewhat more prepared for city life than the average immigrant: they spoke English, most were literate, and indeed, some were well educated. But the majority of them moved (at least at first) into the lower levels of skill in the city labor force. This was particularly true of the blacks who left the farms of the South (where 90 percent had lived) and streamed toward the cities of both North and South. The new availability of more-than-ample numbers of internal migrants collided with the new technology in the cities that produced more goods with fewer men: the expansion of unskilled jobs began to slow just as these flows of rural-to-urban migration peaked.

The political response to these combined trends was a drastic change in our immigration laws, which cut the flow from almost a million a year before the First World War to less than half that number after it—and in proportion to our now larger population, the cut seems even more drastic (Higham 1963). Furthermore, the newer immigrants in the 1950s and 1960s were more skilled and entered the labor force at all levels; thus they had less overall effect on the mobility chances of the native born.

The situation keeps changing. By the late 1970s, the pool of excess farmers had dried up (including Puerto Ricans), and the flow of rural-to-urban migration had become a trickle. Simultaneously, a new phenomenon has appeared: large numbers of illegal or undocumented immigrants, two thirds or more from neighboring Mexico. They slip into the country against the wishes of the authorities, and nobody knows for sure how many there are, although estimates indicate several millions of them. At first they were mainly temporary agricultural workers who came for a few months during harvesttime in Texas and California. But now even those jobs tend more and more to be done by machines, and many undocumented workers are found in Los Angeles and Chicago and New York working in tasks that do not demand high skills. They are especially useful to marginal entrepreneurs (for example, in the garment or restaurant industries) who need cheap workers willing to toil long hours under unsavory conditions without complaining to official inspectors. Native-born workers have higher expectations and tend to refuse such jobs; if unemployed, they can subsist through the work of other members of the family or the welfare system. Thus it is possible to have illegal immigrants working while the unemployment rate among citizens remains high (U.S. Labor 1978: chapter 5).

It is difficult to quantify the exact impact of immigration on the mobility chances of native-born citizens, but the trend line is clear enough: in the earlier years of this century, a significant number of Americans experienced mobility into higher jobs because many lower ones were filled by willing immigrants. In recent years, the overall effect of legal immigration on mobility has become minor, and the effect of illegal immigration is not known for sure but is probably less than the impact of the migration before World War I.

CONCLUSIONS

What can we say about the relative weights of these different causes of mobility? Using the mobility among their five broad strata as a base, Featherman and Hauser calculated that about half the total mobility that was measured in 1962 was caused by structural shifts in the occupational distributions from the generation of fathers to the generation of sons. By 1972, that proportion had fallen to about two fifths, even though total mobility itself had increased slightly, which indicated a more than compensating increase in nonstructural mobility (p. 93—their "circulation mobility" includes all nonstructural mobility).

We estimate that differential reproductive mobility had considerable impact before World War II (at least one third as great as that of occupational shifts) but has become negligible in effect in more recent decades. The influence of immigration has probably been curvilinear: somewhat less than reproductive differentials but still significant through the 1920s, declining markedly until the 1960s, and increasing a little in the most recent years, particularly through the impact of undocumented workers. In all of these estimates, we include the multiplier effects of step-by-step movements without measuring them separately, since they are distributed throughout the system in ways that have not been identified.

The study of mobility tables shows that succession and mobility both occur and that in recent decades the rates of total mobility have not shown much change. Thus the reduced impact of reproduction differentials and immigration have been offset by some increase in shifts within the occupational structure and even more of an increase in circulation or exchange mobility. All of these trends are linked to economic growth at sustained rates, and since 1974, there have been increasing doubts about the ability of the nation to continue those rates.

The discussion in this chapter about intergenerational mobility in the male occupational structure has been designed as a skeleton or framework into which we can fit more specific analyses of topics of interest to be taken up in the next chapter, such as: What about the mobility chances of black people? Where do the careers of women fit into the picture? How important is education for career success? Who goes to college?

SUGGESTED READINGS

Boudon, Raymond. 1974. *Education, Opportunity and Social Inequality.* New York: John Wiley & Sons.
> *Powerful analysis of relation between expanding educational opportunities and rates of social mobility, which shows the connection to be less causal than supposed. Data are from several European countries, but the model is applicable to the United States.*

Goldthorpe, John H. 1977. "Class Mobility in Modern Britain: Three Theses Examined." *Sociology* 11: 257–87.
> *Analysis of contemporary debates on effects of mobility in Britain.*

Horan, Patrick M. 1978. "Is Status Attainment Research Atheoretical?" *American Sociological Review* 43: 534–41.
> *Why ask questions about mobility? Horan says most scholars have started with assumptions derived from a neoclassical, functionalist view of society.*

McClendon, McKee J. 1977. "Structural and Exchange Components of Vertical Mobility." *American Sociological Review* 42: 56–74.
> *A recent attempt to separate the two components of mobility by statistical manipulation of survey data.*

Müller, Walter, and Kurt Mayer, eds. 1973. *Social Stratification and Career Mobility.* The Hague: Mouton.
> *Articles from various countries.*

Pessen, Edward, ed. 1974. *Three Centuries of Social Mobility in America.* Lexington, Mass.: D. C. Heath.
> *Articles on the social history of mobility in various communities.*

Family, education, and career

The transmission of property from generation to generation, in the same name, raised up a distinct set of families, who, being privileged by law in the perpetuation of their wealth, were thus formed into a Patrician order, distinguishable by the splendor and luxury of their establishments. From this order, too, the king habitually selected his counsellors of State; the hope of which distinction devoted the whole corps to the interests and will of the crown. To annul this privilege, and instead of an aristocracy of wealth, of more harm and danger, than benefit to society, to make an opening for the aristocracy of virtue and talent, which nature has wisely provided for the direction of the interests of society, and scattered with equal hand through all its conditions, was deemed essential to a well-ordered republic.

Thomas Jefferson (1821: 38)

7

Jefferson proposed to do away with the aristocracy of wealth by changing the laws of inheritance to encourage men to divide their landed estates equally among all their children and thus eventually break them up into small holdings. And he proposed to establish the aristocracy of virtue and talent, characteristics he assumed were "scattered with equal hand" among all strata, by creating a public school system in the state of Virginia that would provide primary education for all citizens and then select the best students for further training in high schools and universities. In his later years, he founded the University of Virginia as the capstone to this system and was so proud of it that he ordered that his tombstone should record his two greatest accomplishments: the writing of the Declaration of Independence and the founding of the University of Virginia.

From Thomas Jefferson forward, American political leaders have endorsed high rates of mobility. In doing so, they have reflected the general values held by most Americans which accept some inequality in society, believing that people should get different rewards for different kinds of work, but also believing that each generation should start fresh and compete in a "fair" way for those rewards. In other words, we believe that young people ought to have careers based on their own talents and desires rather than have their lives determined by the class positions of their parents; they should have "equality of opportunity" but not "equality of result." Accepting the fact that some aspects of the talent and the desires of the children are inherited from or shaped by the parents, nevertheless we believe that a high degree of equality of opportunity can be achieved through the school system: if all children have access to good schools at all levels, *regardless* of the financial resources of their families, then the graduates should be able to compete on a reasonably fair basis.

The practical means for achieving this end began in our early history with free elementary schools in every village and town, supported at first by churches (more interested in equal access to the

Bible than to economic success) but later by local tax money. Later, free high schools were added, and in most small towns, they are now the most prominent buildings to be seen. In the mid–19th century, free or inexpensive state universities were founded with federal aid (Jefferson was a generation ahead of his times). In recent decades, a variety of new programs have been created, ranging from Headstart classes for poor youngsters before first grade, through vocational and job training, to college scholarships and other forms of affirmative action for bright but economically disadvantaged students. Through more schools and more financial support programs it was thought that most children would be given access to training appropriate to their talents and aspirations, thus increasing equality of opportunity for all.

However, this approach was based on the assumption that the problem could be solved by various government programs that would keep disadvantaged youngsters in school longer, in combination with financial help to poorer schools that would make them "better." But behind that assumption were three beliefs about the way schools worked in the real world:

1. Good schools can overcome handicaps from other social forces, particularly family background.
2. Bad schools can be made better by spending more money on them.
3. There is a close connection between the amount of education a youngster gets and the kind of career she or he will have.

To the degree that those beliefs are not correct, government attempts to increase equality of opportunity through changing the schools to make career competition more "fair" will fall short of their goals.

Recent research has cast partial doubt on all three beliefs. The massive work of James Coleman and his associates in the mid-1960s showed that the money available to particular primary and high schools did not much influence the amount the students knew. Furthermore, what the students did know was more influenced by family background than by anything else the researchers could measure. Indeed, the longer they stayed in school, the more the children of higher-strata families moved *ahead* in their test scores and the children of lower-strata families slipped *behind*. In other words, instead of removing family handicaps, the schools often appeared to accentuate them (Coleman et al. 1966; Averch et al. 1972; Hodgson 1975).

A few years later, the work of Christopher Jencks and his associates reported that the income earned by a man was only loosely related to the number of years he stayed in school (although that was a better predictor than any other single variable that could be measured). A lot of other factors intervened that shaped careers once people left school and started working—so many factors, and so hard to pin down, that Jencks at one point dismissed them as "luck." The implication was that even if we equalized schooling we would not equalize career outcomes very much (Jencks et al. 1972 and 1979).

Both of these researches have become highly controversial. They stimulated new studies and even more debates about just what the studies meant. The issues raised are so essential to the understanding of both succession and mobility, and are so important to policy decisions about how the schools should be managed, that we must examine the discussion in considerable detail (for a cogent critique, see Aaron 1978: chapter 3).

Perhaps the main reason why the connections between family background, education, and career outcome are so debatable is the obvious fact that so many things influence one another: it is hard to separate out just what determines what at each stage of a person's development. To take a few examples: some aspects of intelligence may be transmitted through the genes, but since they do not show up until they interact with environmental forces that shape a child's behavior, we cannot be sure what portion of observed and measured intelligence is genetic and what portion is environmental. (And since the subject involves politically volatile issues connected with race and ethnic background, the research is usually designed to prove a point more than to provide scientific enlightenment.) Indeed, we do not fully understand exactly *how* the early social environment—ranging from nonverbal interaction between mothers and babies, through family styles of speech and reading, to contact with other children in the local neighborhood and the school—shapes those aspects of intelligence that we can measure through tests (and only through standardized tests, with all their faults, can we study large samples and come to any general conclusions). And we do not know very much about how other personality factors, such as energy level, sense of discipline to aim at long-term goals, and ability to deal with other people, combine with intelligence as measured by the tests to influence the outcome of schooling and the impact of schooling on occupational career. Nor do we fully understand how the subtle parts of the school environment, such as the way the teachers stereotype the children into those who are "good learners" and "bad learners," begin to form the self-images of the children and thus influence their ambitions and their behavior. Those stereotypes can be related to sex, to race, or to socioeconomic status: girls are often supposed to be good at poetry, boys at mathematics, blacks at basketball, the poor at auto mechanics, and the rich at medicine, and teachers sometimes tell them so.

Many things in life are going on at once and influencing one another, but systematic research must make some choices and concentrate on a few of them. We will emphasize the standard variables of stratification research and only mention superficially the most relevant aspects of personality and school environment. And we will do so by following a formal model that is based on the idea of a sequence of events in which several measurable traits of earlier years are correlated with outcomes in later years. Instead of just relating father's occupation with son's occupation, as we did in the last chapter, we will follow the various pathways through which the former does and does not influence the latter. This sequence is often called the *process of status attainment*. (It is also often called *the process of stratification*, which is a most inappropriate label; *stratification* refers to the class structure, so the *process of stratification* implies historical events that change the structure.)

A warning to the reader is important at this point: by committing ourselves to the type of formal model we shall use, we help untangle some of the main variables that are at work. However, to handle the large samples we need in order to follow several variables over long periods of time, we automatically oversimplify the real world. There is a great temptation to jump from the model to reality, to forget that when we speak of "education," for instance, all we mean is the number of years of school attended (regardless of the type of school or the style of teaching). Each variable is measured by a particular operational definition that may be picking up a lot of "noise": many aspects of life connected with that definition that we are not aware of. And it may imply to the reader still other characteristics not intended by the researcher that may or may not actually exist. The conclusions stated are based on the statistical manipulation of the variables as defined. The fit between this type of model and the real world is never as good as we would like it to be.

STATUS ATTAINMENT: BLAU AND DUNCAN

We begin by returning to the book by Peter Blau and Otis Dudley Duncan that was introduced in the last chapter. Their analysis of mobility tables was a refinement on earlier work but not a major change. However, the second part of their book was a creative advance that set off a flurry of follow-up studies in this country and abroad. In that new analysis, they turned their attention away from gross amounts of succession and mobility and toward the specific sequence of events that shaped the careers of individual men. And they did so not with tables of cross-classification, which would have become unwieldy, but with a form of regression analysis that produced path diagrams. Much of this analysis was worked out by Duncan, and we shall refer to it by his name.

The simplest form of regression analysis computes the well-known correlation coefficient; it gives an indication of the degree to which one variable is connected with another. If you can completely predict everybody's score on the second, or *dependent,* variable from a knowledge of their score on the first, or *independent,* variable, then the coefficient is 1.00. If there is no relation between the scores of persons on the independent and the dependent variables, the coefficient is 0.00. On most matters that concern social science, there is an in-between relationship, and the correlation coefficients are intermediate.

For example, we can take our group of sons and give each person two scores using the Duncan socioeconomic index (SEI) of occupational prestige discussed in Chapter 2: one for the son's occupation and one for that of his father. The correlation coefficient between the scores for fathers and sons will be about 0.41. Strictly speaking, this allows us to partially predict the scores of sons from the scores of fathers, and we can convey the size or power of that prediction by indicating the percentage of the total variation in the positions of sons that can be accounted for by our knowledge about their fathers.[1] We get this percentage by squaring the correlation coefficient: 17 percent of the variance is explained. That percentage may seem low and suggest that our nation comes close to being an open society in which sons find their own careers without much influence from their fathers, but the reader should suspend judgment at this point. Indeed, although we have here scaled occupations on the Duncan SEI, and in the previous chapter we reported on a set of 17 occupational ranks, in a rough way the correlation coefficient of 0.41 serves as a simple indicator of the overall pattern shown in the last chapter in Table 6–1, and the connection between fathers and sons in that table is not to be dismissed as negligible.

The goal of Duncan was much more ambitious than to measure the relationship between the occupations of fathers and those of their sons: he wanted to trace out the specific pathways of influence. Just *how* did the fathers influence their sons? The model he developed was based on sequence in time, with the assumption that earlier events accounted for later events. Thus, he measured the father's education as an early background factor. Then he measured the father's occupation when the son was 16 years of age, just at the point of deciding about education and career. Then he indicated the son's education by counting the number of years he stayed in school. Then he computed the status index of the son's first job, and finally the job he held at the time of the interview in 1962. Thus, he put five variables into his model.

---

[1] We often tend to substitute *caused by* for *predicted by,* but doing so is dangerous since we need a clear theoretical understanding of the chains of linkage before we can safely speak of causation. Sometimes correlations are coincidences or are caused by a complex chain of influences not revealed by the data at hand.

The first step in building up the model was to calculate the simple or zero-order correlation coefficients among the five variables, and they are shown in Table 7–1. Inspection of the table begins to show the pattern: the most important correlate of a son's current job is his own education; after that, in descending order, come his first job, his father's job, and his father's education. About a third of the variation in the prestige of men's jobs for the whole sample is predicted or explained by the amount of their education; that relationship is the highest in the table, yet still leaves a large residual of unexplained variance.

But then we run into a new puzzle: a man's education is predicted to some degree by his father's occupation (explained variance is about one fifth). So we might well wonder: how important as an independent cause is a son's education? Maybe there is a *chain of causes* at work: father's occupation (which serves as a proxy for all his SES variables) "causes" son's education, which "causes" son's job. If the links in that chain are very tight, then the son's education is merely a mediating or intervening variable that explains the process through which the father influences the son's career but has little independent effect of its own. That is, high-status fathers keep their sons in school and thus assure their success in life. On the other hand, if the linkages between the first two variables are weak, and the last two linkages are strong, then the son's education could have a lot of *independent* influence and indeed could be the key to a position *different* from that of the father. That is, many poor but bright sons use the schools to achieve mobility.

A little further thought produces another complication. Maybe the father's status position influences the son's career more than once. It certainly has some impact on the education the son gets, but perhaps it has an additional impact later in life, helping the son to get a good first job and then advance in his career. After all, some craft unions give preference to the sons of union members in getting admitted,

TABLE 7–1
Simple correlations among five variables, fathers and sons

	Variable			
Variable	First job, sons	Education, sons	Fathers' occupation	Fathers' education
1962 occupational status of sons	.54	.60	.41	.32
First-job status of sons	—	.54	.42	.33
Education of sons		—	.44	.45
Fathers' occupational status			—	.52
Fathers' education				—

Source: Peter M. Blau and Otis Dudley Duncan, *The American Occupational Structure* (New York: John Wiley & Sons, 1967) p. 169.

and people in some businesses and professions can benefit a lot from family connections. Simple or zero-order correlation coefficients merge these two influences of father on son into a single number, the correlation between the occupations of fathers and sons.

The only way to sort out these influences is to create a flow chart in which one follows the son's career through several stages and recalculates the impact of earlier forces on that career at each stage. The goal is to separate out the *special* influence of *each* variable *independent* of the other variables in the model (that is, to assume that they are held constant). If we are sure of the sequence because we have a theory that tells us what comes first and what comes later, eliminating worry over the direction of causality connecting the variables, we can organize the correlations into a special form that produces a path diagram. The model, introduced to sociology by Duncan, is shown as Figure 7–1, and since the events mostly follow each other in time, there can be little argument about the sequence.

Note that most variables are connected by a straight arrow; the coefficient on the arrow shows the relative influence of the first variable on the second, independent of all the other paths in the diagram. For example: father's occupation is linked to son's education with a coefficient of 0.28. That shows the "direct" connection. Furthermore, son's education is connected directly with his current occupation in

FIGURE 7–1
Path coefficients among five variables, fathers and sons

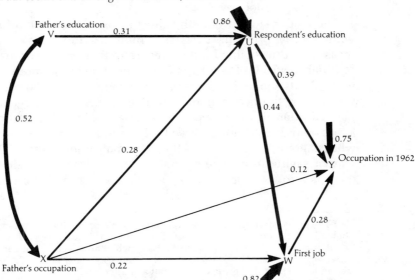

Source: Peter M. Blau and Otis Dudley Duncan, *The American Occupational Structure* (New York: John Wiley & Sons, 1967), p. 170.

1962 with a coefficient of 0.39. Therefore, the "indirect" effect of father's occupation on son's job via the intervening variable of son's education must be a combination of those two coefficients (although not a simple arithmetic sum). But in addition to the indirect influence through education, the father's occupation also influences the son's occupation directly, with a coefficient of 0.12, which shows some small influence that goes through routes *other* than education, such as the father's help to the son's career that comes after schooling is over.

What do these numbers mean? One can read the chart by simply comparing the sizes of the coefficients (or in this version, the thickness of the arrows) in order to get an intuitive grasp of the *relative* strength and weakness of different paths, always remembering the distinction between a simple direct path and a complex indirect path that cumulates influences. One can visualize how the overall relationship between the early variables of parental status and the final dependent variable, son's career, can be decomposed into chains of events.

There are rules for cumulating various coefficients to make statements about how the total variance is decomposed into pathways.[2] Following those rules, we can say that of the total relationship between father's occupation and son's occupation, about one quarter is produced by the direct connection, and another quarter is produced by the indirect connection via education. The rest comes from other indirect connections (such as the impacts of the father's occupation and the respondent's education on the first job, which in turn influences later jobs).

The reader should note the short arrows that come into the chart without any previous ties: each indicates the residual coefficient measuring unexplained influences up to that point. For instance, the residual coefficient for occupation at the time of the interview in 1962 was 0.75; its squared value is 0.56, which means that 56 percent of the variance in the occupational prestige scores of sons remains unexplained after all the independent variables in the model are cumulated, both directly and indirectly. The model "explains" about half of what is going on but leaves the other half unexplained. That is one way of saying in numbers what we have previously said in words: there is a lot of mobility in American society, and the occupational

---

[2] The gross effect of father's occupation on son's occupation, direct and indirect, is shown by the simple correlation coefficient between X and Y, or 0.41, which explains about 17 percent of the variance (since the variables are given in standarized form, an increase in one standard deviation in X produces an increase of 0.4 of a standard deviation in Y). Of that gross effect, about a quarter (0.12 divided by 0.41) is produced by the direct connection. Another quarter is produced by the indirect connection through son's education (0.39 times 0.28, which equals 0.11 divided by 0.41)—the indirect coefficients are multiplied to obtain their cumulative effect. For details see Blau and Duncan 1967: 166–67, and Jencks 1972: 354–56.

positions of men cannot be predicted with great precision from a knowledge of their family backgrounds, *even if you add knowledge about their educations.* That in turn implies that schooling may be important for career but does not completely determine the outcome.

Blau and Duncan warn us that the large unexplained variance does not necessarily mean that the model is weak, since the residual paths are "standing for all other influences on the variable in question, including causes not recognized or measured, errors of measurement, and departures of the true relationships from additivity and linearity, properties that are assumed throughout the analysis . . . . The relevant question about the residual is not really its size at all, but whether the unobserved factors it stands for are properly represented as being uncorrelated with the measured antecedent variables" (Blau and Duncan 1967: 171, 175). Subsequent research does suggest that improvement in measurement techniques to reduce error would increase the explained variance; so the model is somewhat stronger than the numbers suggest (Bielby et al. 1977; Corcoran 1978). Beyond such improvements, the usual temptation is to build in more redundancy (for example, adding the mother's education). Since much of the impact of a redundant variable is already included in some variable in the system with which it is correlated (like father's education), adding the new variable will not greatly change the pattern but will certainly increase confusion to the eye. And it is the pattern which mainly intrigues us: the *relative* weight of the variables. Nevertheless, the unexplained variance is always a challenge to the next investigator who tries to do better.

Let us summarize the results of the Blau and Duncan model. Using simple correlations, they indicated that 17 percent of the variance of the occupational status of sons could be accounted for by the occupational status of their fathers. Furthermore, they showed that the fathers' status explained 19 percent of the variance in the length of education achieved by the sons, which led to the suspicion that part of the function of education was to promote succession rather than mobility: middle-class sons stayed in school longer than working-class sons, and that allowed them to get better jobs (a point strongly emphasized by Bowles and Gintis 1976). The path coefficients showed that the fathers' education and occupation had about equal influence on the sons' education, that the sons' education (including the part of it explained by family background and the part that was independent of family background) was the biggest single influence on sons' eventual occupation, but that there was a small additional influence on career that the family background could continue to assert even after the sons had graduated.

As reported in the last chapter, Featherman and Hauser (1978) repeated the Blau and Duncan survey in 1973. They followed a logic parallel to the earlier study and found that the pattern had changed very little in the intervening 11 years. Indeed, the time lapse had been too short for one to expect much change. However, they were able to note an interesting difference in the trends that separate the races. In the second study, there was a little less direct connection between family background and school attainment and then first job among white men, but a little more among black men, especially younger ones. This indicates that the black community is becoming more heterogeneous and that black fathers have a wider range of status background which they are now able to pass along to their sons, at least partially. We shall give more details about racial differences in a later section, below. (For critiques, see Mueller et al. 1980.)

JENCKS ON INEQUALITY

The new challenges to the conventional wisdom about the equalizing power of the schools, particularly the work of James Coleman and his colleagues, led a group at the Harvard School of Education, under the leadership of Christopher Jencks, to try to integrate most of what was known into one grand model of status attainment that would include more variables than Blau and Duncan studied; the new book was called *Inequality: A Reassessment of the Effect of Family and Schooling in America.* It was published in 1972 and created quite a stir.

Jencks did not collect original data but rather accepted the Duncan results with two useful additions: (1) he interpolated a lot of material from other studies, and (2) he organized it into a series of discrete stages corresponding to points in the life cycle, instead of relying on a single path diagram that summed up the whole process.

Jencks added income as the final dependent variable in the chain rather than occupation, and reported that there is only a moderate zero-order correlation, 0.44, between occupational status and income (using "estimated true" coefficients which adjust the figures upward to compensate for measurement errors, and limiting the sample to native white males of nonfarm background, aged 25 to 64 in 1962). Obviously, men whose occupational titles are the same often earn different amounts of money. There are many reasons for that: varying pay scales in different parts of the country; the increases that come from seniority on the job; variations that come from the size and profitability of the firm or the strength of the union; and the fact that the occupational title itself is only an abstraction that covers different tasks and different amounts of authority. (For recent studies, see Kalleberg and Griffin 1980.)

Jencks also found a correlation of only 0.35 between respondents' education and income and only 0.29 between fathers' occupation and sons' income. Every time we add another variable into a chain of causes and effects, we weaken the connection between the earliest predictors and the final outcome, because at each step in the process other factors are at work (or, "luck" keeps reappearing). Consequently, this new model, which uses income as the final dependent variable instead of occupational prestige, reduced the measured impact of education on life chances.

The Harvard team also wanted to measure somewhat more sharply the "pure" effect of years of schooling, independent of the qualities that students bring with them to the school building. To do so, they added another new variable to the chain: the son's IQ at age 11, on the assumption that it is the best available measure of the talent or "cognitive ability" of the child that reacts with the stimuli of the school. (That got them into the issue of genes versus early socialization experiences in the home as "causes" of IQ, but since schools cannot affect those proportions, we shall pay no attention to the issue here.)

In organizing the vast statistical material from many different studies that is integrated in *Inequality*, Jencks tended to stress a polemic point: economic (occupational and income) inequality in the United States is very large, and simply improving the quality of bad schools and reducing the differences among individuals in the number of years they attend school will not go very far in eliminating the economic differences. He estimated that most—indeed close to three quarters—of the variation in the incomes of adult men cannot be explained by cumulating all the usual predictors: family background, IQ score, years of education, and even job title. He wrote:

> Economic success seems to depend on varieties of luck and on-the-job competence that are only moderately related to family background, schooling, or scores on standardized tests. . . . The fact that we cannot equalize luck or competence does *not* mean that economic inequality is inevitable. Still less does it imply that we cannot eliminate what has traditionally been defined as poverty. It only implies that we must tackle these problems in a different way. Instead of trying to reduce people's capacity to gain a competitive advantage on one another, we would have to change the rules of the game so as to reduce the rewards of competitive success and the costs of failure (Jencks et al. 1972: 8).

In other words, if we really propose to equalize incomes, we must do something that *directly* alters the operation of the labor market to reduce the range of incomes: corporation presidents should receive less, and people who fry hamburgers should receive more. The amount of government intervention required to produce such a result is often called socialism, and Jencks was not afraid of adopting the word. He implied that our national preoccupation with changing the schools was a distraction from the real issue.

The reaction to Jencks's conclusions was strong; he was not faulted on technical grounds, but many critics were unhappy about the implications of the words *luck* and *socialism*. Jencks and colleagues set out on a second round of research, including the integration of several new surveys of careers (including those of brothers) that had since become available. The new book, *Who Gets Ahead?*, published in 1979, is likely to be much less controversial for at least two reasons. First, it gives up the noble attempt of the earlier volume to communicate with the general public and instead offers dry and statistical prose in a highly technical style. Second, the new volume usually avoids the discussion of policy implications. The authors no longer emphasize the difficulty of creating more equality of result; they simply report on the amount of variance in schooling, job, and income that can be explained by different background characteristics.

These policy weaknesses of the book are offset by a prodigious amount of new work, using many new sources of data, that certainly increases the accuracy of the calculations, although it does not dramatically alter the conclusions. Let us report a few of the more significant analyses.

Who Gets Ahead? makes a number of changes in procedure, but the most interesting for our purposes comes from a recognition that the standard SES measures on parents are crude measures of the total effect of family background. Although it gives those measures, it also adds, where possible, a measure based on the similarity of the careers of brothers. Jencks assembled some new data of his own as well as material available in other studies in order to increase knowledge about what happens to boys reared in the same home, although the difficulty of tracing both brothers keeps the samples much smaller than one would like. The resemblance between brothers is a total measure of family influence that is useful but not very specific: it covers shared genes, shared environment in the home and the neighborhood, and the possible influence of one brother on the other. It predicts career outcome somewhat better than the conventional SES indicators, thus reducing the size of that bothersome residual variance.

Jencks and his colleagues also rounded up a number of scores that went beyond the usual IQ scores, including measures of personality. They found that no one of the additional measures was particularly powerful, but a combination of them predicted career outcome about as well as the IQ score by itself and seemed to be adding something new to the mix.

Let us start with the overall conclusion and then break it down into a series of sequences that follow one another. *The resemblance between brothers, or total family background, explained almost half the variance in the occupational statuses of men and a little less than a third of the variance in their incomes.* (If we were able to measure the lifetime earnings of men instead of using only one year as the dependent variable, the predictability would be even higher, since temporary ups and downs would be averaged out.) Obviously, this result is much more powerful than that of Blau and Duncan and suggests more inheritance of position than was previously believed.

The most important single indicator of total family background was the father's occupational status, but that accounted for only a third of the resemblance between brothers. Adding in a string of other demographic variables (education of both father and mother, income of both, family size, and race) adds another third. The remaining third of the variance "is presumably due to unmeasured social, psychological, or genetic factors that vary within demographic groups" (p. 214).

If the schools are to be equalizers, then talented children of poor families must stay in school as long as talented children from rich families. Otherwise, the schools are just mediators or the transmission belts used by privileged families to obtain privileged careers for their children. If we measure talent at a relatively early age and then follow the subsequent paths taken by the children, we can estimate how much of school attainment is a consequence of talent (as measured by the tests), regardless of the socioeconomic background of the students' families. Jencks and his colleagues report that early cognitive test scores explain about 40 percent of the variance in ultimate educational attainment; about two thirds of that is *independent* of the connection between the IQ scores themselves and family background. This implies that there is a lot of variation of talent picked up on the tests even among families of similar social status (indeed, even among brothers), and the variation in talent has a significant amount of influence on educational attainment. However, test scores have far less effect on educational attainment than a completely meritocratic system would require, and they have even less effect on ultimate earnings, predicting only about 5 to 10 percent of their variance, all else being equal. The schools are already more "fair" than the labor market, according to these particular measures.

Who Gets Ahead? spells out some of the details as follows:

> The fact that demographic background affects cognitive skills and educational attainment explains more than half of its effect on occupational status and earnings. . . . (p. 82)
>
> We turn now to explaining *how* ability exercises its influence on an individual's schooling. Higher-scoring individuals [with all other variables constant] are treated differently than lower-scoring individuals, especially in school. Adolescents with high scores are more likely to be in a college curriculum, more likely to receive high grades, more likely to report that their parents want them to attend college, more likely to say their friends plan to attend college, more like to discuss college with teachers, and more likely to have ambitious educational and occupational plans. . . . (p. 106)

> A man's ability in 6th to 11th grade has important effects on his later occupational status, but 60 to 80 percent of the effect is explained by the amount of schooling he gets. (p. 115)

That last paragraph indicates that employers are more interested in the years of schooling than in the cognitive ability itself.

The earlier book reported that once a cohort of youths is in high school, variations in the quality of the schools (measured by expenditure per pupil or degrees held by teachers) do not explain much variation in the eventual educational attainment of the students, independent of their cognitive ability. That suggests that efforts in the courts and legislatures to equalize spending in different school districts will not make much difference in the impact of education on careers, although it might make life pleasanter for the students and the teachers. This conclusion does not deny that some particular schools, or programs within schools, can change the motivations and performance of some students, but it does assert that differences in the quality of schools are subtle matters of leadership and social climate which cannot be measured by standard bureaucratic ratings that in the last instance depend upon the amount of money that is spent.

What about the influence on students of their peers in the same school? There are two types of segregation, often intermixed in practice, that tend to make high schools different from one another: segregation by SES and segregation by race. Although earlier research tended to conclude that segregation by SES raised the aspirations and the attainment (such as college attendance) of pupils who went to predominantly middle-class schools, more careful studies have disputed that result and often find the opposite pattern. In *Inequality*, Jencks evaluated the evidence and found two conflicting forces in the "better," or middle-class, schools: (1) because most of the students are thinking about going to college, aspirations are raised even among the minority of students from poorer families not accustomed to college; (2) the better schools have higher academic standards, and thus the grades of many students are lowered in the overall competition, which tends to lower their aspirations for college. These two forces may cancel out each other.

Concerning racial segregation, Jencks almost threw up his hands in despair. Most of the research compared white and black and mixed schools at a given date. But schools are desegregated under different circumstances, and the effects of those differences on the students is important; consequently, results varied by year and by location. Furthermore, very few studies actually followed groups of black students who moved to predominantly white schools to see how the particular change affected their aspirations and performance. So he said "the most reasonable assumption at present is that racial desegregation [in high schools] makes little or no difference to students' college prospects" (Jencks et al. 1972: 155).

Entering a college that has a selective admissions policy provides some career advantage over a nonselective college, but additional variations in the quality of the colleges do not add to that effect. However, choice of curriculum makes a difference: people preparing to study law or engineering will end up with higher incomes than those who are studying music or poetry.

In a general sense, everybody knows that staying in school pays off—that is, people with more education have higher-status jobs and earn more money. But *how much* difference does it make? And is the difference linear, so that an extra year of high school is worth about the same as an extra year in college? Indeed, is the last year in college, which provides the coveted bachelor's degree, worth something extra?

Studies done after Jencks's first book was written indicate a slightly higher correlation between education and earnings than he first reported, probably due more to methodological improvements than to actual trends in society; the various surveys indicated an average correlation of about 0.40 between years of education and earnings in dollars, without controlling for other influences. In the new book, there is a chapter on education written by Michal Olneck (Jencks et al. 1979: chapter 6), which shows that the relationship is not linear: years in college are worth more than years in high school, particularly if one stays long enough to pick up a degree. Four years of high school bring an increase in dollar earnings over elementary school graduates of about 40 percent; four years of college bring an increase of almost 50 percent over high school graduates. Thus, teachers appear to be correct when they tell students to stay in school because doing so will improve their careers.

But are they really so accurate? We know that family background affects both talent and the length of schooling; maybe it is the family influence that counts, not the impact of the schooling by itself. Olneck estimates that if we control for both family background and IQ scores, the "pure" effect of a high school diploma is reduced by half to about a 20 percent increase in earnings, and the effect of a college degree is reduced to an additional 35 percent in earnings. Notice that the reduction for the controls is greater for the high school years than for the college years. There appears to be a gradual reduction in the impact of background variables as one gets older, so that *once young men get into college,* they are on their own to a greater extent, and the payoff of higher education, especially for those who stay long enough to get the degree, is almost as great for those from poorer families and for those with less measured talent as it is for the others. In the earlier years, education is as much a reflector of family background as an equalizer that offsets family background, but in the later years, education has more independent influence.

These measured effects of education fit with our discussion in Chapter 3 that emphasized a rather sharp break in the occupational system that divides men with college degrees from all others. Employers screen applicants through the simple device of academic credentials, and jobs at the managerial level, even for young people just starting to work who are being selected and trained for such jobs, are given to those with a college degree in hand. Over past decades, we have dramatically increased the level of education for all segments of the population: almost everybody now finishes elementary school, and over 80 percent finish high school. Among those who go no further, there is a large pool of workers, and the jobs they get and the earnings they receive depend more on family background, individual talent, and the oddities of work experience than on a few years more or less of schooling. But at the upper levels of the system, the minority of good jobs goes primarily to those who have received a complete college education, about a quarter of young men and women. And within that select group, the further differential impact of family background or even test scores is rather small in terms of jobs received or dollars earned: it is the degree that counts. Since background has a lot to do with the chance of getting the degree in the first place, we reach a double conclusion: college degrees both protect the privileges of people born into upper-status families and permit some from lower-status families to climb into the elite.

There is a trend at work that might change these conclusions a little: in recent years, the increase in college graduates has somewhat reduced the value of the degree in terms of economic payoff: there are more educated young people competing for the available good jobs. But we do not yet know how that will affect their entire careers, rather than their first jobs (Freeman 1976a; Jencks et al. 1979: 188–90).

Olneck commented:

> Our findings place a number of widespread presumptions in doubt. The most significant of these is that high school dropouts are economically disadvantaged because they fail to finish school. Our results suggest that the apparent advantages enjoyed by high school graduates derive to a significant extent from their prior characteristics, not from their schooling. Unless high school attendance is followed by a college education, its economic value appears quite modest . . . .
>
> Furthermore, while the distribution of elementary and secondary education has become considerably more equal, the distribution of higher education has become somewhat less equal. Since higher education has more impact on earnings than elementary or secondary educa-

tion, at least for those who complete college, the increasingly unequal distribution of higher education may more than offset the effects of equalizing the distribution of elementary and secondary education (Jencks et al. 1979: 189–90).

Careful reading of those paragraphs allows one to understand what seems to be a paradox: in recent decades in the United States (and Europe), the general population's average level of education has improved markedly, and educational inequality has been reduced: that is, the gap between the poorly educated and the average has declined. Yet the inequality in earnings persists as before. More equal schooling has not produced more equal earnings. Reforming the educational system by itself will not reform the economic system. Employers raise their standards and insist on higher credentials for the same jobs that used to go to people with less education. The relative earning power of a college degree remains high (although some first signs of reduction have appeared). And the relative impact of one's family of origin on eventual placement in society remains about the same as before (for a comparative analysis that includes Europe, see Boudon 1974).

SCHOOLS, STUDENTS, AND STATISTICS

One of the main reasons why school reforms have less overall impact on mobility chances than anticipated is the "creaming process." If new high schools or new branches of the state university are built to make education more accessible, the best students from the most advantaged families who are waiting in line will be the ones most likely to enroll. That is, before the change, there were many students who could not get into the existing schools, and they formed a pool of prospective new students. Once the new facilities are available, the most ambitious and talented, and probably the ones from the highest SES families in the previously excluded pool, will take most advantage of the new opportunities. Thus, the average schooling for the community goes up, but the correlation between family background and education does not necessarily change. The new schools get "the cream of the crop" from among those who were previously waiting in line, and the most underprivileged remain outside the door (for one study, see Lavin et al. 1981).

The other main factor that weakens the effect of school reforms on mobility chances is the looseness of fit between years of school (all else held constant) and the final outcome in the form of earned income. The impact of family background plus the unexpected exigencies of what happens on the job considerably weaken the pure influence of education.

Those new high schools and colleges do in fact change the lives of many individuals, so from the practical point of view they are certainly useful. They increase the career chances of the new students (particularly those from disadvantaged groups), give them a sense of real progress compared to their parents, and convince them that the system is more fair than it was. Moreover, those who receive a fuller education are typically better informed, more flexible and more tolerant—desirable qualities in themselves, whatever their effect on mobility. But on the average for the whole society, those new schools do not change the *relative* life chances of many young people from different backgrounds, at least not enough to make major changes in the coefficients of the path diagrams. By emphasizing those coefficients and deemphasizing the number of young people whose lives have been changed, much of the research literature gives a partial impression of social trends that may lead many citizens to the wrong conclusion, such as a vote against school taxes.

The statistical model Jencks and others have adopted from Duncan concentrates on the relative chances of individuals from different backgrounds, and it is perfectly legitimate to do so when discussing the stratification system as a whole or for comparing one such system with another. But the model is an abstraction, and we should never forget the gap between it and the reality experienced by the particular graduates of the new schools. And even in terms of improving the relative chances of some groups compared to the average, certain programs can make a difference. Some small (but expensive) experiments have raised the IQ scores of preschool children from impoverished backgrounds by 20 to 30 points, and some scholarship programs (such as the GI Bill of Rights or special aid for minority students) have increased considerably the college attendance of bright students from poor homes. Indeed, changes can affect groups (such as blacks) and still not significantly alter coefficients for the aggregate of all individuals (Jencks et al. 1972: 14, 358).

In recent years, the study of the status attainment process may have gone too far in its emphasis on this one statistical model. Those who are intrigued with computer manipulation of many variables for large samples of people find path diagrams and similar statistical tools to be an elegant way of presenting lots of output to sophisticated readers. They even like to call it "causal analysis" because it separates out the relative influence of different variables on the final outcome. But from a sociological perspective, it is more descriptive than causal: it maps out the routes different individuals take within a social structure that is assumed to be constant. It tells us little about the causes of that structure or of changes in it. And its guidance for citizens and policymakers is limited by the fact that most of the diagrams cover the whole range of the population instead of concentrating on those particular groups where a change in government programs could in fact alter the lives of underprivileged children (see the debate between Hauser 1976 and Boudon 1976; also Horan 1978).

The aim of most practical reform is to improve the opportunities of some special groups—often small ones with limited impact on national, aggregate statistics—that have previously been unfairly handicapped. Path diagrams can help spot those groups and diagnose the problem. But research designs based on tabular analysis similar to our earlier discussion of mobility tables are also likely to be helpful, for with them we can separate out of the total population those particular groups we wish to help, we can choose the point in the life cycle we hope to influence (such as the decisions made in the last years of high school), and we can study the two or three variables most amenable to policy influence. Furthermore, congressmen, school board members, and parents will be able to understand and participate in the discussion. More complex styles of research are likely to lose readers in this larger audience, and they are the ones who pay the costs of the investigations and have ultimate responsibility for the application of the results. So we should either learn to present complex research in simpler ways or keep the citizens in mind when we set up the original research designs. As an example of how research can be organized in a way that communicates a more vivid sense of practical reality, let us turn to a study that concentrates on a specific point in the life cycle that shapes the careers of so many young people.

WHO GOES TO COLLEGE?

All people with college degrees do not have outstanding careers, but few people (other than athletes and entertainers) achieve important positions without them. We already know that family SES, some additional influences from family background as shown by similarities among brothers, and measured IQ all influence the number of years of school achieved. But how can we use these same variables to explain more precisely why some people go to college and others do not?

The best strategy to follow is a longitudinal approach that starts with a large sample of adolescents in high school and gets information about their test performances, school records, and family backgrounds and then follows them along through the years to see how successive events sort them into alternative paths: different high school curricula, then graduation, then the decision about whether to continue in college, and if so, what type of school is chosen. Such follow-up studies require patience and money, and a fine one from Wisconsin is available, directed by William H. Sewell and reported in

Sewell and Shah (1977) and Sewell and Hauser (1975). Fortunately, this time we can discuss a study that includes females. (For another local study, see Rehberg and Rosenthal 1978.)

The Wisconsin research dealt with 9,000 persons who were high school seniors in 1957; most of them were followed up seven years later. Table 7–2 reports the percentages who started college, organized separately for boys and girls and then divided into quartiles by socioeconomic status and IQ score. Forty-four percent of all the boys started college of some kind, but only 31 percent of the girls. Among the boys, we note (by reading down the "all IQ levels" column) that only 21 percent of those from low-status families continued their education, compared to 73 percent from high-status families. And reading across the "All SES levels" row at the bottom of the table, we note that only 15 percent of the boys from the lowest ability group managed to continue after high school, compared to 74 percent of those from the highest ability group.

But ability and status are related, so it is instructive to study the body of the table, which cross-classifies them. Take, for example, just the group of highest ability, all of whom are intellectually capable of college study. About half of the brightest boys from the lowest status level managed to get into college, compared to fully 91 percent of those from the highest status group. By contrast, among those of lowest ability, the boys from low-status homes had only a 6 percent chance of continuing to study, but those from high-status homes had a 39 percent chance (one wonders how they did in a college classroom). Clearly, status and ability had independent effects; when either one was controlled, the other still made a big difference. Thus individuals who had both variables in their favor were almost sure to go to college; boys who had both variables operating against them were almost sure to avoid college; and those who had one but not the other in their favor made it 40 to 50 percent of the time.

Among girls, the proportions going to college were a little lower for every group. A more elaborate analysis of the data showed that SES counted a little more than IQ as a causative factor among girls, but the opposite was true among boys.

There is some evidence that IQ tests are biased in favor of children from middle- and upper-status families, but the bias is not overwhelming: some children from lower-status backgrounds manage to get good scores, and among them, half of the boys and almost one third of the girls in the Wisconsin sample started college. What factors help us understand why *some* of these poor but bright adolescents continued their education and *others* did not? How can we explain the individual choices in a group that appears to have so much leeway for personal decision? Here we must look to subtle factors of motivation.

TABLE 7–2
Wisconsin high school graduates: Percentage who entered college by sex, SES, and IQ

SES levels	Intelligence levels, males					Intelligence levels, females				
	Low	Lower-middle	Upper-middle	High	All IQ levels	Low	Lower-middle	Upper-middle	High	All IQ levels
Low	6	17	28	52	21	4	6	9	28	9
Lower-middle	12	27	43	59	34	9	20	24	37	21
Upper-middle	18	34	51	72	45	16	26	31	48	31
High	39	61	73	91	73	33	44	67	76	63
All SES levels	15	34	51	74	44	11	23	35	55	31

Source: W. H. Sewell and V. P. Shah, "Socioeconomic Status, Intelligence, and the Attainment of Higher Education," in *Power and Ideology in Education*, ed. J. Karabel and A. H. Halsey (New York: Oxford University Press, 1977), p. 205.

The Wisconsin study, along with others, indicated that *within* any given status level, some families are more ambitious for their children than others (or, to be more precise, that the children perceive such differences and can report them on a questionnaire). The ambition is transmitted to the child through encouragement to succeed in school as a means of getting a better job later on. Children with such encouragement are likely to do a little better than others, particularly if they are talented; the approval and encouragement they receive from teachers and the higher grades they get in school are rewarding and begin to shape self-perceptions as persons who are "college material." That process in turn helps the motivated students to get into college preparatory courses, and such participation in turn increases the chance of making friends with other college-bound students. These encouraging factors of parental ambitions, school performance, and influence of peers and teachers all lead to the formulation of college aspirations and plans. For upper-status students, these pressures toward college are almost automatic, and only those with severe handicaps in intelligence or personality fail to succumb to them. Thus, for upper-status students, the factors described are the "mediating" variables that translate the abstraction of socioeconomic status into particular realities that stimulate and guide behavior. But within lower-status groups, there is enough openness of choice to allow some students, particularly those of high talent with ambitious parents, to aim toward college.

Actually, the factors we are discussing can be observed even before the end of high school (Spenner and Featherman 1978; and articles by Kitsuse and Rist in Karabel and Halsey 1977). For example, an earlier study conducted in the Boston metropolitan area reconstructed the school history of a sample of boys from the first grade through the end of high school (Kahl 1953). Boys with high IQ scores usually had good marks starting with the first grade, but even more, those with low IQ scores had poor marks. Father's occupation did not affect school performance in the earlier grades, but it began to take effect in the fourth grade and, by the time of junior high school, was slightly more important than IQ in predicting performance.

However, some of the bright boys from lower-status homes kept up their motivation and aimed for college. The Boston research indicated that the main reason they did so was the special encouragement they got from home. These were usually homes headed by skilled workers or routine white-collar workers, not by men at the very bottom of the occupational scale. The boys themselves could be divided into two groups, each reflecting to a remarkable degree the values about life held by their parents: those who believed in "getting by" and those who believed in "getting ahead." This basic split showed in their more specific attitudes toward the details of schoolwork, after-school recreation, and jobs. The boys who believed in just getting by generally were bored with school, anticipated some sort of low-level job, and found peer-group activity to be the most important thing in life. The boys who were striving to get ahead took schoolwork more seriously than recreational affairs. Both groups noticed the differences: the nonstrivers said the others "didn't know how to have any fun," whereas the strivers said the others were "irresponsible; didn't know what was good for them."

Two quotations from interviews with parents will show how these contrasting attitudes of the boys were reflections of the values about life, work, and school held by their parents (Kahl 1953: 194–96):

Case A. The father is a bread salesman; he has five children. He is a high school graduate.

> I was never a bright one myself, I must say. The one thing I've had in mind is making enough to live on from day to day; I've never had much hope of a lot of it piling up. However, I'd rather see my son make an improvement over what I'm doing and I'm peddling bread. . . . I think he's lazy. Maybe I am too, but I gotta get out and hustle. . . . I don't keep after him. I have five kiddies. When you have a flock like that, it is quite a job to keep your finger on this and the other thing. . . . I really don't know what he would like to do. Of course, no matter what I would like him to do, it isn't my job to say so as he may not be qualified. I tried to tell him where he isn't going to be a doctor or lawyer or anything like that, I told him he should learn English and learn to meet people. Then he could go out and sell something worthwhile where a sale would amount to something for him. That is the only suggestion that I'd make to him. . . . I suppose there are some kids who set their mind to some goal and plug at it, but the majority of kids I have talked to take what comes. Just get along. . . . I don't think a high school diploma is so important. I mean only insofar as you might apply for a job and if you can say, "I have a diploma," it might help get the job, but other than that I don't see it ever did me any good.

Case B. The father is a foreman in a factory with about 20 men under him. He had three years of high school and is convinced that he would have gotten further ahead if he had had more education.

> Down at the shop, we see a lot of men come in and try to make their way. The ones with the college education seem to succeed better. They seem better able to handle jobs of different sorts. They may not know any more than the other fellows, but they know how to learn. Somehow they've learned how to learn more easily. . . . If they get a job and see that they aren't going to get anywhere, they know enough to get out of it or to switch. They know enough to quit. . . . So that's why I hope my boy will go to college. . . . The college men seem also better able to handle themselves socially. They seem smoother in getting

along with people and more adaptable to new situations. I think that I would have gotten along a lot better myself if I had had that sort of education.

In most instances, the parents who believed in getting ahead were somewhat frustrated: the father had not reached the place in the hierarchy that he had expected and desired. He blamed his failure on insufficient education and was determined that his son would do better. On occasion, the father was satisfied, but the mother was not; she then thought of her husband as a failure and tried to influence the son to outshine him (for further research, see Kohn 1977).

The two basic factors of SES and IQ not only influence the chance of continuing education after high school, they also influence the type of school chosen and the chance to graduate. About one third of all college students start at two-year community colleges. These schools' curricula usually permit some students to transfer later to four-year colleges, but many concentrate on technical courses that prepare students directly for the world of work in positions that are somewhere in the middle of the occupational status range: dental assistants, automobile mechanics, bookkeepers, and the like. Indeed, the whole system of higher education is stratified according to the quality of the education provided and the particular career preparation emphasized, and that hierarchy is matched by the SES of parents of the students (Berg 1970). A national study by the American Council on Education in 1971 provided telling evidence: of all the students who entered the local community colleges, only 12 percent came from families with over $20,000 in income. The public four-year colleges recruited 15 percent of their students from equivalent families. The public universities had 22 percent, and the private universities had fully 42 percent from such families. The relative prestige of the college certificates or diplomas follows a similar ranking, and employers make choices accordingly (Karabel, in Karabel and Halsey 1977).

These studies of college attendance and graduation can be used to give partial support to both of two opposing ideological positions: (1) The American system of higher education is so big and so open that it provides major opportunities for talented youths from poor families to prepare themselves for successful careers that raise them above the level of their parents; and (2) the American system of higher education is sufficiently stratified so that its main function is to reproduce for each generation of children the status positions held by their parents. Does it promote mobility or succession? The answer is: both.

Sewell actually calculated the "loss" of potential talent through the effect of the biases against poorer families and against girls. Using the Wisconsin data from the late 1950s, he estimated that if all children of both sexes had the same chance to go to college as did boys of high SES (that is, if their selection was based solely on talent as shown by the relation between IQ and schooling among high SES males), then 32 percent more young people would have gotten some training beyond high school, 43 percent more would have entered a college, and 47 percent more would have graduated. Those are dramatic figures that indicate the potentials for further improvement in our educational system. (See further: Levine and Bane 1975; Sewell et al., 1976; Karabel and Halsey 1977; Persell 1977; Hurn 1978.)

CAREERS OF BLACKS

In recent decades, black people have made considerable advances in the American educational and occupational systems (partly because of migration from farms to cities and from South to North), although they still lag behind in many respects. For example, at the end of World War II, about two-thirds of white but only one third of black youths were finishing high school. By the mid 1970s, about 85 percent of the whites were graduating compared to 75 percent of the blacks. Both groups were staying in school longer, but the black increase was much more than the white, so the gap between the two races had diminished. Recent college graduation rates showed a larger gap: about 25 percent of the young whites were getting degrees, but only about half that proportion of blacks. Similarly, blacks on the average had moved up the scale of occupations, but the proportions in the highest ranks were still small (Freeman 1976b).

These changes in educational and occupational opportunities mainly benefit young people, and a long time elapses before they show up with strength in averages of income that cover all ages. Thus, on the average, black men earned 53 percent as much as white men in 1959, 58 percent as much in 1969, and 61 percent as much in 1975. Black women did somewhat better by comparison with white women (although women as a whole earned much less than men): black women earned 61 percent as much as white women in 1959, 84 percent as much in 1969, and 88 percent as much in 1975 (Farley and Hermalin 1972; U.S. Census 1976a and 1976b). Young blacks with a good education now are beginning to earn high salaries; however, many young blacks with a mediocre education suffer from extraordinarily high rates of unemployment (see below, Chapter 10).

Since both educational and occupational careers depend partly on family of origin, current changes in opportunities will not have their full effect until a generation or two have passed: to put it bluntly, nothing we do today can actually change the parental background of a young black person. Although we cannot change background in the real world, we can make some statistical experiments that simulate change. Blau and Duncan analyzed the stages of the careers of black men compared to white men and found that even when the lower social origin, education, and first occupation of Negroes have been taken into account, their occupational achievement is still far inferior to that of whites. . . . Negroes are handicapped by having poorer parents, less education, and inferior early career experiences than whites. Yet even if these handicaps are statistically controlled by asking, in effect, what the achievement of nonwhites would be if they had the same origins, the same education, and the same first jobs as whites, their occupational chances are still consistently inferior to those of whites. Thus being a Negro in the United States has independent disadvantageous consequences for several of the factors that directly affect occupational success. The cumulation of these distinct, though not unrelated, disadvantages creates profound inequalities of occupational opportunities for the Negro American (1967: 209).

If one adds the fact that among men holding the same types of occupations, blacks commonly earn less money than whites, the cumulative disadvantages are even greater. *At each stage* of the status-attainment process, blacks have trouble fully translating advantages from a previous to a subsequent step in their careers. Thus extra schooling for blacks does gain them better jobs, but less so than for whites; similarly, better jobs mean higher incomes, but less so than for whites. Various forms of discrimination plague blacks at each point of transition, leading to the final disadvantage in earnings. The most dramatic trends of recent years affecting blacks concern education, where they have made important gains, but the payoff in jobs and earnings is very slow in coming (Featherman and Hauser 1978: chapter 6; Jencks et al. 1979: chapter 7).

Indeed, at every level of education, whether we focus on elementary school graduates or high school graduates or college graduates, black men earned only about 75 percent as much as white men. For women, however, the pattern was different. At lower levels of education, black women earned about 90 percent as much as white women, but those with high school or college educations actually earned a little more than white women of equal schooling, for reasons that are not at all easy to discern. (All of these comparisons make a somewhat dubious assumption that is hard to avoid in dealing with the statistics, namely, that the quality of education received per year of schooling is the same for both races.)

Who Gets Ahead? reports an interesting calculation in chapter 7, written by Joseph Schwartz and Jill Williams. They find that if one performs the mental experiment of assuming that black men had an educational distribution equal to that of white men, but that discrimination in converting schooling to appropriate jobs and incomes remained as it was in the 1970s, then the gap in earnings between the two races would be reduced by 25 to 30 percent. However, if one reverses the thrust of the experiment, so that the educational distributions remained as they are now but that at each level of education the payoff in occupation and income were the same for both races, then the earnings gap would be reduced by 55 to 70 percent. Blacks are gaining as a result of new educational opportunities, but among the men, they would gain much more if on-the-job discrimination could be eliminated (parallel findings are reported by the Michigan Study of Income Dynamics, Duncan and Morgan 1978).

Although blacks still suffer from discrimination at various stages of their careers, change has been sufficient to produce major alterations in the structure of the black community. It is no longer correct to think of that community as predominantly lower class in composition. William J. Wilson estimated that by 1970, black males were divided into roughly equal thirds in occupational level; one third had middle-class jobs, one third had working-class jobs, and one third had lower-class jobs. But he added:

> the impressive occupational gains made by blacks during these [last] three decades have been partly offset by the effects of basic structural changes in our modern industrial economy, changes that are having differential impact on the different income groups in the black community. Unlike more affluent blacks, many of whom continued to experience improved economic opportunity even during the recession period of the 1970s, the black underclass has evidenced higher unemployment rates, lower labor-force participation rates, higher welfare rates, and, more recently, a sharply declining movement out of poverty. The net effect has been a deepening economic schism in the black community that could very easily widen and solidify (Wilson 1980: 142).

One effect of these trends in the underclass is a sharp increase in the number of poor black families headed by women, many of whom receive government welfare benefits. Public consciousness of this segment of the black community has increased at the same time that the black professional and middle class is also growing and solidifying. Some observers believe that the interests of these different social-class levels are diverging and thus weakening the unity of the black civil rights movement. Wilson concluded (p. 182), "Many blacks and white liberals have yet to recognize that the problem of economic dislocation is more central to the plight of the black poor than is the problem of purely racial discrimination."

The difficulties of blacks take on additional political meaning when their situation is compared to that of earlier white immigrants into the country and their sons. Blau and Duncan reported that by the second generation, most European immigrant groups had become completely integrated into the system; indeed, as a whole they did better than some natives (for example, whites born in the South). Thus there seems to be at least partial truth in the widespread belief in the capacity of the American system to absorb outsiders and within a generation give them equal occupational opportunity, but there are stark exceptions: blacks who have moved out of the isolation of southern farms and into the industrial cities of both South and North; Mexican-Americans, who are the descendants of families who have lived for generations in the rural Southwest or of families who have come into the country in more recent decades; Puerto Ricans who have moved to the mainland; and Native Americans (Indians). Equality of opportunity is more equal for some groups than for others.

CAREERS OF WOMEN

It is not easy to make neat comparisons between the status attainment process for women and for men. Obviously, the average family socioeconomic background is the same for both sexes (as it is not when comparing the races).[3] But once boys and girls start school, comparisons get complex. In the past it was assumed that most young women would work a few years, then get married and raise a family. In recent years, the situation has changed in some ways. About half of all white women now have paid jobs, a figure reached by black women a long time ago; however, many of the women who work have part-time jobs. Married women in recent years have tended to have fewer children and to return to work sooner than in the past. As a result, most young women now expect to work during most of their lives, and women increasingly think of education as preparation for a career, including some occupations previously dominated by men (Stromberg and Harkess 1978; Burstein 1979). However, they enter a labor market that is still structured according to historical patterns that tend to segregate women into a limited number of "appropriate" types of jobs (such as secretaries, schoolteachers, nurses). As more women enter the labor force, the competition for these particular jobs intensifies, and wages are pushed down. That may help explain why the average relative earnings of women have actually declined in the last two decades until they are now about 60 percent of those for men.

But the clustering of women into certain occupations is not the whole explanation for lower earnings. Some studies have suggested that the irregular work patterns of many women, who leave the labor force for a period to have children, cause them to lose experience on the job and thus fall behind males of their same age cohort. Yet, the Michigan Panel Study of Income Dynamics reports that only about a third of the wage gap between white women and white men in their large sample can be explained by the effects of past work history and

---

[3] Of course, in more subtle terms than SES, family background is not the same for both sexes: girls are socialized differently from boys with respect to school and career.

years of training completed on the current job (Corcoran in Duncan and Morgan 1978). And almost none of the wage gap can be accounted for by a weaker current labor force attachment, as indicated by absenteeism, plans to quit work, or self-imposed restriction on hours of work or location of job in relation to the home. (Of course, exaggerated assumptions in the minds of employers about these factors may well make a substantial difference, leading them to decide that there is greater risk in giving special training and promotion to women.) More than half of the wage gap remains unexplained by a combination of these factors, a finding supported by other studies which show that comparisons between groups of women and men who are identical in education, work experience, and job title still produce lower earnings for the women (Sawhill 1973; Oaxaca 1973; Stevenson in Stromberg and Harkess 1978).

We do not have many detailed studies of the pathways of status attainment for women that we could compare to the results of research on men by Duncan and Jencks. In fact, the use of their models for women remains controversial. How can we compare daughters with full-time careers to mothers who were housewives? Should we assume that the initial status of daughters is determined by their mothers or their fathers? How can we handle women who try to divide their time between home and job and so seek only part-time work? (For reviews, see Acker 1980 and Glenn and Albrecht 1980).

Facing these problems, researchers have usually created models that make their statistical tasks easier but tend to strain our common-sense perception of reality. We know of no studies that have published a simple outflow table showing the movement from fathers or mothers to daughters. Instead, they present sophisticated indexes, such as the relative rates of mobility for men and women that would have occurred *if* women were distributed among occupational levels in the same proportions as men. Since the most important fact about women's careers is precisely their different occupational distribution, that procedure seems excessively artificial.

Hauser and Featherman (1977: chapter 8) summarize their own and other studies in a few useful observations: the relative influence of parental background status on the educational attainment of women does not differ much from the pattern for men, and the relative influence of education as a determinant of the job level of women does not differ much from that for men, but women earn less from the same type of job than men do. Generally speaking, women marry men who have family backgrounds and educations similar to their own. In fact, one can predict the occupational levels of men almost (but not quite) as well from the positions of their fathers-in-law as from those of their own fathers.

CONCLUSIONS

Since the early days of our republic, reformers have tried to use the schools to offset some of the inequality that emerges from the marketplace and from the family structure. Most particularly, they wanted each generation to start fresh, to have equal opportunity to succeed. In the last two decades, when high school graduation has come close to being universal and college attendance widespread, many observers expected that the dream had about come true. They believed we were coming close to a completely open or meritocratic society in which the level of education reached would be based solely on talent, and the level of occupation and income achieved would be mainly determined by educational preparation.

Reality does not match the model, however, for three main reasons. First, as years of schooling have gone up for *all* segments of the population, including those from black and/or poor homes, *equality* of educational opportunity has improved only modestly. That is, middle-class children have increased their schooling almost as much as lower-class children. (The gap between the races has narrowed more than the gap between the classes.) Thus, average schooling can go up, and even opportunities for the poor can go up, and yet the relation between parental status and children's education can change only a little. (In statistical language, mean years of education for all young people increase, the range from top to bottom narrows, but the correlation between parents and children declines only a little.)

Second, the new educational opportunities in the expanding schools and colleges do not guarantee everybody the career success that was assumed. All levels of diplomas have suffered from inflation: they are not worth what they used to be in occupational terms. So the sons and daughters of poorly educated farmers and miners and factory workers who achieve a high school diploma or junior college certificate discover that the personnel offices have changed the rules and now require more advanced education than previously for any given type of job. The newly acquired education does not buy much more occupational status than the mere literacy of their parents.

Third, although the college degree has now become a prerequisite for most upper-level jobs, the general relationship between years of education and occupational status and income is not as close as is often assumed.

These interconnected trends have been formalized into a convincing model for both the United States and Western Europe by Raymond Boudon. He wrote:

> The principal conclusion . . . is that there is no reason to expect that a considerable increase in educational demand, which is occurring in industrial societies, is connected to an increase in social mobility, even

if accompanied, as it certainly is, by a reduction in unequal educational opportunity . . . The expansion of education . . . has proved ineffective for reducing economic inequality, and it has probably not been any more successful in diminishing social immobility. In this respect, the principal effect of the increase in demand for education appears to be one of requiring the individual to spend more and more time (in school) to realize social aspirations which, themselves, have remained unchanged (1977: 195–96).

There has been theoretical speculation connecting high rates of mobility with a widespread belief among the people that the United States is the land of opportunity, and indeed, with the conviction that the free-enterprise system as it works here is a good one that makes most people content with life. But the models we have been analyzing do not connect so directly with the perceptions of the citizens and thus should not be used for ideological celebration. Individuals may sense that they are getting ahead for a variety of reasons, and perhaps the main one is that the average standard of living has gone up, permitting sons and daughters to live a bit more comfortably than their fathers and mothers. That improvement is not captured by correlation coefficients that connect the status scores of parents and children. Or, to take another example: many blacks have gone to high school and college and gotten good jobs that in fact put them above their parents. Yet, they may or may not concentrate on the improvement over the past instead of noting that their incomes are currently less than those of most whites of comparable education. We cannot deduce their mood from statistics on mobility, for we are never sure what benchmarks people use for judgment when they evaluate their situation in life; it is better to ask them than to guess.

SUGGESTED READINGS

Brittain, John A. 1977. *The Inheritance of Economic Status.* Washington, D.C.: Brookings Institution.
> *A study of the careers of brothers that shows a strong influence of family background on career outcome.*

Duncan, Otis Dudley, et al. 1972. *Socioeconomic Background and Achievement.* New York: Seminar Press.
> *A sequel to Blau and Duncan's* American Occupational Structure, *it adds new variables (including measurements of attitudes) and creates a more complex model, parallel to that of Christopher Jencks.*

Freeman, Richard B. 1976. *The Black Elite.* New York: McGraw-Hill.
> *Analysis of career trends among young blacks with college degrees.*

Goldthorpe, John H. 1980. *Social Mobility and Class Structure in Modern Britain.* New York: Oxford University Press.
> *Report on two large studies of amounts and trends of mobility in Britain, and social consequences.*

Halsey, A. H. et al. 1980. *Origins and Destinations: Family, Class and Education in Modern Britain*. New York: Oxford University Press.
Analyses of the changing educational system and its impact on mobility since World War II.

Levine, Donald M., and Mary Jo Bane, eds. 1975. *The "Inequality" Controversy: Schooling and Distributive Justice*. New York: Basic Books.
Articles evaluating the research of Christopher Jencks and its policy implications.

Wilson, William J. 1980. *The Declining Significance of Race*. 2d ed. Chicago: University of Chicago Press.
Affirms that status among blacks is increasingly a matter of class and decreasingly of race.

Elites, the capitalist class, and political power

Those who hold and those who are without property have ever formed distinct interests in society.

James Madison (1787: 79)

Although we are all of us within history we do not all possess equal powers to make history.

C. Wright Mills (1956: 22)

8

Our interest in this chapter and the one which follows will be the relationship between the class structure and the political system. These chapters deal successively with two aspects of that relationship: political power and class consciousness. The treatment of power focuses largely on those who occupy positions at the top of the class structure and the apex of the political system, an approach which adheres to the emphases in the existing literature and appears to be guided by the inherent logic of the subject. After all, the people at the top are the most likely to occupy themselves with the manipulation of instruments of power. Yet the people beneath them are far from powerless, especially—and here is where class consciousness comes in—when they are united by a shared awareness of common goals. Thus we see these two chapters as complementary and hope readers will do the same.

This chapter covers power structures in the community and nation and examines empirical evidence developed from three competing theoretical perspectives: elite, class, and pluralist. The elite perspective makes a sharp distinction between an organized minority (the elite) which rules and an unorganized majority which is ruled. The class perspective, which is rooted in Marxist theory, also emphasizes the power of a minority, but it is more specific about the identity of the rulers and the structure which creates them: they are the owners of productive wealth, or the capitalist class. The pluralist perspective denies that power is concentrated in one group and maintains that in democratic societies there are multiple bases of power representing the interests of competing groups and no minority can hope to impose its will. Obviously the first two approaches have much more in common with one another than with the third.

HUNTER: POWER IN ATLANTA

Two books published in the 1950s ignited a major controversy among social scientists concerning the degree of concentration of political power in the United States. C. Wright Mills's *The Power Elite* (1956), which we will take up later in this chapter, concluded that national decision making is being concentrated in the hands of a small, unrepresentative elite of corporate, political, and military leaders. Floyd Hunter's *Community Power Structure* (1953) suggested that a parallel tendency is affecting local communities. Those who defended the Mills-Hunter position came to be known as *elite theorists,* in contradistinction to the opposing *pluralists,* who contended that power was so diffused among competing groups that no single group could dominate the others.

Hunter's book is a case study of the structure of power in Atlanta, Georgia (which he called Regional City). Using a new methodology which we will describe shortly, Hunter concluded that a small circle of men, most of them executives in leading banks and corporations or lawyers with corporate practices, made the key decisions in the community. The members of this elite filled the first two levels of a four-tier power-ranking system which Hunter described as follows:

First Rate:	Industrial, commercial, financial owners and top executives of large enterprises.
Second rate:	Operations officials, bank vice presidents, public-relations men, small businessmen (owners), top-ranking public officials, corporation attorneys, contractors.
Third rate:	Civic organization personnel, civic agency boards of directors, newspaper columnists, radio commentators, petty public officials, selected organization executives.
Fourth rate:	Professionals such as ministers, teachers, social workers, personnel directors, and such persons as small business managers, higher paid accountants, and the like. (Hunter 1953: 109)

Note that Hunter placed the top executives above even the highest-ranking public officials (such as the mayor). The text leaves no doubt that he relegated most public officials to the third tier. The men in the third and fourth categories, who were more numerous than those of the upper tiers and more specialized in their concerns, carried into action the policies which were initiated by the "men of decision" above them. Hunter gave an example of how this process operated in the words of one of his informants:

> "Charles Homer is the biggest man in our crowd. He gets an idea. When he gets an idea, others will get the idea. Don't ask me how he gets the idea or where. He may be in bed. He may think of it at breakfast. He may read a letter on the subject. But recently he got the idea that Regional City should be the national headquarters for an International Trade Council. He called in some of us [the inner crowd], and he

talked briefly about his idea. He did not talk much. We do not engage in loose talk about the 'ideals' of the situation and all that other stuff. We get right down to the problem, that is, how to get this council. We all think it is a good idea right around the circle. There are six of us in the meeting.

"All of us are assigned tasks to carry out. Moster is to draw up the papers of incorporation. He is the lawyer. I have a group of friends that I will carry along. Everyone else has a group of friends he will do the same with. These fellows are what you might call followers.

"We decide we need to raise $65,000 to put this thing over. We could raise that amount within our own crowd, but eventually this thing is going to be a community proposition, so we decide to bring the other crowds in on the deal. We decide to have a meeting at the Grandview Club with select members of other crowds.

"When we meet at the club at dinner with the other crowds, Mr. Homer makes a brief talk; again, he does not need to talk long. He ends his talk by saying he believes in his proposition enough that he is willing to put $10,000 of his own money into it for the first year. He sits down. You can see some of the other crowds getting their heads together, and the Growers Bank crowd, not to be outdone, offers a like amount plus a guarantee that they will go along with the project for three years. Others throw in $5,000 to $10,000, until—I'd say within 30 or 40 minutes—we have pledges of the money we need. In three hours the whole thing is settled, including the time for eating!"

Mr. Treat paused for a moment, then continued: "There is one detail I left out, and it is an important one. We went into that meeting with a board of directors picked. The constitution was all written, and the man who was to head the council as executive was named—a fellow by the name of Lonny Dewberry, a third-string man, a fellow who will take advice."

The investigator asked how the public was apprised of the action. Mr. Treat said: "The public doesn't know anything about the project until it reaches the stage I've been talking about. After the matter is financially sound, then we go to the newspapers and say there is a proposal for consideration. Of course, it is not news to a lot of people by then, but the chamber committees and other civic organizations are brought in on the idea. They all think it's a good idea. They help to get the council located and established. That's about all there is to it." (Hunter 1953: 173–74)

Notice that the proposal moved from a small circle of men to a slightly larger group which met informally at an upper-class men's club. By the time it became public knowledge, the key decisions had been made. Moreover, the men publicly identified with the project were not those who had taken the initiative.

How did the structure of power in Atlanta relate to the community's class structure? Hunter did not use *social class* or related terms, but he was obviously suggesting that the city's upper class (represented by wealthy businessmen) stood at the top of the power structure. The relationship of other classes to the creation and implementation of public policies is less clear, although there are some hints scattered through the book. For example, Hunter indicated that one or two labor leaders—whom we might consider representatives of the working class—were regarded as influential by his informants. He also found that leaders of the largely working-class or lower-class black community (still subject to segregation in the 1950s) were able to negotiate certain concessions from the city because they represented a growing black electorate. However, these observations do not lead to any systematic explanation of how these two sets of leaders or the people they represented were related to Atlanta's political system. Hunter's implicit position was that middle- and lower-class Atlantans were so isolated from the exercise of power that their influence was of minor significance.

THE REPUTATIONAL METHOD AND ITS CRITICS

Hunter's book was influential in two ways, both of which gained it friends and enemies. One was its critical attitude toward American institutions. If Hunter is right, political democracy is weak in the face of economic inequality; middle- and lower-class citizens cannot hope to match the power of the wealthy. The other source of influence was the book's innovative technique for identifying community leaders. The new procedure, which came to be known as the "reputational method," was widely imitated and just as frequently attacked. Taking a clue from earlier community studies, Hunter systematically recorded the opinion of community members about power standings just as Warner and Hollingshead had done for prestige standings.

Hunter started by putting together lists of Atlanta's major political officeholders; executives and officers of leading business, professional, civic, and fraternal organizations; plus major wealthholders and "society" leaders—175 people in all. These lists were then presented to 14 "judges," knowledgeable about the community, who were asked to select the top leaders on each list. Forty names, on which Hunter found broad consensus among the judges, emerged from this process. Finally Hunter interviewed a substantial proportion of the 40 and asked the following question:

> If a project were before the community that required *decision* by a group of leaders—leaders that nearly everyone would accept—which 10 on the list would you choose? (p. 62)

This final poll yielded a select group of approximately 20 leaders who were regarded as influential by the leaders themselves.

The reputational technique provided a quick way to identify community leaders, which contributed to its popularity. However, pluralist critics raise multiple objections to the procedure. They charge that Hunter and his followers:

1. Assume what needs to be proven. By asking their informants *who* the decision makers are, researchers are implicitly assuming the existence of a small, decision-making elite. According to political scientist Nelson Polsby, the proper question is not Who runs the community? but Does *anyone* at all run the community? (Polsby 1970: 297).

2. Equate a reputation for power with power itself. The information which researchers using Hunter's technique receive from informants could well be inaccurate because informants misperceive the power structure.

3. Assume that a single elite deals with a broad range of issues. Decision makers may well be specialized in their interests and powers, thus forming a system of multiple elites, perhaps representing different segments of the community.

4. Assume that leaders form a cohesive elite. The identification of leaders does not tell us whether leaders agree on issues and exert their power in a concerted fashion.

5. Downplay the role of formal political institutions by largely ignoring the role of city government, political parties, and elections.

6. Base research on an asymetrical (one-sided) conception of power, which is virtually implicit in a narrow focus on the identity of leaders. Policy makers may, in fact, find themselves compelled to take the probable reactions of others groups into account as they make decisions. If this is the case, power is in some sense reciprocal.

Hunter's critics were formally less concerned with his conclusions than with how he had reached them. Yet many of their criticisms implied that community power is dispersed rather than concentrated and the reputational approach is defective because it is incapable of detecting such dispersion, Pluralist researchers proposed a methodological alternative designed to meet these objections. Instead of focusing on the identification of putative *decision makers*, they insist that students of community power should be studying *decision making*, by examining how representative community issues are resolved. If it can be shown that a well-defined group consistently triumphs over opposition in these matters, the existence of a dominant elite has been demonstrated. Otherwise, the pluralists contend, it must be assumed that power is divided among competing groups and shifts from one to another as the issue which is the focus of debate changes.

(For criticism of the reputational approach see Dahl 1967, Polsby 1970, Aiken and Mott 1970.)

DAHL: POWER IN NEW HAVEN

The best-known piece of research employing a decisional methodology is Robert Dahl's study of New Haven, Connecticut, *Who Governs?* (1961), which was presented as a pluralist refutation of Hunter's work as well as Mills's examination of the national power structure. Although Dahl focused on New Haven politics in the mid-1950s, he prefaced his work with a glance backward at the preceding two centuries of the city's history. Over that period, Dahl found, New Haven's power structure had been transformed in several stages from oligarchic (rule by the few) to pluralistic. He based this conclusion on an examination of the social characteristics of elected officials. (Note that Dahl's method in this instance is neither reputational nor decisional but what we call *positional*. Power is attributed to individuals by virtue of the positions they hold. And Dahl assumed that elected positions were the most important.)

For decades after its foundation, New Haven was ruled by professional men drawn from a small circle of established patrician families. In the mid–19th century, power shifted to members of the emergent entrepreneurial class. The typical New Haven mayor of the new period was an industrialist, of more modest origins than his patrician predecessors, but of the same colonial New England stock. After 1900, men whom Dahl designated "ex-plebs" predominated. The ex-plebs had risen from working-class or lower-middle-class families of recent immigrant origins, often gaining public office on the basis of support from their ethnic brethren. The officeholders of the new era were often lawyers or businessmen, but they were not drawn from the major law firms or large corporations which had produced the public officials of earlier generations.

Dahl believed that yet another transformation of New Haven politics was taking place as he carried out his research in the 1950s. Social mobility and cultural assimilation appeared to be undermining the social basis of "ethnic politics." What would take its place? One possibility was new politics based on class interests, previously diluted by ethnic loyalties. But Dahl argued that complex urban problems would require technical solutions and therefore influence would flow to

> technicians, planners, professional administrators, and above all to professional politicians with capacities for building durable coalitions out of traditionally non-cooperative and even mutually suspicious social strata. The new men in local politics may very well prove to be the bureaucrats and experts—and politicians who know how to use them (Dahl 1961: 62).

In other words, the political finesse of the professional politician and the technical expertise of the urban expert would dampen potential class conflict while resolving the problems of the city. This assertion runs directly counter to Hunter's insistence that in Atlanta, at least, the influence of urban professionals was circumscribed by the power of a small elite.

The core of Dahl's book is an examination of community decision making in three issue areas: (1) party nominations for political office, (2) urban renewal planning, and (3) public education. Dahl was interested in establishing who the decision makers were in each of these areas and, more specifically, who had successfully introduced or vetoed key policy initiatives.

Dahl's most general conclusion was that New Haven did not have the pyramidal power structure which Hunter described for Atlanta; rather power in New Haven was diffused among a variety of groups and individuals. Thus, Dahl determined that leaders in any one of the three issue areas were unlikely to be influential in either of the other two. Among 50 major leaders, only 3 exerted influence in more than one area. All of them were public officials: the mayor, his predecessor, and the chief of the redevelopment agency (Dahl 1961: 181). Leaders, in other words, are specialized. Moreover the sources of leadership are diverse. In none of the issue areas were leaders predominantly drawn from a "single homogeneous stratum of the community" (Dahl 1961: 182).

Two "strata" were the focus of particular attention in Dahl's study. Shying away from social class or terms suggestive of class, he labeled them "economic notables" and "social notables." The notables were New Haven's top wealth and prestige classes. By Dahl's account, the two were discrete groupings with little overlap: only 5 percent of the individuals on his combined list of notables fell into both categories (Dahl 1961: 68). (This conclusion, to which we will return below, is clearly at odds with the findings of the community prestige studies we examined in Chapter 2.)

Dahl was interested in the notables because of the significance which had been attributed to them by the elite theorists. One test of their importance for New Haven's power structure was representation among the 50 leaders influential in the three issue areas. Dahl counted only seven economic and social notables on this list. To these few might be added an additional four "leaders" which were actually corporations that had influenced specific decisions.

Dahl's research convinced him that the social notables had largely withdrawn from the public arena that had in earlier epochs been dominated by their patrician ancestors. The economic notables appeared to be more active, but their participation was largely limited to the one issue area which was of particular interest to them, urban renewal. Even in this context, their influence did not seem overwhelming. A careful examination of key urban renewal decisions led Dahl to conclude that

> the Economic Notables, far from being a ruling group, are simply one of the many groups out of which individuals sporadically emerge to influence the policies and acts of city officials. Almost anything one might say about the influence of the Economic Notables could be said with equal justice about a half dozen other groups in the New Haven community (Dahl 1961: 72).

Thus, Dahl did not find a concentration of community power in the upper class, but neither did he see an even distribution of influence throughout the class structure. He attributed little or no direct influence over important government decisions to those below the line "dividing white-collar from blue-collar occupations" (Dahl 1961: 230). None of the 50 key leaders, for example, had a blue-collar occupation. Influential individuals, Dahl reported, were typically drawn from "middling social levels" (Dahl 1961: 229).

One of Dahl's principal arguments is that the diffusion of power in the course of New Haven's history from a small patrician class to a broad middle sector was related to the changing distribution of political resources, such as wealth, prestige, knowledge, electoral attractiveness, and control of media. In the initial period most politically useful resources were concentrated in the hands of the patricians. Gradually a system of "dispersed inequalities" emerged, under which the distribution of most resources remained unequal, but no one group monopolized all resources. The distinction between social and economic notables, for example, suggested the separation of wealth from prestige. Furthermore, the ethnic politician and the urban planner gained power with new types of political resources: ethnic identity and technical expertise.

THE DECISIONAL METHOD AND ITS CRITICS

The response to Dahl's work in some ways paralleled the earlier reaction to Hunter's study. The book especially appealed to those who saw in it a sophisticated vindication of American democracy. If Dahl's New Haven did not quite fit the idyllic world of the traditional high school civics text, it did maintain that power was not wholly concentrated in a small, upper-class elite and that most citizens of whatever class had access to some significant political resource. Moreover, *Who Governs?*, like *Community Power Structure*, popularized a method of inquiry. The decisional method was widely imitated, but like the reputational technique, it did not escape criticism. Among the principal objections raised were the following:

1. The conclusions of a decisional community power study are necessarily dependent on the specific decisions selected for inves-

tigation. Yet there are no generally accepted criteria for specifying a list of community issues which is in some sense "representative" of local power arrangements. Dahl, for instance, has been criticized for selecting education as an issue area since, as he concedes, the city school system is of little interest to the notables who generally live in the suburbs, are therefore prohibited from holding school board positions, and typically send their children to private or suburban public schools (Dahl 1961: 70). The party nomination process is likewise a questionable test of community power since it involves a matter of institutional procedure rather than conflict over public policy alternatives.

2. The decisional method is biased toward attributing power to the public officials and civic leaders who are most formally and actively associated with each issue area. It is least likely to uncover a small elite of the sort described by Hunter, which is quietly involved in a broad array of issues, setting the basic goals which a larger group of more specialized leaders publicly pursue.

3. By focusing specifically on decisions, Dahl's method misses the significance of latent concerns which are not allowed to become public issues requiring decisions. For example, when Hunter studied community power in Atlanta, most questions involving equity for black citizens were in this category of "nondecisions." By manipulating public opinion or institutional procedures (such as the operation of legislative committees) the powerful are frequently able to suppress consideration of matters they prefer to ignore. (For criticism of decisional method see Aiken and Mott 1970; Bonjean and Grimes 1974; Domhoff 1978; Bachrach and Baratz 1974.)

DOMHOFF: NEW HAVEN RESTUDIED

Recently one of Dahl's critics among class theorists, G. William Domhoff, reexamined New Haven politics in the 1950s. Domhoff's book, *Who Really Rules?* (1978), refutes several of Dahl's principal claims, including the notion of a sharp distinction between economic and social notables and the idea that the economic notables had relatively little influence over New Haven's urban renewal program.

Domhoff argued that the formal criteria which Dahl employed to define membership in his top economic and prestige classes were narrow and substantively questionable. Such errors could well lead to mistaken conclusions about the relationship between the two groups and their respective roles in local affairs. Dahl had defined the social notables as the families represented at New Haven's annual debutante ball. This standard delineated a top prestige class consisting of less than 0.1 percent of the population, well below the estimates in most community studies including an earlier New Haven study conducted by Dahl's Yale colleague, Hollingshead (with Redlich 1958). Following Hollingshead's conclusion that membership in prestigious private clubs was the best indicator of membership in New Haven's upper class, Domhoff redefined the social notables as the members of the top three clubs in the area. This criterion expanded the top prestige class to approximately 1 percent of the population.

Dahl's class of economic notables consisted of the owners of local property with high assessed value and the officers of the largest business enterprises operating in New Haven. Domhoff redefined the economic notables in terms of a network of interrelated business interests at the core of New Haven's economy. He isolated the network through an analysis of "interlocking directorates." An interlock exists when two corporate entities are linked through an individual who holds positions in both, typically by sitting on two boards of directors. Domhoff found that virtually all of New Haven's largest business enterprises, banks, and corporate law firms were linked in this fashion to a *single* corporate network. At the center of the network were 10 organizations, most of them banks, which were extensively linked to the others. Interestingly enough, at least two of Dahl's informants had stressed the power of the First New Haven Bank, the most heavily interlocked organization, describing it as a key part of the local " 'power structure,' " whose backing was "necessary for anything that happens in this town" (Domhoff 1978: 18–19).

Domhoff's economic notables were the individuals who held top positions in any of the organizations linked to the corporate network, approximately 300 people. Defined in this way, the top economic class was approximately twice the size of Dahl's original group, with fewer small-business owners and fewer local managers of big corporations headequartered outside of New Haven. In other words, Domhoff ended up with the leaders of the largest local enterprises.

Nearly 60 percent of New Haven's economic notables were also social notables, according to Domhoff's criteria (Domhoff 1978: 30). Moreover, individuals who held a higher-than-average number of network positions or were associated with organizations which were central within the network were more likely to be social notables. Domhoff, then, was able to demonstrate the existence of a network of economic notables which, particularly at its core, overlapped substantially with the world of social notables. By doing this, he knocked down part of the support for Dahl's argument that power in New Haven could not be concentrated in a single elite because of dispersed inequalities in the distribution of different political resources.

Domhoff chose to reexamine Dahl's conclusions about decision making in urban renewal because he regarded it as the most significant of the three issue areas considered by Dahl; although Domhoff did not point it out, it is also the issue that would be most likely to concern the pocketbooks of the rich and thus the most likely one to get them active in decision making. (See also a book on the same subject by one of Dahl's associates: Wolfinger 1973).

Dahl portrayed the program as the work of a newly elected Democratic Mayor, Richard C. Lee, and his redevelopment chief. The role of the economic notables, by this account, was essentially passive. They had been unable to promote or even agree on a redevelopment program prior to Lee's election, and the mayor found himself required to "bargain, threaten, reward, and maneuver endlessly" to gain the cooperation of the notables and others who were crucial to his plan (Dahl 1961: 79). Although the notables were well represented on a "citizens action committee" appointed by the mayor, the committee had little real influence. Domhoff challenged this view of urban renewal in New Haven with the help of documentary material, such as correspondence and minutes of meetings which were unavailable when Dahl did his research.

According to the evidence presented in *Who Really Rules?* the New Haven urban renewal effort was actually shaped by the prior initiatives of certain upper-class interests, both national and local. Nationally, Domhoff traced the story back to the late 1930s when a national debate over urban renewal policy set those who would emphasize building adequate housing for the poor against those who were concerned with preserving downtown real estate values and anxious to replace central city slums with commercial and other nonresidential structures. The first alternative was backed by labor and liberal groups, the second by major business interests. By the early 1950s, it was clear that the second alternative had emerged victorious.

Domhoff sketched the activities of three national organizations, all business dominated, which played key roles in defining and promoting the conservative urban renewal alternative: (1) the Urban Land Institute, put together by real estate, financial, and other corporate interests to research urban land uses and provide advice to cities interested in central city redevelopment; (2) the U.S. Chamber of Commerce, which carried on national lobbying on urban renewal issues and showed its local affiliates how to design renewal programs beneficial to downtown business interests; and (3) ACTION (American Council to Save Our Neighborhoods), a public relations effort launched in 1954 with strong corporate participation and the blessing of the Eisenhower administration. ACTION regarded New Haven as a demonstration project and apparently helped the city to obtain the highest per capita urban renewal funding in the country (Aiken and Mott 1970: 198).

Locally, Domhoff stressed the activities of the New Haven Chamber of Commerce which, he concluded, was dominated by members of his network of economic notables. In the early 1940s, the chamber persuaded a reluctant mayor to appoint a special commission to develop a comprehensive renewal plan. The commission was headed by a business executive active in the chamber and produced a plan which, without essential modification, became the basis for the renewal program of the 1950s. After the war, an independent redevelopment agency was set up by the city. The agency's board was dominated by business figures. Its minutes suggest that the Chamber of Commerce was the only group which took an active interest in its proceedings. Immediately after Lee's election in 1953, the chamber began to press the mayor-elect for action on the urban renewal program. Lee was already familiar with the chamber's views on the matter since he had been employed by the organization in the early 1940s when its interest in urban renewal first emerged.

Domhoff did not challenge Dahl's interpretation of the Citizen's Action Committee appointed by Mayor Lee. Documentary evidence indicates that the committee was regarded by all concerned as public relations window dressing. Nor did Domhoff directly question the leadership role ascribed to Lee by Dahl, but his research demonstrated that the business community had shaped and promoted the renewal well before Lee ever came to office.

In sum, *Who Governs?* substantially underestimated the influence of business interests on urban renewal in New Haven.[1] Dahl was apparently misled by the unjustifiably restrictive way he defined his economic notables, by his lack of access to relevant documentary evidence, and by his failure to consider national developments which molded local events. The last concern points to a significant problem of theoretical perspective. Dahl appears to have proceeded on the assumption that the power structure of New Haven was self-contained. Domhoff reminded us that communities are integrated into a larger society and therefore potentially subject to the decision making of national elites.

COMPARATIVE COMMUNITY POWER STUDIES

Ultimately, the power structures of Atlanta or New Haven are of minimal importance to people outside Atlanta and New Haven. They are of wider interest only if studying them can tell us something about community power generally. For this reason, scholarly interest in this field has turned to comparative analyses of the dozens of individual community power studies which have been done since the publication of Hunter's book (Walton 1970; Clark 1971; Bonjean and Grimes

---

[1] Domhoff also argues that Dahl underestimated the influence of Yale University (located in New Haven) on the redevelopment program, though his evidence in this regard seems less compelling.

1974). The object of such studies is to search out systematic patterns in the variations among communities. Researchers have been especially interested in determining the community characteristics which are associated with pluralistic versus pyramidal (elite-dominated) power structures.

One of the best comparative studies is Walton's (1970) analysis of research covering 61 separate communities. Walton tested a long list of hypotheses about community power which had been suggested by earlier work. Among his principal conclusions was one which confirmed the suspicions of many who were familiar with the literature: investigators who employed the reputational technique (typically sociologists) were most likely to uncover pyramidal power structures, and those who used the decisional method (generally political scientists) were most likely to find pluralistic configurations. It would seem that many investigators were predisposed toward one or another image of the power structure before research had even begun and, perhaps unwittingly, chose the method that tended to verify their assumptions. In order to avoid the spurious results which might be introduced by this tendency, Walton based his conclusions on a multivariate analysis which controlled for the method employed by the researcher.

One important finding relates directly to social class. Walton found a general agreement in the studies he analyzed that decision makers are "overwhelmingly" recruited from the upper-middle class and include a particularly high proportion of business leaders. Another key finding concerns the influence of local affiliates of large corporations. Walton determined that communities in which a high proportion of business firms are absentee-owned are the most likely to have pluralistic power structures. Local managers of national firms tend to stay out of town politics, since their future careers are within the corporation not the community. Local business leaders, on the other hand, have deep roots in the community, along with the knowledge and connections which make them effective participants in politics. In fact, they are likely to have inherited a family tradition of involvement in community affairs.

The perspective of the affiliate manager is reinforced by the parent corporation's own attitude toward local politics. Within the community, the corporation's concerns may include taxation, water supply, labor relations, and police protection. But these matters are typically settled before the local plant is established, and the corporation may simply shift its operations elsewhere if it becomes dissatisfied with conditions. Firms engaged in extractive operations (for example, mining) are an important category of exceptions to this generalization. Such firms cannot easily pull up stakes and leave, and they are often deeply involved in local politics (Goldstein 1962).

Absentee firms appear to encourage pluralistic power arrangements by reducing community dependence on local business interests without becoming directly involved in local politics. However, Walton's finding should not obscure the extent to which community affairs are indirectly but powerfully shaped by national corporate interests. A corporation's implicit threat to rechannel investments away from a community is a potent influence on local decision making, even when corporate managers are not among community decision makers. Moreover, corporate interests may collectively influence local communities by shaping national policies which affect them. Domhoff's portrayal of the development of urban renewal policy is a relevant example. Thus, a community may be inclined toward pluralistic decision making and yet have few critical decisions to make. We must shift our focus to a national level of power if we are to fully understand the forces which shape local communities.

MILLS: THE NATIONAL POWER ELITE

C. Wright Mills's book, *The Power Elite* (1956), was published shortly after Hunter's community study and provoked a parallel controversy on national power arrangements. Mills, whose work on the middle class we referred to in Chapter 3, was a major critic of American civilization during the 1950s, a self-satisfied era in our national life which Mills characterized "a material boom, a nationalist celebration, a political vacuum" (Mills 1956: 326). Mills's conception of the national power structure centered on the growing significance of three major interlocking institutions: the modern corporation, the executive branch of the federal government, and the military establishment. He saw each of these institutions becoming enlarged and centralized. A few hundred major corporations were taking the place of thousands of smaller competing firms which once typified the economy. The federal executive had gathered enormous powers and resources previously nonexistent or scattered among other units of government. The military, once small and decentralized, had developed into a colossal bureaucracy commanding a war machine of unprecedented scale and destructive power. (For recent evidence supporting Mills with regard to these trends, see Dye 1979: 21–22, 53, 80).

As the corporations, the federal government, and the military grew, they eclipsed and subordinated other institutions (Mills 1956: 6):

> No family is as directly powerful in national affairs as any major corporation; no church is as directly powerful in the external biographies of young men in America today as the military establishments; no college is as powerful in the shaping of momentous events as the National

Security Council. Religious, educational, and family institutions are not autonomous centers of national power; on the contrary, these decentralized areas are increasingly shaped by the big three in which developments of decisive and immediate consequence now occur.

The implication which Mills drew from these trends was that the basis of national power had become control over the three key institutions. Those who sit at the "commanding heights" of the corporate, political, and military hierarchies make the critical national decisions. Who are they? In the corporations, an amalgam of very rich families with corporate-based fortunes plus the ranking executives of the top national firms, whom Mills collectively labeled the "corporate rich"; in the federal government, the president, vice president, cabinet, heads of major agencies, and members of the White House staff; among the military, the generals and admirals. These three institutional elites together constitute the power elite.

Mills argued that the emergence of a national elite undercut important traditional bases of power. As we saw in the preceding section, community elites decline in importance as the power of national institutions grows. Investment decisions which are crucial for a community may be made in a distant corporate boardroom. Even the significance of wealth as a power resource is reduced. Very sizable personal fortunes are of trivial significance relative to the assets of any major national corporation. However, the largest family fortunes, such as those of the Rockefellers, Mellons, or Fords, are typically invested in national corporations, and in this form, wealth retains its significance as a basis of power.

Mills conceived of the political system as consisting of three tiers. The top tier is, of course, the power elite. The bottom tier, which Mills labels "mass society," encompasses the great majority of the population. Subject to large-scale national institutions which are beyond their control or comprehension and misinformed by media which are dominated by national elites, the members of the mass are passive participants in the political system. Between the mass society and the power elite are "the middle levels of power" comprising a multitude of competing interest groups from labor unions to the gun lobby, whose most typical arena of conflict is the Congress. The middle levels of power are the source of most political news, but they are not the locus of the most important political decisions. In the welter of competing interests, none can impose itself. This "semi-organized stalemate," as Mills characterized it, only serves to reinforce the dominance of the power elite.

The key decisions are, of course, reserved for the power elite. But which are the key decisions? Mills is unambiguous on this point. Two issue areas are of sweeping importance: national economic policy and military affairs–foreign policy. These matters unmistakably, often brutally, intrude into the lives of ordinary men and women as boom or bust in the economy and peace or war abroad. Mills saw decision making in both areas receding from the Congress to the executive branch of government, where the viewpoints of corporate and military elites are richly represented. He was keenly aware of the terrible fact that a small circle of men had assumed the right to launch a cataclysmic nuclear war. And, while most economic decisions under capitalism had always been private decisions, Mills felt that the leaders of major national corporations were much freer to determine their own course than were their smaller predecessors, subject to the restraints of a competitive market. We might add that since the publication of Mills's book, the emergence of the multinational corporation places many important economic decisions even further beyond the control of national politics (Barnet and Muller 1974).

Mills's conclusions were clearly influenced by the period during which he was writing. The country had recently come out of World War II and was entering a period of protracted cold war. General Eisenhower, a military man, was in the White House, and other officer-heroes were serving in civilian posts. These transitory developments probably led Mills to overestimate the significance of the military sector of his power elite. In the postwar world, the country faced a series of key decisions in foreign policy and international economic policy which could be dominated by a handful of men if the major corporate, political, and military institutions they represented were in agreement. But even as Mills wrote, new issues were emerging, such as the civil rights question, which could not be easily contained at the elite level of power but would have to be fought out at the middle level, particularly in Congress, and even in the streets.

MILLS, HIS CRITICS, AND THE PROBLEM OF ELITE COHESION

Much of the criticism which has been directed at elite theory in the community-power literature is also relevant to Mill's work. For example, pluralists have argued that Mills's methodology, like Hunter's, is flawed by a failure to examine actual decisions as a test of the power of the elite. In this section, we will focus on the substantive issue which has provoked the most debate among Mills's readers, the problem of elite cohesion—that is, the extent to which the members of a hypothesized elite hang together in pursuit of common objectives and in opposition to other groups. (For other lines of criticism, see the community-power discussion above and Domhoff and Ballard 1968.)

The cohesion issue was effectively posed in a classic essay by Dahl, directed at both Hunter and Mills, which accused the elite theorists of "confusing a ruling elite with a group that has a high *potential for control"* (Dahl 1967: 28). To be politically effective, potential for control must be coupled with "potential for unity." Thus, Dahl contended, the American military has the potential to impose a dictatorship on the nation but that potential means nothing unless military leaders are in agreement on that objective. The implication is that Mills defined an elite in terms of key positions in organizations which control important resources (potential for control) without ever demonstrating a political consensus among the members of the elite (potential for unity).

Mills's pluralist critics are clearly predisposed to the belief that unity among power contenders is difficult to achieve, especially in contemporary America. This inclination was strikingly illustrated in the best-known pluralist alternative, David Riesman's version of the American political system developed in a more general book on American society and culture, *The Lonely Crowd* (1953). In the course of his treatment of national power, Riesman asked two questions: "Is there a ruling class left?" and "Who has the power?" His answers were, respectively, no and no one. As the first question implies, Riesman believed that the country had had a ruling class in the past. Early in the history of the republic, it consisted of the landed gentry and mercantile interests which made up the federalist leadership; and, later, of captains of industry. But by the 1950s, the ruling class had been supplanted by an amorphous constellation of "veto groups," organized representatives of specialized interests including "business groups, large and small, the movie-censoring groups, the farm groups and the labor and professional groups, the major ethnic and major regional groups" (Riesman 1953: 246). The veto groups are distinguished from the powerful of previous eras by their inability to take positive initiatives to impose their own will. Feeling themselves powerless, chary of offending other groups, their function is largely defensive, "to neutralize those who might attack them" (Riesman 1953: 247).

How can any decision be taken in such a political context? Is anyone in charge? Riesman's reply was that leadership may be needed to initiate something new or halt something in progress, but little leadership is needed to maintain the status quo. To the extent that anyone exercises power, it is in terms of very specific and narrow issues. Power which might be effective over a broad range of issues or in the face of big questions which affect the nation as a whole is smothered by the action of the veto groups.

Mills characterized Riesman's amorphous power structure as "a recognizable although a confused statement of the middle levels of power, especially as revealed in congressional districts and in Congress itself" (Mills 1956: 244). Power at that level is indeed a semi-organized stalemate. In Mills's view, Riesman was guilty of a mindless empiricism which equated all interest groups and all issues. To describe the corporate elite and the Polish-American lobby as two veto groups misses the point. Clearly, certain groups are more powerful than others; moreover some groups may recognize a community of interest with others, thus creating a definite structure of power. As we have seen, Mills was only interested in the big economic and foreign policy questions and regarded most of the issues which consume the attention of the middle levels as trivial.

Cohesion presented a particular problem for Mills. He had to demonstrate both that the three distinct elites are internally cohesive and that they are drawn together into a single power elite. Mills did present a series of mechanisms through which elite unity might be achieved. They fall into essentially two categories, social-psychological and structural. The social-psychological mechanisms include similarities in origins, education, career, and lifestyles which produce "a similar social type" and contribute to ease in informal association (Mills 1956: 19). Mills presented evidence on these topics for each elite. He noted that elite men tend to be drawn from upper-class or upper-middle-class, urban, white, Protestant families and that they are likely to be educated in Ivy League schools. There is a significant overlap between the world of the power elite and upper-class "society" with its elaborate links among "proper" families, select prep schools, class values, and notions of style. (These commonalities, as Mills conceded, apply more to the civilian elites than to the military.)

In addition, members of the three elites have similar career experiences even if they do not move through the same institutions. The experience of managing a large organization is shared by the corporate rich, the "political directorate," and the chiefs of the Pentagon. The character of modern bureaucratic life has tended to blur the distinction between leadership in a large corporation, a civilian department of government, and an army. Mills contended that these shared elements of background and careers and the considerable material rewards attached to elite position tend to make members of the power elite conscious of the differences between themselves and the great mass of the population and to draw them together; they develop a form of upper-class consciousness which leads them to view the world from a similar perspective.

The structural mechanisms of cohesion examined by Mills concern the more-or-less-formal connections between institutions. One critical link is the interchange of personnel among the three institutions, especially the movement of representatives of the corporate world into and out of top political positions, a question we explore at greater length below. Another tie between these two is the dependence of political candidates on financing from the corporate rich, which we will also examine further. The military is closely allied with the corporations, who are its suppliers, while militaristic foreign policy pursued by the political directorate strengthens its ties to the generals and admirals. All three elites are, of course, compelled to consider each other by virtue of the inevitable interdependence of institutions operating on such a scale.

While pluralists remain unconvinced by Mills's treatment of the problem of cohesion, a Marxist critic appears to suggest that Mills has been all too successful in demonstrating elite unity. In an essay entitled "Power Elite or Ruling Class?" Paul Sweezy observed quite accurately that there is an unresolved tension in Mills's book between two views of the elite. The first is based on social class: Mills provided evidence that "those who occupy the command posts do so as representatives or agents of a national ruling class which trains them, shapes their thought patterns, and selects them for their positions of high responsibility" (Sweezy 1968: 123). Much of the evidence Mills presented for elite unity seems to point in this direction, especially the material on social background and recruitment patterns. The second view emphasized three "major institutional orders"; here Mills approached the corporate, military, and political realms as distinctly separate domains with autonomous leadership which comes together to form the power elite. Sweezy was highly skeptical of the second view, particularly given the evidence that Mills presented for the former. The American military, Sweezy contended, is firmly under civilian control, and the political elite is dependent on the class that rules the corporation; thus, the justification for thinking in terms of institutional elites collapses. Mills never dealt at length with this line of criticism, although in a breezy reply to critics on the left, he commented, "They want to believe that the corporation and the state are identical. . . . I don't believe it's quite that simple" (Mills 1968: 224).

THE NATIONAL CAPITALIST CLASS: ECONOMIC BASIS

Sweezy's criticism suggests an alternative to both the Millsian and pluralist views of national power: the identification of power with the class which controls income-producing wealth, the capitalist class. This conception, which has its roots in Marx, is similar to Mills's economic elite but assumes that the "corporate rich" have largely subordinated competing elites to their will. We have chosen the term *capitalist class* in preference to Sweezy's *ruling class* so as to avoid the implicit suggestion about political arrangements.

Tentatively, we can define the capitalist class as consisting of people who receive more than half of their income from property sources. Although such people surely exist at all income levels, only at very high levels—on the order of several hundred thousand dollars

TABLE 8–1
Distribution of corporate stock by income level*

	Percent held by highest earners			
Year	1 percent	5 percent	10 percent	50 percent
1958	52	74	83	96
1971	51	67	75	92

* Does not account for 20 to 25 percent of stock held by institutions.
Source: Marshall E. Blume et al., "Stockownership in the United States,"
Survey of Current Business, November 1974, pp. 16–44.

a year—does dependence on property income become the predominant pattern (see Table 4–3). A basic division within this class is that between local and national capitalists. The locals are led by the community's most affluent business owners, such as bankers, real estate investors, and department store owners. The national figures are those who own and/or manage the major corporations—those Mills dubbed "the corporate rich."[2] In the remaining pages of this chapter, we will explore the economic and social bases of the capitalist class and examine the mechanisms through which it makes its influence felt in national politics. Since we have touched on the local capitalist class in the community studies we reviewed earlier and our interest here is national power, we will restrict most of the discussion which follows to the national sector of the capitalist class.

In Chapter 4, we examined data indicating that wealth in general, and income-producing assets in particular, are highly concentrated in the United States. Here we will focus more narrowly on the corporate holdings of the rich. Tables 8–1 and 8–2 allow us to establish two crucial facts about corporate wealth in the United States: (1) there is an extremely high and relatively stable concentration of corporate shareholding in the United States, and (2) corporate stock constitutes a high proportion of the total wealth of the very rich. The first table indicates that the top 1 percent of income earners hold a majority of all the stock in private hands. The table also establishes a strong connection between high income and corporate stockholding. The second table, which examines the holdings of the top 3.5 percent of wealthholders, points to a sharp difference between the merely comfortable and the truly wealthy. Those with the largest fortunes have the highest percentage of their total investment in business enter-

---

[2] For some purposes the national sector of the capitalist class can be conceived as divided into two sub-groupings: (1) those who are tied to the smaller corporations oriented toward domestic markets and have few investments abroad; they tend to be more conservative and less internationalist in political perspective, and (2) those who are linked to the larger multinational corporations with extensive investments abroad; they are more internationalist and more liberal on certain political issues.

TABLE 8–2
Mean value of assets of top wealthholders by net worth, 1969

Size of net worth	Cash	Corporate stock	Corporate and foreign bonds	Government bonds	Life insurance equity	Mortgages and real estate	Noncorporate business	Other	Total
$ 50,000–99,999	$15,834	$15,931	$617	$2,507	$2,498	$37,379	$4,840	$6,677	$86,283
$ 100,000–299,999	26,999	18,970	1,823	5,547	3,221	62,753	9,100	13,841	142,254
$ 300,000–999,999	52,446	253,638	6,664	27,794	5,652	133,001	26,003	50,713	555,911
$ 1,000,000–4,999,999	93,288	1,076,166	25,035	129,256	10,007	248,073	72,870	249,537	1,904,237
$ 5,000,000–9,999,999	207,369	4,333,277	61,349	950,482	20,450	569,207	231,367	1,128,950	7,502,451
$10,000,000 or more	382,655	10,340,755	96,689	1,873,132	24,611	869,909	3,409,317	2,547,905	19,544,973

Source: U.S. Internal Revenue Service *Statistics of Income, 1969: Personal Wealth Estimated from Tax Returns* (Washington, D.C.: U.S. Government Printing Office, 1973), and Leonard Beeghley, *Social Stratification in America: A Critical Analysis of Theory and Research* (Santa Monica, Calif.: Goodyear, 1978), p. 221.

prises, particularly corporate enterprises. We might draw a line somewhere around $300,000. In the wealthholding class just below this figure, "corporate stock" and "noncorporate business" constitute approximately 20 percent of total holdings; for the class just above the line, they encompass 50 percent; but for the tiny minority with fortunes in excess of $10 million, such holdings exceed 70 percent of net worth. (Note that the figures in this table can be doubled to bring them up to approximate 1980 values.)

Even these data tell us relatively little about the very largest American fortunes. For that purpose, we turn to a list compiled by *Fortune* magazine in 1968 of 66 individuals with estimated personal wealth in excess of $150 million (Table 8–3). This list is, of course, slightly out of date. For example, the two billionaires included have since died, and some new fortunes worthy of inclusion have been accumulated in recent years (see, for example, Louis 1973, 1979). However, a more serious deficiency is the focus on individuals rather than extended families. The estimates include the assets of each individual's spouse and minor children but not those of other relatives. In fact the largest private fortunes combine the holdings of a number of separate but related households. These family groupings are generally based on descent from a founding ancestor who accumulated the initial fortune, typically during the late-19th-century expansion of American capitalism (Gilbert 1981). For instance, the six Rockefellers on the *Fortune* list are all grandchildren of the late John D. Rockefeller of Standard Oil fame, and the total value of the Rockefeller fortune (including holdings of family members not listed) has been estimated at $5.0 billion. Other families well represented on the *Fortune* list include the Du Ponts ($7.6 billion), the Mellons ($4.8 billion), and the Fords ($2.0 billion) (Lundberg 1968: 132–77).

TABLE 8–3
Fortune's list of centimillionaires

$1 billion to $1.5 billion:
  J. Paul Getty, Getty Oil Company
  Howard Hughes, Hughes Tool, real estate
$500 million to $1 billion:
  H. L. Hunt, independent oil operator
  Dr. Edwin H. Land, Polaroid
  Daniel K. Ludwig, shipping
  Ailsa Mellon Bruce
  Paul Mellon
  Richard King Mellon
$300 million to $500 million:
  N. Bunker Hunt, independent oil operator; son of H. L. Hunt
  John D. MacArthur, Bankers Life & Casualty
  William L. McKnight, Minnesota Mining & Manufacturing
  Charles S. Mott, General Motors
  R. E. (Bob) Smith, independent oil operator, real estate

TABLE 8–3 (*continued*)

$200 million to $300 million:
Howard F. Ahmanson, Home Savings & Loan Association
Charles Allen, Jr., investment banking
Mrs. W. VanAlan Clark, Sr. (Edna McConnell), Avon Products
John T. Dorrance, Jr., Campbell Soup
Mrs. Alfred I. Du Pont
Charles W. Engelhard, Jr., mining and metal fabricating
Sherman M. Fairchild, Fairchild Camera, IBM
Leon Hess, Hess Oil & Chemical
William R. Hewlett, Hewlett-Packard
David Packard, Hewlett-Packard
Amory Houghton, Corning Glass Works
Joseph P. Kennedy
Eli Lilly, Eli Lilly & Company
Forrest E. Mars, Mars Candy
Samuel I. Newhouse, newspapers
Marjorie Merriweather Post, General Foods
Mrs. Jean Mauze (Abby Rockefeller)
David Rockefeller
John D. Rockefeller III
Laurance Rockefeller
Nelson Rockefeller
Winthrop Rockefeller
Cordelia Scaife May, Mellon family
Richard Mellon Scaife
DeWitt Wallace, *Reader's Digest*
Mrs. Charles Payson (Joan Whitney)
John Hay Whitney

$150 million to $200 million:
James S. Abercrombie, independent oil operator, Cameron Iron Works
William Benton, *Encyclopedia Britannica*
Jacob Blaustein, Standard Oil of Indiana
Chester Carlson, inventor of xerography
Edward J. Daly, World Airways
Clarence Dillon, investment banking
Doris Duke
Lammot Du Pont Copeland
Henry B. Du Pont
Benson Ford, Ford Motor Company
Mrs. W. Buhl Ford II, Ford Motor Company
William C. Ford, Ford Motor Company
Helen Clay Frick, daughter of Henry Clay Frick
William T. Grant, W. T. Grant variety stores
Bob Hope, Hollywood
Arthur A. Houghton, Jr., Corning Glass Works
J. Seward Johnson, Johnson & Johnson
Peter Kiewit, construction
Allan P. Kirby, Woolworth heir, Allegheny Corp.
J. S. McDonnell, Jr., McDonnell Douglas, aircraft
Mrs. Lester J. Norris
E. Claiborne Robins, A. H. Robins, drugs
W. Clement Stone, insurance
Mrs. Arthur Hays Sulzberger (Iphigene Ochs), *New York Times*
S. Mark Taper, First Charter Financial Corp.
Robert W. Woodruff, Coca-Cola

Source: Arthur M. Louis, "America's Centimillionaires," *Fortune* 77 (May 1968), p. 156.

The economic power of such wealthy clans comes from the fact that the bulk of their fortunes are jointly administered (although individual members may also maintain separate investments). Family holdings may center on a single enterprise (Ford) or encompass a network of linked interests typically revolving about a bank. For example, the Mellons control the Mellon Bank of Pittsburgh, and the Alcoa, Carborundum, and Gulf Oil corporations (Lundberg 1968: 150–54; Herman 1981: 217–21).

The concentration of personal wealth is paralleled by the concentration of wealth in the corporations themselves. The dominant position of the largest corporations which Mills observed seems to have been further consolidated since he wrote. In 1950, shortly before the publication of *The Power Elite*, the 100 largest—among nearly 200,000 industrial corporations—already controlled approximately 40 percent of all industrial assets; by 1976 their share had grown to 55 percent. The 500 largest industrial firms account for over three quarters of the jobs in manufacturing (Szymanski 1978: 36). In the 1950s, mergers among some of the nation's largest banks increased concentration in the financial sector; by 1976, the 50 largest banks held 66 percent of all banking assets (Dye 1979: 20–21; Fitch and Oppenheimer 1970).

However, as the concentration of corporate assets has grown, stockholding in individual companies has become dispersed. The largest corporations have hundreds of thousands of stockholders, and diffusion of stock ownership is so great that individual holdings of even 5 percent of total stock are uncommon. One result of this tendency is a change in the relationship between the ownership and management of large corporations. Firms which once would have been controlled by families or small groups of investors are now typically dominated by their top officers, who are seldom owners of proportionally large blocks of company stock but rather people who have worked their way up through the ranks. A major study conducted recently by Edward Herman of the University of Pennsylvania's Wharton School of Business and Finance indicated that 64 of the 100 largest industrial corporations were controlled by hired managers; an additional 14 were controlled by some combination of managers and "outside" members of the board of directors (who are most typically officers of other corporations); and only 22 of the firms were controlled by owners (Herman 1981: 60).

Some writers detect in these developments a "managerial revolution," which they conceive in terms of a sharp split between the interests of stockholders and corporate managers (Berle and Means 1932; Burnham 1941; Galbraith 1967). From this viewpoint, a manager who is neither an owner nor subject to the dictates of owners is free to substitute personal goals for those of the stockholders. According to these theorists, the traditional owner-entrepreneur operated a firm with one consideration in mind: profit. The professional manager is not quite free to ignore profit but, with little direct stake in the corporation's earnings, may pursue a broader array of objectives including corporate growth, technological progress, the welfare of employees and customers, and public esteem for self and company. One well-known writer was so moved by this image of corporate high-mindedness that he dedicated an essay to celebrating "The Soulful Corporation" (Kaysen 1957).

Mills's conception of the corporate rich consisting of both top executives and major stockholders is a direct response to these ideas, which pose yet another problem of elite cohesion. What has taken place, he insists, is not a "managerial revolution" but a "reorganization of the propertied class . . . into a new corporate world of privilege and prerogative" (Mills 1956: 147). There has been a diffusion of stockholding in individual corporations, but (as we have demonstrated) the ownership of corporate stock remains concentrated among the top few percent of wealthholders. As a result "the narrow industrial and profit interests of specific firms and industries and families have been translated into the broader economic and political interests of a more genuinely class type" (Mills 1956: 147). The professional manager is included in the new propertied class. He shares the privileges, interests, and outlook of the established rich.

Contemporary evidence bears Mills out on this point. A survey conducted by *Fortune* magazine in 1976 showed that the chief executives of the 800 top industrial, financial, and retail corporations had a median income in excess of $200,000 (nearly $350,000 in the 100 largest industrial firms), high enough to place them along with the traditional rich in the closing seconds of the income parade. The executives do share with stockholders a direct interest in the profitability of the corporation. Although few chief executives hold substantial proportions of the outstanding stock in the corporations, 75 percent of those in the survey held at least $100,000 in shares, and 30 percent held over $1 million worth. Moreover, the direct stake of the executive in the corporation does not end with stockholding. Chief executives typically receive a substantial part of their annual compensation in the form of a bonus tied to the profit and stock performance of the corporation (Herman 1981: 91–98).

In addition to the direct incentives offered to executives, there are other forces upholding the interests of owners in the management of corporations. For one, major stockholders have not been wholly eliminated as an influence in the corporate world. As indicated above, Herman's study of the top 100 nonfinancial corporations showed that 21 percent were controlled by owners (Herman 1981: 60). An earlier *Fortune* survey of the top 500 firms concluded that 30 percent were family run. It is probable that proprietary interests are even stronger below this level of firm size. Even in the large firms which are management dominated, there are frequently small blocks of stock which are still substantial enough to allow their owners influence over some key decisions (Herman 1981: 60, 101–2; see also Zeitlin 1974).

In addition, managerial behavior is constrained by forces outside the corporation which indirectly represent capitalist class interests. Poor economic performance by a publicly held firm may limit its access to credit and may subject managers to the risk of removal through a corporate takeover. The influence of those whom Herman labels "the wealthy investor community" is subtle and pervasive:

> Several score institutions and several thousand wealthy investors account for a great deal of stock ownership, and this group is informed and powerful. Many top officers and outside directors are members of this wealthy investor community, and its interests filter into corporate attitudes, ideology, and standards in a variety of ways—directly through substantial representation on boards and in some cases by outright control; indirectly through transactions with financial interests and continuous inquiries and suggestions from owners and creditors and their representatives (brokers, security analysts). (Herman 1981: 101)

If this community is unhappy with the economic performance of a firm, its managers see the price of their stock falling, encounter increasing difficulties in obtaining credit, and face the risk of displacement through a corporate takeover. But the ideological influence to which Herman refers operates on a more subtle plane. The attitudes of the investor community pervade the boardrooms and executive offices so as to focus all discussion on profit-oriented performance criteria. All other considerations are simply "ruled off the agenda" (Herman 1981: 102). This orientation has been thoroughly inculcated in a manager by the time he or she has risen to the top ranks of the corporation. If anything, the professional manager appears to be under greater pressure to conform to orthodox business standards than the founding entrepreneurs or their heirs (Herman 1981: 103).

There is, then, little support for the idea of a "managerial revolution," at least in the sweeping form that it has been put forward by some writers. Corporations are typically run by their managers, but this does not appear to alter corporate goals. Since managers share the objectives and rewards of wealthy stockholders, it seems reasonable to accept Mills's conception of a capitalist class consisting of owners and managers tied to a corporate system.

An elaborate web of association ties the members of this class to one another and reinforces their common perspective. Interlocking directorates connect the largest firms to a vast national network of banks and corporations (Dooley 1969; Pennings 1980; Koenig et al.

1979). The leaders of the corporate world encounter each other through industry organizations, business lobby groups, participation in government advisory groups, service on the boards of foundations and related nonprofit organizations, and connections to the institutions of upper-class society which we describe in the next section (Herman 1981: 187–242; Dye 1979).

THE NATIONAL CAPITALIST CLASS: SOCIAL BASIS

Parallel to the economic basis for a national capitalist class in the corporate economy there is a social basis in an upper-class social world built on prestige and exclusive patterns of association. Among the institutions identified with this world are the select prep school, the *Social Register,* and the proper metropolitan men's club. These three have, in fact, been widely used by researchers as formal indicators of upper-class membership (Domhoff 1970: 9–23).

We have already described the appearance of the *Social Register* in early industrial America, when the new rich were being socially merged with the established upper classes. Although occasionally capricious in its inclusions and exclusions, a century after its creation, the *Social Register* remains, in Mills's words, "the only list of registered families . . . the nearest thing to an official status center that this country, with no aristocratic past, no court society, no truly capital city, possesses . . ." (1956: 57).

A small circle of prestigious prep schools, such as St. Paul's (New Hampshire), Hotchkiss (Connecticut), Foxcroft (Virginia), and Chapin (New York), drew their students from upper-class families (Domhoff 1970: 9–32). These day schools and boarding schools tend to be concentrated in the Northeast, but they draw many students from throughout the country. They are secular or nominally Episcopalian (the religious affiliation most common in the upper class) and traditionally single-sex institutions, although many have become coeducational in recent years. A few are older than the republic, but most were founded or experienced their major expansion around the time the *Social Register* appeared. They have, moreover, served a similar function: the integration of old prestige and new money (Baltzel 1958: 292–319).

Prep school graduates are informally referred to as "preppies," a term with mixed undertones of admiration and contempt, which is used more loosely to refer to various aspects of an upper-class lifestyle (Birnbach 1980). The extension of the term is not inappropriate. Admission to one of these select institutions is indicative of acceptance to upper-class status. The style and values the prep schools inculcate in their students equip them for participation in an upper-class social community. The network of personal ties which develop among prep school students and their families will serve them well in their subsequent careers and social lives.

The prep schools contribute to a pattern of upper-class endogamy by bringing students and their siblings into contact with potential marriage partners, both directly and through debutante parties and other upper-class social functions to which prep school students are likely to be invited. A study of weddings covered on the *New York Times* society page, a traditional monitor of upper-class social life, found that 68 percent of the brides and grooms were either listed in the *Social Register* or had attended an exclusive prep school. Twenty-four percent of the marriages were between individuals both listed in the *Social Register* (Blumberg and Paul 1975). This is a high figure, given that the *Register* covers less than 0.5 percent of the national population, but it misses the full extent of upper-class endogamy. Since 68 percent of the new spouses can be considered upper class by the two criteria mentioned, the level of endogamy should be more than 36 percent. (This figure is based on the extreme assumption that all non-upper-class individuals in the study are marrying upper-class individuals, thus diluting endogamy.)

Most major metropolitan areas have one or two men's clubs, such as New York's Knickerbocker, San Francisco's Pacific Union, or Philadelphia's Philadelphia Club, with a distinctly upper-class membership. The major clubs perform much the same function as the *Social Register* and the prep schools: they indicate who can be considered part of "proper society." They also provide an informal setting where upper-class associations can be developed and maintained and, on occasion, important business or political matters can be discussed free from outside scrutiny (Baltzell 1958: 336–54; Domhoff 1970, 1974).

The prep schools, top universities, and metropolitan men's clubs draw not only from their own regions but from a national upper-class population. For example, over 30 percent of the members of San Francisco's Bohemian Club reside outside the San Francisco area (Domhoff 1974: 30). The national scope of the upper class is also evident in marriage patterns; the society page study referred to earlier found that 54 percent of the marriages reported were intercity (Blumberg and Paul 1975: 74). The *Social Register*, perhaps in recognition of the national character of the upper class, has recently abandoned its city-by-city editions and begun publishing a single national edition.

To what extent is the national social class we have been describing identical with the national wealth class examined in the previous section? We would be surprised if the two did not overlap substantially, since our studies of wealth and prestige on a local level suggest an intimate connection. In Chapter 3 we noted that virtually all of the founders of great fortunes in the late 19th or early 20th centuries had traceable descendants listed in the *Social Register* by 1940. More recently, Blumberg and Paul (1975) tabulated occupational data on the fathers of brides and grooms in their society page study; nearly 60 percent of the men whose occupations were identified were corporate executives. Using *Social Register* listings, education at top prep schools, and membership in the exclusive metropolitan clubs as criteria, Domhoff (1967: 51) found that 53 percent of the directors of the top manufacturing and financial corporations could be classified as upper class.

Using slightly broader criteria, Dye concluded that only 30 percent (1979: 170) of the presidents and directors of major corporations were of upper class *origins*. But his data show that 75 percent of men in these positions belong to at least one of the top clubs, which would make them upper class by Domhoff's criteria and indicates an effort by socially established members of the capitalist class to draw managers of lesser class origins into upper-class society. What these studies demonstrate at the very least is substantial overlap between the top wealth and prestige classes at the highest levels of American society.

For the student of national power arrangements, the significance of the link between upper-class society and corporate wealth is related to the problem of cohesion raised earlier. The achievement of consensus on specific policy issues and more generally the maintenance of class solidarity is made earlier because those who own and control the major concentrations of national wealth encounter each other in a private sphere of informal relations. The schools and clubs are merely the outer manifestations of this realm whose deeper meaning resides in shared experience, mutual intimacy, and the bonds of friendship and kinship that produce a consciousness of common identity and shared values. Domhoff points to group dynamics research in social psychology which has established that physical proximity among the members of a group, frequent association, a group reputation of high prestige, and an informal atmosphere all contribute to group solidarity. These are characteristic features of the upper-class world we have been describing and prepare us for another basic conclusion of the same research: "members of socially cohesive groups are more open to the opinions of other members and more likely to change their views to those of other members" (Domhoff 1974: 89–90, 96). Baltzell, in his earlier study of upper-class Philadelphia, made a related point which he phrased in terms of social control: An upper-class community inculcates and sustains "a mutually understood code of conduct" in its members. Upper-class people are especially subject to the "norms and sanctions of their peers. A man caught in an act of dishonesty or disloyalty fears, above all, the criticism of his class of lifelong friends" (Baltzell 1958: 61).

MECHANISMS OF CAPITALIST CLASS POWER: PARTICIPATION IN GOVERNMENT

In the next few pages, we will discuss the institutional mechanisms which extend the power of the capitalist class well beyond the economic sphere which is its immediate concern. Among the most potent of these mechanisms is direct participation in national government, especially at the top levels of the executive branch. Although few recent presidents have been drawn from the upper class, they have typically placed upper-class men in key cabinet positions and leaned on them for advice. Journalist David Halberstam captured the essence of this dependence in the opening pages of a perceptive book on the Kennedy-Johnson years. He records a meeting between John F. Kennedy, the month before he took office, and Robert Lovett, a Wall Street investment banker with impeccable social credentials and elaborate corporate connections—in Halberstam's words, "the very embodiment of the Establishment." Kennedy tried to persuade Lovett, a Republican who had voted for Kennedy's opponent, to accept a major cabinet post:

> Lovett declined regretfully. . . , explaining that he had been ill. . . . Again Kennedy complained about his lack of knowledge of the right people, but Lovett told him not to worry, he and his friends would supply him with lists. Take Treasury, for instance—there Kennedy would want a man of national reputation, a skilled professional, well known and respected by the banking houses. There were Henry Alexander at Morgan, and Jack McCloy at Chase [Manhattan Bank], and Gene Black at the World Bank. Doug Dillon too. Lovett said he didn't know their politics. Well, he reconsidered, he knew McCloy was an independent Republican, and Dillon had served in a Republican administration, but, he added, he did not know the politics of Black and Alexander at all (their real politics of course being business). At State, Kennedy wanted someone who would reassure European governments: they discussed names, and Lovett pushed, as would Dean Acheson, the name of someone little known to the voters, a young fellow who had been a particular favorite of General Marshall's—Dean Rusk over at [the] Rockefeller [Foundation]. He handled himself very well, said Lovett. The atmosphere was not unlike a college faculty, but Rusk had stayed above it, handled the various cliques very well. A very sound man (Halberstam 1972: 16–17).

Ironically, the three top cabinet appointments made by Kennedy, a liberal Democrat, reflected the advice of Lovett and others like him. As secretary of the treasury, he chose C. Douglas Dillon, an investment banker connected with Dillon, Read, and Company, a major

Wall Street firm started by Dillon's father; as secretary of defense, Robert McNamara, who had just been made president of Ford Motor Company; and as secretary of state, Dean Rusk, then president of the Rockefeller Foundation, a man with many admirers in corporate circles (Burch 1980: 175–77).

Cabinet recruitment studies show that Kennedy's appointments followed a pattern established by his predecessors and maintained by his successors. Cabinet officers are overwhelmingly drawn from the top of the class structure, most notably from the national capitalist class and the national prestige class we have been describing. Mintz (1975) examined the social and occupational backgrounds of people who served in the cabinet between 1897 and 1973. She found that nearly two thirds of the fathers of cabinet officers had had professional or managerial occupations. Seventy-eight percent of the cabinet officers themselves had been corporate officials or partners in corporate law firms; at least 60 percent could be classified as members of a national upper class on the basis of *Social Register* listings, exclusive prep school attendance, or membership in any one of a long list of selective social clubs; and over half of the cabinet members fit both categories.

Using slightly different criteria, Burch concluded that nearly two thirds of cabinet officers and major diplomatic appointees from 1933 to 1980 were linked to the corporate world or sizable family fortunes (Burch 1980: 378–84). The occupational backgrounds of the men covered by Burch's study were as follows:

Lawyers 29%
Big businessmen 27
Small businessmen 4
Government service 21
Other 19

Clearly, most ranking federal officials were lawyers, big businessmen or government career people. Burch noted a substantial representation of corporate lawyers and investment bankers in the first two categories and suggested, as have Mills and others, that such men play a crucial mediating role between business and government akin to the coordinating roles they play within the corporate world. Our own, more focused survey of the men who held the top cabinet posts (State, Defense, and Treasury) from Kennedy's inaugural cabinet in 1961 through Reagan's in 1981, reveals that 60 percent were drawn from major industrial corporations, financial institutions, or corporate law firms *(Who's Who in American Politics 1979; Who's Who in America 1980)*. But if the corporations are well represented among top federal decision makers, there is no parallel representation of labor. Burch (1980: 377) found that since 1913 only six men have served in the cabinet who were in any way connected with the labor movement. Most served for short terms and all but one were secretaries of labor.

It is common practice for cabinet officers to return to the corporate world after leaving public office (Salzman and Domhoff 1979). They resume law practice, often becoming lobbyists for big business, or they become corporate executives. Their experience and connections in government are put at the service of their business associates. And indeed, many cycle themselves more than once in and out of government, maintaining links between the two worlds. One cabinet officer under President Reagan links Mills's big three institutions: Alexander Haig has been a general, head of the civilian staff of the White House, a corporate president, and secretary of state.

What can be said about the class background of Congress? The occupational origins of the House of Representatives are presented in Table 8–4. The majority of House members, like the majority of cabinet officers, have come to national office from careers in law or business. The representation of blue-collar workers or white-collar employees has been scanty indeed. Evidence going back to the beginning of the century (1906) shows that this recruitment pattern has been utterly consistent (Nagle 1977).

The Senate has a similar recruitment base. Ninety-four percent of the senators in the 92d Congress (1971–72) were professionals (70 percent lawyers) or business owners prior to entering politics; a small percentage were farmers or ranchers; none held working-class or lower-middle-class positions. Morever, few senators could be described as self-made men. Two thirds of the senators' fathers were professionals or businessmen; only 15 percent were manual workers, the occupational status of the majority of males employed during the lifetimes of these fathers (Zweigenhaft 1975).

These data suggest that the senate is at the very least an upper-middle-class institution. But a significant minority of senators can be described as upper class. In the 92d Congress, 20 percent qualified on the basis of social credentials, including *Social Register* listings, prep school attendence, or membership in exclusive clubs. The corresponding figure for the House was 5 percent (Zweigenhaft 1975: 124).

TABLE 8–4
Occupations of members of the House of Representatives (percent)

Occupation	1948	1952	1956	1960	1964	1968	1970
Lawyer	58%	51%	49%	48%	52%	66%	52%
Business owner	13	22	21	23	20	12	16
Farm owner	5	7	9	3	6	2	4
Manager	—	2	4	—	4	6	8
Professional	16	13	13	26	10	10	14
White collar	2	2	2	—	4	2	2
Other	5	2	2	—	4	—	4
Total	100	100	100	100	100	100	100

Source: John Nagle, *System and Succession: The Social Bases of Political Elite Recruitment* (Austin: University of Texas Press, 1977), p. 74.

An Associated Press report concluded that there were at least 37 millionaires among the 100 Senators in 1979 (Alexander 1980: 23). The wealthiest included two freshman senators, John Danforth (of the Ralston Purina family) of Missouri and H. John Heinz III (of the "57 Varieties" family) from Pennsylvania, both worth somewhere between $7 million and $17 million. The net worth of the average senator was $440,000 (Green 1979: 225).

Congress, then, is recruited from the upper levels of the class structure, although the typical congressman appears to be drawn from a stratum a notch below that of the typical cabinet officer. The congressman is also more likely to be a career politician rather than a top executive or corporate lawyer on temporary assignment. The law and business backgrounds of many congressmen suggest a smaller-scale, more localized version of the corporate world so richly represented in the cabinet. If the cabinet is recruited from the national capitalist class, the Congress draws on the local capitalist classes.

What do cabinet and congressional recruitment patterns tell us about national politics? It certainly cannot be argued that class background allows us to predict the political behavior of individual decision makers. For example, Edward Kennedy and Barry Goldwater, two of the wealthiest men in the Senate, stand at opposite ideological poles of mainstream American politics. But we have already seen that the behavior and opinions of people in the aggregate are shaped in important ways by class position; in the next chapter, we will see that this generalization is applicable to politics. Moreover, we have noted how informal association shapes receptivity to opinions. The congressman whose personal associations are largely upper class or upper-middle class is likely to be more open to viewpoints common at the top of the class structure than to those prevalent toward the bottom.

The precise effect of these tendencies is not easy to gauge but in Chapter 9 we will point out certain issues, such as medical care and unemployment, which are of much greater concern to working-class people than to those above them. The failure of the United States to develop an adequate system of public health care or mechanisms to deal with the highest levels of unemployment in the industrial world is quite probably related to the recruitment patterns of cabinets and congresses.

MONEY AND POLITICS

The most obvious political resource available to the rich is money, used to finance legitimate political activities or, on occasion, to purchase illegitimate influence over officeholders. In some periods of American history, the application of political cash has produced blatant distortions of public life. For example, in 1913 a lobbyist for the

National Association of Manufacturers (NAM) publicly acknowledged that he had bought legislative favors with bribes and influenced House leaders to appoint congressmen favorable to NAM to House committees and subcommittees (*Congressional Quarterly* 1976: 654, 662). More recently, the Watergate revelations, which drove Richard Nixon from office, included evidence that a decision to raise milk price supports had been exchanged for huge campaign donations from milk producers, that the Nixon reelection committee had accepted money from foreign interests in violation of federal law, and that a long list of major corporations had made illegal campaign donations (Alexander 1980: 73–80). Nixon also had followed the traditional practice of using high-level jobs to reward major contributors. Ruth Farkas, a sociologist and member of the board of a New York department store, made one of the largest donations to the campaign and was subsequently appointed ambassador to Luxembourg. According to congressional testimony, Ms. Farkas had turned down an earlier offer of the ambassadorship to Costa Rica with the objection, " 'Isn't $250,000 an awful lot of money for Costa Rica?' " (Alexander 1980: 58).

The publicity generated by the abuses of the Nixon campaign and the accelerating cost of running for office produced pressure for campaign financing reform, and significant legislation was passed in the 1970s. The new laws limit individual campaign donations to $1,000 per candidate in each election and $25,000 annually to all federal candidates; restrict group donations, which must be made through registered Political Action Committees (PACs), to $5,000 per candidate per campaign; provide for federal financing of presidential campaigns on a matching basis; and require public disclosure of campaign donations and expenditures.

But, as interpreted by the courts, the legislation does not limit *independent* expenditures which individuals or groups make on behalf of a candidate, as long as they do not coordinate their spending with the candidate's campaign organization. Nor do the laws limit the amounts that candidates or their families spend on their own campaigns, except in the case of presidential contenders who accept federal financing. The significance of self-financing can be appreciated in the recent election to the Senate of H. J. Heinz III and the reelection of John D. Rockefeller IV to the governorship of West Virginia. Heinz covered 90 percent of his primary campaign expenditures with "loans" from his personal fortune, outspending his opponent two to one; by the end of the general election he had loaned his campaign $2.5 million (Alexander 1980: 22). Rockefeller used an incredible $12 million of his own money, nearly $30 for every vote he received and 11 times the amount spent by his opponent, former governor Arch Moore (*U.S. News and World Report*, December 15, 1980).

The major effect of the legislation of the 1970s is to constrain the influences of very rich individuals on candidates while increasing the political weight of certain organized groups, including corporate groups. In 1972, some individuals gave hundreds of thousands of dollars to political candidates. Contributions on anything like that scale are no longer legal (Alexander 1980: 53). But wealthy contributors have been superseded by the PACs. By 1978, PACs were spending three times as much as the major parties. Three categories of PACs—labor, business, and "ideological"—have played especially significant roles. Although the new legislation maintained existing prohibitions on the direct use of funds from corporate and union treasuries to finance political activities, it allowed them to use their own money to form and administer PACs which solicit donations from union members or corporate executives and stockholders. Unions had long used PACs to support prolabor candidates, but the recent legislation eased certain restrictions on corporate use of PACs and produced lightning expansion of corporate PAC activity in the late 1970s. By 1980, business groups were for the first time outspending labor groups and appeared to have much stronger growth potential (*New York Times,* August 4, 1981; Green 1979: 9).

The ideological PACs range from committees concerned with specific issues, such as abortion, to those with broader political concerns, such as the right-wing Conservative Political Action Committee (NCPAC). The latter, one of the top money raisers in 1980, contributed significantly to the defeat of several liberal senators in the 1980 election, through focused, independent (and therefore legally unlimited) spending in selected races. The removal of these men contributed to a decisive rightward shift in the political complexion of the upper chamber. In general, the conservative PACs have been outspending their liberal opponents, igniting labor union fears of a well-financed political assault by an alliance of business interests and conservative ideological groups (Malbin 1979: 32; Alexander 1980: 90).

Clearly, campaign finance reform has not severed the traditional connection between wealth and politics, although it has certainly altered the character of the relationship between them. The limit on individual campaign donations—still relatively high from the viewpoint of middle-income people—compels political fund raisers to shift their focus slightly downward in the class structure. Congressmen, who still depend on individual contributors for the greater part of their campaign financing, will probably be spending more of their time at upper-middle-class cocktail parties (unless they depend on direct-mail solicitation, a technique most likely to produce results for candidates at the extremes of the ideological spectrum) (Malbin 1979: 26).

Koenig (1980) argued convincingly that the corporate core of the national capitalist class is the principal beneficiary of recent legislation. Although the very rich individuals among them have had the political power of their personal fortunes reduced, the class as a whole has probably enhanced its influence. The various corporate committees do, in fact, tend to contribute to the same sympathetic candidates (*Congressional Quarterly* 1980: 3408). Thus, for the upper class, the reorganization of political giving is a phenomenon parallel to the earlier reorganization of corporate ownership: both contribute to upper-class cohesion by making class interests and power more collective and less individual. At the same time, campaign financing reform contributes to the legitimacy of the political system by eliminating some gross forms of corruption without undermining the ability of the corporations to use campaign money to assure business-oriented government.

BUSINESS LOBBIES

What corporate interests do not achieve through direct participation in government or by financing political campaigns, they may attain by persuading public officials to adopt (or abandon) particular policies. Especially since the emergence of the modern corporate economy, business representatives have devoted elaborate efforts to shaping the decisions of Congress and the federal departments and regulatory agencies which carry legislation into practice. The terms *lobby* and *lobbyist* are often employed to cover these efforts, although in their strictest sense, they refer only to organizations or individuals professionally engaged in influencing legislators. At the turn of the century, as the case of the NAM lobbyist cited earlier suggests, business lobbies—backed by abundant flows of cash—moved Congress with dependable ease. In recent decades, major business lobbies have generally employed more subtle methods, in part because competing interests are better organized and the possibilities of unfavorable publicity are greater. (On contemporary lobby techniques, see Green 1979: 27–59 and *Congressional Quarterly* 1976: 653–67).

Currently the principal business lobby organizations in Washington are the U.S. Chamber of Commerce and the Business Roundtable. Recently merged with the National Association of Manufacturers, which was known as the representative of the smaller manufacturing corporations, the chamber gains its special strength from its ability to mobilize pressure on members of congress through its 2,500 local affiliates. The local capitalist class, which dominates the affiliates, is likely to include important elements of the power structure in a legislator's home district, as well as people who belong to the same social networks as the legislator. When the Washington office wants to pressure senators or representatives on a particular vote, it can systematically mobilize letters, phone calls, and personal visits from a local business owner, a legislator's former law partner, a college fraternity brother, or a fellow member of the local country club.

The Business Roundtable consists of the chief executive officers (CEOs) of approximately 200 of the largest corporations. Its power is based on the formidable resources controlled by these corporations and the prestige of those who lead them. The roundtable typically operates more quietly than the chamber. Its stock-in-trade is the personal visit from a CEO and the carefully crafted economic study or legal brief supporting its position. The leaders of the roundtable have access to congressmen and senators and even to the president—entree which no ordinary lobbyist could hope to duplicate. A congressional aide commented, "A visit from a CEO has an unbelievable impact, as perhaps it should. It shows a commitment" (Green 1979: 29).

The power of these two groups was demonstrated in 1978 when they collaborated with other business lobbies to fight a bill creating a consumer protection agency. The legislation had already passed the House or Senate on five separate occasions; it was backed by the president, the speaker of the House, and 150 consumer, labor, and other groups, and it had been supported two to one by the public in surveys conducted by the Harris organization. As part of its campaign, the Roundtable had retained Leon Jaworski, a highly paid, Washington-wise lawyer known for his role as a special prosecutor in the Watergate investigation, to lobby against the legislation, and employed the North American Precis Syndicate to disseminate prepared editorials and cartoons to some 4,000 newspapers across the country, never acknowledging the business group as the source. According to the syndicate, the material was used approximately 2,000 times. Two undecided congressmen told lobbyists for the bill that they were for the first time receiving sizable contributions from small-business groups encouraged by the U.S. Chamber of Commerce. Another representative was informed by his campaign finance chairman that his biggest contributors were against the legislation. A Florida congressman expressed fear that "the Chamber will run a candidate against me in the primary." The bill failed in the House 227 to 189 (Green 1979: 53–56).

There are, as pluralist writers would remind us, a multitude of lobby groups operating in Washington, many of them directly opposed to business lobbies on key issues. But their mere existence is not confirmation of the pluralist image of the political order as an athletic league in which all major social interests are represented with more-or-less-equal strength. Some interests are not represented at all. Others cannot compete in the same league as the representatives of business (as the fate of the consumer agency bill suggests). Business lobby efforts are certainly better financed and probably better organized than those of any other sector of the society. The chamber alone had an annual budget of $20 million in 1978; the American Petroleum Institute, which represents the major oil companies, spent $30 million (Green 1979: 28, 34). Eighty percent of the 1,000 largest corporations maintain their own representatives in Washington.

The superior organization of business interests is in part a reflection of a more general phenomenon referred to earlier; people toward the top of the class structure have higher rates of social participation. Only a minority of blue-collar workers are members of labor unions, but virtually every business belongs to some representative organization.

The authoritative Washington journal *Congressional Quarterly* in its *Guide to Congress* noted that two broad lobby coalitions confront each other over most critical legislation: a conservative alliance led by the major business groups and a liberal alliance generally led by labor unions and civil rights groups. In the next chapter, we will have an opportunity to assess the relative strengths of these two camps when we examine some recent legislative conflicts over legislation affecting labor unions.

POLICY-PLANNING GROUPS

A step removed from the conflictual world of political campaigns and legislative battles is a quieter and less visible realm of organizations dedicated to formulating and disseminating broad proposals for national policy. We have already noted the influence of one of them, the Urban Land Institute, which was set up to study urban renewal prospects. Like that institute, the most influential policy organizations—groups such as the Council of Foreign Relations, the Council for Economic Development, and the Business Council—have been created and financed by the corporate elite, which plays a prominent role in their activities. A social-network analysis of the boards of major corporations, memberships of exclusive men's clubs, and participants in key policy-planning organizations reveals an elaborate pattern of overlap (Domhoff 1975). The major foundations, such as Rockefeller, Lilly, Kellogg, Mellon, and Kresge, although broader in their concerns, perform similar functions and are also tightly connected with the national capitalist class (Dye 1979; Domhoff 1967: 64–71).

The Council on Foreign Relations, the most widely known of the policy organizations, was founded at the close of World War I by a group of eastern bankers, lawyers, and academicians conscious of

America's expanding role in world affairs. Today the majority of its 1,500 members are financiers, executives (especially from the largest banks and corporations), and lawyers, but academics and journalists are also well represented. The council publishes *Foreign Affairs*, the most prestigious journal in the field, along with books and pamphlets on varied foreign policy questions. But the core of the CFR program consists of study groups which bring executives, government officials, military officers, and scholars together to define policy alternatives in specific areas of concern. Frequently, ideas which emerge from these groups become national policy. For example, council groups played a key role in planning three major international institutions which appeared after World War II: the International Monetary Fund, the World Bank, and the United Nations. The move toward reorienting American policy toward China also began in council groups. The influence of the council is magnified by the fact that its members frequently hold top foreign-policy posts. By the council's estimate, one third of its members served in official capacities over a 20-year period (Domhoff 1978: 64–67; 101–9).

Another function of the council is to back the careers of intellectuals sympathetic to corporate interests and filter out those who are unsympathetic. The career of former secretary of state Henry Kissinger is illustrative: Kissinger moved from a university position to Washington via an active role at the Council on Foreign Relations and close ties to the Rockefeller family (Lundberg 1975; Collier and Horowitz 1976). His predecessor from the Kennedy-Johnson years, Dean Rusk, moved to State from the presidency of the Rockefeller Foundation. As we have seen, Rusk was urged on Kennedy by a representative of the corporate establishment. The policy organizations also provide a private, informal setting in which corporate leaders can seek a consensus on significant policy questions before they become public issues.

INDIRECT MECHANISMS OF CAPITALIST-CLASS INFLUENCE

Capitalist-class influence over government is not limited to the direct means we have been describing: recruitment to decision-making positions, campaign financing, lobbying, and domination of policy-planning institutions. The capitalist class can also affect government policy indirectly through its control of the economy and the mass media. A defining characteristic of a capitalist society is the existence of a relatively small class which controls most productive wealth and therefore independently makes investment decisions which can decisively affect the welfare of other classes. Although governments in capitalist societies have limited control over what business leaders do, their political fortunes are closely linked to business decisions. The connection is typically phrased in terms of "business confidence." If business leaders lack confidence in a government or its policies, they are not likely to risk their capital in new investments. The resulting decline in aggregate level of investment will soon be reflected in a rising level of unemployment, which, in turn, will subject the government to pressure from an electorate dissatisfied with the state of the economy. If the government wants to rectify the situation without making basic changes in the capitalist economic order, it must find a way to regain the confidence of investors. What sorts of government policies are likely to alienate business confidence? Basically, any which threaten business profits, from "excessive" taxation of corporate income to the imposition of expensive regulations designed to reduce pollution or guarantee worker safety. The precise factors which lead to a loss of confidence are less important than the essential fact that this mechanism gives the capitalist class an indirect veto over government policy.

Two aspects of the business-confidence veto are particularly worth noting. One is that it can influence a government in the absence of an actual curtailment of investment. The mere risk of such action is enough to persuade decision makers to reconsider a proposed policy. In fact, the possible effect of government action on investor behavior is frequently raised as an issue in public policy debates. The other is that the veto mechanism does not require conscious, concerted action by members of the capitalist class to be effective. Isolated investment decisions made on the basis of an objective assessment of potential risk and profitability may collectively produce a downturn in business activity and subject a government to popular pressure (Bloch 1977).

Governments are also subject to the limits imposed by private control of the mass media through which people receive information about public affairs. In the United States, virtually all significant media are owned by the local and national capitalist classes (though they might just as well be organized as cooperatives, like the respected French paper Le Monde, as semiautonomous public bodies, like the British Broadcasting Company, or as organs of political parties like a number of European papers). Control of the media has become highly concentrated, and the principal media companies are now counted among the largest corporations. The three television networks which provide Americans with most of the news they hear are represented on the Fortune list of major industrial corporations, as are the publishers of the country's two most prestigious dailies, the New York Times and the Washington Post, and the two most important newsmagazines, Time and Newsweek (owned by the Post). Nine newspaper chains control one third of total circulation, and most newspapers get their national and international news from two sources,

United Press International and the Associated Press (Dye 1979: 98–99).

Capitalist-class influence over the media is not limited to the power of ownership. Since the media are operated for private profit and most of their income comes from corporate advertising, media managers are sensitive to pressure from advertisers. The networks are additionally subject to the influence of the affiliated stations which broadcast their programs to local audiences. Thus, Edward R. Murrow's brilliant and controversial current affairs program, "See It Now" on CBS television, was forced off the air after its corporate sponsor withdrew and no regular replacement could be found. In the 1950s, programs which dealt with the issue of racial discrimination or employed black actors could not appear on network television because corporate sponsors refused to be associated with them and some affiliates (particularly in the South) refused to carry them. There are, however, relatively few confrontations between advertisers and networks over such matters. As an executive of a major advertising agency explained, direct interference by the advertiser is seldom necessary "because the producers involved and the writers involved are normally pretty well aware of what might not be acceptable" (Barnouw 1978: 54; see also Tuchman 1974).

As the ad man's comment suggests, the main power which the capitalist class exercises over the media is the power to impose implicit limits on what is "acceptable." The media, in turn, operate on their audiences, not by imposing specific ideas, but by defining the subjects which are appropriate for consideration and delineating the range of reasonable opinion. In other words, they define the public agenda. (Their ability to do so is increased by the concentration of media control). Thus, until the late 1950s, racial inequity was not a national issue, though it was most certainly a serious national problem. To this day, the question which so troubled Mills, the possibility that our leaders are pursuing policies which carry us toward nuclear annihilation, has not been raised in a serious fashion by the major media.

CONCLUSIONS

We began this chapter by reviewing studies of community power structures. Although we reached no definitive resolution of the debate between elite or class and pluralist views, we did learn that local decision makers are overwhelmingly drawn from the upper and upper-middle classes and that local affairs are strongly influenced by the decisions made by national elites, especially corporate elites.

The latter conclusion forced us to think about national power structures. We examined the work of C. Wright Mills, which alerted us to institutional developments which have tended to concentrate power in the leadership of huge organizations. Within Mills's power elite, the corporate sector appeared to be dominant over the political and military sectors. This led us to focus our attention on the national capitalist class, and we learned the following: a small class controls most corporate stock, and although major corporations are typically run by their top executives, there is no division of interest between these hired managers and big stockholders who do not hold such positions; we may regard the two groups, as did Mills, as members of a single class. There is considerable overlap between the national capitalist class and the national upper class represented by such institutions as the *Social Register* and exclusive men's clubs and prep schools; the upper class provides some of the social glue which binds the members of the capitalist class together. Finally, the national capitalist class has powerful means to shape national politics; these include placement of its members in top decision-making positions, campaign financing, lobbying, creation of policy-planning organizations, exercise of the business-confidence veto, and control of the public agenda through the mass media.

However, even so formidable an array of political resources cannot, as a pluralist would be quick to point out, be considered definitive evidence of capitalist-class domination. Any such broad conclusion would have to be based on a more comprehensive analysis of the political system than is possible within the bounds of this book. We are, however, committed to examining how social classes participate in the political system and how they interact in the political arena. With those goals in mind, we will amplify the picture we have painted here in the next chapter, which deals with class consciousness and conflict between classes in electoral and industrial contexts.

SUGGESTED READINGS

Aiken, Michael, and Paul E. Mott, eds. 1970. *The Structure of Community Power*. New York: Random House.
  Important collection of community power studies.

Bottomore, Tom. 1966. *Elites in Modern Society*. New York: Pantheon Books.
  Short, lucid survey of elite theory.

Domhoff, G. William. 1979. *The Powers that Be*. New York: Vintage Books.
  Synthesis of recent empirical work on the capitalist class.

Domhoff, G. William, and Hoyt B. Ballard, eds. 1968. *C. Wright Mills and the Power Elite*. Boston: Beacon Press.
  Excellent set of critical essays on Mills' power elite thesis.

Gold, David, et al. 1975. "Recent Developments in Marxist Theories of the Capitalist State." *Monthly Review* 27 (October): 29–43 and (November): 36–51.

Neat summary of recent debates among Marxist scholars concerning the character of the relationship between the capitalist class and the state.

Mosca, Gaetano. 1939. *The Ruling Class.* New York: McGraw-Hill.
  Classic theoretical work on political elites.

Pareto, Vilfredo. 1935. *Mind and Society.* New York: Harcourt Brace Jovanovich.
  Elite theory, reflecting influence of Mosca.

Rose, Arnold M. 1967. *The Power Structure: Political Process in American Society.* New York: Oxford University Press.
  A pluralist counterattack on Mills and Hunter.

Truman, David. 1971. *The Governmental Process: Political Interests and Public Opinion.* 2d ed. New York: Alfred A. Knopf.
  A classic pluralist interpretation of American politics.

Useem, Michael. 1980. "Corporations and the Corporate Elite." *Annual Review of Sociology* 6: 41–77.
  A recent review of the research literature.

Zeitlin, Maurice. 1977. *American Society, Inc.: Studies of the Social Structure and Political Economy of the United States.* 2d ed. Chicago: Rand-McNally.
  Useful collection covering the distribution of wealth, corporate ownership and control, and the national power structure.

Class consciousness and class conflict

I believe that leaders of the business community, with few exceptions, have chosen to wage a one-sided class war today in this country.

Douglas Fraser, president of the
United Auto Workers (1978)

9

We owe the concept of class consciousness to Karl Marx. Its role within his theory was pivotal, joining individual experience to broad social structures and transforming alienated individual resentment of the capitalist present into decisive striving for the socialist future.

Class consciousness implies an *awareness* of membership in a group defined by a relationship to production, a sense that this shared identity creates *common interests* and a common fate, and, finally, a disposition to take collective *action* in pursuit of class interests. At some points in his work, Marx implied that only a group whose members experience such a consciousness can be defined as a class. Elsewhere he carefully distinguished between a *class-in-itself* and a *class-for-itself*. The first is a class in a formal, definitional sense; its members share a social position (defined by the analyst) but are unaware of their common situation. The latter is a class in an active, historical sense: its members are aware of common interests; they engage in militant action focused on goals which they conceive as being in direct opposition to those of other classes, indeed, are defined by that opposition. Thus, embodied in Marx's conception of class consciousness— especially in the notion of a class-for-itself—is the expectation of class conflict.

In its fullest sense, class consciousness is not just an aspect of public opinion ("What percentage of blue-collar workers supported Roosevelt?") but an intense, collective involvement in the events of a critical historical juncture. It develops out of a long series of strikes against bosses who exploit workers and riots against authority that brutalizes the masses. It culminates in urban mobs roaming the streets and burning the buildings that symbolize upper-class domination and in peasants seizing the land they work, and it ends with a revolutionary seizure of power in the name of the oppressed: Paris in 1871, Mexico in 1910, Moscow in 1917, Peking in 1948, Havana in 1959.

Revolution is rare, but simmering class struggle is endemic. Slave revolts, violent strikes, local mobs on a rampage—these occur regularly in many societies. And more institutionalized and controlled forms of class struggle, such as union organizing campaigns and political movements that seek legislative power to help the underprivileged, are considered a normal and healthy part of a democratic society. Historians study past revolutions; sociologists usually focus on the early stages in the development of class consciousness, which could, under very specific historical circumstances, lead toward revolutionary consciousness but is more likely to result in peaceful change or historical stagnation. In this chapter, we will examine the extent to which people are aware of sharing a class identity and class interests, the social factors which advance or retard the development of this consciousness, and its relationship to political opinion and behavior. The final sections of the chapter will focus on class conflict as reflected in two arenas: electoral politics and labor relations.

MARX AND THE ORIGINS OF CLASS CONSCIOUSNESS

One of Marx's major objectives was to isolate the social forces which could produce the transformation of a class-in-itself into a class-for-itself; he hoped that by understanding the process he could determine how to intervene and speed it up. Specifically, he asked, What inherent tendencies of capitalist society are likely to produce a class-conscious proletariat? Here are the factors which are especially stressed in his work:

1. *Concentration and communication.* The process of industrialization in capitalist society concentrates the proletariat in big cities, working-class neighborhoods, and large factories. This process promotes communication among workers, leading to a recognition of common problems and facilitating efforts at political organization.
2. *Deprivation.* Marx expected a progressive impoverishment of the proletariat, if not in an absolute sense, at least relative to the rising productive capacity of the industrial economy and the wealth of the bourgeoisie.
3. *Economic insecurity.* Marx was convinced that the proletariat's sense of deprivation would be exacerbated by the periodic experience of unemployment during the downturns in the capitalist economy, which, he observed, is quite subject to boom-and-bust cycles.
4. *Alienation at work.* Marx identified the mindless, repetitive, unsatisfying quality of factory-type labor with capitalism. (For a modern rendition of this argument, see Braverman 1974). Such

labor is fundamentally at variance with human nature as Marx understood it and therefore is a spur to the development of class consciousness.

5. *Polarization.* The swings of the capitalist economy drive smaller enterprises out of business; their owners are forced into the proletariat, while control of the economy becomes further concentrated at the top. The result is the steady depletion of the middle ranks and the corresponding development of a society polarized between a miniscule, affluent bourgeois minority and an impoverished proletarian majority.

6. *Homogenization.* Within the proletariat, Marx observed a lowering of skill levels and therefore an equalization of wage levels produced by adaptation to the simple requirements of machine tending in the modern factory. This tendency leads to a less stratified, more homogeneous proletariat, which, because of its shared condition, is all the more disposed to unified political action.

7. *Organization and struggle.* In order to defend itself, the proletariat would be drawn increasingly into working-class parties and labor organizations. Participation in such organizations and the experience of struggle against capitalist employers and the bourgeois state and its police and armies would promote the development of hostile class consciousness and revolutionary struggle.

The revolutions which Marx's theory anticipated in the advanced industrial countries never came. However, class-based revolutions in industrializing agrarian states (Mexico, Russia, China, for example) have been a characteristic feature of 20th-century history. In the industrial nations, working-class parties and labor movements reshaped political systems and economic life. In both cases, the factors listed above have significantly changed events. Understood as variables which can depend upon specific circumstances, they can even help us understand the failure of revolution in the advanced countries. For example, the homogenization of the labor force which Marx predicted did not occur, as we saw in Chapter 3. Although property relations become polarized in the sense that most productive property was concentrated in the hands of a small minority, the relative differentiation of the bureaucratically organized occupational structure and the substantial range in incomes even among manual workers inhibited the emergence of a sense of common identity and the shared experience which are the basis of class consciousness. Furthermore, the profits from imperialist trade helped avoid the impoverishment of the industrial workers. We might say that Marx was sociologically correct in identifying the key processes, even if he was historically wrong in predicting their outcome.

LEGGETT: WORKING-CLASS CONSCIOUSNESS IN DETROIT

We begin our examination of the processes that generate class consciousness with one of the few recent studies in the United States that used systematic field study material to isolate some of the determinants of working-class awareness and hostility. John C. Leggett studied blue-collar workers in Detroit in order to find the specific differences that made some of them much more class conscious and politically aggressive than others. He reported on interviews with nearly 400 manual workers; they made up random samples of seven neighborhoods with distinctive ethnic compositions, allowing comparisons between blacks, Poles, and northwest Europeans.

Four criteria, which Leggett regarded as successively more stringent indicators of attitudes, were used to measure levels of class consciousness: class verbalization, skepticism, militancy, and egalitarianism. *Class verbalization* was indicated by class references in responses to a series of open-ended political questions, all devised to avoid any mention of class. For example, interviewees were asked which political party they preferred and why. The following was considered a class-conscious response: "[The Democratic Party] It's more for the working people. The Republicans are for business people and the corporations" (Leggett 1968: 163). *Skepticism* was measured by answers like "rich people," "big business," or "the upper class" in response to the question, "When business booms in Detroit, who profits?" *Militancy* was determined by an affirmative reply to an item requiring the respondent to imagine himself among working-class people who were planning protest action against landlords over high rents and poor housing: would he take part in protest activities, such as picketing? *Egalitarianism* was indicated by agreement with a statement to the effect that wealth in the country should be divided up more equally.

Leggett found that the four criteria formed a Guttman scale in the sense that most of those who gave class-conscious responses to the more restrictive items (e.g., egalitarianism) gave similar answers to all the weaker items (e.g., verbalization). Seventy-five percent of the respondents fit this pattern. The scale runs through five successive levels of class consciousness: class indifferents, class verbalizers, skeptics, militant radicals, and militant egalitarians. Class indifferents were those who gave no class-conscious responses. The rather extravagant labels given to the two highest categories refer, respectively, to those who responded affirmatively to the militancy item but negatively to the egalitarianism item and those who responded affirmatively to both. Leggett classified one third of the men inter-

viewed as militant radicals or egalitarians, a little over half as verbalizers or skeptics, and the remainder as indifferents.

Leggett was particularly interested in two sources of class consciousness, economic insecurity and working-class organization, both
suggested by Marx. He considered "uprootedness"—the experience
of being torn out of an agrarian region and thrust into an urban
industrial milieu—to be one source of economic insecurity. His
reasoning was that "the prepared," workers from industrialized regions, would not be plagued by the problems of adaptation to economic life which would plague "the uprooted," who should therefore
exhibit higher levels of class consciousness. Two subgroups within
the sample could be classified as uprooted: Southern-born blacks and
European-born Poles and Ukrainians. When uprooted members of
these two groups were compared with prepared members of the same
groups, it became clear that uprootedness did in fact contribute to
class consciousness. Fifty-two percent of the uprooted were class
militants (fell into the top two categories) as against 22 percent of the
prepared. Further analysis of the data established two significant
points: (1) workers who were not only from agrarian regions but
actually had farm experience were more class conscious than the uprooted generally, and (2) that tendency was increased among those
who joined labor unions in the city. Sixty-four percent of the men
who combined these characteristics were class militants (calculated
from Leggett 1968: figure 4–4, p. 64).

Leggett also found a significant difference in class consciousness
between the employed and unemployed, another confirmation of the
economic-insecurity thesis: 46 percent of unemployed versus 31 percent of employed workers were class militants. But a more complex
picture involving specific relationships among employment status,
race, and union organization lies behind this average result. Unemployed whites were more militant than employed whites; blacks were
more militant than whites; and union members were more militant
than nonunion workers. However, the difference between the employed and the unemployed for the entire sample was artificially
inflated by the overrepresentation of blacks among the unemployed.
Ironically, unemployed blacks were not more militant than employed
blacks, in part because employed blacks are more likely to be members of labor unions.

Leggett investigated two further aspects of economic insecurity:
the personal effects of the depression of the 1930s and of downward
mobility. On the assumption that the experience of the depression
would be a continuing source of radicalization (for which there was
already some support in voting studies), he compared workers who
were adolescents or adults during the 1930s with younger workers.

There was a small but measureable differentiation in class conscious-ness: 39 percent of the depression generation and 30 percent of younger workers were class militants.

Although some have speculated that the experience of downward mobility from middle class to working class might produce a heightened working-class militancy born of resentment over lost position, Leggett's research offers no support for this notion. In the Detroit sample, manual workers with middle-class fathers exhibited a substantially weaker working-class consciousness than nonmobile workers, which suggests the stability of class values developed in the course of middle-class socialization and the hope of regaining middle-class status. Since about 18 percent of working-class men have middle-class fathers (Featherman and Hauser 1978: 150), this tendency suggests that downward mobility contributes significantly to the dilution of working-class consciousness.

Black workers in Detroit revealed much higher levels of class con-sciousness than whites: 57 percent of the blacks were militants com-pared to 22 percent of the whites. Leggett found more class militants among blacks than among any other group or subgroup, and the difference between blacks and whites exceeded every other compari-son he recorded in the book. Leggett used blacks as an example of a *marginal minority*, which he defined as a "sub-community of workers who belong to a subordinate ethnic or racial group which is unusually proletarianized and highly segregated" (Leggett 1968: 14). Such groups are subject to greater economic insecurity than the general population. They are more or less culturally homogeneous and rela-tively isolated from middle-class contacts. Their members typically live in ethnic neighborhoods and belong to ethnically identified for-mal organizations—churches, social clubs, political groups. These so-cial features might be expected to amplify working-class conscious-ness. They were partially shared by communities of Polish and Ukrainian workers, whom Leggett classified as *semimarginal* and who were, in fact, much more class conscious than workers of British and German descent, though less so than blacks.

In an effort to sort out the relative importance of different sources of class consciousness, Leggett performed a correlational analysis of eight different predictors of class consciouness: race-ethnicity, union membership, uprootedness, downward mobility, generation, skill level, employment status, and personal income. A multivariate analysis showed that the eight factors collectively explained a re-spectable 40 percent of the variance in the scale of class conscious-ness. Most of the result could be attributed to three key factors: race-ethnicity, union membership, and uprootedness.

Ultimately the reason for studying class consciousness is the as-sumption that it influences political behavior. Leggett measured the political effect of class consciousness by asking respondents whether they had backed Governor G. Mennen Williams (1948–60), a progressive who was identified as prolabor and supportive of liberal economic measures and civil rights initiatives. He found that Williams was supported by 76 percent of the class militants in the Detroit sample but only 50 percent of the verbalizers and class indifferents. Again there was a significant race difference: 76 percent of blacks were for Williams, against 59 percent of whites (Leggett 1968: 122). Largely because of his civil rights stands, black support of Williams was so broad that level of class consciousness made little difference. Leggett did not indicate whether race hostility influenced white workers' reactions to Williams, although he could have easily done so given the data he had at hand.

The relatively mild items on the Detroit questionnaire certainly do not tap the intense common commitment and revolutionary drive that Marx had in mind when he wrote of class consciousness. Nor do the responses Leggett recorded reveal any desire to test the limits of existing capitalist society. But he did show that Detroit workers were aware of class and class interests and that this consciousness was reflected in their political behavior. He also demonstrated that consciousness was advanced, as Marx led us to expect, by working-class organization and economic insecurity. However, the Detroit study uncovered sources of economic insecurity whose significance was underestimated by Marx. Current unemployment and memories of the depression fit neatly with Marx's focus on the boom-and-bust dynamics of the capitalist economy, but the same cannot be said of uprootedness and marginal minority status. In this chapter, we will frequently return to the theme of ethnic subordination suggested by the last factor.

THE ORIGINS OF WORKING-CLASS CONSCIOUSNESS IN COMPARATIVE PERSPECTIVE

Empirical studies of class consciousness such as Leggett's are relatively rare, in part because they typically depend on data gathered through costly surveys. But there is another way of getting at the origins of class consciousness: instead of looking at the social correlates of class-oriented opinion, we can look at the correlates of class-oriented political behavior represented in voting patterns. This admittedly back-door approach to the topic is justified by the evidence we have from Leggett and some of the other authors we will be discussing that class consciousness does in fact predict voting behavior; besides, this focus has the distinct advantage of turning dozens of voting studies from all the world's democracies into grist for our mill.

Here we will limit ourselves to looking at influences on working-class voters. Later in the chapter, we will look at voting from a slightly different perspective involving all classes.

Our task is simplified by the fact that two sociologists, Lipset (1960) and Szymanski (1978), have synthesized the relevant research. Nearly all the studies they examined present data on working-class support for leftist or liberal parties—in the United States, the Democratic party; and in Europe, communist and socialist parties. We can summarize much of what Lipset and Szymanski found with the following list of social correlates of leftist/liberal voting among workers:

Lower skill level.

Unemployment.

Union membership.

Larger city.

Larger workplace.

Economically advanced region.

Minority ethnic or religious group.

Specific occupations:
  Miner, fisherman, sailor, longshoreman, forestry worker.

Male.

Working-class origin.

These variables, some of them already familiar from Leggett's research, point to several general forces which shape working-class consciousness. One concerns the relative opportunities for intraclass and interclass communication. When working-class people have substantial interaction with one another and live in near isolation from members of other classes, they are most likely to develop a common identity and political consciousness. Most of the occupations listed above fit this description in the extreme. Workers in these jobs are not only likely to vote left, they are also very prone to militant labor action. Kerr and Siegel (1954), in a classic study of industrial conflict in 11 countries, found that workers in the mining, maritime and longshore, lumber, and textile industries have the highest propensity to strike. One characteristic distinguishes workers in these sectors from the employees of less strike-prone industries: they are concentrated in what the authors term "an isolated mass" (Kerr and Siegal 1954: 191–93):

> They live in their own separate communities: the coal patch, the ship, the waterfront district, the logging camp, the textile town. These communities have their own codes, myths, heroes, and social standards. There are few neutrals in them to mediate conflicts and dilute the mass. All people have grievances, but what is important is that all members of each of these groups have the same grievances. . . . The employees

form a largely homogeneous, undifferentiated mass—they all do about the same work and have about the same experiences. Here you do not have the occupational stratification of the metal or building crafts, of the hotel or restaurant, or of the government bureau. . . . In these communities there are not the myriad of voluntary associations with mixed memberships which characterize the multi-industry town. . . . The employer throws out few lines to these workers. He is usually an absentee owner who "cuts out and gets out" in the logging business or exhausts a mine. . . . The worker is as detached from the employer as from the community at large. The union becomes a kind of working-class party or even government for these employees, rather than another association among many.

Several of the variables on our list contribute in ways less dramatic than the creation of an isolated mass to intraclass communication and semi-isolation. In large factories, blue-collar employees may seldom see, much less interact with, managers. Similarly in larger cities, workers are likely to live in class-segregated neighborhoods and have few social contacts with middle-class people. Class origins can also contribute to isolation, since people of working-class origins are likely to have working-class kin and spend much of their leisure time with them. By contrast, the tendency of middle-class origins to dilute class consciousness was shown by Leggett's data.

Contemporary labor unions are regarded by many leftist intellectuals as conservatizing institutions. Judged by their potential to create a revolutionary consciousness in workers, this is certainly an accurate characterization. Nevertheless, voting data from eight countries demonstrated a consistent association between union membership and support of leftist parties (Szymanski 1978: 71).

The influence of economic insecurity is also reflected in some of the variables of the list. This is obviously the case with unemployment, but also with low skill level, minority ethnic status, and the specific occupations indicated, since workers with these characteristics tend to have the lowest job security.

Interestingly enough, income per se is not included among the variables. Were we considering all classes, income would be an important predictor of political attitudes, but *within the working class*, its influence is quite inconsistent. We might expect the poorest workers to have the strongest complaint against the system. On the other hand, the poor are frequently politically uninformed and too distracted by problems of the moment to concern themselves with larger matters. Szymanski (1978: 57) presented relevant evidence on working-class voting in seven countries. In three cases, higher income was associated with stronger support for the left, in three the reverse was true, and in one the relationship was irregular. In Leggett's study (1968: 182) the correlation between income and class consciousness was close to zero. Two careful empirical studies, conducted in the United States and Britain, of the so-called *embourgeois-ment* thesis—the notion that workers tend to adopt middle-class values and political attitudes as they become more affluent—ended up rejecting the idea (Hamilton 1967; Goldthorpe et al. 1968). Only when people move to middle-class jobs do they begin to change their views in a consistent way.

Alienation at work, another factor in the development of class consciousness, is represented on our list by skill level and size of workplace. Unskilled and semiskilled workers are the most frequently subject to close discipline at work, especially in large-scale industrial settings where they are likely to be engaged in repetitive tasks within a minutely fragmented division of labor. It is not surprising that such workers are the least satisfied with their jobs and the most likely to support the left.

As we have indicated, minority ethnic or religious status is often a source of leftist political attitudes because it is often associated with economic and social deprivation. But even members of minority groups who are economically secure, such as middle- and upper-income Catholics and Jews in the United States, tend toward the left. This may in part reflect the intergenerational transfer of allegiances developed during less propitious times. The attitudes of Jewish and Catholic descendents of the new immigrants are consistent with this explanation. But a sense of deprivation based on continuing prestige differences may also be responsible for the maintenance of a political gap between majority and minorities in many countries.

The reference to gender on our list of variables may seem incongrous, yet there is substantial evidence indicating that women are more conservative than men. Szymanski (1978: 100) cited evidence from elections in 11 countries consistently showing that women were less likely to support leftist parties. However, the political differences between men and women in the United States are relatively trivial, at least where economic issues are at stake (Szymanski 1978: 99–102). Since working-class socialization places the greatest emphasis on gender differences, we would expect sex differentials in political attitudes to be greatest in the working class. Both Szymanski and Lipset associated female conservatism with traditionalism which involves acceptance of the world as it is and submission to authority—in the family, the factory, the community, and the church.

The correlates of support for the left among blue-collar voters suggest, then, that intraclass communication and class isolation, labor organization, income insecurity, alienation at work, the situation of ethnic minorities, and freedom from traditional values are all fundamental to the development of working-class consciousness. Returning again to our summary of Marx's sociology of class consciousness, we find all but the last two factors presaged in his work. Even ethnicity and traditionalism received occasional, though begrudging, recognition there. He seems to have regarded both as remnants of a lost world which would be rapidly swept away by the growth of modern society; a century after his death, it appears that he was wrong. More generally we can reaffirm our initial assessment: Marx succeeded as a sociologist even where he failed as a prophet.

RICHARD CENTERS AND CLASS IDENTIFICATION

Our concern with class consciousness is based on the idea that it provides a link between objective class position (measured in terms of occupation, income, or wealth) and political behavior. That is, we assume that people who recognize and articulate their class position are more likely to promote their class interests. The most systematic and sustained effort to investigate this linkage on a national scale grows out of the work of Richard Centers (1949), who focused on one aspect of class consciousness, *class identity*, or the sense of belonging to a particular social class.

Centers began by noting that in previous public opinion surveys (such as the famous one conducted by *Fortune* magazine in 1940), about 80 per cent of Americans consistently called themselves middle class. Some popular writers seized upon these figures to proclaim that America was almost completely a middle-class country—that if we had any class consciousness at all, it simply meant that we mostly thought of ourselves as belonging to the same big group. But Centers noticed that the figure quoted came from the following survey item, which offered only three alternatives:

What social class do you consider that you belong to?
1. Upper class
2. Middle class
3. Lower class

He also noticed that when respondents were asked the question in open-ended form (without a specific list of answers from which to choose), many called themselves working class. Centers made a reputation for himself by changing the wording of the fixed answers, adding working class as one of the possible replies. When he asked a nationally representative cross section of 1,097 adult white men in 1945 which class they belonged to, offering them the four alternative answers, he got the following replies:

Upper class	3%
Middle class	43
Working class	51
Lower class	1
Don't know	1
"Don't believe in classes"	1
Total	100%

In subsequent samples, he got almost the same distribution. Centers rightly concluded that Americans do not like the term *lower class* and that this dislike was the main conclusion to be drawn from the *Fortune* survey, not that they actually thought of themselves as overwhelmingly middle class. His confidence in the results of the surveys was strengthened by the fact that only a tiny minority of respondents refused to accept one of the labels suggested in the question: even fewer were inclined to deny the existence of social classes. Centers was moved to say, "The authenticity of these class identifications seems unquestionable" (Centers 1949: 78). Since 1945, numerous national surveys—we treat some of them below—have employed questions modeled on Center's forced-choice class-identification item, obtaining similar but not identical results.

A few years after Centers published his findings, Kahl and Davis (1955) examined class identification as part of a Cambridge, Massachusetts, study. Before posing Centers's question, the investigators asked their respondents to describe the class system "in this part of the country" in their own words, and followed with an open-ended class-identification question which avoided giving answers to interviewees: "What social class do you think you are in?" The response to Center's item was just about what he had obtained nationally, but the preliminary questions elicited a very different pattern of replies. Responding to the open-ended items, over 20 percent of the sample denied the existence of class or answered using occupational or other categories unrelated to Centers's class categories. Among those who spontaneously selected labels that were on Centers's list, middle class was the most popular choice. However, many of these middle-class identifiers shifted to working class when presented with the forced-choice question, as did many who initially avoided class labels.

These findings throw cold water on Centers's confident assertion quoted above. We can assume that the forced-choice question is in some sense a measure of class consciousness since, as we will see, responses to it are related to both class position and political attitudes. However, the Cambridge research tells us that we cannot use the answers as literal descriptions of the way people freely conceive of their own class positions.

CORRELATES OF CLASS IDENTIFICATION

What types of persons chose the particular labels offered in class-identification surveys? Centers regarded occupation as the principal basis of class identification. When he sorted respondents by occupation, he found that 70 percent or more of professionals and businessmen considered themselves middle class, while over 70 percent of manual workers considered themselves working class. A series of election year surveys conducted from 1956 to 1968 by the University of Michigan's Survey Research Center (SRC) obtained similar results (Schreiber and Nygreen 1970). But as even these figures indicate, there was not complete consensus. Center's data conform to a pattern which is by now familiar: the results were fairly clear-cut at the extremes of the class structure but somewhat ambiguous in the middle. In particular, over a third of sales and office workers among Centers's respondents and about half among the SRC respondents labeled themselves working class (Centers 1949: 86, Hamilton 1975).

Centers's view that occupation is the main determinant of identification is supported by Hodge and Treiman's (1968) analysis of 1964 SRC survey. They found that occupation (of the family's main earner) was a stronger predictor of class identification than either family income or respondent's education, but the three variables considered together left much of the variance in class identification unaccounted for. Objective class position seemed to be a crucial but not decisive determinant of this aspect of class consciousness.

Hodge and Treiman experimented with several additional variables in an effort to isolate other influences on class identification, but they only found one additional factor which was significantly and independently related to class identification: patterns of association. The class positions of friends, neighbors, and kin proved to be strong influences on the formation of class identification. The data available to measure this variable were somewhat crude but serviceable; the survey simply determined whether respondents had *any* friends, *any* neighbors or *any* relatives in several broad occupational categories. For example, 57 percent of those who had high-status friends, neighbors, and kin, but no low-status contacts in any of these categories, identified themselves as upper or upper-middle class. Only 7 percent of those in the opposite situation did so. Of course, the contacts of a respondent can partly be explained by his or her status, but not entirely so: Hodge and Treiman found association to have an independent influence on class identification. Put differently, your class identification depends partly on your objective class position and partly on whom you know. Together, occupation, income, education, and association explain only about one fifth of the variance in class identification.

MARRIED WOMEN AND CLASS IDENTIFICATION

Centers's original class identification surveys referred only to men, but the SRC data cover both men and women. If we are interested in the relationship between objective class position and identification, the inclusion of women raises an intriguing problem: do working wives base their class identification on their husband's occupation, their own occupation, or some combination of the two? Hodge and Treiman implicitly allowed for the influence of the wife's job on the self-placement of both spouses when they measured earnings in terms of *family* income. But by defining occupation for all respondents as "main earner's occupation"—the husband's in most house-holds—they ducked the questions posed above.

TABLE 9–1
Percentage of women reporting middle-class identification, by own and husband's occupation

Occupation of wife	N	Occupation of husband				
		Professional, technical, and managerial	Clerical and sales	Craftsmen and foremen	Operatives, service, and laborers	All occupations
Professional, technical, and managerial	127	85	67	56	44	72
Clerical and sales	213	69	48	32	27	45
Operatives, service, and laborers	213	35	50	24	15	22
All occupations	553	73	52	35	21	43

Source: Kathleen V. Ritter and Lowell L. Hargens, "Occupational Positions and Class Identifications of Married Women," *American Journal of Sociology* 80 (1975): 939.

Table 9–1, drawn from a paper by Ritter and Hargens (1975), considers the effect of both spouses' occupations on the class identification of wives. Their data are from four SRC surveys, conducted between 1960 and 1970, which asked respondents to choose between working-class and middle-class identification. The table indicates that both a woman's own occupation and her husband's influences her choice. For example, reading down the leftmost column shows that the proportion of wives of professionals who identify themselves as middle class falls off appreciably as the woman's own occupational rank declines. A comparison of the polar cases—professional wives with husbands in the lowest blue-collar positions and professional husbands with wives in such occupations—suggests that the effect of husband's position is slightly greater. After further analysis, Ritten and Hargens concluded that the influence of wife's occupation and husband's occupation on her self-placement are probably close to equal. They also find a significant, though less powerful, influence of a woman's father's occupation on her own class identification.

Ritter and Hargens do not estimate the effect of wives' occupations on the overall pattern of class identification—their impact on both men and women, independent of other variables we have examined. Furthermore, this effect is limited by the fact that wives' and husbands' occupations are correlated with one another. As we would expect, the data showed very few respondents in the high-low polar categories alluded to above. Only about 17 percent of the wives of white-collar men hold blue-collar jobs; while the proportion of wives of working-class men holding white-collar positions is significantly larger, it is likely that such women are concentrated in the lowest sorts of clerical or sales positions. The keypunch operator and the salesclerk at Woolworth's come to mind.

We may speculate that women and men answering the class identification question are not simply weighing two occupations but are thinking in terms of a standard and style of living, a set of associations, and particular values and attitudes that are shared by the members of a household. Traditionally, all of these things were largely dependent on the husband's job, and it was reasonable to assume that the class positions of most individuals were socially fixed by the characteristics of the (male) heads of their families. But as women's labor force participation rates have risen and permanent dependence on two incomes has become a critical fact of life for many families, the traditional assumption has become a dubious notion. Ritter and Hargens' findings are consistent with the idea that the family continues to be the relevant basis of class position, but the standing of families is no longer solely dependent on the activities of men.

TRENDS IN CLASS IDENTIFICATION

The continuing use of class identification questions modeled on Centers in national surveys opens the possibility of plotting long-term trends in the pattern of self-placement. We would be interested in any shift in the pattern because it could indicate that Americans were becoming less or more or somewhat differently class conscious.

Any attempt to measure such trends runs into a methodological problem: we have to be sure that the successive studies we use are in fact comparable. Kahl and Davis (1955) demonstrated that open-ended and forced-choice items produce very different results, but even relatively minor alterations in the wording of forced-choice items can affect the response (Schreiber and Nygreen 1970). However, there are two series of national surveys which repeatedly administered the same question to compatible national samples, the Survey Research Center election year series to which we have already referred and the General Social Surveys carried out by NORC. The SRC surveys covered white males age 21 and over. Some of the results are reported in Table 9–2.

The SRC surveys measured class identification with the following item (Schreiber and Nygreen 1970: 349):

> There is quite a bit of talk these days about different social classes. Most people say they belong either to the middle class or the working class. Do you ever think of yourself as being in one of these classes? (If yes) Which one? (If no) Well, if you had to make a choice.

In 1968, "being in" was changed to "belonging in."

The shape of the data is clear enough: the proportion of respondents labeling themselves working class expanded until 1960 and then dropped below the 1956 level. The proportion calling themselves middle class followed an opposite trajectory.

If, as it appears, the proportion of working-class identifiers was declining in the 1960s, to what can this be attributed? A common explanation is the shifting occupational structure. We could reasonably expect the expansion in white-collar employment to be paralleled by a decrease in the number of working-class identifiers. But Schreiber and Nygreen's SRC data allow us to discard this idea. The percentage drop in working-class identifiers from 1960 to 1968 was the same among manual workers as it was for the sample as a whole, down from about 85 to 76 percent. So the change did not depend on any occupational reshuffling; something else was going on. But it was a short-run tendency, as shown by the NORC surveys from the 1970s which indicated that the pattern of class identification was not changing during that decade (Table 9–3), despite further growth of

TABLE 9–2
Class identification in SRC surveys, 1956–1968 (percent)

Class	Survey year				
	1956	1958	1960	1964	1968
Middle class	39%	39%	33%	43%	45%
Working class	58	60	65	53	52
Don't know	1	*	*	1	2
Reject idea of class	2	1	2	2	1
Total†	100	100	100	100	100

* Less than 0.5 percent.
† May not add to 100 due to rounding. Sample sizes range from 483 to 667.
Source: E. M. Schreiber and G. T. Nygreen, "Subjective Social Class in America: 1945–1968," *Social Forces* 48 (1970): 351.

nonmanual occupations. The General Social Surveys carried out by NORC included an item quite similar to Centers's question:

> If you were asked to use one of four names for your social class, which would you say you belong in: the lower class, the working class, the middle class, or the upper class?

The responses, which were quite stable over the period covered, show that Americans are still slightly more likely to call themselves working class than middle class. Since the wording of the NORC item is quite similar to that employed by Centers in 1949, it is tempting to make comparisons. The NORC results suggest that the proportion of middle-class identifiers has not changed, but the lower-class identification has grown a few percent at the expense of working-class identification. This apparent change may, however, simply reflect differences in the samples: NORC covered all people over 18, not just white men.

In sum, there is no evidence of a consistent trend altering the pattern of class identification over the three decades since Centers's original survey, in spite of very sweeping changes in the occupational structure.

CLASS IDENTIFICATION, POLITICAL OPINION, AND VOTING

Our interest in class identification, like our concern with class consciousness generally, stems from the idea that consciousness is a link between class position and political attitudes and behavior. After Centers had satisfied himself that class identification was closely correlated with occupation, he went on to explore its relationship to

TABLE 9–3
Class identification in NORC surveys, 1972–1978 (percent)

Class	Survey year		
	1972	1975	1978
Upper class	2%	3%	2%
Middle class	44	44	45
Working class	47	48	47
Lower class	7	5	5
No class; don't know	0	*	*
Total†	100	100	100

* Less than 0.5 percent.
† May not add to 100 due to rounding. Sample sizes about 1500.
Source: National Opinion Research Center, *General Social Surveys, 1972–1978: Cumulative Codebook* (Chicago: University of Chicago Press, 1978), p. 125.

ideological differences. For this purpose he constructed a "conservatism-radicalism battery" of six questions, which he administered to respondents in the national surveys discussed earlier (Centers 1949):

1. Do you agree or disagree that America is truly a land of opportunity and that people get pretty much what's coming to them in this country?
2. Would you agree that everybody would be happier, more secure, and more prosperous if the working people were given more power and influence in government, or would you say that we would all be better off if the working people had no more power than they have now?
3. As you know, during this war many private businesses and industries have been taken over by the government. Do you think wages and salaries would be fairer, jobs more steady, and that we would have fewer people out of work if the government took over and ran our mines, factories, and industries in the future, or do you think things would be better under private ownership?
4. Which one of these statements do you most agree with? (1) The most important job for the government is to make it certain that there are good opportunities for each person to get ahead on his own. (2) The most important job for the government is to guarantee every person a decent and steady job and standard of living.
5. In strikes and disputes between working people and employers, do you usually side with the workers or with the employers?
6. Do you think working people are usually fairly and squarely treated by their employers or that employers sometimes take advantage of them?

He then scored each question according to whether the answer favored the working people and government intervention (radical) or employers and individual initiative (conservative). Each question was weighted equally, and an additive score was computed for every respondent showing whether his answers were predominantly in one direction or the other. Centers ended up with five categories of persons: ultraconservative, conservative, indeterminate, radical, and ultraradical.

The questions in Centers's battery do not form a scale in the sense that Leggett's ideological battery does; for example, two persons giving conservative answers to four out of the six questions will not necessarily answer the same four questions conservatively (Case 1953). The criterion of scalability that Centers applied was much less rigorous; he intercorrelated the answers to the specific questions and found that they tended to hang together. It seems permissible to use the battery as a first approximation toward politico-economic attitudes, but it is a limited tool. After all, different issues will divide people along different lines; people who are conservative in the sense that they oppose labor unions may be radical in support of women's rights.

How do conservatism and radicalism relate to class identification? *Perhaps the main finding of Centers was that answers to the identification question were predictive of answers to the ideological battery.* Let us contrast the percentages of self-labeled middle-class and working-class persons who fell into the various ideological categories (Centers 1949: 20):

	Middle class	Working class
Ultraconservative	35%	12%
Conservative	33	23
Indeterminate	21	33
Radical	7	19
Ultraradical	4	13
Totals	100%	100%

The conservative persons were more likely to come from the middle class, the radicals from the working class (all five differences within rows were statistically significant). The overall tetrachoric correlation between class identification and ideology is .49 (it is slightly higher for urban than for rural persons). Note, however, that the differences are due entirely to the middle-class persons, who were conservative and consistently avoided radical answers. But the working class gave as many conservative as radical answers (and a great many working-class persons were "indeterminate," which means they gave inconsistent answers).

Centers further discovered that if he held occupation constant and varied class identification, he got substantial variations in ideology. Thus business, professional, and white-collar people were generally conservative, *but those who called themselves middle class were much more so* than the minority who called themselves working class. Similarly, the minority of manual workers who called themselves middle class were more conservative than the rest of the manual workers, who called themselves working class (though this difference was less marked than the preceding one). The details are shown in Table 9–4. Comparisons such as these led Centers to say that his data supported the "interest-group" theory of social class behavior, for it seemed that appropriately class-conscious members of a stratum had attitudes more typical of that stratum than did the minority whose objective occupational status and subjective identification were at variance.

TABLE 9–4
Occupational stratum, class identification, and conservatism-radicalism

Stratum and class identification	N	Conservatism-radicalism (percent)			
		Conservative	Indeterminate	Radical	Total
Urban business, professional and white collar:					
Middle class	298	74	20	6	100
Working class	100	47	30	23	100
Urban manual workers:					
Middle class	83	37	30	33	100
Working class	318	25	34	41	100

Source: Richard Centers, *The Psychology of Social Classes*, (Princeton, N.J.: Princeton University Press, 1949), p. 126.

We might add, "Almost, but not quite." Careful inspection of Table 9–4 discloses that one gets slightly better prediction of ideology by varying occupation than by varying class identification. This is neatly summarized by Centers's tetrachoric correlation coefficients: The correlation between identification and ideology is 0.49, whereas that between occupation and ideology is 0.56. True, the difference is small, but if class consciousness were an intervening variable between occupation and ideology, the difference should go in the opposite direction. That is, if occupation produces class consciousness, which in turn produces ideology, then people who have "false consciousness" should have false beliefs—i.e., manual workers who consider themselves middle class should have middle-class beliefs. The data show that their beliefs are in between but closer to those of other workers than to those of business people. A cautious interpretation of the data would suggest that both class consciousness and ideology tend to be consequents of occupational position, but the sequence of causation between class consciousness and ideology is not clear. Futhermore, there is much causation left entirely unexplained after both predictors have been used.

RECENT STUDIES OF CLASS IDENTIFICATION AND POLITICS

Since the publication of Centers's work, other researchers have examined the relationship between class identification and ideology using data from the SRC election surveys. In their classic study, *The American Voter* (1960, 1964), Angus Campbell and his SRC colleagues found a stronger independent relationship between class identification and political orientation than is evident in Centers's data. Using the two-step SRC identification item, they distinguished between respondents who indicated that they had previously thought of themselves as belonging to the middle or working class and those who had not done so but were willing to choose one or the other "if you had to." The former were labeled "class aware" to distinguish them from those who were only inclined to identify with a class when required to by the question. The latter constituted about one third of the 1952 and 1956 survey samples the researchers employed.

The Michigan group found that occupation and class identification were about equally efficient as predictors of political attitudes or voting preference. This finding parallels Centers's results. However, class awareness proved to be a substantially stronger predictor of the political variables than was occupation. In other words, class awareness is a kind of "super" class identification which comes closer to measuring "true" class consciousness and looks more like a direct link between objective class position and personal politics. Among the class aware there was a fairly strong association between class identification and liberal or conservative stances on such issues as government responsibility for full employment. Among the unaware the association was relatively weak. A similar pattern emerges with regard to Democratic or Republican partisanship, with the aware working class most likely to vote Democratic. In effect, the less-developed class consciousness of the unaware dilutes class polarization in politics. According to the researchers, the fact that some association between class identification and political orientation is evident among the unaware probably reflects the influence of friends and kin among whom "attitudes 'appropriate' to the individual's class may be taken on without recognition of their class relevance" (Campbell et al. 1964: 194).

The Michigan group also made comparisons between those whose class identification was consistent with their occupational positions and the "misidentifiers," such as manual workers who chose the middle-class label. For *both* groups, voting behavior was associated with class identification, although the correlation was weaker for the misidentifiers. Except among those with a very low level of interest in politics, the misidentifiers were more likely to vote with the subjective class label they had chosen than with their objective class position. This conclusion strengthens Centers's argument for class identification as a critical link between class position and political behavior.

A more recent piece by Avery Guest (1974) examined political orientations with the 1956 through 1968 SRC data. Guest did not consider objective class position at all but focused instead on the aware-unaware distinction in class identification introduced by the Michigan group. His reanalysis of the data revealed a more complicated picture than the Michigan researchers had recorded. In brief, he found that class awareness operated in the expected fashion among working-class identifiers but produced unanticipated results among middle-class identifiers.

Guest divided respondents into four class identification-awareness categories and used these categories to analyze responses to questions dealing with government responsibility for job creation, medical care, and education (Table 9–5). As a quick scan of the table will show, class identification was consistently associated with the positions taken on these issues: working-class identifiers were much more likely to give liberal responses than were middle-class identifiers.

If awareness functions as a super class identification, we would expect the four respondent categories to be arrayed on a liberalism-conservatism spectrum with the class aware at the ideological extremes as follows: aware working class, unaware working class, unaware middle class, aware middle class. In fact, working-class aware persons were the most likely to take liberal positions on these issues, followed by the working-class unaware. But in most cases, the aware middle class was closer than the unaware middle class to the working-class (liberal) end of spectrum. In other words, the unaware middle class was the most consistently conservative in its responses.

TABLE 9– 5
Domestic issue liberalism, by level of class awareness

	Percent agreeing with liberal position			
Issue	Aware working class	Unaware working class	Aware middle class	Unaware middle class
Employment guarantee:*				
1960	71	57	53	54
1968	36	28	29	28
Medical care:†				
1960	76	54	44	50
1968	65	59	54	55
Aid to education:‡				
1960	65	53	51	53
1968	31	28	25	33

* 1960   "The government in Washington ought to see to it that everybody who wants to work can find a job."
   1968   "In general, some people feel that the government in Washington should see to it that every person has a job and a good standard of living. Others think the government should just let each person get ahead on his own."
† 1960   "The government ought to help people get doctors and hospital care at low cost."
   1968   "Some people say the government in Washington ought to help people get doctors and hospital care at low cost; others say the government should not get into this."
‡ 1960   "If cities and towns around the country need help to build more schools, the government in Washington ought to give them the money they need."
   1968   "Some people think the government in Washington should help towns and cities provide education for grade and high school children; others think that this should be handled by the states and local communities."
Source: Avery M. Guest, "Class Consciousness and American Political Attitudes," *Social Forces* 52 (1974): 500.

Voting preferences followed the same pattern: the aware working class was the most likely to vote Democratic and the unaware middle class was the least likely to do so. Here there is an interesting twist. In the years when the Democrats were victorious, the gap in electoral preferences between the aware and unaware in each identification class narrowed. Guest contended that this happens when class issues have become more salient and tend to polarize people regardless of their level of class awareness. On the other hand, the Republicans, whose conservative ideology tends to appeal to a relatively small constituency drawn from the upper-middle and upper strata, thrive when the focus is on personalities or issues without clear class implications.

The effect of class awareness conforms neatly to Marxist expectations where the working class is concerned: the group which appears the most class conscious is the most likely to recognize its class interests and act (vote) accordingly. In short, the most conscious are the most militant.

Why shouldn't the same formula hold for the middle class? Guest offers no satisfactory answer, and perhaps the issue can only be resolved through more careful scrutiny of the data. We would want to know, for example, whether there were any significant social differences between the aware and the unaware. Perhaps the class identification question means something different to working-class and middle-class identifiers. When some respondents say that they have already thought of themselves as belonging to the working class, they are asserting more than an identity; they are recording their prior recognition of shared political interests. Those who have previously thought of themselves as middle class may have simply recognized themselves as "average" and therefore without distinctive political interests. On the other hand, the unaware middle-class identifiers may have had some other self-identification (businessman, professional?) which, without referring explicitly to class, is connected to class interests. And as always, mobility from one class to another must be suspected as an important additional influence.

FRAMES OF REFERENCE

The various sets of data concerning self-identification or class consciousness in America, and the connections between identification and ideology, do not automatically fit together, because the researchers used different techniques. However, if we borrow some general ideas from social psychology, and also attempt to apply to American data some interpretations that were first suggested by British researchers exploring very similar data which they gathered, we can arrive at a tentative synthesis.

Elizabeth Bott has pointed out that "people do not experience their objective class position as a single clearly defined status." We might add that such clear definitions are the result of calculated decisions on the part of academic researchers; *they* are the ones who create concepts like "upper-middle class" or "bourgeoisie" and through hard thinking attach some specific empirical criteria for membership (granted, they may start with words in popular usage, but by the time they have finished their ratiocinations, the original words have taken on new meanings). Naturally, they endow their concepts with connotations that derive from the researchers' own general philosophy; thus Warner thought of strata of prestige and the Marxists of actual or latent conflict groups. Then the researchers go into the field and try to discover the degree to which the populace thinks as the concepts suggest they should, and the investigators feel a growing sense of triumph the more closely they can fit the data to the concepts.

But, said Bott:

> When an individual talks about class he is trying to say something, in a symbolic form, about his experiences of power and prestige in his actual membership groups both past and present. These membership groups—place of work, friends, neighbours, family, etc—have little intrinsic connection with one another, especially in a large city, and each of the groups has its own pattern of organization. The psychological situation for the individual, therefore, is one of belonging to a number of segregated, un-connected groups, each with its own system of prestige and power. When he is comparing himself with other people or placing himself in the widest social context, he manufactures a notion of his general social position out of these segregated group memberships. . . . The group memberships are not differentiated and related to one another; they are telescoped and condensed into one general notion (1954: 262).

The man—or woman—in the street is aided in conceptualizing by ideas and terms that have diffused into popular culture from intellectual debate. Thus, especially in Europe, there are many factory workers who have been subjected to long propaganda that stems from Marxist ideology; naturally, they not only use class-conflict terminology, they actually perceive their own position and interpret their everyday experiences in conflict terms. Similarly, the American middle classes have been bombarded with propaganda about our equality and absence of classes. Consequently, they tend to perceive as individual differences experiences that a European would see as common class experiences.

Therefore, any individual's self perception in a stratification order is a combination of (1) actual experiences in a wide variety of contexts in many membership groups and (2) verbal theories about society, which are usually vague and somewhat contradictory commonsense notions that have filtered down from the theorizing of intellectuals and propagandists. Consequently, the social reality of identification that we are studying is complex rather than simple, and when we simplify it (as we must for certain purposes) into categories like middle class or working class, we do violence to the original facts. The simpler and neater the scheme, the further it is from reality.

Let us complicate the picture even more. Bott went on to point out that

> the individual performs a telescoping procedure on other people as well as on himself. If they are people who have the same, or similar, group memberships as himself, he is likely to feel that they have the same general position and belong to his own class. If they are outsiders, his knowledge of them will be indirect and incomplete so that there is plenty of room for projection and distortion. . . .
>
> The suggestion advanced here is that there are three steps in an individual's creation of a class reference group: first, he internalizes the norms of his primary membership groups—place of work, colleagues, friends, neighbourhood, family—together with some more hazy notions about the wider society; secondly he performs an act of conceptualization in reducing these segregated norms to a common denominator; thirdly, he projects his conceptualization back on to society at large. . . . The main point is that the individual himself is an active agent. He does not simply internalize the norms of class which have an independent external existence. He takes in the norms of certain actual groups, works them over, and constructs class reference groups out of them (1954: 263–65).

Finally, Bott reminded us that because the conceptualizations were both hazy and tied to a variety of actual experiences in the life history of an individual, they could shift in the course of an interview. Sometimes respondents would think in terms of the people they knew in their hometown as children; sometimes of their workmates; sometimes of their dreams for their own children. These shifts, plus those of the forms of the questions being asked, would lead them to shift frames of reference.

The interviews that Bott conducted in London paralleled the American data and showed at least four different models of the class structure that could be used by different respondents or by the same respondent at different points in an interview:

1. Two-valued power models.
2. Three-valued prestige models.
3. Many-valued prestige models.
4. Mixed power and prestige models.

The power model tends to be reduced to a two-level system because it takes two to make a fight, and respondents tend to think primarily of themselves (and their colleagues) versus all the rest. Respondents whose own experiences had involved considerable conflict would be likely to think of a two-level system of conflict. *But they would almost all be members of the working class.* Middle-class persons—even those with a personality predisposition to conflict—would have certain experiences and interests that would make it difficult for them to accept the Marxist conception. For one thing, most of their personal conflicts would have been with other members of the middle classes; they compete as individuals with other individuals. They would want to feel that their success was a result of personal qualities, such as intelligence and ambition, so that they could claim full credit for their positions. If they feel something of a failure, they may blame it on bad luck or even the unfairness of the higher-ups—but they still must acknowledge that some people (manual workers) are even worse off; so they resist the notion of basic class conflict between haves and have-nots. They do not want to have to identify with the workers in order to blame the bourgeoisie and the system for their troubles.

People who think in terms of prestige, and who recognize the possibility of rising and falling, almost inevitably use a model with at least three levels. Prestige implies someone above you and someone below you. Only the really "down and out" will admit that they are on the bottom; self-respecting workers will always look down on bums beneath them and gain psychic satisfaction from their own superiority. Thus, contented workers who do not stress conflict and who feel some personal success will think in terms of at least a three-valued prestige hierarchy with themselves in the middle, bums on the bottom, and business and professional men on top. Middle-class persons also use the three-valued model, but they shift the dividing lines between the levels and lump all workers together as the ones below them and recognize the upper class as the group on top. You can almost always get a person who uses a three-valued system to make finer distinctions just by pushing the questioning; as you narrow the focus of attention to any part of the system, the respondent begins to think of subtler differentiations among persons. *The prestige concept, unlike the power idea, is infinitely divisible.*

Bott suggested that the three-valued prestige model is most common among the people who think of themselves as belonging in the middle. She found that the many-valued model was used by those who placed themselves in the working class but felt some incompatibility in their position. Thus, those who were somewhat better educated than their colleagues or who had aspirations to a more cultured outlook would admit that they were occupationally rather near the bottom but saw themselves as intellectually higher up. They would resolve the difficulty by seeing a society of many layers, with themselves second from the bottom and more like the level above them on some characteristics than on others.

The mixed prestige-power models were used by intellectuals who tried to reconcile Marxist theories with the more complex facts of contemporary life (see also Bott 1964 and Ossowski 1963).

We can now hypothesize that the men in the Cambridge sample who shifted from "middle" on the open-ended questions to "working" on the closed probably used the many-valued prestige model in their thinking. They knew they were occupationally in the working class, but when they had the chance to think in other terms (such as education or values) they could see themselves as toward the middle of a complex system. Those who denied class at first but then called themselves workers when forced to make a choice also probably thought of a many-layered system without clear lines of demarcation. Those who stuck to "middle class" through both forms of the questions were most likely to use the three-layered model. Those who remained with "working class" through both forms probably came closest to the power model which simplifies and consolidates shades of difference.

ELECTIONS AND THE DEMOCRATIC
CLASS STRUGGLE

Although no advanced industrial country has experienced the convulsive class revolution envisioned in the *Communist Manifesto*, most have passed through periods of bitter class confrontation and continue to experience less dramatic, institutionalized struggles over conflicting class interests. Class conflict is especially evident in two realms: electoral politics and labor relations. Most of the remainder of this chapter will be devoted to these areas.

Elections in modern democracies have been characterized as manifestations of "democratic class struggle" in recognition of the representative role of political parties (Anderson and Davidson 1943; Lipset 1960: chapter 7). Synthesizing the available evidence in 1960, Seymour Martin Lipset wrote:

> Even though many parties renounce the principle of class conflict or loyalty, an analysis of their appeals and their support suggests that they do represent the interests of different classes. On a world scale, the principal generalization which can be made is that parties are primarily based on either lower classes or the middle and upper classes (p. 230).

In most parliamentary systems, parties can be arrayed on a spectrum from right to left, with the former upholding the interests of the privileged classes and the latter attacking them on behalf of the less fortunate.

TABLE 9–6
Political preference, by occupational class, five countries (percent)

France: Voting in 1973 legislative elections

Occupational class	Party					Total
	Communist	Socialist	Center	Gaullist	Other	
Businessmen	12	22	22	36	8	100
Executives, professionals	11	22	20	39	8	100
White-collar workers	17	29	19	23	12	100
Blue-collar workers	33	27	14	22	4	100
Farmers	8	19	16	49	9	100

Sweden: Voting in 1968 election.

Occupational class	Party						Total
	Communist	Social Democrat	Center party	People's party	Conservative	Other	
Upper management and professionals	0	14	16	27	39	4	100
Small business	0	31	24	22	16	7	100
White collar	1	43	14	24	15	3	100
Foremen	2	71	7	11	6	3	100
Workers	2	75	10	7	3	3	100

Germany: Party affiliation, 1967

Occupational class	Party				Total
	Social Democrat	Free Democrat	Christian Democrat	Other	
Self-employed middle class	14	8	58	20	100
Salaried employees	34	4	45	17	100
Workers	49	1	33	16	100

Great Britain: Party affiliation, 1969

Occupational class	Party			Total
	Labor Party	Conservatives	Other	
Professionals	18	76	6	100
Businessmen	23	69	8	100
Office workers.............................	37	54	9	100
Skilled workers.............................	50	40	10	100
Semiskilled and unskilled workers....................................	54	35	11	100
Welfare recipients	51	36	13	100

United States: Party affiliation, 1981 (percent of those expressing preference)

Occupational class	Party		Total
	Democratic	Republican	
Business and professional......................................	55	45	100
Clerical and sales	71	29	100
Skilled manual...	72	28	100
Semiskilled and unskilled manual	76	24	100

TABLE 9–6 (continued)

United States: Presidential vote, 1976 and 1980

	1976			1980			
Occupational class	Democrat (Carter)	Republican (Ford)	Total*	Democrat (Carter)	Republican (Reagan)	Independent (Anderson)	Total*
Professionals or managers	41	57	98	33	56	9	98
Clerical, sales	46	53	99	42	48	8	98
Blue-collar workers	57	41	98	46	47	5	98
Union member in household	65	34	99	47	44	7	98

* Does not total 100 due to missing data.
Source: For France: Stanley Rothman et al., *European Society and Politics: Britain, France and Germany* (New York: West Publishers, 1976). For the United States: *Gallup Report*, August 1980; and Marlene M. Pomper ed., *The Election of 1980* (Chatham, N.Y.: Chatham House, 1981). For others: Richard Rose, ed., *Electoral Behavior: A Comparative Handbook* (New York: Free Press, 1974).

The class constituencies of major parties in Western democracies can be read from the data in Table 9–6. The French system is multiparty. Business owners, executives, and professionals tend toward the right-wing Gaullist party. White-collar workers are spread across the spectrum. Blue-collar workers are mainly Communist and Socialist. The Swedish voting pattern is quite similar.

The German, British, and American systems are dominated by two big parties. In each country, one of them is more popular among the business and professional strata and the other is more popular among manual workers. Clerical workers, once again, are divided in loyalty.

As these data suggest, the alignment of classes to parties is typically unmistakable but less than precise. Many people, as we have seen, are not conscious of their class interests, and many parties are imperfect class representatives, in part because they play other representational roles. Political parties frequently have ethnic, religious, or regional bases which crosscut their class associations.

Among the countries covered here, the United States presents the loosest relationship between classes and parties. Every other country has at least one party which identifies itself as socialist (the Communist, Socialist, Social Democratic, and Labor parties) and regards itself as a partisan of the working class. The Democratic party sometimes labels itself liberal (never socialist) and claims to be the representative of the "common man," but it is rather coy about making explicit appeals to class. This difference is reflected in the weaker class bias in American party loyalties. The simplest comparisons are with Germany and Great Britain, since they have two-party systems. Note that in both cases the percentage gap in working-class or upper-middle-class party affiliation is substantially larger than the corresponding differentials in the American system.

A variety of explanations has been advanced for this American "peculiarism" (some of which we will explore later in this chapter), but the most immediate cause is the role of ethnicity in American politics. The American party system is rooted in the relationships among class, ethnicity, and politics as they were worked out in the period 1928–48. Samuel Lubell (1956) has interpreted this period in a classic study of electoral behavior. Lubell described what might be called the emergence of the urban, ethnic working class. The generation preceding 1925 witnessed the greatest mass immigration that this country has ever experienced, and most of the newcomers went to work in the factories of the big cities. Simultaneously, many farmers were streaming into the cities where they could make more money in the new industries; during and after the First World War, this internal migration included hundreds of thousands of Negroes. By the 1920s, these people and their children were becoming voters in great numbers, and for the first time, the urban workers approached dominance in national politics, for it was not until then that more people lived in cities than on farms. And these urban workers were primarily Democrats; by 1928, the Democrats outvoted the Republicans in most of the big cities. It is Lubell's central thesis that, although economic issues have always been important in our politics, in earlier years they were more closely connected with regional interests and conflicts, but by 1928 the parties had taken on the color of class parties, with the Republicans representing business (and successful farmers) and the Democrats representing workers (and unsuccessful farmers). This one split tended to override regional differences and divisions based on noneconomic issues, though of course they were still significant:

> Never having known anything but city life, this new generation was bound to develop a different attitude toward the role of government from that of Americans born on farms or in small towns. To Herbert Hoover, "rugged individualism" evoked nostalgic memories of a rural self-sufficiency in which a thrifty, toiling farmer had to look to the marketplace for only the last fifth of his needs. The Iowa homestead on which Hoover grew up produced all of its own vegetables, its own soap, its own bread. . . .
>
> In the city, though, the issue has always been man against man. What bowed the back of the factory worker prematurely were not hardships inflicted by Mother Nature but by human nature. He was completely dependent on a money wage. . . . A philosophy that called for "leaving things alone" to work themselves out seemed either unreal or hypocritical in the cities, where nearly every condition of living groaned for reform. . . . If only God could make a tree, only the government could make a park. (Lubell 1956: 33–34)

Franklin Delano Roosevelt, who came to office in 1933 in the depths of the Depression, was the first president to take advantage of these developments. He built an electoral coalition of Catholic and Jewish immigrants and their sons and daughters, blacks, and working-class people generally. This backing and the emergency situation of the Depression enabled him to obtain passage of the New Deal economic reform and welfare legislation.

The Democratic Party which emerged from the New Deal period was a party with strong working-class support but not a working-class party. Ethnicity blurred class lines. Most white Protestant workers supported the Democrats, but some of them (more than among Jewish or Catholic workers) favored the Republicans. The Democratic party also had important upper-class backers, drawn from the "ethnic rich"—men such as John F. Kennedy's multimillionaire father Joseph, a Catholic, or Jewish financier Bernard Baruch. The ethnic rich bankrolled the party, and although they were probably more ideologically flexible than their Protestant counterparts in the Republican party, they were nonetheless a conservatizing influence on their own party. Moreover, in the prosperous years after the Second World War, many of the children and grandchildren of immigrants moved into middle-class and upper-middle-class positions, but most retained their affiliation with the Democratic Party. This further diluted the class identity of the party, and on economic issues, moved it toward the center. Indeed, many of the working-class Democrats, enjoying the benefits of both the New Deal reforms and the postwar prosperity, tempered their previous liberal beliefs.

HAMILTON: CLASS AND POLITICS IN THE UNITED STATES

Richard Hamilton (1972) has produced the most elaborate class analysis of the American electorate in recent years. He took both class and ethnicity into account throughout his work. Although Hamilton's study is largely based on the 1964 SRC election survey, it is still worth serious consideration, for two reasons: first, Hamilton presented more-detailed class-ethnic comparisons than are available in any other published source, and second, the 1964 presidential election is a convenient test of political feelings, since conservative Republican Barry Goldwater and his liberal Democratic opponent Lyndon Johnson presented voters with a more clear-cut ideological choice than is available in most elections.

Hamilton employed three measures of political orientation: party identification, preference in the 1964 presidential election, and responses to a series of questions designed as indicators of domestic liberalism. The questions dealt with support for federal aid to education, government responsibility for medical care, a guarantee of jobs and a basic living standard, and denial that the "government has gotten too powerful (Hamilton 1972: chap. 3). Responses to such items in national surveys typically reveal liberal majorities (see *New York Times*, May 3, 1981, p. 1 for a recent example). However, there are significant variations depending on phrasing. For example, in the 1964 SRC survey, a majority favored a job guarantee, but only a minority backed the proposal which combined both job and living-standard guarantees (Hamilton 1972: 89–93).

Responses to the party identification and presidential preference items are shown in Table 9–7. (The results are fairly consistent with more recent, though less detailed, tabulations—see tables 9–4 and 9–5 and Nie et al. 1976: chap 13.) Note that Hamilton divides respondents into white Protestants and "others." The latter category includes blacks, Catholics, and Jews and, given this denominational division, most Hispanics and descendents of the "new" immigrants. (We will adopt a verbal shorthand and call these two groups *WASPs* and *Ethnics*). He creates four classes by distinguishing middle from working class (manual and nonmanual) and then splitting each of them into upper and lower on the basis of income.

The basic pattern in the table is easy to anticipate: lower classes and Ethnics are more Democratic in both party identification and voting than higher classes and WASPs. But note that political orientation is much more decisively structured by class among the WASPs than among the Ethnics. We can get a sense of the relative significance of class and ethnicity here by comparing intraclass differences between WASPs and Ethnics with intraethnic differences between adjacent classes. In most cases, ethnic differences are greater.

Let's take a closer look at Hamilton's conclusions about individual class-ethnic groupings. One of his basic points is that upper-middle-

TABLE 9–7
Party preference by class and ethnic group

Class	WASPs	Ethnics
Percent affiliated with Democratic party:*		
Upper-middle	42%	62%
Lower-middle	59	83
Upper-working	67	78
Lower-working	71	89
Percent voting for Johnson:		
Upper-middle	37%	74%
Lower-middle	52	84
Upper-working	68	76
Lower-working	81	92

* Of those expressing preference.
Source: Richard Hamilton, *Class and Politics in the United States* (New York: John Wiley and Sons, 1972), p. 437.

class WASPs constitute an especially reactionary segment of the electorate. They are the only grouping with a Republican majority and were alone in their strong support for Barry Goldwater in 1964 (subtract Democratic percentages in Table 9–7 from 100 to obtain percent Republican). There is an immense political gap between WASPs and Ethnics in this class. Upper-middle-class Ethnics were solidly Democratic in their party identification and voting. Their reactions to domestic issues were generally liberal and, in fact, much closer to those of working-class WASPs than to those of upper-middle-class WASPs.

We have already referred to Hamilton's (1966) work on the "marginal" or lower-middle class. There is especial interest in the politics of this class for at least two reasons. One is that it includes clerical workers, the largest and fastest-growing major occupational grouping and thus of considerable importance for the future of American politics. The other is that the members of this class have frequently been portrayed, in both American and European contexts, as clinging fiercely to their "marginal" or insecure middle-class status (Mills [1961], for example, wrote of "status panic") and therefore open to right-wing, extremist movements which promise to protect their social standing.

In fact, as Hamilton has shown, about half of the members of this stratum do not even identify themselves as middle class. A majority—both among WASPs and Ethnics—regard themselves as Democrats and voted against Goldwater, and in general, they are more liberal than the upper-middle class. They are not all right-wing.

Hamilton (1966; 1972: chap. 9; 1975: chap. 3) demonstrated that class origin is a key to lower-middle-class politics. People with middle-class fathers, especially among WASPs, are more likely to be Republican and adopt conservative positions than those with working-class backgrounds. (Interestingly enough, class background seems to make little difference in the politics of members of the upper-middle class). Hamilton described what he characterized as a "Republican core group" consisting of upper-middle-class WASPs and "second generation" members of the lower-middle class.

The Republican core is characterized by overwhelmingly conservative positions on domestic issues and gives solid support to conservative candidates (Goldwater received 84 percent of their vote). They are, by Hamilton's estimate, a relatively small proportion of the middle classes, but they are distinguished by a high level of interest in politics, decisive political convictions, a strong sense of political efficacy, and consistent participation in elections (see Table 9–10 in Hamilton 1972: 360). Hamilton believed that the Republican core is an "isolated mass" in the sense we applied earlier in this chapter to certain highly class conscious and militant working-class populations.

Cut off from other groups, only vaguely aware of the problems faced by less privileged persons, the members of the Republican core reinforce one another in a common commitment to "a peculiar and distinctive world outlook" (Hamilton 1972: 361). Hamilton did not, in fact, present evidence of the social isolation of this group. However, some of the material in our earlier chapter on association appears to support his contention.

Hamilton's treatment of the politics of the working class includes a discussion of the *embourgeoisment* thesis (which, as we noted earlier in this chapter, he refuted) and an examination of the influence of labor unions on the politics of their members. As we can by now anticipate, union members are more likely to identify themselves as Democrats and vote Democratic. The differences were greatest in large cities, suggesting that unions are most able to influence their members in the relatively more class-segregated social milieu that the city provides. Among blue-collar workers in big cities outside the South, 84 percent of union members considered themselves Democrats, but only 57 percent of nonmembers did so (Hamilton 1972: 321). However, Hamilton's data indicate that unions have no clear influence on workers' issue stands. And judging from the past three decades of presidential elections, unions have a consistent but not especially powerful influence over their members. From 1952 to 1980, members of union families (which, of course, include some white-collar workers) gave 4.5 percent more of their votes to Democratic candidates than did manual workers generally (*Gallup Report*, December 1980).

In this book, we have repeatedly concerned ourselves with locating the major divisions in the class structure. Hamilton (1972) had something to say on this issue. He rejected the widely held notion that the most significant class cleavage, for political purposes at least, is the manual-nonmanual split. In the past, when there were proportionately few white-collar workers and they were well differentiated in economic and cultural terms from blue-collar workers, this traditional conception seemed fairly safe. But we have seen many indications that such distinctions are blurring, especially in the middle of the class structure. Hamilton believed that the main political cleavage is the division between the upper-middle class and the rest of the population. Party affiliation is consistent with his view, but voting preferences do not quite fit Hamilton's conception, since ethnic membership alters the picture: the clearest division among the Ethnics is *within* the working class, or at least it was in 1964. However, the material on trends in class voting which we will analyze below indicates that the lower-middle-class voters have moved away from the upper-middle class and closer to the working class in the elections since 1964.

There is a paradox, of which he is well aware, in Hamilton's analysis of American political orientations. As he and others have noted, most Americans tend toward liberalism on economic, or bread-and-butter, issues. Although increasing numbers of people regard themselves as political independents, there are still twice as many Democratic identifiers as Republican identifiers (Gallup 1980: 31). According to Hamilton, only the members of a relatively small middle-class WASP minority are consistently conservative and Republican in their political opinions and behavior. How is it, then, that liberal Democrats are not consistently elected to office and liberal policies, such as national health care, are not enacted despite majority support in opinion surveys? Part of the answer to this question lies in matters we treated in the last chapter—campaign financing, the class background of officeholders, the influence of the capitalist class on government decision making—which are beyond the scope of Hamilton's work. But he did point to several factors which are more directly related to public opinion and electoral behavior.

Of key importance is the fact that people toward the top of the class structure are much more likely to vote than those toward the bottom. This is particularly true of the conservative Republican core as defined by Hamilton. They are also better informed politically and more likely to participate in various sorts of political activities. The 1980 election provided a telling example of their electoral weight: according to the *New York Times/CBS* exit poll, 40 percent of the voters were professionals or managers and only 17 percent were blue-collar workers, proportions wholly out of line with their respective representation in the labor force (*New York Times*, November 6, 1980).

Hamilton also argued that voters are not presented with clear issue choices in elections. And voter concerns are not always reflected in public discussion. Using the SRC surveys from the 1950s, Hamilton showed that a majority of the electorate favored national health care legislation, which nonetheless failed to become a political issue. Yet much attention in the media and in politics was focused on domestic and international Communist subversion, matters which surveys at the time showed to be of relatively minor concern to the public (Hamilton 1972: chap. 3).

TRENDS IN CLASS PARTISANSHIP

In recent years, some writers have detected what they regard as a decline in the relationship between social class and party support (Abramson 1978; Lipset 1981: 503–21; Ladd and Hadley 1978; for alternative interpretations see Knoke 1976, Flanigan and Zingale 1975, Davis 1978). Such a trend could indicate a waning of class consciousness or a reduction in the significance of elections as arenas of democratic class conflict. The evidence most frequently cited for this interpretation is the changing class pattern in presidential elections.

The curves in Figure 9–1 represent the presidential preferences of three occupational classes in elections since World War II. Note that the curves have never crossed or even touched and that since 1952 they have always shifted in the same general direction. These features indicate a certain consistency in political behavior: class differences have been maintained over the entire postwar period, but polarization has rarely been so great that classes exhibited sharply divergent reactions to a candidate.

The 1948 election was clearly exceptional. The class differentials recorded that year were not only higher than in the years that followed, but they diverged similarly from the experience of the 1930s and early 1940s (Cantril 1951: 602; Alford 1963). Since 1952 the differential between the working class and the upper-middle class (indicated by the numbers under the lower curve) has been fairly stable, with the exception of 1972 when all classes joined in rejection of Democratic candidate George McGovern and class polarization narrowed appreciably.

FIGURE 9–1
Voting in presidential elections by occupational class

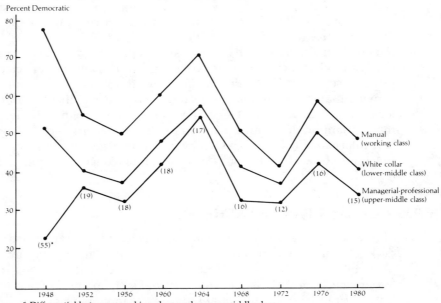

Percent Democratic

* Differential between working class and upper-middle class.
Sources: *Gallup Report,* December 1980; Campbell et al., 1954.

One important change is evident over the postwar period. As we observed above, the lower-middle class has pulled away from the upper-middle class. Since 1972, it has occupied a position midway between the other two classes. It is this shift which is largely responsible for the impression that class voting has diminished, particularly since the most common measure of polarization is the Alford Index based on the difference between manual and nonmanual voters (Alford 1963).

In sum, class voting is not declining, but the pattern of class partisanship is shifting, probably because the position of the lower-middle class within the class structure is changing.

CLASS CONFLICT AND THE LABOR MOVEMENT

The preceding pages focused on electoral politics as an arena of "democratic class struggle." Here we shift our attention to industrial conflict, the confrontation between capitalists and laborers in the workplace. American labor history has been distinguished by an ironic combination of violent struggle and limited class consciousness. Violence has grown out of tenacious capitalist resistance—not so much to specific economic demands as to the very right of workers to organize labor unions. The class consciousness of American workers has been limited in the sense that they and their leaders have typically sought circumscribed goals—basically union recognition, economic security, and decent working conditions. Labor unions, as we will see, have played a key role in supporting the passage of liberal welfare measures whose main benefits have flowed not simply to their own members but to working-class and lower-class people generally. But they have rarely sought a fundamental reordering of economic and political relationships designed to benefit the working class, which is to say that they have not developed a socialist class consciousness. In both ways, the American experience differs from that of industrial democracies generally. Elsewhere, employer resistance has been less evident, and the labor movement has been more committed (in rhetoric at least) to a socialist transformation. In regard to the first point, a leading historian observed on the eve of the New Deal:

> Employers in no other country, with the possible exception of those in the metal and machine trades of France, have so persistently, so vigorously, at such costs, and with such a conviction of serving a cause opposed and fought trade unions as the American employing class. In no other Western country have employers been so much aided in their opposition to unions by the civil authorities, the armed forces of government, and their courts. (Lorwin 1933: 355, cited in Greenstone 1977: 19)

Nearly a half century later, an American labor economist writing on industrial conflict in Europe noted, "The resistance of U.S. employers to unionizing efforts has no serious counterpart in Europe today" (Kassalow 1978: 97, cited in Brody 1980: 248).

In Chapter 3, we sketched the history of the labor movement up to World War I. A brief review of the decades which followed will place contemporary developments in a meaningful framework. World War I was a period of rapid expansion for the unions, especially those belonging to the American Federation of Labor (AFL), which had formed a wartime political alliance with the Wilson administration. Free to organize workers without government or employer harassment, the AFL unions grew from 2 million to 4 million workers in two years (Brooks 1971: 134).

Coasting on its wartime momentum, the AFL continued to grow and gained some important strike victories in the immediate postwar period. But a reaction soon set in, fed by a national "red scare." In 1919, 300,000 steelworkers nationwide went out on strike, protesting 12-hour workdays and bare-subsistence wages. The response of employers and the federal and local governments which supported them was decisive and often brutal (Brooks 1971: 139–44; Boyer and Morais 1975: 202–9).

The steel strike collapsed after three bitter months. Its fate was indicative of what was to come in the 1920s. In particular, it revealed many of the weaknesses of working-class consciousness and organizations and many of the techniques used by the capitalists to resist unionization. The strike revealed a working class divided by differences in skill level, race, and ethnicity. Blacks were used as strikebreaking workers. Language diversity kept many immigrant workers from communicating with one another or with native-born members of their class. All these divisions were systematically exploited by employers.

Clearly violence played a major role in the suppression of strikes. Violence in turn depended on the fact that local and national authorities sided with the capitalists. In effect, civil liberties were routinely suspended in strike situations. Without the normal protection of the laws, workers could be physically intimidated (often by thugs hired for this purpose), union organizers harassed, and leaders jailed. Much of this activity was coordinated by special firms that sold "union-busting" services (Litwack 1962: 95–115).

Resistance to the labor movement was so effective in the 1920s that the proportion of the nonagricultural labor force organized in unions declined from approximately 20 to only 10 percent (Brooks 1971: 148). Most of the core which remained by 1930 was in the relatively conservative AFL craft unions, which showed little interest in organizing the masses of less-skilled mass-production workers employed in large-scale industry. At this late date even the legal right of workers to bargain with their employers through labor unions remained in doubt. In short, there was little to indicate that the American labor movement was on the verge of an era of militant action, dynamic growth, and expanding national power.

The change, of course, came with the Great Depression and the concomitant shift in national politics, particularly during the years 1933 to 1937. A labor historian has described this period as "the highwater mark of class struggle in modern American history" (Davis 1980: 47). Indeed, many historians believe that without the legal reforms that were produced by the struggles of the period, all-out revolution would have ensued. The transformation of labor relations which emerged from this period was clearly the product of a clash between intense worker militancy and dogged capitalist resistance. When the United Textile Workers declared an industrywide strike in 1934, *Fibre and Fabric*, the New England trade journal, declared, "A few hundred funerals will have a quieting influence" (*Fortune* 1937: 122). Before this bitter, violent strike had completed its three-week run, thousands of National Guard troops had been mobilized in seven states, and 12 strikers and 1 deputy had been killed. The union lost.

But during these years, there were more labor victories than defeats. Some of the most significant were gained through a new tactic, the sit-down strike; workers forced concessions from employers by taking physical control of the workplace. First used in the rubber industry in 1936, the innovation, which appealed to the militant mood of workers at the time, spread rapidly. One labor official remembers 1937 as the year he received calls daily saying, "My name is Mary Jones; I'm a soda clerk at Liggett's; we've thrown the manager out, and we've got the keys. What do we do now?" (Brooks 1971: 180).

By 1938, the right to union representation had been written into law through the National Labor Relations Act, known as the Wagner Act, and unions had successfully established themselves in the mass-production industries, such as steel, automobiles, rubber, and electrical goods, which stood at the center of the American economy. A conjunction of social and political developments made these accomplishments possible. Of critical importance were the developments which helped overcome the division within the working class and the labor movement which had plagued earlier unionization drives. The significance of ethnic differences declined as the sons and daughters of immigrants joined the labor force. No longer cut off from one another by language barriers, more confident of their place in American society than their parents had been, and more demanding of their rights, these second-generation Americans helped recast labor relations just as they contributed to the revamping of national electoral politics.

Differences between skilled workers and unskilled and semiskilled in manufacturing did not disappear, but a barrier to unionization was removed when the CIO (Committee for Industrial Organization) was formed within the AFL in 1935 with the explicit purpose of organizing workers on an industry-by-industry basis rather than on the craft basis that was typical of the AFL unions. The following year the more-aggressive CIO broke with the tradition-bound AFL, retitling itself the Congress of Industrial Organizations. The CIO strove to remove another source of weakness by organizing both black and white workers.

As CIO organizers set about their task, the American working class was in an extraordinarily militant mood. The story of the drugstore soda clerk may be apocryphal, but it suggests the atmosphere of the times. The rank and file frequently ran ahead of union organizers, who found themselves forced to restrain premature action they were not in a position to support. Working-class solidarity grew to the extent that big strikes attracted workers from other industries and localities, who came to offer moral and even physical support (Greenstone 1977: 44).

The key to the worker militancy of the 1930s was the experience of the Depression. We have seen that economic insecurity feeds class consciousness. The insecurity that workers experienced during this period was connected to the breakdown of the entire economic system. The confidence that workers had had in their employers was shattered by the recognition that even such powerful companies as U.S. Steel and General Motors were subject to the vagaries of the marketplace. When capitalists responded to the Depression by laying off workers, reducing benefits, and speeding up work, they lost the loyalty of many workers. Typical were the reactions of an elderly Ford worker who complained that he had devoted his working life to "helping to create a millionaire," and an unemployed machinist about to lose his home who concluded, "The bankers and industrialists who have been running our country have proved their utter inability, or indifference, to put the country in a better condition" (Brody 1980: 77).

But neither the reduced factionalization nor the growing militancy of the working class could have accomplished the transformation of industrial relations of the 1930s without the changed political context represented by the New Deal. As the experience of the 1920s made clear, if government was hostile to labor, or at least so indifferent as to ignore patently illegal forms of employer resistance, unionization was impossible. The new state of affairs was clear from the passage of the Wagner Act in 1935. The act guaranteed the right of workers to form labor unions, prohibited employers from interfering with the exercise of that right, and set up a National Labor Relations Board (NLRB) thereafter to ensure that these provisions were carried out in practice. Shortly thereafter the LaFollette Civil Liberties Investigating Committee began hearings "which, through exposure, largely neutralized the repressive weapons heretofor used in the fight against trade unionism" (Brody 1980: 139).

Both the labor act and the LaFollette investigation would have been unthinkable under earlier administrations. Ironically, neither was encouraged by Roosevelt, whose own attitude toward labor was ambivalent (Brody 1980: 138–46). He did not initiate many of these reforms but was so dependent on working-class political support that he was forced to go along with them.

THE POSTWAR ARMISTICE

The organizational base which the labor movement had built in the 1930s was strengthened during World War II, through close cooperation between the government and the unions in support of the war effort. By 1945, approximately 36 percent of the nonagricultural labor force was organized (Dubofsky 1980: 9). A wave of strikes (which had been prohibited during the war) in 1945 and 1946 gained substantial wage increases for workers, in sharp contrast to the repression of unions in the wake of World War I.

Yet the labor movement was not, as some thought at the time, invulnerable. In 1947, capitalist-class interests gained passage of an important piece of antilabor legislation, the Taft-Hartley Act. In the next couple of years, as a new "red scare" developed, an upheaval within the labor movement resulted in the removal of Communists and other leftists from the positions of leadership they had held in some unions and the explusion of a number of left-leaning unions from the CIO. The Taft-Hartley Act made it easier for employers to resist union organizing, while the loss of the left deprived the union movement of its most effective organizers, people who had played a major role in the union drives of the 1930s. Both contributed to the collapse of a major organizing effort in the South and severely weakened other efforts to extend union coverage.

Despite these defeats, the labor movement had for the first time established a secure place for itself. In the process, it had significantly reformulated the relationship between the capitalist and working classes in key areas of the economy. Unionization not only provided mechanisms to press for better wages and hours but also afforded some control over working conditions and protection from the traditional petty tyranny of the foreman. Though the majority of workers were never represented by unions, the unionization of some firms and industries posed an implicit threat which tended to constrain the behavior of capitalists in other sectors.

If the 1930s represented a period of explicit class conflict during which these changes were forced on the capitalist class, the decade after the war was the time when the details of a class armistice were worked out. When leaders of the major labor organizations met in Washington with key business representatives in 1945, their purpose was to "lay the basis for peace with justice on the home front." The conference was convened by President Truman at the suggestion of conservative Senator Arthur Vandenberg, who told the president, "Responsible management knows that free collective bargaining is here to stay. . . . and that it must be wholeheartedly accepted" (Brody 1980: 175).

Although many business leaders were willing to accept the existence of unions, they were determined to preserve for the capitalist class what they termed the "right to manage." At stake was participation in decisions regarding such matters as investment (including plant openings and closings), product design and production methods, and the pricing of final products. Had labor gained a share in these decisions, as did some contemporary European unionists, the labor movement would have been able to meaningfully concern itself with employment and other basic economic questions. Unions would thus have been able to represent, not just their own members, but the working class more broadly. That "property rights" in fact remained the dominant influence was demonstrated over the next decade; business did not so much as concede to unions the right to examine the books of the enterprises with which they bargained. The right to manage gradually ceased to be an issue (Brody 1980: 173–213).

By the late 1950s, the shape of the industrial peace was unmistakable. Unions were firmly established among blue-collar workers at the core of the economy in heavy industry. Here they could gain substantial benefits for their members as long as they did not interfere with management prerogatives—benefits which would allow a large segment of the working class a life of relative affluence. "The labor movement," concluded auto union leader Walter Reuther, "is developing a whole new middle class" (Brody 1980: 192). Serious industrial conflict was banished to the periphery of the economy—to the smaller firms, weaker economic sectors, and backward regions (especially the South). If such conflict was relatively infrequent, that was in good measure because the labor movement had grown satisfied and unaggressive. By the end of the decade, the giant AFL-CIO (the two had remerged in 1955) was behaving, in the words of labor economist Richard Lester, as a "sleepy monopoly" (Dubofsky 1980: 8).

Oddly enough, labor came to play a more dynamic role in national electoral and legislative politics than it did in the workplace. During the 1930s, the labor movement began to cast off its traditional "volunteerism," the determination to steer clear of politics except when its own direct interests were involved. In the postwar period, labor emerged as a major supporter of the Democratic party and a broad array of liberal social and economic programs. Writing in the late 1960s, David Greenstone (1977) concluded that the relationship between labor and the Democratic party, although unofficial, had come close to that between Social Democratic parties and labor unions in some Western European countries. The political goal of the activists within the labor movement was "to complete the transformation begun by the New Deal and make the Democrats the genuine party of the common man in America" (Brody 1980: 229). Having assumed this burden, labor came to represent not just union members but the working and lower classes generally.

Labor was politically active in two broad arenas, electoral and legislative. In the former, the labor movement promoted liberal candidates, both within and on behalf of the party, raised a substantial part of the party's campaign money, and fielded thousands of campaign workers. In areas such as Detroit where unions were especially strong, the party and the union's political organization became virtually indistinguishable (Greenstone 1977: 119–40). In Washington, labor maintained a formidable lobbying apparatus which, during the 1960s and early 1970s, played a major role in obtaining passage of liberal legislation in such areas as civil rights, health care, minimum-wage protection, public employment programs, nutrition programs for the poor, and occupational health and safety (Greenstone 1977: xvii–xxiii, 319–60). Clearly, the benefits of such legislation flow toward the lower portions of the class structure. Ironically, union lobbyists could not match their successes in social legislation with victories in labor legislation, such as the long-sought repeal of bothersome portions of the Taft-Hartley Act.

As we indicated in the preceding chapter, union lobbyists became the leaders of broad liberal coalitions which confronted business lobbies and other conservative groups over critical pieces of legislation. In effect, a class cleavage ran through the center of national legislative politics. Although that cleavage disappeared from view over many issues (such as the Vietnam war which imposed severe strains on labor's relationship with the Democratic party), it was still apparent in the struggles over budget and tax policies in the early months of the Reagan administration.

THE FUTURE: A RENEWAL OF
CLASS CONFLICT?

Recent years have brought widely recognized signs of a decline in the economic and political strength of the labor movement. Concurrently, there are indications that the labor-business truce worked out at the end of World War II is breaking down. In particular, members of the capitalist class have launched an increasingly aggressive campaign against the labor movement, which some alarmed union labors have characterized as a one-sided class war.

The clearest indication of the dilution of labor's strength is the decreasing proportion of the labor force represented by unions. Although the labor movement continued to grow in absolute numbers as the work force expanded, in relative terms membership had sunk to less than a quarter of nonagricultural workers by 1978 (Serrin 1981). Moreover, the results of representation elections conducted among workers by the NLRB revealed the declining effectiveness of organizing efforts: the proportion of union victories slid steadily from 80 percent in 1946 to 47 percent in 1977 (Brody 1980: 248). These developments were underscored by signs that labor's power in Washington was waning. In the 1976–78 congressional session, labor suffered several unanticipated legislative defeats, one of which we will discuss shortly, and in the 1980 election, a number of labor's closest friends were defeated by conservatives hostile to union interests.

Labor's problems stem in good measure from the basic shifts in the economy and occupational structure which we discussed in Chapter 3. The bastion of union power, built up in the 1930s, is in the manufacturing sectors, which are now in relative decline. To the extent that new jobs are being created in industry, they tend to be located in the so-called Sunbelt—a band of boom areas running across the southern tier of the country—much of which covers states which are openly hostile to unions. At the same time, employment growth has been strongest among those categories of workers who are the most difficult to organize: white-collar employees, service workers, employees of small establishments, and women workers. (By no small coincidence, most of these are also groups which we have noted to be among the least class conscious.) The only area in which the unions seemed to be making significant gains was in the public sector labor force, especially among teachers and white-collar employees of federal, state, and local bureaucracies. But public sector employment has been leveling off in recent years. In short, labor's natural economic base is shrinking. Unless union organizers become much more effective in attracting those whom they have traditionally failed to reach, the erosion will continue (Dubofsky 1980: 8; Estey 1980: 15; Troy and Sheflin 1980: 18).

The most dramatic recent demonstration of the political decline of the unions came with the defeat of the 1978 Labor Law Reform Bill. Although regarded by both labor and business as a critical test of strength, the bill was fairly modest in its intent, which was to restore the effectiveness of the 1935 Wagner Act. Over the years, employers had discovered that they could stave off union organizing efforts by legal maneuvering and other tactics designed to discourage union activists and postpone representation elections. The longer delays stretched out, the greater the probability that a union drive would collapse. The basic provisions of the bill were designed to guarantee speedy elections to determine whether workers wanted union representation, ensure prompt decisions from the NLRB in unfair labor-practice cases, and stiffen penalties for violation of existing labor laws, such as the firing of union sympathizers.

The bill evoked one of the most extensive and expensive lobby campaigns in the history of the republic. The AFL–CIO spent $3 million on its campaign in support of the bill. A coalition of business groups, including the Business Roundtable, National Association of Manufacturers, U.S. Chamber of Commerce, and National Federation of Independent Businessmen spent approximately $5 million to secure its defeat. Some 20 million pieces of mail were generated by the two campaigns (Cameron 1978: 80). Both made extensive use of state and local affiliates to pressure congressmen, who found themselves deluged by communications from businessmen and labor leaders in their states or districts (Cameron 1978; Green 1979: 51–53).

The reform bill glided through the House and found strong majority support in the Senate. However, senators sympathetic to business mounted a determined filibuster to keep the matter from coming to vote (an ironic parallel with the problems the bill was intended to remedy), and business lobbies applied strong pressures to sustain the filibuster. Labor supporters failed by two votes to gain the 60 percent of the Senate needed to close debate.

Unionists were stunned by both the undemocratic character of their defeat and by the composition of the coalition which had confronted them. They were used to the idea that the lesser capitalists represented by the Independent Businessmen, the Chamber of Commerce, and the NAM harbored strong antiunion sentiments. But the fact that the Business Roundtable—representative of the largest American corporations, the firms with which the unions had made their peace in the 1950s—would support initiatives designed to thwart union organizing came as a terrible revelation. It opened old wounds. In the midst of the conflict over the bill, Lane Kirkland, a ranking AFL–CIO official who later became president of the federation, had charged the corporations with embarking on "a campaign to kill the hopes of the most oppressed and deserving workers in this country. It is class warfare. . . ." (Zeitlin 1980: 32). Shortly after the Senate defeat, Douglas Fraser (1978), president of the United Auto Workers, resigned from the semiofficial Labor-Management Group in Washington with a direct attack on his Business Roundtable colleagues in the group: "I believe leaders of the business community, with few exceptions, have chosen to wage a one-sided class war today in this country. . . . The leaders of industry, commerce, and finance in the United States have broken and discarded the fragile, unwritten compact previously existing during a past period of growth and progress."

Fraser accused corporate America of resisting social legislation designed to help the underprivileged, of indifference to the welfare of the public and its own employees, of working to subvert the democratic process for self-serving ends, and of desiring the elimination of labor unions. With regard to the last issue, Lane and Fraser and other labor leaders were, by 1978, ready to see the defeat of the labor reform bill as part of a broader business attack on the unions which had been brewing for some time. They were aware, for example, that the NAM had launched a new "Committee for a Union-Free Environment," that the shift of jobs toward the Sunbelt was in part fueled by the determination of corporations to escape to an environment less friendly to the unions, and that even the largest corporations were taking advantage of the services of an aggressive new breed of labor consulting firms.

The new consultants posed an intriguing contrast with the union-busting industry of the 1920s and 1930s. The firms which supplied tear gas, small weapons, and strike-breakers have been supplanted by practioners of manipulation, sophisticated in their application of social scientific knowledge. For example, the consultants show management how to convey to employees an artificial sense of participation in company decisions and how to use systems of subtle rewards and punishments to influence employee attitudes or create anxieties which work against the union. Employers are advised to avoid certain categories of workers because they are more likely to be receptive to union appeals. Consultants also instruct corporations in the advantages they can glean from calculated violations of labor law (Langerfeld 1981). It is not surprising that charges of illegal discrimination by employers against union members brought before the NLRB have increased sixfold since the mid-1950s (Brody 1980: 248).

If a new round of class conflict is breaking out, does it all come, as Fraser suggests, from management maneuvers? In the course of the 1970s, there was an upturn in the number of strikes and an increase in the proportion of so-called wildcat strikes and strikes over working conditions. Workers are also more frequently rejecting the contracts negotiated with corporations by their union leaders, suggesting dissatisfaction among the rank and file. But these developments are not easy to interpret. They may simply be a reflection of the stiffening attitude of the capitalist class rather than an indication of a newly developing militant consciousness among workers (Naples 1981: Lipsky 1981; Rosenberg and Weisskopf 1981).

In the early 1980s, it is clear that the capitalist class, both local and national, has gained the initiative. The decline of the unions in the economy and in national politics are closely related phenomena, representing an inversion of the experience of the 1930s. Current developments threaten to alter the balance of power between the working class and the capitalist class that has stood for a generation.

CONCLUSIONS

This chapter has examined one central theme: class consciousness. Marx first raised the issue, since he believed that subjective awareness of one's objective position in the property and occupational system would lead to a sense of belongingness with others of similar position and promote conflict with those above or below. Those experiences in turn would generate political beliefs or ideologies that interpreted the world and suggested appropriate forms of organized action to advance class interests.

Contemporary sociologists have used Marx's views to create specific hypotheses that could be tested in empirical research. They wanted to explain the origins of class consciousness as indicated in various forms of verbal response, including use of class terms of self-identification, and they wanted to pinpoint the consequences of identification for political belief and action. They have consistently found in the United States and other countries that objective position in the occupational system is an important influence on identity, with manual workers usually considering themselves to be working-class people and nonmanual workers calling themselves middle class. These terms carry connotations much broader than just a classification of jobs: they imply a way of life, a set of friends, a system of values. And they cover all members of a family not just the principal breadwinner, whose job is usually used to define class membership. In the United States, very small percentages of people consider themselves either upper class or lower class (or poor); almost half put themselves in the working class, and a slightly smaller proportion are middle class.

But identification flows from other causes besides occupation, and so it reflects more than one social fact of life. Particularly important is racial or ethnic membership. When people belong to a minority group that suffers from discrimination that leads to economic insecurity and social stigma, they respond by identifying with other underdogs in the system. And underdogs in general develop ideologies of liberal or leftish tone that demand changes in society to promote more equality and justice. These ideologies are even more pronounced among individuals and groups who have had these additional experiences: uprootedness, such as movement from one country to another or from farm to city; a high rate of interaction within their own group and isolation from other groups; two or three generations of similar social status; and membership in organizations, especially unions, that promote class conflict. All of these specific indicators, except perhaps for aspects of ethnicity, can be deduced from Marx.

Those who feel deprived in society and identify with others like themselves not only develop ideologies that clarify their position and verbalize their indignation, they join political parties to advance their interests through the vote (and if the parties are repressed and the circumstances grave, they may move toward revolutionary activity). In the Western democracies, the use of legal political activity has had marked success in reducing the workday, protecting unions, advancing the process of collective bargaining to raise wages, and providing various forms of social security. In the United States, the party of the underdog has been the Democratic party; its following comes particularly from the working class and from ethnic supporters, and it is closely tied to organized labor.

Sometimes these various social forces come into contradiction: for example, a person from a subordinate ethnic group may achieve superordinate occupational position. The result is that all the correlations between occupation, ethnicity, identification, ideology, union and party membership, and voting become blurred by cross pressures. People in reality do not have completely neat and consistent social characteristics that permit neat and consistent predictions of all their political beliefs and behaviors.

Outside of electoral politics, the main avenue for advancing the interests of the working class has been the organization of labor unions for direct confrontation with employers. In the initial stages, particularly in the United States, the capitalists fought labor organization with bitter violence, calling upon private detectives and the repressive arms of the government—the police and the militia—to help them. Many people were killed and injured. Eventually, the right to organize was granted by law and recognized by the owners of big business in most branches of basic industry. The struggle then turned to specific matters of wages and working conditions and led to great improvements for workers in the organized industries, some of which have spilled over and aided other workers. But the successes were greatest in basic industry, and the proportion of workers engaged in that sphere is going down. The struggles of the future will turn more and more to people in white-collar and service occupations, government as well as private, and the outcome is uncertain.

SUGGESTED READINGS

Aronowitz, Stanley. 1973. *False Promises: The Shaping of American Working Class Consciousness*. New York: McGraw-Hill.
  The development of working-class consciousness in historical perspective, emphasizing the effect of consumer culture on working-class views.

Brody, David. 1980. *Workers in Industrial America: Essays on the 20th Century Struggle.* New York: Oxford University Press.

> *A lively introduction to the history and historiographic literature of the labor movement in the 20th century.*

Ladd, Everett Carll, Jr., and Charles D. Hadley. 1978. *Transformations of the American Party System: Political Coalitions from the New Deal to the 1970s.* New York: W. W. Norton.

> *In contrast to the view developed in this chapter, the authors argue that the significance of social class in electoral politics has declined sharply.*

Laslett, John M., and Seymour Martin Lipsett, eds. 1974. *Failure of A Dream? Essays in the History of American Socialism.* New York: Anchor Books.

> *Attempts to explain the relative weakness of socialism in American social consciousness and political history.*

Ossowski, Stanislaw. 1963. *Class Structure in the Social Consciousness.* New York: Free Press.

> *A systematic account of competing basic conceptions of class structure in the history of Western social thought.*

Thompson, E. P. 1963. *The Making of the English Working Class.* New York: Vantage Press.

> *Classic historical portrayal of the development of working-class consciousness.*

The poor, the underclass, and public policy

The new poverty is constructed so as to destroy aspiration; it is a system designed to be impervious to hope. The other America does not contain the adventurous seeking a new life and land. It is populated by the failures, by those driven from the land and bewildered by the city, by old people suddenly confronted with the torments of loneliness and poverty, and by minorities facing a wall of prejudice.

Michael Harrington (1962: 10)

A federal interagency committee is quietly examining the possibility of doing away with the use of the word "poverty" and of recomputing the income figures used to define the poor. Apparently directed by the Office of Management and Budget, the group is working on the assumption that the number of poor in the nation is exaggerated because their income statistics do not include nonmoney income received in the form of food stamps, medical care, and other government subsidies. . . . A government source said: "Poverty is a value-laden, highly politicized word, and that's not the kind of word we like."

New York Times (April 7, 1973)

10

During the 1950s, the country experienced a decade of steady economic growth, and once the Korean War ended, it seemed that prosperity could continue even in times of peace. The country was in a satisfied, perhaps a smug mood, as symbolized by its choice of president: Dwight D. Eisenhower, war hero, family man, everybody's favorite father figure—the man with the friendly smile. His main political program was a desire not to do anything dramatic that might upset the good mood.

Only a few critics seemed worried about the state of domestic economic affairs. Among them was John Kenneth Galbraith, iconoclast among the economists. He wrote a book called *The Affluent Society* (1958), and some people mistakenly assumed from the title that he was celebrating prosperity. But his main message was that the new affluence was creating new problems that were not being noticed by public policy: a built-in, permanent tendency for inflation; old cities decaying without sufficient investment for proper renewal of public services; and a new type of poverty. The "old" poverty was mainly experienced by European immigrants who had swarmed to our mines, factories, and cities and were given the lowest and toughest jobs. The immigrants may have suffered deprivation but not loss of hope: through time, they felt, they would learn the language and the skills that would elevate them in the hierarchy, and their children would emerge from the public schools as full-fledged Americans who could easily enter the mainstream of society. The new poverty, according to Galbraith, affected two types of persons: individuals who suffered from one or another personal handicap (bad health, inadequate education, low intelligence) and who should be helped by social security or social welfare but were not being adequately supported; and individuals living in islands of poverty in areas of the country untouched by the new prosperity—for example, the Appalachians, peopled with subsistence farmers and underemployed coal miners, or the inner-city slums to which the rural poor were moving in large numbers. These people and their children needed help from deliberate government action; economic growth by itself was leaving them behind.

Then came a stronger statement: Michael Harrington's *The Other America: Poverty in the United States* (1962). He estimated that over 40 million Americans were poor and that the new prosperity was not helping them but in many instances was actually making their situation worse.

> One might summarize the newness of contemporary poverty by saying: These are the people who are immune to progress. But then the facts are even more cruel. The other Americans are the victims of the very inventions and machines that have provided a higher living standard for the rest of the society. They are upside-down in the economy, and for them greater productivity often means worse jobs; agricultural advance becomes hunger (1962: 12).

Harrington's book was widely read by members of the new Kennedy administration in 1963, including the President and his influential brother, Robert, who had been shocked by the misery he had seen in West Virginia during the electoral campaign. Galbraith became an advisor to the President. The new political leaders found that members of the federal bureaucracy concerned with unemployment and welfare policies knew about a lot of poverty that was not widely recognized by the public; so did a few members of Congress and their research staffs who had data on malnutrition, disease, alcoholism, drug addiction, and juvenile delinquency. With the arrival of the new administration, poverty and its various forms of pathology came back into public discussion. These leaders were Democrats, heirs to Roosevelt's New Deal, and their political constituencies thought of themselves as liberals devoted to constant social betterment. If the New Deal had not fully solved the problems of poverty, they proposed to move forward with new impetus—but cautiously, since members of this younger generation of Democrats were pragmatists more than ideologues.

Their approach was to divide the problem into two parts: (1) the situation of the unfortunates with personal handicaps, who might need more help through modest improvements in the welfare system of cash support and social services, including better training for those lacking in job skills; and (2) the ablebodied unemployed, who would be helped most by a faster growth in the general economy to reduce the unemployment rate below the 5 to 6 percent level typical of the Eisenhower years. A large tax cut was introduced as a means of stimulating economic expansion, as a way "to get this country moving again." (Note that this approach ignored a central thesis of Harrington, namely, that economic progress itself created as much poverty as it eliminated by introducing new and more efficient technologies in agriculture and industry that increased production but eliminated workers.)

The macroeconomic policies did have a small effect: in the early 1960s, the unemployment rate went down a little. In the late 1960s, it went down even further as we became involved in Vietnam and again moved toward a wartime economy. The decade as a whole enjoyed the greatest economic prosperity and growth in the nation's history.

Furthermore, there were improvements in the welfare system, partly designed during the Kennedy years but fully enacted under Lyndon B. Johnson, along with a series of measures to create equal political and economic rights for minorities. The former measures were labeled by Johnson the War against Poverty; combined with civil rights legislation, they expressed his call for a Great Society. He phrased the basic philosophy in his own grandiloquent way (June 26, 1964; quoted in Levitan and Taggart 1976: 3):

> We stand at the edge of the greatest era in the life of any nation. For the first time in world history, we have the abundance and the ability to free every man from hopeless want, and to free every person to find fulfillment in the works of his mind or the labor of his hands.
>
> Even the greatest of all past civilizations existed on the exploitation of the misery of the many.
>
> This nation, this people, this generation, has man's first chance to create a Great Society: a society of success without squalor, beauty without barrenness, works of genius without the wretchedness of poverty. We can open the doors of learning. We can open the doors of fruitful labor and rewarding leisure, of open opportunity and close community—not just to the privileged few, but to everyone.

THE PERSISTENCE OF POVERTY

Yet despite more than a decade of rapid economic progress, despite a lower unemployment rate, despite a series of measures aiding minorities, particularly blacks, to improve their training and gain access to better jobs, many people felt that the problems of poverty were getting worse instead of better. They responded to the symbols that reached the mass media: there were riots in the black ghettos; all the measures of juvenile delinquency and adult crime were going up; the number of families on welfare "exploded." To take just the last indicator: in 1940, about 382,000 families were getting assistance under the largest form of relief: Aid to Families with Dependent Children, which in most instances meant helping a mother with small children but no husband. In the following two decades, that figure slightly more than doubled, to 803,000 families in 1960. But in the single decade of supposed prosperity that followed, it jumped to

2,550,000 families (U.S. Census 1975: I, 301). Why was a period of economic expansion accompanied by a dramatic growth in the number of families on welfare? Why did the government have to spend more money to help poor people in a decade of marked prosperity?

The way the question is posed carries a double meaning:

How much poverty exists in America?

Why are the public and the government concerned about it?

It is impossible to consider one meaning separate from the other. The very definition of poverty is a cultural act: every society and every epoch defines it in a different way. And nobody bothers to define it and then to measure its extent unless it is perceived as a "problem" that somebody, probably the government, ought to worry about. Consequently, the programs the government designs to deal with poverty become the definition of poverty: when welfare grows, so does poverty. When the government had no such programs, before the New Deal, there was little public awareness that poverty was a problem. The poor may have suffered, but the society at large paid little attention.

Welfare is not the only indicator that reaches public and official attention, of course. Delinquency and crime are often believed to express, at least in part, the deprivations and the angers created by poverty. High infant mortality rates for some parts of the population (people on isolated, marginal farms or in city ghettos) compared to the general average indicate poor nutrition and inadequate medical care (for more information on hunger, see Kotz 1979). And obviously, political protest is a clear sign of tension. That protest can be in the form of organized movements attempting to change public policy, like the civil rights movement or progressive parts of organized labor. Or it can express itself in spontaneous riots in the streets (National Advisory Commission on Civil Disorders 1968). The causes of protest are often ambiguous, since it can be stimulated by certain forms of progress: if the average standard of living is increasing but some groups are not moving forward, their sense of justice becomes outraged, and they demand a share of the new prosperity. By contrast, if there is no economic growth, even the poor can get accustomed to their lot and take it for granted. Protest usually reflects progress that is unequally distributed in ways that are perceived as unfair.

Sociologists not directly connected with government programs are likely to think in comparative terms: for them, poverty is a style of life that is far below the general average or mainstream for the society in question. Thus in a country like India, where the general standard of living is meager, those considered poor would have to be in acute misery, perhaps actually starving to death. In the United States a century ago, a large family could live in a city apartment of three or four rooms with no bath and no hot water, seldom eat meat, be unable to send its children beyond the eighth grade in school, and still not be viewed as impoverished, since much of the working class lived that way. So long as one or two of the family members had a job and the rent and grocery bills usually got paid, the family was normal. If the workers lost their jobs and the landlord threw the whole family out on the street, then they became classified as poor, and some relief agency (probably a private, religious group) might move in to give them a temporary helping hand.

When a family has to struggle to get along but most of the time manages to obtain the essentials of living as defined by the standards of their day and their class, they tend to keep up hope and strive to improve their lot in the future. They encourage their children to stay in school, they attempt to save a few dollars when times are good, they hold up their heads in pride of accomplishment—the mere fact of being able to take care of themselves. When circumstances conspire against them so that year after year they fail to meet these standards, they are likely to turn apathetic. They give up hope for the future and just think about meeting the problems and perhaps gaining the small satisfactions that today presents. They do not plan, they simply exist. Here is what one mother in a migrant farm worker family told Robert Coles of her life:

> We tried three times (to settle), you know. My husband and me, we tried to stay there in Arkansas and work on his place, the boss-man's, but he couldn't pay us nothing from now on, because of the machinery he'd bought himself. Then we tried Little Rock, and there wasn't a job you could find, and people said go North. . . . and then the man came through, from one of the big farms down here, and he said we could make money, big money, if we just went along with him and went down to Florida and worked on the crops, just the way we always did, and that seemed like a good idea, so we did. And with the kids, one after the other, and with needing to have someplace to stay and some food and money, we've been moving along ever since, and it's been a lot of moving, I'll say that, and I wish one day we'd find there was nothing for us to do but stop, except that if we did, there might not be much food for that hot plate, that's what worries me, and I'll tell you, it's what my boy will say and my girl—they tell me that if we didn't keep on picking the crops, well then we'd have nothing to eat, and that wouldn't be worth it, sitting around and going hungry all the time. And I agree with them on that. So, we keep going, yes sir, we do. . . . The kids do a lot, and I'd rather they could be working at something else, later, like I said before, but I doubt they will. (Coles 1971: 59)

When eligible, many impoverished families turn to the welfare system for help. That system is designed to provide a minimum level of existence but is forced to be stingy about it—partly because those who work hard for their living do not want to subsidize beyond the barest essentials others who do not have adequate work, and partly because those in positions of power do not want to create a system that will reduce the pressures forcing the poor to accept the lowest jobs in society, like migrant farm labor, that most people would avoid if they had any choice.

In sum, the trends of the 1960s that brought poverty into public attention as a major issue were intimately connected with advanced technology, expanding prosperity, higher aspirations about the definition of a mainstream style of life, somewhat greater opportunities for minorities—and at the same time, segments of the population that were not able to participate in the good life, who felt that they were being unfairly deprived, and who turned in increasing numbers to the welfare system and to various forms of protest. These were the people who lived far enough below the mainstream level to be defined as poor in the contemporary United States, although their physical conditions of existence were better than those suffered by people classified as poor in the past. The more affluent the average style of life, the more painful it was to be poor.

Among the many factors advanced to explain why so many people were living below a level considered acceptable in the contemporary United States, three were of central importance:

1. Internal migration of 20 million persons from rural zones, many forced out of agriculture by modern machines, who moved to the cities in the decades from 1940 to 1970 and created a labor pool that could not readily be absorbed in good urban jobs; one fifth of them were blacks from the South. Since they lived in the cities, they were visible instead of hidden in the countryside where they could be ignored. And since they were citizens, they had legal rights and could organize to demand them.

2. The system of production was changing as factories became more automated. Manufacturing jobs for persons of low skill were shrinking as a proportion of the labor force, and many antiquated factories in the older cities were closing and shifting their production either to small towns or to foreign countries. Therefore, an excess of job seekers was competing for a diminishing supply of positions. A disproportionate number of those without jobs were from minority groups, American citizens living in the slums originally built for foreign immigrants.

3. The system of social security and welfare that had grown up over the years was not as effective as often believed. It was a patchwork of different programs designed for different categories of people, and many were not being adequately helped.

Given the obvious link between government programs to aid the poor and the very definition of poverty, we will examine the two together. We will see how the government experts in the 1960s agreed upon a formal definition of poverty, how they used it to measure the extent and estimate the causes of poverty, and how it became a benchmark to determine the success of the war against poverty. And we will see how the government programs to end poverty that were formalized in the 1960s had roots in the past and consequences in the future.

THE NEW DEFINITION OF POVERTY

When President Kennedy came to office in 1961, he was under pressure from civil rights activists and from other liberal constituencies in the Democratic party to take a new look at racial discrimination and at persistent poverty. Bureaucratic studies in his adminstration, supported by academic research, gave substance to Harrington's position that there were still millions of people living in misery—indeed, some in hunger—in the United States. Since the general living standards were rising steadily, it seemed to many that the nation could finally afford to completely eliminate poverty.

The war against poverty required a coordinated plan that would lift everybody above the threshold of acceptable living standards, both by helping poor people get better jobs and by integrating various parts of the existing system of piecemeal public welfare that left many needy people without assistance. For some, basic education and job training would be required; for others, improvements in the systems of social insurance and social welfare. In order to measure the size of the problem and to test the effectiveness of remedial measures in the coming years, an official definition of poverty was needed, something the government had never before enunciated. Using the definition, a census could be taken indicating the number of people who were poor; then the specific causes of their poverty could be analyzed, and programs could be designed or redesigned to help them.

The policymakers adopted an old idea from the private charities and local public welfare offices that had always needed some guidelines to help them decide who to help and how much to give. There was a tradition going back to the beginning of the century based on the idea of a "market basket" of cheap but nutritious foods that would keep a family alive, along with other essential items, including enough rent money to keep them from being evicted. Usually, no long-term expenses (such as furniture) were included, as the charity help was considered to be a minimum to tide people over a temporary emergency. Year after year, different groups calculated the items that ought to go into the market basket and then went to the store to find out how much the items would cost. This procedure produced minimum subsistence budgets; people in trouble were helped up to the level of those sparse budgets.

In more recent years, Mollie Orshansky in the Social Security Administration had been doing similar budget studies to help evaluate the adequacy of pension levels, aided by the Department of Agriculture's estimate of the cost of minimum nutrition during temporary crises, which often assumed that the homemaker was a sophisticated dietitian who never wasted a penny (Orshansky 1965). Using these several studies as a rough guide, the President's Council of Economic Advisors announced that as of 1963 a family needed about $3,000 a year in income to escape poverty; that figure became the famous "poverty line." (Council 1964). It followed a rule of thumb that had been used before: the cost of simple food times three, based on the fact that poor people tend to spend about one third of their income on food. Shortly thereafter, the government recalculated the figure to include variations in family size and rural or urban residence, and it set the line at $3,130 for a nonfarm family of four. Every year since then, the figure has been adjusted to reflect changes in the cost of living, using the consumer price index. This definition of poverty was not expected to be used as a guideline for dispensing grants under each specific program but rather as a measurement of the overall effectiveness of the total war against poverty. However, in recent years, it has been adopted as a guide for federal grants to local governments based on the proportion of local people who are poor.

Unfortunately, the government planners overlooked one thing: there really is no completely objective way to calculate a minimum subsistence budget and thereby draw a poverty line, even if one tries to do so by some supposed biological standards of nutrition. Contemporary cultural values always intercede and help define what is appropriate, and when the general standard of living goes up, so do ideas about the minimum that is acceptable to maintain subsistence. Therefore, the 1963 standard should have been adjusted in later years for two trends: (1) changes in the cost of the items in the market basket and (2) changes in the content of that basket. The government has made only the first of these adjustments.

The relativity of the concept of subsistence was demonstrated dramatically by Oscar Ornati and his colleagues at the New School for Social Research; their investigations were conducted before the government officially defined poverty but published just afterward (Ornati 1966). They examined budgets calculated by local charity agencies going back to 1905. They found that two types of standards were used for welfare purposes: (1) the "subsistence" budget, or the absolute minimum for survival on a *temporary* basis; (2) an "adequacy" budget, which was a little higher and was often used as the cutoff point above which families were no longer eligible for welfare services other than money payments. In addition, the local agencies often calculated a third figure, a "comfort" budget, which represented the amount necessary for a simple but decent standard of living for routine civil service and other workers. The adequacy budget approximates the lower budget for employed workers used by the Department of Labor beginning in 1920, and the comfort budget approximates its intermediate budget—as described in detail in Chapter 4.

Ornati then plotted these budgets over the years to see how their content changed. Let us concentrate on the subsistence level. Remember, in each year the local budget makers started anew and tried to calculate the barest possible minimum. They usually began with ideas about nutrition and then added the other short-run necessities, such as rent. They did not think explicitly about a proportional relationship to average incomes, yet retrospective vision shows they had that in the back of their minds. Ornati controlled for inflation by recalculating all the budgets in terms of the 1960 value of the dollar, and he found that the subsistence budgets had increased from about $1,700 to about $2,700 in real terms in the years from 1914 to 1960, an increase of 59 percent. Herman P. Miller has calculated that the real average income of all families and individuals went up about 78 percent in the same period (Miller 1971: 38). Thus, the subsistence budgets increased in real value at almost the same rate as the general standard of living of the country.

The change can be made more concrete by considering a few items included in the subsistence budgets. Comparing a 1908 calculation for Fall River, Massachusetts, with a 1960 budget for welfare recipients in New York City, Ornati showed that the high-protein food allowance for a family of four had gone up from about 22 pounds to almost 55 pounds, while the farinaceous (flour-based) foods had declined from 47 to 34 pounds. The housing allowance had doubled in constant dollars: it permitted four rooms with a toilet but no bath in 1908, but five rooms and a complete bathroom in 1960. There was no provision for electricity in 1908, but by 1960, even the charity cases were allowed lights, a refrigerator, and an iron (Ornati 1966: 151).

Lee Rainwater made some additional calculations from the Ornati data by comparing them to average disposable personal income (after taxes). He found that the family subsistence budgets tended to be about 40 percent of the average disposable income for four persons in any given year (there were, of course, some small variations from year to year). The adequacy budgets tended to be 55 to 60 percent of the average disposable income (Rainwater 1974: 46), close to what the U.S. Department of Labor now calls a "lower" budget for workers.

When thinking about the Ornati conclusions, Rainwater had a splendid additional idea. Instead of just using the definition of poverty created by the budget experts, he wondered about public opinion and took a look at old data from Gallup polls. He discovered that the same question had been asked every year since 1946: "What is the smallest amount of money a family of four needs to get along in this community?" He found that it tended to be between 50 and 55 percent of average family disposable income, or more generous than allowed by the budget makers thinking about subsistence (which, after all, was perceived as temporary relief not longer-term need). Although there was a little variation from year to year, there was no long-term change: it was the same 50 percent in 1969 that it had been in 1947. In other words, the public thought of poverty as a stable fraction of the average income, as did the budget makers in an unconscious way, but the public was a little more generous in setting the ratio than were the experts.

Now we can return to the government's decision in 1963. The $3,130 set as the poverty line for a family of four was 37 percent of the average disposable personal income for families of four persons in that year. Thus, without realizing it, the government followed a tradition of more than half a century of experts by defining poverty as anything less than about 40 percent of the average disposable income: the budget makers of 1963 defined poverty in almost the same ratio to the average income as did their predecessors in 1905.

Since 1963, most scholars have used a slightly different measure of the average, so let us switch to that benchmark, namely, the median money income of multiperson families, a figure that gets wide publicity every year.[1] It is calculated before taxes are paid but after cash transfer payments have been received. In 1963, it was $6,250, which meant that the poverty line of $3,130 was 50 percent of the median. In the 1960s, the median increased markedly in real terms (after inflation); in the 1970s, it increased quite a bit in money terms but only slightly in real terms. In 1978, the median income for all families was $17,640, and the poverty line was set at $6,660, which came to only 38 percent of the median, a drop of 12 percentage points (Table 4–4, above; U.S. Census 1980c: 464).

By freezing the content of the market basket the poor were supposed to buy, while average Americans were buying more and better items, the government had increased the gap between the two levels. Under the official definition, to be poor in 1978 meant that a family was further below the mainstream than a poor family had been in 1963. Thus the irony: when the federal government decided for the

---

[1] This excludes single individuals living alone; their income averages less than half that of families, and the poverty line for them is appropriately lowered. The median income for nonfarm families of four is about 15 percent higher than that for all families, and would be the exact comparison to the poverty line that is given here, but that median is not readily available for all years, so we substitute the figure for all families.

first time to declare war on poverty, it changed the rules and adopted an absolute definition of the level of living that determined the poverty line (except for changes in the cost of living), whereas both experts and the public had always previously used a relative definition that allowed the poor to improve at about the same rate as everybody else. The government made it easier to "win" the war on poverty in statistical terms by making it harder to be classified as poor.

It is also interesting to look at the legal minimum wage for employees of businesses engaged in interstate commerce. It is set by act of Congress not by bureaucratic experts. The original idea behind it was to produce a "living" wage for an unskilled workingman responsible for supporting a family, although that is hardly the way it works in reality. In 1963, the minimum wage was $1.25 an hour. If a person had worked 40 hours a week and 52 weeks a year—which is rarely the case for unskilled workers—he or she would have earned $2,600 a year, which came to 83 percent of the poverty line for a family of four. In 1978, the minimum was set at $2.65 an hour, or $5,510 a year. That also brought home 83 percent of the family poverty budget (but 163 percent of the poverty budget for a single individual living alone). Thus a family could have a hardworking but low-skilled breadwinner and still be poor. Add on the effects of many weeks of unemployment during the year, and it is easy to understand why we have a lot of "working poor" in the country.

To sum up the material on the budget-making process, we note that there had been a long tradition by local relief agencies of calculating subsistence (or survival, or poverty) budgets in terms of the food and rent and other unavoidable expenditures necessary to keep a family going during a temporary emergency. Parallel to it was a tradition of the federal Labor Department of devising a minimally adequate or lower-level budget for steady but unskilled workers and their families, and another more comfortable or intermediate level for mainstream working-class families. Regardless of the technical procedures used for calculating these budgets, it turned out that they kept a steady ratio to the average standard of living: as the average increased, the various budget levels increased roughly in proportion. In more recent years, when the public was asked about the minimum for getting along, they also pegged it as a ratio to the average. When the poverty line was officially set by the federal government in 1963 for the first time, it was put near the traditional level, at just about half the median money income for all families. But since then, the items in the budget have been frozen, and so its relationship to the median income and to the Labor Department's budgets has steadily declined. In the eyes of the federal government, poverty now gets further from the mainstream as the years pass by.

HOW MANY POOR?

In studying trends in the amount of poverty, we are usually forced to use the government's official definition because it is the base of most available statistics. Occasionally, private scholars reorganize the data using alternative definitions, such as half the median family income.

By the official definition (adjusted through time only for changes in consumer prices), these are the trends in the size of the population living in poverty in the United States—calculated on the basis of money income before taxes but after cash transfers (U.S. Census 1980b: 491):[2]

1963: 36 million persons, or 20 percent of total population.
1965: 33 million persons, or 17 percent of total population.
1970: 25 million persons, or 13 percent of total population.
1972: 24 million persons, or 12 percent of total population.
1978: 24 million persons, or 11 percent of total population.

Scholars at the University of Wisconsin's Institute for Research on Poverty have published data using a relative definition of poverty that approximated (but was not identical to) one half of median family income, and they have provided many useful comparisons using both the official and the relative definitions. They found that 30 million people were poor by relative standards in 1965, a figure that grew to 33 million by 1972 as the population increased. In both years, the percentage of poor was almost 16 percent, and indeed it will remain so as long as the distribution of income around the median does not change. Since the distribution has remained essentially stable for two decades or more, we can assume that by 1978 approximately 34 million Americans were below the poverty line defined in relative terms, or 10 million more than the official count. The same scholars calculated that it would have cost $12.5 billion in additional transfer payments in 1972 to bring all persons up to the official poverty line, an average of $510 each. Using the relative definition, it would have cost $19.3 billion, or $597 per person (Plotnick and Skidmore 1975: chap. 4).

Yet conservative critics assert that the government's definition of poverty is too generous, because it does not count noncash benefits in the form of food stamps, medicare, and housing subsidies. If these are included, and two additional corrections are made for the facts that (1) people tend to underreport their incomes when talking to the Census Bureau, and (2) transfer payments (government cash benefits)

---

[2] A retrospective calculation, using the official definition, indicated that 44 million persons, or 29 percent of the population, were poor in 1949.

are not taxed the way wages are, then it is possible to juggle the figures to make them suggest that only 3 to 5 percent of our citizens are poor. Using that approach, Martin Anderson asserted that:

> The "war on poverty" that began in 1964 has been won. . . . Any Americans who truly cannot care for themselves are now eligible for generous government aid in the form of cash, medical benefits, food stamps, housing and other services. (Anderson 1978: 15)

Unfortunately, such a statement can only be believed by a person who manipulates statistics to make a point and ignores all other aspects of social reality. For instance, these statistics average out all payments for medicare and housing subsidies and allocate the average to all families. But most poor families are ineligible for housing subsidies, and no family gets cash for medicare, which pays directly to doctors and hospitals for treatment of the indigent sick. According to this approach, the sicker the poor get and the richer their doctors become, the less poverty there is in the United States!

Anderson's use of the word *generous* for government aid contradicts direct studies of families living on welfare or attempting to survive on the minimum wage; they show a level of misery that must be called poor in the United States of the 1980s. Actually, poverty in the social sense involves factors that go beyond cash budgets. Long-term, persistent poverty that exceeds temporary crises includes social definitions that degrade people and classify them as unworthy of public and personal respect, which in turn saps their energies and their efforts to live as citizens rather than outcasts. Especially since almost half the people officially counted as poor are children, no amount of statistical "correction" can remove the social problem and the political issue (for qualitative studies, see Harrington 1962, Liebow 1967, Rainwater 1970, Stack 1974, Sheehan 1976; regarding children, see Keniston et al. 1977).

Regardless of one's threshold definition of poverty, it is crucial to make the distinction between temporary and long-term deprivation. Many people fall below the poverty line during a given year as a result of temporary circumstances: loss of a job, physical injury, breakup of a marriage. When they get back on their feet, they are no longer poor. Others remain poor for many years. Some of them can never work because they are too old or are physically or mentally disabled. Others who work from time to time have so little technical or social skill that they cannot keep for long a job that pays enough to get them above the margin with some sense of security and anticipation for the future. Some who work regularly at wages close to the minimum level have too many children to feed. Some others (much exaggerated in the press) make a calculated career of living off government benefits that allow them to survive but never approach the mainstream.

Richard Coe has analyzed data from the University of Michigan's Panel Study of Income Dynamics that follow a large sample of families over the years to see how their circumstances change. He reported that of the people who were poor (by the official definition) in 1975, only 11 percent had been poor in *all* of the previous nine years. On the other hand, about a quarter of the total sample had been poor in at least *one* of those years (Duncan and Morgan 1976 and 1978).

Combining those figures with government data, we can estimate that a *quarter of the population lives close to the risk of occasional poverty, that 11 to 12 percent are poor in a given year, and that at least 3 percent of all Americans are stuck in poverty for a very long time.*

In a parallel approach that counted people on welfare (AFDC), Martin Rein and Lee Rainwater started with the observation that welfare is primarily directed toward female-headed families and their children. Using the same University of Michigan Panel Study data, they followed the experiences of all women in the sample who were from 18 to 54 years of age in 1968—the people who potentially might need welfare. Projecting the experience of those women to all women of the same age in the country, they calculated the following figures (Rein and Rainwater 1977):

Total, women 18–54 years of age	50,000,000	100%
Go on welfare at least once in 10 years:	(7,000,000)	(14)
Stay on welfare 4 years or less	3,500,000	7
Stay on welfare 5 to 8 years	2,730,000	5
Stay on welfare 9 or 10 years	770,000	2

They conclude that welfare serves to tide many women over short-term crises, but only a relatively small number of women—less than a million—should be called a permanent "welfare class" who stay on for nine years or more.

The government calculates a different way and reports that of those who are on welfare at a given moment, 24 percent have been on the rolls for six years or more (U.S. Census 1980c: 358). That would indicate about 850,000 women in 1977—about 2 percent of the age group that is eligible for welfare, almost the same as the estimate of Rein and Rainwater.

WHO IS POOR?

Arguments about the total number of individuals or families who should be classified as poor are endless since they depend upon the perceiver's eye. However, once we agree upon some definition "for the sake of the argument," then we can turn to significant questions that have empirical answers: What kinds of people are poor? What makes them poor? What can be done to alleviate their poverty?

Since most of the data come from the government, let us use the official definition. Table 10–1 shows the distribution of poverty; it starts with the total number of individuals (or families) who fall below the poverty line (after transfer payments have been received), and then gives the breakdown into various social characteristics. We learn that there are more than twice as many poor whites as poor blacks; that 40 percent of the poor are children and 13 percent are elderly; that about half the poor families are headed by a man, and half by a woman. These data contradict two popular stereotypes: (1) that the poor are mostly black; (2) that the poor mainly reside in families with a mother as head and no father in residence. We are thus warned that poverty and welfare are not synonymous, since most of the families receiving welfare are in fact headed by a woman.

Another way to approach the data is to ask: If you belong to a certain social group, what is the chance of your being poor? This life chance is called the risk (or rate, or prevalence, or incidence) of poverty, and it is shown in Table 10–2. Here we learn that while 11 percent of all families and unrelated individuals are poor, 25 percent of nonwhite families are poor. Thus there is a correlation between race and some of the direct causes of poverty, such as low wages and underemployment. We also learn how important the government's transfer programs are in putting people just above instead of below the poverty line: if one *excluded* these payments, then the percentage of families below the line would more than *double*. For the *elderly*, it

TABLE 10–1
The distribution of poverty, 1978

		Millions	Percent
a.	*Total poor persons*	24.5	100%
	Race: White	16.3	66
	Black	7.6	31
	Other	.6	3
b.	*Total poor persons*	24.5	100
	Age: Over 65 years	3.2	13
	18–64 years	11.6	47
	Under 18 years	9.7	40
c.	*Total poor families*	5.3	100
	Family head: Male	2.6	50
	Female	2.7	50

Note: Based on money income after transfers but before taxes.
Source: U.S. Bureau of the Census, *Characteristics of the Population below the Poverty Level: 1978,* Current Population Reports, 1980, series P-60, no. 124, p. 2.

TABLE 10–2
The risk of poverty, 1976

	Percent poor	
Population category	Before taxes, before transfers	Before taxes, after transfers
All families and individuals	26%	11%
Unrelated individuals	46	22
Multiperson families	18	8
White families and individuals	23	10
Nonwhite families and individuals	42	25
Head under 65	17	11
Head over 65	58	13

Source: U.S. Bureau of the Census, *Social Indicators, 1976* (Washington, D.C.: U.S. Government Printing Office, 1977), p. 468.

would more than *quadruple*. The war on poverty has not yet been won, but certainly some progress has been made through the government's efforts.

So far the figures suggest that a part of poverty is a consequence of the fact that some of the elderly citizens still do not have enough pension income to keep them above the poverty line, although this group is much smaller than it used to be. The bulk of poverty, however, is connected with adults of working age (and their children) who either do not have jobs or do not receive enough pay, as detailed below. Two important social characteristics are correlated with these factors: race and sex. If a family is headed by a black or by a woman, then its chances of being poor are dramatically increased. Roughly speaking, being black instead of white *doubles* the chance of being poor, but being a female head of family instead of a male head *quintuples* the risk (U.S. Census 1980d: 2).

POLICIES TO ALLEVIATE POVERTY: TRANSFERS VERSUS JOBS

Suppose the citizens of the United States decided that the government should take Lyndon Johnson's goals seriously and make every possible effort to eliminate poverty. What *could* be done? What are the logical alternative policies?

The simplest definition of poverty is that it is life without enough money. The simplest way of eliminating a shortage of funds is to send a check. Consequently, some people (including the most conservative of economists, Milton Friedman) have long maintained that the government should give every poor family enough money to bring them above a minimum standard of living. The mechanism for doing so already exists: most families declare their incomes every year to the Internal Revenue Service and pay a tax based on the size of their incomes. Proponents of this direct approach to end poverty say that, along with levying a tax on those with enough income, the IRS could send a check to those without adequate earnings. If such a plan were adopted, some or even all of the existing systems of social insurance and social welfare could be eliminated, from social security pensions, through unemployment insurance, to Aid to Families with Dependent Children, or AFDC. The savings in administrative costs would be large, and the simplification of procedures would grant dignity to the recipients. As indicated above, the additional costs to the U.S. Treasury (not even counting administrative savings) would not, in relation to the total budget, be very great. In a straightforward economic sense, the federal budget could afford to end poverty.

Why then hasn't it been done? Indeed, both presidents Nixon and Carter proposed a limited version of this plan, but it never came to a vote in the full Congress. The reasons are intricate and will be explained in detail below. In general, they stem from the interests of special constituencies: some want to preserve the pool of underemployed people in order to help businesses that need cheap workers; others want to keep the present mix of welfare programs; others are morally outraged by the idea of a guaranteed minimum annual income, or negative income tax, as this approach is usually labeled, which seems to them to turn Uncle Sam into Santa Claus.

Another approach to poverty is to assert that it is not just a question of inadequate income. For those who are able to work but do not have jobs that provide decent wages, the most important thing is to help them get such jobs. A job is a social role, not just a source of money. It signifies that a person is a responsible adult, able to care for himself or herself, worthy of being considered a full and participating citizen in the community, and often a good parent who provides for children. A check from the government is not a socially adequate substitute for a job for those who are defined as people who ought to work.

Therefore, we must ask: how much of the total amount of poverty in the United States is directly connected with unemployment or underemployment—that is, inadequate work over a period of time with good enough pay to bring a person and a family above the official poverty line? If we exclude young children, adolescents in school, and the elderly, we will find that there were 13.5 million poor persons of working age in 1978 (grouped in 4.6 million households). However, 2.3 million were ill or disabled and unable to work; another 3.6 million were busy keeping house and in most instances had small children at home. That leaves 1.0 million who did not work because they could not find or did not look for jobs. Another 6.6 million did work at least part of the year. Indeed, 1.7 million of them had full-time jobs for 40 or more weeks during the year and still did not bring home enough money to avoid poverty; the rest either had part-time jobs or suffered from long periods of unemployment (U.S. Census 1980d: 61; see also Schiller 1980).

These figures suggest that almost half of the poverty among persons of working age that remains after transfers is connected with disability or family duties that keep people out of the labor force (and such poverty should be corrected by improvements in the transfer system). A little more than half is connected with unemployment, underemployment, and substandard wages.

During the Kennedy administration, it was thought that a tax cut could stimulate employment to such a degree that large numbers of people would be brought out of poverty. The tax cut may have helped a little, but the unemployment rate did not go below 5 percent until Vietnam War expenditures increased in the second half of the decade (the goal was a rate of 3 percent). And all during the 1970s, it ranged between 5 and 9 percent. In any given month in 1980, a little over 7 million persons were unemployed (since the labor force was close to 100 million persons, the figures in millions can be used as approximations to percents). However, only a quarter of them were out of work for more than 15 weeks. On the other hand, 22 million persons were unemployed at least once during the year. Many of these were covered by unemployment insurance, but many were not—especially the women and young people who were entering the labor force for the first time or reentering after a lengthy period of withdrawal. And 60 percent of the unemployed (especially the teenagers) lived in households with another person who had a job (all figures from *New York Times*, May 9, 1981). Obviously, all unemployment does not create poverty, but there would be much less poverty if the unemployment rate could be kept lower so that more poor heads of households and other persons in them could readily get and keep jobs. And lower unemployment would tend to drive up wages for persons at the bottom of the skill hierarchy, especially if combined with an increase in the legal minimum wage.[3]

In recent years, it has become increasingly clear that the private economy cannot maintain reasonably full employment and that those who suffer the results over long periods of time are primarily people of low skill (Aaron 1978: chap. 3). Two policies have been suggested to help them: give them job training to increase their skill, and create government-supported jobs to take up the slack in the demand for labor. As long as unemployment is above the minimum, or "fric-

---

[3] The official unemployment figures exclude many discouraged people who have stopped looking for jobs (Moses 1975).

tional," rate (people changing jobs or entering the labor force and requiring a little time to find a job), job training may give some people a better chance to compete, but it will not have any effect on reducing overall poverty, for the newly trained will simply take jobs away from other workers. Job *training* must be combined with job *creation*, either in the private or the public sector. Both goals were sought under the CETA (Comprehensive Employment and Training Act) programs of the 1970s, which set up training program activities and also gave money to local governments to help them hire unemployed people and give them useful tasks; about a million persons were helped under these programs in 1980.

In sum, the various possible alternative policies for ending (or markedly reducing) poverty are these:

The government could send checks to all those with incomes below a minimum to bring them up to that level.

It could improve job training for people of low skill.

It could stimulate the economy to increase the total number of jobs in the private sector.

It could create more jobs in the public sector.

It could increase the minimum wage.

It could increase the size of transfer payments to those unable to work full-time so that they all reach a minimum income level.

Some other ideas have been discussed (such as the system of family allowances used in certain countries) but have never had enough popularity to be translated into serious proposals in the Congress. The big issues in public policy relate to the proper mix in the approaches listed and to the total amount the government can afford to pay without creating too high a tax burden or too much inflation or reducing the incentive to work. These are political issues: in each instance, some group will benefit, but another group will pay more in taxes or other costs.

The nature of the political struggles about various policies to alleviate poverty can best be understood through a brief history of what the government has actually done and the fate of major specific proposals for new programs. It all started with the Great Depression of the 1930s.

THE BEGINNINGS OF WELFARE: ROOSEVELT

The Depression hit the nation with devastating effect: the unemployment rate was above 20 percent from 1932 through 1935 and did not go below 15 percent until the eve of war in 1940—and simultaneously, the wages of those with jobs were pushed down. Per capita income was cut by a third. Private charities were overwhelmed, and the attempts of local governments to provide some form of assistance were totally inadequate. With the election of Franklin D. Roosevelt in 1932, the federal government moved quickly and devised entirely new approaches to the problems of unemployment and poverty (Piven and Cloward 1971: chap. 2 and 3). The first step was direct "relief" in the form of cash payments to any family in desperate need, financed by "emergency" grants from the federal to the state governments, which made up their own rules of distribution within broad federal guidelines. In 1934, one sixth of the population was receiving assistance. In addition, the Civilian Conservation Corps provided some jobs for unemployed young men in reforestation and similar projects.

By 1935, it was decided to expand the job programs and phase out direct relief. The Work Progress Administration was set up to finance all sorts of construction projects and other activities, mainly organized by local governments. From 2 to 3 million people (mostly men) were employed in the later years of the decade by the WPA and another million people in other projects (U.S. Census 1975: I, 339). The responsibility for direct relief was turned back to the states and localities, but with some help in the form of "categorical" programs in which the federal government would share the costs of support for impoverished people classified as unemployable for specific reasons: the blind, the physically or mentally disabled, the elderly, and mothers with small children and no husbands to provide for them. It was assumed that much of the aid dispensed under these programs would eventually fade away as the new programs of the federal social security system took hold.

The core of that new system was OASDI—Old Age, Survivors and Disability Insurance. Enrolled individuals (and especially in the earlier years, not everyone was included) would receive full coverage after 10 years of contributions made by employees and employers to the trust funds. Retired persons would get permanent pensions, as would those who were disabled to the point of not being able to work. Widows and orphans (survivors) of insured workers would get benefits. There was also established a system of unemployment insurance administered by the states under federal guidelines that would give temporary payments to insured workers during periods of layoff, usually up to 26 weeks. All insurance-type benefits were automatic entitlements to those enrolled and did not require the means test to demonstrate the impoverishment that was required for direct relief.

Each of these new programs dealt with a piece of the general problem of distress—that is, with a special category of people. Some programs emphasized care for the elderly; others gave help to young mothers without husbands; others offered temporary payments to workers between jobs, or provided jobs for the unemployed that were expected to end with the return to "normalcy." Some were based on a means test, others were viewed as insurance or entitlements. Nobody thought in simple and direct terms of providing enough money to bring *all* poor people up to some standard of minimum decency. Consequently, the programs overlapped in some ways but failed to integrate in others. Some people who were not poor received payments (especially old age pensions), and others who were living in misery found themselves ineligible for any help.

POSTWAR YEARS

By the end of World War II and the years of prosperity it produced, the scene had changed. The social security system was beginning to pay out large sums to the elderly, and since it was viewed by the public as an insurance program that returned to them in the form of pensions money that they had earlier contributed in the form of premiums, it was not stigmatized as "relief" and was popular among all segments of society. (Actually, it is a program that taxes workers to pay retirees, but most people do not think of it that way.) The "make-work," or special public jobs, had disappeared. The unemployment compensation system was working smoothly and was taken for granted. When Eisenhower was elected in 1952, we learned that these programs were no longer connected with a partisan New Deal but were accepted by the Republicans, who had earlier opposed them.

In the 1960s, the Kennedy and Johnson administrations added three significant new programs: food stamps (poor families could buy, for cash, stamps that were redeemable at the grocery store for food worth more than the cost of the stamps); medicare (insurance to cover hospital and doctor bills for the elderly, regardless of their income); and medicaid (free medical insurance for the poor, regardless of their age).

The combination of social security pensions for the elderly, plus AFDC for poor families with children, plus some other cash assistance programs, had made a significant dent in officially defined poverty by the mid-1970s: the number of families below the poverty line had dropped to 11 percent (it would have been 26 percent without these programs). And the noncash programs, such as the food stamps and medical payments, helped some more. But as the programs developed, so did opposition to some of them, particularly the means-tested ones that were defined by the public as "welfare."[4] (The social insurance programs remained popular.) There was a

---

[4] In a "means-tested" program the applicant must prove to the authorities that he or she is poor enough to be eligible for help.

growing public feeling that too many people were taking advantage of welfare and that the cost to the U.S. Treasury was too great. Opponents said these programs "were getting out of control," that there was too much "fraud and abuse," that the nation could no longer afford to solve social problems by "throwing money at them." Before the war on poverty had gone very far, a resistance movement emerged.

The main debate concerned AFDC, partly because it was growing so fast (especially during the 10 years following 1964) and partly because of widespread suspicion that many families were taking advantage of it who really were not eligible for help—or should not be. By 1970, the number of families on welfare had grown to 2.5 million; by 1975 another million had been enrolled, adding up to more than 11 million individuals, counting children. Three quarters of those families were headed by a woman; three quarters lived in metropolitan areas; a little less than half were black. In New York City alone, the proportion receiving welfare grew from 1 in 30 people in 1960 to 1 in 6 in 1970.

As suggested above, the migration of many poor farmers *to* the cities, coupled with the flight of low-skilled manufacturing jobs *from* the cities, were underlying economic causes for the growth in the welfare rolls, despite general prosperity. But there were social and political causes as well. The proportion of black families in the nation that were headed by a woman jumped from 21 percent in 1960 to 35 percent in 1975; there was also an increase in white female-headed families. Thus, there was some increase in the number of persons who became eligible for welfare. But the largest increase in enrollment came because the administration of the program (not the law) adjusted to political pressure, as indicated by Piven and Cloward:

> The welfare explosion occurred during several years of the greatest domestic disorder since the 1930s—perhaps the greatest in our history. It was concurrent with the turmoil produced by the civil rights struggle, with widespread and destructive rioting in the cities, and with the formation of a militant grass-roots movement of the poor dedicated to combatting welfare restrictions. Not least, the welfare rise was also concurrent with the enactment of a series of ghetto-placating federal programs (such as the anti-poverty program) which, among other things, hired thousands of poor people, social workers, and lawyers who, it subsequently turned out, greatly stimulated people to apply for relief and helped them to obtain it. (1971: 198)

In other words, the welfare system served as a mechanism for buying social peace: when those who were left out of prosperity finally began to scream, they were given a modicum of help. By 1975, the process had run its course: most of the eligibles had been signed up, the rolls had stopped growing, and the resistance movement had grown stronger than the protest movement.

ATTEMPTS TO REFORM WELFARE: NIXON

The first suggestion for major reform in the design of the welfare system (beyond mere tinkering with eligibility rules) emerged in the early part of the Nixon administration in 1969. One impetus for change was the dismay about the overlap in various programs and the discrepancies in the rules from one area to another that stemmed from local options in the way the system was administered. In some states, no benefits could be paid to a woman with a husband living in the house; in others, she would be eligible if her husband was unemployed. The level of payments under both AFDC and its accompanying medicaid and food stamps were set very low in the Southern states, but in other places, the same programs paid *as much as 10 times more.* Although there was little research evidence to support the idea, many officials were convinced that these discrepancies caused people to move north to get higher benefits, and the governors and mayors in those states demanded changes. Furthermore, the complexity of the total system, which mixed cash benefits, food stamps, and many other noncash benefits and services (family advice, job training, housing and medical subsidies, etc.), created a large bureaucracy of social service workers who were accused of soaking up more and more of the money and interferring more and more in people's lives.

Many experienced administrators in the federal government had been advocating a simplified procedure that would combine various categories of people (mothers, unemployed fathers, elderly not sufficiently supported under social security, permanently disabled) and various types of benefits into a single cash payment based solely on financial need. Furthermore, they wanted it administered according to national standards that would be the same everywhere, probably run by the federal Social Security Administration (possibly even by the Internal Revenue Service). Obviously, they were thinking along the lines of a negative income tax or guaranteed minimum annual income. In principle, it seemed gloriously efficient and appropriate to a computer age that preferred to standardize life according to automatic criteria. And it would only cost $5 to $10 billion extra at first and might eventually cost less as it cut administrative overhead and presumably increased the incentive to work (by making reduction in payments gradual as earned income increased so that everybody would always gain by having some sort of job).

Nixon was elected as a conservative who would stress work rather than welfare, but he hoped to soften his harsh political image by supporting efficient government aid for the poorest families. He liked the idea of simplifing the system by combining several programs into a single national cash grant based on need, if it could be done without too much additional cost to the U.S. Treasury. But Nixon realized that such a concept was politically dangerous, since it implied that people would get something for nothing and that some of those who were able to work might refuse to do so. So he carefully added two stipulations: (1) his program was basically a substitute for AFDC, not a plan for everybody, and thus it would be limited to low-income families with children (with or without a father present); (2) it would contain a work requirement such that ablebodied persons refusing to accept jobs would lose benefits. The plan was formulated by experts in the bureaucracy coordinated by Daniel Patrick Moynihan, who had served President Kennedy as assistant secretary of labor and was brought back to Washington as Nixon's urban affairs advisor.

The scheme was labeled the Family Assistance Plan and was introduced early in 1969. It would provide a cash grant of $1,600 to a family of four with no income, plus $860 worth of food stamps, bringing the minimum guaranteed income to a level of $2,460 (considerably less than the poverty line that year of $3,800). All states would have to pay this minimum (using mostly federal money), and those that were currently paying more would have to supplement their grants so that no family would lose income. If the family had a person able to work (that is, not disabled and not the sole person available to care for very small children), then that person would have to register as willing to accept a job, or the payments would be reduced; this feature allowed Nixon to call his plan "workfare instead of welfare." When a family had some income from a job, they could keep $720 of it without having benefits reduced. After that, the benefits would be reduced 50 cents for every extra dollar earned—the equivalent of a 50 percent marginal tax rate on additional earnings. This would blur the distinction between families on welfare and families earning some but not enough money and was thought to provide an incentive for people to work even if they were getting some benefits. The following examples show how earned income would reduce government payments until they were phased out completely (for a family of four):

Earned income	Family assistance	Total cash income
0	$1,600	$1,600
$2,000	960	2,960
4,000	0	4,000

The poorer families would also be eligible for up to $860 in food stamps. It was estimated that the additional cost to the government would be about $5 billion but that the plan would be much simpler to administer than existing welfare programs. (It was separately but simultaneously proposed to combine categorical aid to the elderly, blind, and permanently disabled into a single federal program.)

When first introduced, the new plan received the support of the National Association of Manufacturers, the AFL–CIO, and every former secretary of health, education, and welfare, both Republican and Democrat. It quickly passed the House of Representatives by a wide margin. But then the troubles began in hearings in the Senate Finance Committee, headed by Senator Russell Long of Louisiana. It was noted that the number of people getting some form of government payment would double, even though most of the newcomers would be getting small grants to supplement low earnings—the working poor. It was also argued that the 50-cent reduction in government benefits for each additional dollar earned was a very high tax rate that might reduce the incentive to work rather than increase it, and furthermore, that such a rate was unfair, since those earning enough to start paying income tax only had to share 14 percent of their earnings with the government. The fact that existing AFDC rules reduced payments 67 cents per dollar earned was not emphasized, probably because it was assumed that most female welfare recipients did not work at all, whereas in fact many did; as a group, welfare recipients got only half of their total income from government benefits. Furthermore, in order to limit the program, Nixon did not fold into the cash grants most of the other forms of benefits (food stamps, medicaid, etc.). The result was a series of incongruities, or "notch" problems: when earned income fell a dollar, some people would become eligible for benefits worth hundreds of dollars. Thus people with almost identical incomes would in fact be receiving quite disparate forms and amounts of help from the government.

To these arithmetic difficulties were added political issues. The liberals said the plan was much too stingy, offering a level of support far below the poverty line and below that currently paid in many states. They argued that, although those states would be required to supplement the plan at first, they would be tempted to phase out the supplements over the years and pay at the new, nationally established minimum level. Furthermore, the liberals were deeply suspicious of any plan introduced by their worst enemy, Richard Nixon. The conservatives answered that any increase in the basic benefit level would very rapidly increase the number of working poor receiving partial payments, that it would be easy to have a third or more of the population getting "handouts," and that the costs to the U.S. Treasury could be enormous. And the Southerners were worried that any increase in the existing low levels of AFDC in their region would reduce the supply of poor people available as seasonal workers on farms during the harvest season and would also have the tendency to push up the low local wage rates that were attracting many manufacturing firms to move down from the northern states. The plan was debated to death: it never emerged from the committee and suffered the same fate when reintroduced the following year with some modifications (Moynihan 1973, Anderson 1978).

Nevertheless, the search for a workable form of guaranteed minimum income continued. The government sponsored a series of local experiments to test the impact of various similar schemes on the amount people actually did reduce their efforts to earn money from jobs. The initial results, from an experiment in New Jersey, indicated that work reduction would be minimal and that people liked the new system. But later results from Denver and Seattle were more discouraging: if families were guaranteed enough cash to supplement earnings and bring income up to the official poverty line, but earnings above that line caused a 50-cent-per-dollar reduction in benefits, it was found that husbands worked about 6 percent less than they would under the old system, that wives worked 23 percent less, that female heads of families worked 12 percent less, and that teenagers in the family reduced their part-time work by about one third. Furthermore, there was startling evidence that, instead of encouraging families to stay together by removing the incentive for the father to leave home and make the mother eligible for AFDC, the new system actually increased separations, probably because unsatisfied wives were more sure of support under the experimental rules and felt more free to evict their husbands (U.S. Senate 1978).

ATTEMPTS TO REFORM WELFARE: CARTER

Before these new research results were fully available, the Carter administration entered office, and yet another team tried to face up to what was then considered to be "the welfare mess." Incongruities between different programs and different regions were still the main causes of concern, and many people were worried about the demoralizing effects of long-term payments to single mothers that seemed to be ensuring the country a permanent welfare class. A report to a Congressional committee stated:

> Our income security programs are shaped by at least 21 committees of the Congress and by 50 state legislatures, by six cabinet departments and three federal agencies, by 54 state and territorial welfare agencies and by more than 1,500 county welfare departments, by the U.S. Supreme Court and by many lesser courts. (*New York Times*, April 3, 1977)

The results, said the report, encouraged family separations, discouraged work when people would lose more than they gained, kept people from saving any money (which would make them ineligible for continued help), kept many poor and hungry people from getting food stamps because they had to pay cash for them (even though the stamps were worth more than the money), and created enormous disparities of support for people in different places.

The Carter team came in with a program that was not too different from the Nixon proposals. However, they recognized one significant fact that had been pushed aside earlier: the key problem was not "forcing" people to work but providing jobs when they did not exist. So the Carter plan called for the creation of almost a million and a half jobs to be added to local governments with federal money at wages close to the legal minimum. These jobs, along with training programs, would be part of CETA (Comprehensive Employment and Training Act). Benefits to families would follow the Nixon scheme, although at a slightly more generous level. Food stamps would no longer require a cash payment, and the rules would be the same in all parts of the country. Some money would be given to the working poor through a very modest "income tax credit," a form of negative income tax administered by the Internal Revenue Service (it already existed but would be expanded). All states would have their current contributions to the system reduced as the federal share increased, which generated local political support. (*The New York Times* front-page headline on August 7, 1977, read, "Carter asks New Welfare System with Emphasis on Required Work; New York could save $527 million.") When the full program was phased in, by 1980, it was expected to cost about $34 billion, which was only about $6 billion above projected expenditures under existing programs.

What were the results? The Nixon administration had succeeded in obtaining only one major reform: categorical aid for the needy elderly, blind, and permanently disabled, previously a hodgepodge of local programs partly subsidized by the federal treasury, was reorganized in 1974 into the federal Supplemental Security Income, or SSI, administered in most states by the Social Security Administration. The Carter administration succeeded in eliminating the cash payment for food stamps, it expanded the number of people involved in CETA programs, and it increased tax credits. But AFDC was not changed; the Congress never seriously debated the issue. The various committees, agencies, and states continued to run their mixture of programs (see Levitan and Taggert 1976, and Levitan 1980).

In the fiscal year ending October 1, 1977, the total income support system cost the federal government $164 billion, and state and local governments an additional $22 billion, as shown in Table 10–3. Welfare benefits for both AFDC and SSI came to a total of $16.6 billion and helped about 16 million individuals. Food stamps were costing $4.5 billion and served 18 million recipients. Medicaid for the poor cost $17.2 billion and paid the bills for almost 25 million patients. But all of these were dwarfed by social security, which paid out $84.1 billion to 34 million people; medicare for those people cost an extra $21.2 billion. The Carter budget requested an additional $4 billion for various CETA programs for a little less than a million persons. It is not known exactly how many families were drawing support under more than one program.

The net effect of these programs for reducing poverty in the preceding year is shown in Table 10–4. Excluding CETA jobs but including noncash benefits, it shows that officially defined poverty was

TABLE 10–3
Welfare and social insurance expenditures (federal, state, and local, fiscal year 1977)

	Recipients (millions of persons)	Payments ($ billions)		
		Federal	State and local	Total
Welfare				
Cash benefits:				
Aid to families with dependent children	11.5	5.7	4.6	10.3
Supplemental security income	4.1	4.7	1.6*	6.3
Veterans' and survivors' non-service-				
connected pensions		3.1	—	3.1
Earned income tax credit		0.9	—	0.9
General assistance	1.0	—	1.3	1.3
Total		14.4	7.5	21.9
In-kind benefits:				
Food stamps	18.0	4.5	—	4.5
Child nutrition and other Department of				
Agriculture food assistance		3.3	—	3.3
Medicaid	24.7	9.7	7.5	17.2
Housing assistance		3.0	—	3.0
Basic educational opportunity grants		1.8	—	1.8
Total		22.3	7.5	29.8
Total welfare		36.7	15.0	51.7
Social insurance				
Cash benefits:				
Old age, survivors, and disability insurance				
and railroad retirement	34.0	84.1	—	84.1
Special compensation for disabled coal miners		0.9	—	0.9
Unemployment compensation†	7.0	15.2	—	15.2
Veterans' and survivors' service-connected				
compensation		5.7	—	5.7
Workers' compensation‡		—	6.7	6.7
Total		105.9	6.7	112.6
In-kind benefits:				
Medicare	22.0	21.2	—	21.2
Total social insurance		127.1	6.7	133.8
Total welfare and social insurance§		163.8‖	21.7	185.5

* Excludes state administered supplements.
† Benefits are paid from federal fund financed by federal and state taxes.
‡ Administered by states and usually financed by employers.
§ Excludes federal civil service pensions.
‖ Gross national product was $1,900 billion; thus federal costs for welfare and social insurance were 8.6 percent of GNP, and total costs were 9.8 percent of GNP.
Sources: For dollars: George J. Carcagno and Walter S. Corson in Joseph A. Pechman, ed., *Setting National Priorities: The 1978 Budget* (Washington, D.C.: The Brookings Institution, 1977), p. 253. For recipients: *New York Times*, April 2, 1977; *U.S. News & World Report*, May 18, 1981.

TABLE 10–4
Effect of income-support programs on poverty (fiscal year 1976)

	Families in poverty*	
Alternative	Number (thousands)	Percent of all families
No income transfer (before taxes)	20,237	25.5
Social insurance income† (before taxes)	11,179	14.1
Social insurance and money transfer income‡ (before taxes)	9,073	11.4
Social insurance, money, and in-kind transfer income§ (before taxes):		
Medicare and medicaid excluded	7,406	9.3
Medicare and medicaid included	5,336	6.7
Social insurance, money, and in-kind transfer income (after taxes)	5,445	6.9

* Families are defined to include unrelated individuals as one-person families.
† Social insurance programs included are social security and railroad retirement, government pensions, unemployment compensation, workers' compensation, and veterans' compensation.
‡ Money transfer income programs are veterans' pensions, supplemental security income, aid to families with dependent children.
§ In-kind transfer income is the imputed value of food stamps, child nutrition and housing assistance, and medicare and medicaid.
Source: Based on studies of the Congressional Budget Office as reported by George J. Carcagno and Walter S. Corson in Joseph A. Pechman, ed., *Setting National Priorities: The 1978 Budget* (Washington, D.C.: The Brookings Institution, 1977), p. 225.

reduced from 25.5 percent of families and single individuals to 6.9 percent of families and individuals. Social security, not welfare, was the most important reason.

The debates of the Nixon and Carter years made key issues much clearer to the experts:

1. A simple program based mainly on cash grants in the style of a negative income tax runs into certain unavoidable choices that are politically impossible to resolve (at least in the short run):
   a. To keep the costs within bounds, either the initial payment level must be kept low (and liberals protest), or the marginal tax rate on earnings must be set high (which conservatives protest because it reduces work incentive). As soon as the initial payment level begins increasing, the number of working poor eligible for partial payments goes up at a fast rate.
   b. To function with a minimum of "notch" incongruities, all the noncash programs must be folded into a single cash scheme, but that means that special constituencies in favor of food stamps for nutrition, or medical care for the sick, or housing subsidies to save the cities, all protest.
2. The problem of unemployment among the poor who go on welfare cannot be solved either by a work requirement (which has proven ineffective) or by a relatively low marginal tax rate on earnings to maintain incentive. It is deeply connected with the inadequate supply of jobs at decent wages for low-skilled people,

and that problem appears to be getting worse as technology gets more sophisticated.

3. A program that would bring all families in the country up to the official (but inadequate) poverty line, and that permitted an appropriate combination of welfare plus work, is threatening to low-wage industries and regions, and they will oppose it. The bitter struggles of farmers against those attempting to form labor unions to help migrant agricultural workers shows the depth of such opposition.

ATTEMPTS TO REFORM WELFARE: REAGAN

The Reagan administration began with a new set of goals. They accepted all the difficulties listed above that had defeated attempts to restructure and simplify the system; indeed, Martin Anderson, who had served briefly in the Nixon administration and then written a persuasive book in 1978 arguing against restructuring, was the man put in charge of domestic planning by President Reagan. The new leaders wanted to reduce expenditures, not improve the system. They proposed to tighten all the rules in the existing system to make it cheaper and to eliminate any parts of it that seemed expendable. There were two undefined limits put on this process: (1) social security was not to be changed much, since it was said to be based on the insurance principle and people had the right to their benefits (and they represented a huge block of vociferous voters); (2) the "truly needy" should be supported by a "social safety net."

The main Reagan economic thrust was not directed toward helping the poor but rather toward pleasing the middle class, which was restive after years of inflation and was demanding a reduction in government expenditures and taxes. Since it was also part of the Reagan philosophy to sharply increase defense outlays, social programs had to be cut in compensation. The Reagan view reflected much public opinion, which felt that inflation was caused by government expenditures, and that government had been growing too fast. It is true that during the 1960s when the economy was thriving, total federal government expenditures did grow from about 18.5 percent of the gross national product in 1960 to 20.5 percent in 1970—partly from social and partly from military increases (state and local expenses went up even faster). In the next decade, as the Vietnam War phased out, military expenditures were reduced, but social expenditures increased, until the final budget reached 22.8 percent of GNP in 1976. During the Carter administration the outlays stabilized at about 22 percent of GNP. The federal government had stopped growing, but the Reagan administration wanted to reduce it.

Starting with Carter's budget projections for the fiscal year ending October 1, 1982, the Reagan team initially proposed:

1. Cutting the total budget outlays from $740 billion to $696 billion, or 6 percent.
2. Increasing defense by at least $4.4 billion.
3. Reducing education, employment, and social services by $8.7 billion. CETA would be cut by two thirds, food stamps by 11 percent, AFDC by 10 percent, medicaid by 5 percent.

Each of these cuts in particular programs does not seem by itself to be such a major revision of emphasis, but since many poor families would experience several cuts simultaneously, the overall effect on them would be large, especially for the working poor. Unfortunately, the statistics are inadequate to predict in advance exactly how large the net effect would be and which families would suffer most—but political decisions are made in terms of public mood rather than careful estimates. For instance, no provision was made in the budget for increased costs that will be required to offset the unemployment of people eliminated from CETA who will need AFDC and food stamps. And the cuts for fiscal year 1982 were but a prelude: the administration wanted to cut income tax rates 30 percent in three years and simultaneously increase military spending. To reach that goal, much more drastic cuts in social programs would be required in an attempt to contain the huge deficit.

TRANSFERS IN COMPARATIVE PERSPECTIVE

The United States spends less on income support programs than most European countries. Exact comparisons are difficult because of the diversity of systems, but one estimate for 1975 suggests that our welfare and social insurance transfers, plus some additional programs not shown in Table 10–3, amounted to 11.5 percent of our GNP. Equivalent expenditures in France (which had direct grants to all families with children, regardless of income) came to 20 percent of its GNP, and West Germany and Sweden spent just over 16.5 percent (excluding additional costs for general medical care). The United Kingdom was just under the United States in proportionate expenditures (Rein and Rainwater 1980: Table 5–4). The same study estimates that our expenditures for these programs doubled as a proportion of GNP in the decade between 1965 and 1975.

The time trends for all these countries suggest a growing demographic problem: even with no change at all in the systems, expenditures will grow because the proportion of the population that is aged and retired will increase substantially. Thus payroll taxes on the young must increase, or benefits to the elderly will have to be cut (Ross 1979). This problem will be slightly offset by a relative decrease in the proportion of children and thus, presumably, in children in families on welfare and/or requiring public education.

IS THERE A PERMANENT UNDERCLASS?

The previous discussion has several times introduced the distinction between poverty that arises from temporary difficulties of the individual or the economy—a period of high unemployment, or the pains of family disruption or illness—and the poverty that is based on permanent or at least long-term problems. Since the Great Depression, periods of sharp recession have generally been rather short; and so long-term poverty is often viewed as the fault of the individuals involved: they are assumed to be unskilled or unmotivated or permanently disabled. The welfare system, particularly supplemental security income, is supposed to take care of the permanently disabled. Thus, the biggest group of "problem" families comprises the ones thought to be able to work but who do not work steadily for one reason or another. And some observers believe that their children learn the way of life of their parents, and that these problem families in fact become a permanent underclass of people who perpetuate their style of life through the generations. The typical image of such a family discussed in the mass media consists of a middle-aged woman without a legal husband who lives on AFDC in a public housing project in an inner-city slum with her many illegitimate children, including unwed teenaged daughters who have their own babies.

Is this image a false stereotype or a true picture? There are two types of studies that address the question: (1) researches on the labor market, particularly those stimulated by the theory of the dual labor market, which analyze the facts of continuing unemployment and underemployment in the midst of general prosperity; (2) researches on poor families designed to follow them over a long period of time, often through more than one generation, to find out if they remain poor through the years, and if so, why.

There is little doubt that there are a lot of marginal, low-level jobs in the secondary labor market that pay wages close to the legal minimum, suffer an unusually high rate of layoff on the part of employers sensitive to small swings in the business cycle, and experience absenteeism and quitting on the part of employees.[5] People who hold such jobs may be able to support a single individual with them but not a family on a stable basis. Industrial jobs of this type are declining as a proportion of the labor force, but unskilled service jobs are increasing, so the two trends partly cancel each other. However, the industrial jobs tend to pay more, as emphasized in *The New York Times* (April 18, 1981):

> Between 1950 and 1980, when overall employment increased 114 percent, jobs declined by 5 percent in the automobile industry, 14 percent in mining, and 34 percent in general manufacturing. Employment in

---

[5] Not all jobs are covered under the federal minimum, and some pay even less.

the wholesale and retail trades rose 119 percent; in restaurants, bars, and fast-food emporiums, 220 percent; . . . and in the service trades, which include hotels and motels, laundry services, beauty shops, and janitorial services, 228 percent. . . . These (service) jobs generally pay about half as much as the old factory jobs that are disappearing.

If all low-paying jobs were held by people as stepping-stones, as opportunities to start work and then move up to better positions as the incumbents gained in skill and experience, then such jobs would not create a permanent underclass of people stuck in poverty. But unfortunately, many of these marginal jobs are defined by both employer and employee as dead ends. They are routinized, boring, and often degrading. Employers hire people at the lowest possible wage and assume that they are getting unreliable workers not worth careful training. As long as there are a lot of unemployed people waiting in the job queue, the employer gets used to the idea of high turnover and does not bother to attach workers to the firm on a long-term basis through training, promotion, fringe benefits, and so on. He would rather cut costs to the bone, be able to lay off at will, and, when needed, hire somebody else (Thurow 1975: chap. 4; chap. 4 above).

Who gets the marginal jobs? Mostly, people who cannot get any better jobs and take the leftovers. Thus they are usually untrained and often from groups that are discriminated against in the primary labor market, where employers prefer to select categories of applicants which they assume are better risks for permanent attachment to the firm. Given past traditions and prejudices, the primary employers choose people with high school diplomas or additional training, and they tend to be suspicious of blacks and Hispanics—and for many jobs, of women—thus pushing them into the secondary labor market (Aaron 1978: chap. 2; Laws 1979).

Those individuals who have held a succession of marginal jobs are likely to lose heart. They come to accept the employers' definitions and think of themselves as hard-luck cases who are not going to get anywhere in life. Their ambition is reduced, their discipline is weakened, and they learn to take life as it comes (Davis 1946). They accept marginal jobs from time to time, then they apply for welfare, then they may make some money in a street hustle, and so on (Liebow 1967; Rainwater 1970; Stack 1974; Sheehan 1976). In this way, bad jobs get linked with certain people, and the result is an underclass.

But do they so routinize this style of life as to create a "culture of poverty" that is taught to their children, as suggested by Oscar Lewis (1966)? Or do they continue to behave as rational economic actors who will improve their situation whenever the outside world gives them a chance (Valentine 1968; Ryan 1971)? Any social worker experienced in the life of the poor knows of problem families with a history of generations of misery, who have given up hope. Thus, the stereotype is sometimes matched by real people. But the issue for those concerned with the society as a whole and with public policy becomes one of probabilities: what percentage of poor people become stuck in the underclass? Can anything be done about it?

We have already discussed one study that gives a clue to the amount of inheritance of poverty through the generations. The father-son comparisons of Featherman and Hauser, shown in Table 6–1, indicated that more than a quarter of the sons of farm laborers remained in low categories of jobs: service workers, farmers, and laborers. However, about half of them moved into semiskilled and skilled manual jobs, and about a fifth became white-collar employees. The sons of urban laborers did a little better: only a fifth of them remained in labor or service occupations; about half became semi-skilled or skilled manual workers, and more than a quarter climbed into the white-collar ranks.

The Department of Labor recently commissioned a study by Mary Fish to review and synthesize all the best information on the careers of poor people and their children (Fish 1978). Here are a few of her conclusions:

1. About half of the working poor at any one time (not welfare recipients) are likely to stay in poverty most of their lives; about a quarter climb out permanently, and another quarter move back and forth across the line. "Chances of the family of a low-income employed household head moving up are greater if the worker is white and male and the family is not large" (p. 3).

2. "The welfare cases—particularly women who receive Aid to Families with Dependent Children (AFDC)—represent three groups of people: a small group of hard-core unemployed who spend most or all of their working years on welfare (10 percent); a larger group who move back and forth between low-income employment and welfare (40 percent); and a final group who are temporarily on welfare because they are down on their luck (50 percent). Most importantly, however, the children of welfare households do not necessarily perpetuate a welfare pattern. About one half of the children who grow up in homes which are permanently poor will eventually move out of poverty" (p. 2).

3. "People leave welfare when the income they can receive from wages enables them to achieve a higher standard of living. If employment is available at or above the minimum wage and a low future unemployment rate is anticipated, people are more apt to leave the welfare rolls and not return. AFDC mothers with the highest education and/or more recent job experience leave welfare more quickly than other mothers" (p. 2).

These studies show patterns that are congruent with what we know about mobility and succession at all levels of the class hierarchy. Wherever a person is born, the circumstances of family life are such that the child will reproduce to some degree the lives of parents: rich tend to remain rich, poor tend to stay poor. The closer the child is to the extreme of top or bottom, the more likely it is that succession at the same level will occur. But the probabilities are not completely determining of life chances: if half the children of the poor remain poor, the other half do not.

Once we determine the probabilities on the basis of circumstances in general (the social structure), then we can look more closely at individual cases to assess why some poor individuals fall into the 50 percent who stay put and others fall into the 50 percent who are able to climb out of poverty. And here we can assume that personal characteristics play an important role, just as they proved to do in selecting those who went to college in the stratum where the probability of going was 50-50, as described in Chapter 7. Energy levels, intelligence, social skills, attitudes and values and sheer luck separate individuals from the same stratum or even the same family into different styles of behavior. Some of those styles reinforce parental class position, others tend to lead children into paths of life different from the parents' (for good examples, see Whyte 1943: chap. 3).

It is this combination of general probability from structural position and its attendant circumstances, along with individual characteristics, that allows us to better understand the total pattern of life in the underclass. Unfortunately, much of the research literature is phrased in polemic terms: one view says that the culture of poverty exists and constrains life chances; the other says that individuals are so adaptable that once they are given economic opportunity they will seize it, and thus one should never "blame the victim" but only the society. Both views have elements of the truth, and careful phrasing of the connections between circumstance and motivation can help us avoid the extremes of the polemic dilemma.

Indeed, circumstance itself is always changing. In those years when the economy is thriving and there are not too many new entrants into the labor force (such as a time of war), the chances improve for most poor people to better their job situation. But even then, some people are more likely than others to be at the end of the job queue and either get the worse jobs or none at all: uneducated blacks and Hispanics, the newest migrants to the city, people who have been at the bottom so long that they have lost steady work habits and the discipline that comes from realistic and realizable hopes for the future. These people, many of them born into poverty, form the core of the underclass, but they are less than half of the people who are below the poverty line at any one time.

Public policy finds it hard to reach and help this "hard-core" group. Whenever a new scheme is devised to give job training or apprenticeship experience, the administrators of the scheme are under pressure to come up with good results. They tend to look at those in the queue and, just like employers, pick out the best; they skim off the cream of the crop. Thus the programs may have some success, but the hard core is left behind. To help these people requires a degree of patience, ingenuity, and devotion that bureaucratic programs rarely muster (Levin 1977). The underclass will continue until we have a prolonged period of very low unemployment combined with a more committed and persevering set of programs directly aimed at those hardest to help.

CONCLUSIONS: POVERTY AND INEQUALITY

Much of this chapter has discussed a single, underlying issue: how many people in the United States live in misery as a result of inadequate income—how many are poor—and how can they be helped by government action?

But as the discussion unfolded, it became increasingly clear that the very definition of poverty was a crucial and highly debatable issue in itself. For some, poverty is a life measured by certain "objective" indicators of malnutrition, poor housing, lack of medical care. But for others, poverty is a life too far below the mainstream of contemporary America, which breeds misery from relative deprivation and social degradation—even though no biological measures of malnutrition and illness are present. The conservative political view is likely to adopt the first definition and support austere government programs of a "safety-net" variety so that nobody starves in America. The liberal political view is likely to demand a set of policies that will reduce the distance from the top to the bottom of the social hierarchy; it maintains that excessive inequality is harmful in itself, both to the people who suffer and to the society at large, even if nobody falls below the minimum of the safety net.

Those who measure poverty by minimum "objective" indicators of level of living claim that most poverty has been eliminated from America. They either use the official statistics that show a reduction of poverty from 20 percent of the population in 1963 to 11 percent in 1978, or they go further and redefine income to include noncash aspects of the transfer and welfare system and thus come up with figures for poverty as low as 3 to 5 percent of the population. The obvious policy consequences of such a view are being unfolded by the Reagan administration: tinker with the welfare system to take care of the remaining 3 to 5 percent and at the same time reduce benefits to others to bring them down to the minimum definition.

Those who measure poverty by extremes of inequality, commonly using as a rule-of-thumb definition an income of less than half the median for all Americans, assert that the percentage of poor has remained stable at 16 to 20 percent and that the number of poor has increased with the growth of the population. For them, appropriate policies would have to start with a restructuring of the labor market to reduce the overall unemployment rate and most particularly to increase the demand for workers at lower levels of skill and simultaneously to increase their relative wages. If necessary (and it does seem necessary), they would support government jobs to absorb any workers that the private sector is unable or unwilling to employ. And then they would improve the transfer system to bring all recipients closer to the relative poverty line, whether they work or not.

The ultimate basis of decision rests on ethical grounds and cannot be solved by empirical analysis: what kind of a society is just? Yet some aspects of the discussion would be helped by better empirical knowledge and sharper theoretical understanding: how much would justice cost the taxpayer? How much can we reduce inequality without reducing the competitive elements that generate economic efficiency (Okun 1975; Thurow 1980)? How far can the government go in controlling the private economy to solve social problems without creating an unbearable bureaucratic machine? At what point do we begin to pay for increased equality by decreased liberty? At what point does injustice threaten the stability of the system and destroy liberty?

SUGGESTED READINGS

Aaron, Henry J. 1978. *Politics and the Professors: The Great Society in Perspective.* Washington, D.C.: The Brookings Institution.
> *Neatly summarizes the research of the 1970s on various aspects of poverty and government intervention.*

Janowitz, Morris. 1976. *The Social Control of the Welfare State.* New York: Elsevier.
> *The political problems of handling distributive justice are analyzed.*

(Kerner Report): National Advisory Commission on Civil Disorders. 1968.
> *Official report of a Presidential Commission on causes and cures of riots in the black ghettos.*

Moynihan, Daniel P., ed. 1969. *On Understanding Poverty: Perspectives from the Social Sciences.* New York: Basic Books.

Sundquist, James L., ed. 1969. *On Fighting Poverty: Perspectives from Experience.* New York: Basic Books.
> *These companion volumes, written by outstanding experts, sum up the academic and practical perspectives of the 1960s.*

Townsend, Peter. 1979. *Poverty in the United Kingdom.* Berkeley: University of California Press.
> *A good source for a comparative view.*

The American class structure: A synthesis

The "structure" in the title of this book refers to those patterns of convergence among the variables that create social classes. The patterns are tendencies, "ideal types," never fully realized in any one situation but discernible when one steps back from detail to think about underlying forces. We constantly emphasize the influence of economic forces on social and political consequences, but do not neglect points of feedback where social facts shape economic trends.

Preface to this book

11

The sentences from the Preface quoted above suggested that this book was going to emphasize several social classes, groups of people at various levels of the socioeconomic hierarchy created by the convergence of key structural patterns. Yet, we have gone from chapter to chapter analyzing one or two variables at a time—income, prestige, occupation, association, education, consciousness, power—and frequently treated them as continuous gradations from low to high. Only occasionally have we reported on attempts to cut a continuum into distinct levels, and the observant reader will have noticed that the levels discussed in different chapters do not always exactly match one another. Thus, we have so far avoided a simple and consistent answer to the most often asked question about stratification: how many classes are there? It is time to rectify the omission and answer the question.

Why has so much of contemporary research used continua of status instead of distinct classes? Perhaps for two reasons: (1) modern statistics usually prefers scales based on continua to feed into computers and (2) it is hard to find good criteria that permit sharp divisions within each variable that could be used to define clear-cut levels or classes. These two reasons flow from the fact that most empirical studies on American stratification have been descriptive researches seeking intercorrelations among easily observed and measured social variables in the contemporary world. We have only a few studies that seek the underlying structural causes of those variables and the historical trends which change their relative strength.

By contrast, theoretical speculation about historical trends usually finds it more revealing to think about underlying or latent categories rather than superficially observable variables. Often the categories are abstract or "ideal" types that are defined by the clustering of several intertwined characteristics. Thus Marx alerted us to the basic division between owners and nonowners of the means of production in all societies. But his meaning of the contrast between capitalists and proletarians in modern society depended upon the presence of high technology, an advanced division of labor, and well-organized capital and labor markets, and only in that specific context did he analyze the social and political consequences of the conflict of interest between the two social classes, and predict the final outcome. It did not bother him that at any one moment of history the distinction between the two classes might in fact be blurred and many individuals might have ambiguous positions (such as land-owning peasants or urban shop-keepers). He was concerned with the trends toward the maturation of capitalism and its eventual overthrow and not with the placement of individuals in the hierarchy. Indeed, his genius consisted in sensing many trends and their implications even before they were fully observable in the real world.

Besides the contrast between history and the present scene, there is another feature which distinguishes between categories and variables (as we noted in an earlier chapter when discussing the perception of classes by ordinary citizens); namely, the mental process of symbolization. When they think of the system as a whole, people are likely to truncate a lot of observations into simplifying symbols: the rich, the middle class, and the poor; the bosses and the workers; the people with a college education versus those without; the people with clout and the nobodies; "us" versus "them". These symbols create a limited number of groupings: dichotomies, trichotomies, occasionally four or five levels. But beyond that, the symbols lose their power as organizing devices for thought and conversation.

In general, respondents tend to talk about the system in terms of these symbols or stereotypes. Yet when they are asked to look more carefully at themselves and their neighbors, the same people can notice many distinctions that are more subtle than the symbolic categories. They describe neighbors who have a little more money than themselves but are not rich; they see some who have lots of money but not much influence; they notice others without much money but with advanced education and good prospects for the future. Thus both sociologists and citizens can alternate between a broad and categorical style of synthesis, and a detailed and minute style of analysis.

The gulf between historical or theoretical material organized into broad categories, and contemporary or descriptive material expressed in minute and measurable variables, has plagued the literature on stratification for many years. It makes the theoretical discussions appear abstract and often unprovable, and the empirical presentations seem picayune and atheoretical. Yet the two approaches must be integrated in order to provide a satisfactory view of the stratification hierarchy, one that links sophisticated research with the perspectives of the citizens who live in the system and also with the best theorists

who have pondered its nature, and we make an attempt at synthesis
in this chapter. But to do so, we must impose our own views on the
data; there is no simple way in which the facts speak for themselves.

HOW MANY CLASSES ARE THERE?

After seeing the material presented in earlier chapters, the reader
can anticipate the initial response to the question about the number of
classes that exist in the United States: it all depends on your viewpoint. The authors view the class structure as growing out of the
economic system. We start with the recognition that there are three
basic sources of income available to households in this country:
capitalist property, labor force participation, and government transfers. The second of these (which, as we know from the income
parade, accounts for most of the income of most of the people) is
shaped by the fact that our economy depends on an occupational
division of labor organized into bureaucratic units. Occupational
placement is linked in turn to educational preparation. Source of
income, along with experiences on the job and in consumption communities, are verbalized as symbols of the system and the niches
which people occupy within it. One of the key aspects of a person's
perception of place in the system is anticipation of change in the near
future: is one stuck or is there a chance to advance? Another involves
the degree of independence in carrying out one's work activities.

Combining the criteria of source of income, occupation, and educational credentials, plus the related processes of symbolization, we can
create an "ideal type" picture of the class structure. The several
criteria tend to cluster in a pattern that identifies six classes in the
contemporary United States:

1. A capitalist class, subdivided into nationals and locals, whose
    income is derived largely from return on assets.
2. An upper-middle class of university-trained professionals and
    managers (a few of whom ascend to such heights of bureaucratic
    dominance that they become part of the capitalist class).
3. A middle class of people who follow orders on the job from those
    with upper-middle class credentials, yet have sufficient voca-
    tional skills to make good livings and enjoy a comfortable,
    mainstream style of life. They usually feel secure in their situation
    and may look forward to some movement up the hierarchy. Most
    wear white but some wear blue collars.
4. A working class of people who are less skilled than members of
    the middle class and work at highly routinized, closely super-
    vised, manual and clerical jobs. Their work provides them with a
    relatively stable income sufficient to maintain a living standard

just below the mainstream, but they have little prospect of advancing in the hierarchy since they typically lack the necessary educational credentials. Thus they concentrate on achieving security through seniority rather than on ambition.

5. A working-poor class consisting of people employed in low-skill jobs, often in marginal firms. The members of this class are typically laborers, service workers, or low-paid operators. Their incomes leave them well below mainstream living standards. Moreover, they cannot depend on steady employment, and far from anticipating advancement, they are at risk of dropping into the class below them.

6. An underclass, whose members have little or no participation in the labor force. They may work erratically or at part-time jobs, but their lack of skills, incomplete education, and spotty employment records make it difficult for them to find regular, full-time positions. Some receive income from illegal activities. Many depend on government transfers for their support. Symbolically, their loose relationship to the labor market and dependence on government handouts anchor them at the bottom of the prestige order.

There are two cutting points that are the least obvious: that between the middle and working classes and that between the working poor and the underclass. Let us examine these divisions in some detail.

The distinction between working poor and underclass becomes difficult when we consider the tendency of some individuals to move repeatedly back and forth across this boundary. Yet the distinction seems worth maintaining. As we move up or down in the hierarchy, away from the boundary, the problem of oscillating mobility is less serious. Moreover, the symbolic difference between having a job, even a marginal one, and welfare dependence is clear; recall, for example, that Coleman and Rainwater's respondents separated these two groups in their judgments of prestige classes.

The line between middle class and working class has been blurred by trends which have reduced the traditional differences between blue-collar and white-collar employment. A declining income differential, the increasing routinization of clerical tasks, and the corresponding drop in the prestige value of a white collar per se, have all served to close the gap between shop and office. Viewed in terms of major occupational groupings, the problem centers on the sales, clerical, and craft categories. Our way of dividing these between middle and working class is based on a distinction between workers whose jobs are highly routinized, closely supervised, low in prerequisite training or education, and low in pay, and those who are in the opposite situation. On this basis, we had no trouble placing semi-professional jobs and the lowest-paid managerial jobs in the middle class or operatives in the working class. The assembly-line character of modern office work and the low salaries associated with most clerical jobs led us to place clerical workers in the working class. We split sales workers into two groups: those engaged in retail work and "others." The latter group includes insurance salesmen, real-estate agents, manufacturers' representatives, and other people who work quite independently and have much higher incomes than the retail workers. Our decision to place most craft workers and foremen in the middle-class is based on similar considerations. They are well paid, skilled, and relatively independent in their work. Moreover, the prestige attached to such occupations places them well above other blue-collar workers. Details on average education, income, and prestige for each of these occupational categories were given in Table 3–3.

In summary, we are suggesting a model of the class structure based on a series of qualitative economic distinctions and their symbolization. From top to bottom, they are: ownership of income-producing assets, possession of sophisticated educational credentials, a combination of independence and freedom from routinization at work, entrapment in the marginal sector of the labor market, and limited labor force participation.

Our scheme is illustrated in Table 11–1. If we round off the numbers from the distributions of each variable treated separately and do a little guessing, we can estimate that the capitalist class includes about 1 percent of the population; the upper-middle class, about 14 percent; the middle and working classes, 65 percent; and the working poor and underclass, 20 percent. We can exemplify this model by going into a little more detail about each of the six classes and relate our definitional criteria to material that has been discussed earlier in the book.

CAPITALIST CLASS

The very small class of super-rich capitalists at the top of the hierarchy has an influence on economy and society that vastly outpaces their reduced numbers. They make investment decisions that in turn open or close employment opportunities for millions of others; they contribute money to political parties, and they often own newspapers or television companies, thereby gaining impact on the shaping of the consciousness of all classes in the nation. The capitalist class tends to perpetuate itself: it passes on assets and styles of life (including networks of contact with other influentials) to its children. This creation of lineage is of sufficient importance to them that they are active in creating and supporting preparatory schools and univer-

TABLE 11-1
Model of the American class structure: Classes by typical situations

Proportion of population	Class	Education	Occupation	Income, 1978	Budget level (Labor Department)
1%	Capitalist	Prestige university	Investors, heirs, executives	$300,000, mostly from assets	—
14%	Upper Middle	College, often with postgraduate study	Upper managers and professionals; medium businessmen	$30,000 or more	Above higher budget
65% {	Middle	At least high school; often some college or apprenticeship	Lower managers; semi-professionals; sales, nonretail; craftspeople; foremen	About $20,000	Intermediate budget
	Working	High school	Operatives; low-paid craftspeople; clerical workers; retail sales workers	About $15,000	Between intermediate and lower budgets
20% {	Working poor	Some high school	Service workers; laborers; low-paid operatives	Below $10,000	Under lower budget
	Underclass	Primary school	Unemployed or part-time; welfare recipients	Below $7,000	Under poverty line

sities for their children and for carefully selected newcomers who can be socialized into their world view.

The super-rich operate on the national and international scene. They have less prominent counterparts in local communities—the people who own the local banks, department stores, and newspapers. They too are capitalists and belong in this class, albeit at the margins.

Our definition produces a very small top class: those who own massive productive assets. After a generation or two, those assets are often distributed among so many heirs that a larger group of less rich and less powerful people ensues. If one studies local communities and counts all those who have a prominent name and live in big houses and belong to the best country club, one will emerge with a larger group (perhaps double or triple our 1 percent). But if one focuses on assets of sufficient size to grant the economic power that we consider crucial, then the group shrinks in size, which explains the difference between our estimate and those of Warner or Coleman and Rainwater.

UPPER-MIDDLE CLASS

Apart from the very top echelon, the capitalist-proletarian distinction has lost much of its force in modern society: history has proven Marx wrong when he predicted a trend toward simplification into an ever-sharper distinction between the two classes as the driving force of social change. Weber, who lived until 1920, was able to see this more clearly than Marx, who died in 1883. Weber wrote:

> One must therefore distinguish between "propertied classes" and primarily market-determined "income classes." Present-day society is predominantly stratified in classes, and to an especially high degree in income classes. But in the special *status* prestige of the "educated" strata, our society contains a very tangible element of stratification by status. Externally, this status factor is most obviously represented by economic monopolies and the preferential social opportunities of the holders of degrees. . . . Today, the certificate of education becomes what the test for ancestors has been in the past, at least where the nobility has remained powerful: a prerequisite for equality of birth, a qualification for a canonship, and for state office. (1946: 301 and 241)

Of course, Weber was also somewhat limited by the vision of his epoch. But he noticed that through education, particularly the university degree, one could obtain both the opportunity for an important job in the church or the state and entry into high society, which still had overtones in Germany from the days of the nobility. In America, the degree is still the key to high bureaucratic position and to high prestige status in the community, but since the proportion of the population which gets degrees has so dramatically expanded, the prestige of the degree has somewhat diminished. And of course, more people now hold high positions in business than in the church.

The more society bureaucratizes, the more it tends to use educational credentials at all levels to sort people out into careers, at least at the beginning. The formality of this process is striking. For example, the current Chinese government civil service, heir to a tradition that long antedates Mao Tse-tung, continues to use 24 distinct grades or levels of jobs, despite ideological ideas of equality; the United States federal civil service has 18 grades; and the General Electric Corporation, considered a model of modern management, recognizes 28 levels of managers and 14 levels of workers. Each of these grades has a different pay scale and different responsibilities. They do not all specify exactly the educational credentials to match the job and the pay, but they usually use educational credentials to sort out beginning applicants into the level that would be most appropriate for them. Afterwards, experience on the job, additional training courses (sometimes at outside schools, sometimes in courses run internally by the management), and demonstrated abilities combine to determine who stays put and who moves up.

The upper-middle class is the group in our society most shaped by formal education. A college degree is usually the minimum requirement, and increasingly post-graduate study in business management, law, engineering, or medicine is required. Currently, more than 20 percent of young people get college degrees, and at least half of them pursue some additional training; about 16 percent of all adults have a degree.

If we turn to occupational statistics, we will recall that Table 3–4 showed 16 percent of the current labor force classified as professionals and technicians, and another 11 percent as managers, officials and proprietors. But a further breakdown in Table 3–5 indicated that only 43 percent of the first group are true professionals, the rest being semiprofessionals and technicians who work under supervision and do not receive the highest salaries. A somewhat similar proportion of the managerial group are in subordinate positions. We estimate that only about 14 percent of the total work force has the combination of university degrees, authority on the job, and high income to qualify for the upper-middle class.

The extent to which adolescents in high school (urged on by their parents and teachers) so often strive to prepare themselves for upper-middle class jobs is a clear indication that these positions have become the symbols of success that motivate so many Americans. They may not grant prestige equivalent to a title of nobility in the Germany of Max Weber, but they certainly represent the sign of having "made it" in contemporary America. The incomes of households in this group range upwards of $30,000 a year (more than twice the median in 1978, as shown in Table 4–4) and tend to increase with age; they are sufficient to purchase houses and cars and travel that become public symbols for all to see and for advertisers to portray with words and pictures that connote success, glamour, and high style. Those who have reached this level of success are likely to convince themselves that they deserve what they receive, that they have earned morally just rewards from the diligent use of superior talent. Sometimes they may grow anxious from the strains of competition, but in general, they are satisfied that they have achieved a proper share of the American dream.

MIDDLE CLASS

We have remarked before that a stratification hierarchy is clearest (and incidentally, mobility the weakest) at the extremes. When we move toward the center, distinctions become blurred, people move more often during their lives from one slot to another, and symbolizations become ambiguous. This is particularly true at the point where the middle class and the working class intersect—or better, overlap—so the reader should not expect precision of classification.

It takes at least a high school diploma to get most middle-class jobs, but the diploma is a prerequisite more than a guarantee of such employment. About 85 percent of the total adult population has a high school diploma and perhaps some training beyond it short of a four-year college degree. Those with the best schooling have the most chance to become the semiprofessionals, technicians, and lower-level managerial people we mentioned above—about 12 percent of the work force. They are joined in the loose grouping we call the middle class with the upper two thirds of those classified as salespeople and craftspeople—another 23 percent of the work force. Typical household incomes for this level, as shown in Table 4–4, would be around $20,000 a year, but there is considerable variation, particularly if more than one person in the household is working. The range is from about $15,000 to $30,000. Styles of life, or consumption patterns, thus range from the intermediate up to the higher levels that are detailed in Table 4–1. Jobs are relatively secure, even during periods of recession, and younger members of the class are likely to be working in situations where some opportunities to advance in the hierarchy are available.

Symbolization of the middle class tends to get confused by an ideological tradition which says that most Americans are middle class. It is a "good," mainstream sort of phrase that a lot of people adopt—including those who are both higher and lower in the hierarchy than the ones we are trying to discuss at this point. Thus most surveys show 35 to 50 percent of our population identifying with the term and only about two percent willing to call themselves upper class, as shown in Tables 9–2 and 9–3. If we subtract about 15 percent for the upper and upper-middle classes as we have defined them, then the size of the remaining middle class according to self-identification would be from 20 to 35 percent of the population. Using a composite of various symbols that people use to classify not only themselves but their neighbors, Coleman and Rainwater decided that 33 percent were middle class, an estimate we accept.

WORKING CLASS

The core of the working class is easy to identify: factory operatives, who make up 15 percent of the work force. But they are joined by lots of others whose work lives and incomes are not markedly different, such as clerks and salespeople whose tasks are routine and mechanized and require little skill beyond literacy and a short period of on-the-job training (some 14 percent of the work force), and the better-paid persons in the service jobs (another 3 percent). Individuals easily move among these classifications, and often one member of family wears a blue and another a white collar, and nobody much notices the difference. Households typically earn $15,000 or less (the national median in 1978 was $13,800). The consumption style of life is described in the Department of Labor's lower budget.

In opinion surveys, almost half the population usually chooses the label working class for themselves, but evidence indicates that some do so because they particularly dislike certain alternative terms, such as lower class. The detailed procedures of Coleman and Rainwater arrived at a figure of 37 percent for the working class, some of whom we will put among the working poor. Thus our estimate for the working class comes to about 32 percent of the population.

In general, working-class families earn less than middle-class families, and more particularly, they are less secure in their incomes. The working class is more susceptible to lay-offs in time of recession, since employers have less invested in their training and experience. Insecurity of work often is combined with a subjective feeling of vulnerability from lower levels of education: relatively few members of the group have training beyond a high school diploma, and over a third (especially the older ones) did not graduate. Yet by contrast with those below them in the hierarchy, working-class people generally anticipate that lay-offs will be temporary and that most of the time they can support their families in a simple but decent manner.

WORKING POOR

In 1978, the government called 11 percent of the population poor, and studies that follow families over time show that in a nine year period some 25 percent of them fall below the poverty line at least once. Of the total work force (and many of the poorest and most discouraged people have withdrawn from it), between 6 and 8 percent are likely to be unemployed at any one moment, and about 20 percent are likely to be unemployed at least once during any given year. Thus it appears that about one fifth of our population lives under duress: they oscillate in income from just above to below the poverty line, they are threatened with periodic unemployment, or they have no chance to work at all. Those among them—probably a little more than half—who are often working but not earning on a steady basis enough money to bring them close to the mainstream style of consumption, we label the working poor; those who depend primarily on the welfare system for cash income we call the underclass.

The working poor include the unskilled laborers, most of those in the service jobs, and some of the lower-paid operatives (especially in marginal firms). Their incomes depend on the number of weeks a year they are employed and on the number of workers in the family. Most families would feel fortunate in a year that brought in $10,000. Some adults have finished high school; a great many have not. They are unable to save money to cover contingencies, and thus insecurity is a normal part of their lives. The one part of the welfare system that has been most beneficial to them has been the Food Stamp program. Once retired, they are entirely dependent on their Social Security pensions, for it is unlikely that they have been enrolled in a private retirement plan that could supplement the government payments.

UNDERCLASS

Those who are seldom employed and are poor most of the time form the underclass in our society. They suffer long-term deprivation from low education, low employability, low income, and eventually, low self-esteem. For a great many, their problems are magnified because they belong to minority groups who are stigmatized and suffer discrimination in the labor market, or they are women without husbands who must make their way in a job world that pays them less than men. Those who cannot get and keep jobs that pay enough to live on are dependent on the welfare system of the government.

The conditions of life in the underclass are sufficiently difficult and demeaning that it is hard—although not impossible—for children to get enough education and enough hope to climb up to higher levels. The future chances for avoiding a life of poverty for these children are about 50-50.

The descriptions of the six classes just given are summarized in Table 11–1. It is clear that no single variable can be used to delineate these classes, so our synthesis is based on a combination of several variables. We believe that they tend to form patterns that are caught by our scheme in a way that is meaningful in two senses: (1) it is congruent with much of the research literature that goes into detail on one or two variables at a time, as well as with the more qualitative community studies that tend to combine many variables into symbolic groupings; (2) it is congruent with the way most Americans tend to see the system and their place within it. Of course, we are thinking here in terms of averages, of typical situations; many individuals and families are hard to place in the scheme, either because they are higher in position on one variable than on another, or because they are mobile, or because more than one member of a family works and they have disparate jobs.[1]

IS THE STRUCTURE CHANGING?

In the first edition of this book, published in 1957, a five-class structure was used as a summary device in Chapter 7. The differences between that scheme and our present one are worth noting.

First, the earlier version put only 9 percent of the population into the upper-middle class, whereas we now believe closer to 14 percent belong there. The change reflects a continued upgrading of technical skills in the labor force that increases the proportion of jobs that demand high training and pay commensurate high salaries.

Second, we have redrawn the lines between those classes who are below the upper-middle category, creating a slightly smaller middle class (earlier labeled lower-middle), a slightly smaller working class, adding a new category of working poor, and using the more graphic term *underclass* for those at the bottom. The persistence of long-term underemployment and the growth of the welfare system may be the main causes of our revised view.

Third, the earlier edition approached the structure in a somewhat different manner. It gave more emphasis to the community studies of prestige and association, and the various researches on consciousness and value systems. Starting with those descriptive observations, it worked its way back to the underlying occupational structure. We have reversed the direction of emphasis in the new version. We pay more attention to capitalist ownership and to the occupational division of labor as the defining variables, and then treat prestige, association, and values as derivative. This difference in viewpoint reflects shifts in the general orientation of the discipline of sociology more than a change in the facts as such.

---

[1] These difficulties of exact status placement and their consequences on consciousness and behavior have been studied under the phrases "status crystallization or status consistency," but the results have been inconclusive (Lenski 1954; Jackson and Burke 1965; Landecker 1981).

Apart from these differences, we believe that the basic structure of today is strikingly similar to the one 25 years ago. There are slow and steady changes that modify aspects of the structure but do not radically change its shape or nature. Perhaps it is worth noting a few of those trends.

Within the capitalist class, there are various tendencies in contradictory directions. The biggest corporations are swallowing up many of the smaller ones and increasing their dominance in the economy. Since the end of World War II, the portion of U.S. manufacturing industry controlled by the 200 largest firms has grown from 45 percent to 60 percent. In 1980 alone, 44 billion dollars was spent by big firms in the acquisition of other firms (*Time*, August 3, 1981: 26). The same type of consolidation is taking place among banks and other financial institutions as various firms merge to create ever-bigger giants.

Yet, new small firms keep emerging, and some of them (especially in the most sophisticated technological areas, such as microcomputers and genetic engineering) can grow quickly into multimillion-dollar enterprises. Other small businesses in retailing and services are important for the creation of employment: two thirds of all new jobs in the last decade were created in firms with fewer than 100 workers (*Time*, August 3, 1981: 27).

At the same time that big industry continues to consolidate, stock ownership becomes increasingly dispersed. Capital accumulation (other than that internal to firms from reinvested earnings) comes more and more from the combined savings of millions of persons in the form of pension funds and other fiduciary investors. Some people call this a trend toward "people's capitalism." But the opposite side of the coin is that the trend often makes it easier for the large capitalists, who may own from 1 to 10 percent of the stock in a given firm, to control the decisions, since they are the only stockholders who are active in management.

Turning to the division of labor, we have already noted that occupational shifts continue to expand the proportion of jobs at the upper-middle level of the class hierarchy. Some of the prosperity from economic growth is distributed to the population by allowing people to move up in the hierarchy, while another part is distributed by increasing the material level of living of all classes a little each decade. Especially significant in the last 25 years has been the opening of more upper-middle-class jobs to people previously discouraged from seeking them: women and minorities. White males still dominate these jobs but less so each year.

The increasing participation of women in the labor force has had many impacts on the system. The education of men and women is becoming more alike; the types of jobs they seek are no longer quite as distinct. The working wife has decreased the birth rate, increased the prosperity of many families, and changed consumption styles in various ways. Incidentally, the working wife has made the job of sociological research more difficult, since the placement of a family in the class system is always harder when more than one member of it is working, especially if they have jobs at different levels of the hierarchy.

Finally, a word about those at the bottom. Although their material resources have increased in an absolute sense, largely through the expansion of the federal system of transfer payments, both social security and welfare, the relative social degradation appears to have gotten worse for those of working age. The more technical and better-paying the average job becomes, the more degrading it is to be a person with no vocational skill, frequent unemployment, and recurring dependence on welfare. Such people are further from the mainstream than before, and their resentment is probably increasing. It is in this social sense even more than in the purely economic sense of material level of living that our society has failed to integrate a significant segment of our people.

Bibliography

Aaron, Henry J. 1978. *Politics and the Professors: The Great Society in Perspective.* Washington, D.C.: The Brookings Institution.

Abbott, Edith. 1936. *The Tenements of Chicago, 1908–1935.* Chicago: University of Chicago Press.

Abramson, Paul R. 1978. "Class Voting in the 1976 Presidential Election." *Journal of Politics* 40:1066–72.

Acker, Joan R. 1980. "Women and Stratification: A Review of Recent Literature." *Contemporary Sociology* 9:25–35.

Ackerman, Frank; Howard Birnbaum; James Wetzler; and Andrew Zimbalist. 1971. "Income Distribution in the United States." *Review of Radical Political Economics* 3:20–43.

Aiken, Michael, and Paul E. Mott, eds. 1970. *The Structure of Community Power.* New York: Random House.

Alexander, Herbert E. 1980. *Financing Politics: Money, Elections, and Political Reform.* 2d ed. Washington, D.C.: *Congressional Quarterly Press.*

Alford, Robert. 1963. *Party and Society.* Chicago: Rand McNally.

Allen, Frederick Lewis. 1952. *The Big Change.* New York: Harper & Row.

Anderson, Dewey, and Percy Davidson. 1943. *Ballots and the Democratic Class Struggle.* Stanford, Calif.: Stanford University Press.

Anderson, Martin. 1978. *Welfare: The Political Economy of Welfare Reform in the United States*. Stanford, Calif.: Hoover Institution Press.

Antonovsky, Aaron. 1967. "Social Class and Illness: A Reconsideration." *Sociological Inquiry* 37:311–23.

Archibald, Katherine. 1953. "Status Orientations among Shipyard Workers." In *Class, Status, and Power*, edited by Reinhard Bendix and Seymour M. Lipset. 1st ed. Glencoe, Ill.: Free Press.

Aronowitz, Stanley. 1973. *False Promises: The Shaping of American Working Class Consciousness*. New York: McGraw-Hill.

Atkinson, A. B. 1975. *The Economics of Inequality*. Oxford: Clarendon.

Averch, H. A., et al. 1972. *How Effective Is Schooling? A Critical Review of Research*. Santa Monica, Calif.: Rand Corporation. Also published by Educational Technology Publications, Englewood Cliffs, N.J., 1974.

Bachrach, Peter, and Morton S. Baratz. 1974. *Power and Poverty: Theory and Practice*. New York: Oxford University Press.

Baltzell, E. Digby. 1958. *Philadelphia Gentlemen*. New York: Free Press.

Barnet, Richard J., and Ronald E. Muller. 1974. *Global Reach: The Power of the Multinational Corporations*. New York: Simon & Schuster.

Barnouw, Erik. 1978. *The Sponsor: Notes on a Modern Potentate*. New York: Oxford University Press.

Beck, E. M.; Patrick M. Horan; and Charles M. Tolbert, II. 1978. "Stratification in a Dual Economy: A Sectoral Model of Earnings Determination." *American Sociological Review* 43:704–20.

Beeghley, Leonard. 1978. *Social Stratification in America: A Critical Analysis of Theory and Research*. Santa Monica, Calif.: Goodyear.

Bell, Daniel. 1976. *The Coming of the Post-Industrial Society*. New York: Basic Books.

Beman, Lewis. 1976. "The Last Billionaires." *Fortune* 94:132–37, 226–29.

Bendix, Reinhard, and Seymour Martin Lipset, eds. 1953. *Class, Status, and Power*. 1st ed. Glencoe, Ill.: Free Press. (2d ed., New York: Free Press, 1966).

Berg, Ivar. 1970. *Education and Jobs: The Great Training Robbery*. New York: Praeger Publishers.

Berle, Adolf A., Jr., and Gardiner C. Means. 1932. *The Modern Corporation and Private Property*. New York: Commerce Clearing House

Bielby, William T.; Robert M. Hauser; and David L. Featherman. 1977. "Response Errors of Black and Nonblack Males in Models of Intergenerational Transmission of Socioeconomic Status." *American Journal of Sociology* 82:1242–88.

Birnbach, Lisa, ed. 1980. *The Official Preppy Handbook*. New York: Workman.

Blau, Francine D. 1975. "The Data on Women Workers, Past, Present and Future." In *Women Working*, edited by Ann H. Stromberg and Shirley Harkess. Palo Alto, Calif.: Mayfield.

Blau, Peter M., and Otis Dudley Duncan. 1967. *The American Occupational Structure*. New York: John Wiley & Sons.

Bloch, Fred. 1977. "The Ruling Class Does Not Rule: Notes on the Marxist Theory of the State." *Socialist Revolution* 7, (no. 1): 6–28.

Bluestone, Barry. 1974. "The Poor Who Have Jobs." In *The Sociology of American Poverty*, edited by Joan Huber and H. Paul Chalfant. Cambridge, Mass.: Schenkman.

Blumberg, Paul M., and P. W. Paul. 1975. "Continuities and Discontinuities in Upper-Class Marriages." *Journal of Marriage and the Family* 37:63–77.

Blume, Marshall E.; Jean Crockett; and Irwin Friend. 1974. "Stockownership in the United States: Characteristics and Trends." *Survey of Current Business,* November, 16–44.

Bonafede, Dom. 1981. "A $130 Million Spending Tab is Proof—Presidential Politics is Big Business." *National Journal* 13:50–52.

Bonjean, Charles M., and Michael D. Grimes. 1974. "Community Power: Issues and Findings." In *Social Stratification: A Reader,* edited by Joseph Lopreato and Lionel S. Lewis. New York: Harper & Row.

Bott, Elizabeth. 1954. "The Concept of Class as a Reference Group." *Human Relations* 7: 259–86.

————. 1964. *Family and Social Network.* London: Tavistock.

Bottomore, Tom. 1966. *Elites in Modern Society.* New York: Pantheon Books.

Boudon, Raymond. 1974. *Education, Opportunity and Social Inequality.* New York: John Wiley & Sons.

————. 1976. "Comment on Hauser." *American Journal of Sociology* 81: 1175–87.

————. 1977. "Education and Social Mobility: A Structural Model." In *Power and Ideology in Education,* edited by Jerome Karabel and A. H. Halsey. New York: Oxford University Press.

Bowles, Samuel, and Herbert Gintis. 1976. *Schooling in Capitalist America.* New York: Basic Books.

Boyer, Richard, and Herbert Morais. 1975. *Labor's Untold Story.* 3d ed. New York: United Electrical Workers.

Bradburn, Norman. 1969. *The Structure of Psychological Well-Being.* Chicago: Aldine.

Braverman, Harry. 1974. *Labor and Monopoly Capital.* New York: Monthly Review Press.

Bremner, Robert H. 1956. *From the Depths: The Discovery of Poverty in the United States.* New York: New York University Press.

Brittain, John A. 1977. *The Inheritance of Economic Status.* Washington, D.C.: The Brookings Institution.

Brody, David. 1980. *Workers in Industrial America: Essays on the 20th Century Struggle.* New York: Oxford University Press.

Bronfenbrenner, Urie. 1966. "Socialization through Time and Space." In *Class, Status, and Power,* edited by Reinhard Bendix and Seymour Martin Lipset. 2d ed. New York: Free Press.

Brooks, Thomas. 1971. *Toil and Trouble: A History of American Labor.* 2d ed. New York: Dell Publishing.

Burch, Philip H., Jr. 1980. *Elites in American History: The New Deal to the Carter Administration.* New York: Holmes and Meier.

Burnham, James. 1941. *The Managerial Revolution.* New York: John Day.

Burnight, Robert G., and Parker G. Marden. 1967. "Social Correlates of Weight in an Aging Population." *Milbank Memorial Fund Quarterly* 45: 75–92.

Burstein, Paul. 1979. "EEO Legislation and the Income of Women and Non-Whites." *American Sociological Review* 44:367–91.

Caldwell, Steven, and Theodore Diamond. 1979. "Income Differentials in Mortality: Preliminary Results Based on IRS-SSA Linked Data." In *Statistical Uses of Administrative Records,* edited by Linda DelBene and Fritz Scheuren. Washington, D.C.: U.S. Social Security Administration.

Cameron, Juan. 1978. "Small Business

Trips Big Labor." *Fortune* 98 (July) : 80–82.

Campbell, Angus; Gerald Gurin; and Warren E. Miller. 1954. *The Voter Decides*. Evanston, Ill.: Row, Peterson.

———. 1960. *The American Voter*. New York: John Wiley & Sons. (Abridged edition, 1964.)

Cantril, Hadley. 1951. *Public Opinion*. Princeton: Princeton University.

Caplow, Theodore. 1980. "Middletown Fifty Years After." *Contemporary Sociology* 9:46–50.

Caplow, Theodore, and Bruce Chadwick. 1979. "Inequality and Life Styles in Middletown, 1920–1978." *Social Science Quarterly* 60:366–68.

Case, Herman M. 1953. "Guttman Scaling Applied to Centers' Conservatism-Radicalism Battery." *American Journal of Sociology* 58:556–63.

Centers, Richard. 1949. *The Psychology of Social Classes: A Study of Class Consciousness*. Princeton, N.J.: Copyright 1949 © renewed by Princeton University Press. Excerpt and Tables 36 and 42, pp. 78, 120, and 126 reprinted by permission of Princeton University Press.

———. 1953. "Social Class, Occupation and Imputed Belief." *American Journal of Sociology* 58:546.

Cicourel, A. V., and J. I. Kitsuse. 1977. "The School as a Mechanism of Social Differentiation." In *Power and Ideology in Education*, edited by Jerome Karabel and A. H. Halsey. New York: Oxford University Press.

Clark, Terry. 1971. "Community Structure, Decision-Making, Budget Expenditure, and Urban Renewal in 51 American Communities." In *Community Politics*, edited by Charles Bonjean et al. New York: Free Press.

Cohen, Jere. 1979. "Socio-economic Status and High School Friendship Choice: Elmtown's Youth Revisited." *Social Networks* 2:65–74.

Coleman, James S., et al. 1966. *Equality of Educational Opportunity*. Washington, D.C.: U.S. Government Printing Office.

Coleman, Richard P., and Lee Rainwater, with Kent A. McClelland. 1978. *Social Standing in America: New Dimensions of Class*. Copyright © 1978 by Basic Books, Inc. By permission of Basic Books, Inc., Publishers, New York.

Coles, Robert C. 1971. *Migrants, Sharecroppers, Mountaineers*. Boston: Little, Brown.

Collier, Peter, and David Horowitz. 1976. *The Rockefellers: An American Dynasty*. New York: Holt, Rinehart & Winston.

Congressional Quarterly. 1976. *Guide to Congress*. 2d ed.

———. 1980. "Democrats May Lose Edge in Contributions from PACs." 38:3405–9.

Corcoran, Mary. 1978. "Measurement Error in Status Attainment Models." Unpublished paper. Ann Arbor, Michigan: Institute for Social Research.

Corey, Lewis. 1935. *The Crisis of the Middle Class*. New York: Covici-Friede.

———. 1953. "Problems of the Peace: The Middle Class." In *Class, Status, and Power*, edited by Reinhard Bendix and Seymour Martin Lipset. 1st ed. Glencoe, Ill.: Free Press.

Coser, Lewis. 1978. *Masters of Sociological Thought*. 2d ed. New York: Harcourt Brace Jovanovich.

Council of Economic Advisors. 1964. *Economic Report to the President*. Washington, D.C.: U.S. Government Printing Office.

Coxon, Anthony, and Charles Jones. 1978. *The Images of Occupational Prestige*. New York: St. Martin's Press.

Cullen, John B., and Shelley M. Novick. 1979. "The Davis-Moore Theory of Stratification." *American Journal of Sociology* 84:1424–37.

Curtis, Richard F., and Elton F. Jackson. 1977. *Inequality in American Communities.* New York: Academic Press.

Cutright, Phillips. 1968. "Occupational Inheritance: A Cross-National Analysis." *American Journal of Sociology* 73:400–16.

Dahl, Robert A. 1961. *Who Governs? Democracy and Power in an American City.* New Haven, Conn.: Yale University Press.

———. 1967. *Pluralist Democracy in the United States.* Chicago: Rand McNally.

———. 1979. "Who *Really* Rules?" *Social Science Quarterly* 60:144–51.

Davis, Allison. 1946. "The Motivation of the Underprivileged Worker." In *Industry and Society,* edited by William Foote Whyte. New York: McGraw Hill.

Davis, Allison; Burleigh B. Gardner; and Mary R. Gardner. 1941. *Deep South: A Social-Anthropological Study of Caste and Class.* Chicago: University of Chicago Press.

Davis, James. 1978. "Study of Categorical Data Over Time." *Social Science Research* 7:151–79.

Davis, Kingsley, and Wilbert E. Moore. 1945. "Some Principles of Social Stratification." *American Sociological Review* 10:242–49.

Davis, Kingsley; Wilbert E. Moore; et al. 1966. "The Continuing Debate on Equality." In *Class, Status, and Power,* edited by Reinhard Bendix and Seymour Martin Lipset. 2d ed. New York: Free Press.

Davis, Mike. 1980. "The Barren Marriage of American Labour and the Demo-cratic Party." *New Left Review,* no. 124:45–84.

Demerath, N. J., III. 1965. *Social Class in American Protestanism.* Chicago: Rand McNally.

Dinitz, S.; F. Banks; and B. Pasamanick. 1960. "Mate Selection and Social Class: Change in the Past Quarter Century." *Marriage and Family Living* 22:348–51.

Doeringer, Peter B., and Michael J. Piore. 1971. *Internal Labor Markets and Manpower Analysis.* Lexington, Mass.: D. C. Heath.

Domhoff, G. William. 1967. *Who Rules America?* Englewood Cliffs, N.J.: Prentice-Hall.

———. 1970. *The Higher Circles: The Governing Class in America.* Englewood Cliffs, N.J.: Prentice-Hall.

———. 1974. *The Bohemian Grove and Other Retreats.* New York: Harper & Row.

———. 1975. "Social Clubs, Policy-Planning Groups, and Corporations." *Insurgent Sociologist* 5 (3):173–95.

———. 1978. *Who Really Rules? New Haven and Community Power Reexamined.* New Brunswick, N.J.: Transaction Books.

———. 1979. *The Powers that Be: Processes of Ruling Class Domination in America.* New York: Vintage Books.

Domhoff, G. William, and Hoyt B. Ballard, eds. 1968. *C. Wright Mills and the Power Elite.* Boston: Beacon Press.

Dooley, P. 1969. "The Interlocking Directorate." *American Economic Review* 59:314–23.

Dotson, Floyd. 1950. "The Associations of Urban Workers." Unpublished Ph.D. thesis, Yale University.

———. 1951. "Patterns of Voluntary Association Among Urban Working Class Families." *American Sociological Review* 16:687–93.

Drake, St. Clair, and Horace R. Cayton. 1954. *Black Metropolis.* New York: Harcourt Brace Jovanovich.

Dubofsky, Melvyn. 1980. "The Legacy of the New Deal." *Executive* 6 (Spring):8–10.

Duncan, Gregg, and James N. Morgan, eds. 1976, Vol. IV. 1978, Vol. VI. *Five Thousand Families: Patterns of Economic Progress.* Ann Arbor: Survey Research Center, Institute of Social Research, University of Michigan.

Duncan, Otis Dudley. 1961. "A Socioeconomic Index for All Occupations," and "Properties and Characteristics of the Socieconomic Index." In *Occupations and Social Status,* edited by Albert Reiss. Glencoe, Ill.: Free Press.

————. 1966. "Methodological Issues in the Analysis of Social Mobility." In *Social Structure and Mobility in Economic Development,* edited by Neil Smelser and Seymour Martin Lipset. Chicago: Aldine.

Duncan, Otis Dudley, and Beverly Duncan. 1955. "Residential Distribution and Occupational Stratification." *American Journal of Sociology* 60:493–503.

Duncan, Otis Dudley; Archibald O. Haller; and Alejandro Portes. 1968. "Peer Influences on Aspirations: A Reinterpretation." *American Journal of Sociology* 74:119–37.

Duncan, Otis Dudley, et al. 1972. *Socioeconomic Background and Achievement.* New York: Seminar Press.

Dye, Thomas R. 1976. *Who's Running America? Institutional Leadership in the United States.* Englewood Cliffs, N.J.: Prentice-Hall.

————. 1979. *Who's Running America? The Carter Years.* 2d ed. Englewood Cliffs, N.J.: Prentice-Hall.

Edwards, Alba M., and U.S. Bureau of the Census. 1943. *U.S. Census of Population 1940: Comparative Occupational Statistics, 1870–1940.* Washington, D.C.: U.S. Government Printing Office.

Edwards, Richard. 1979. *Contested Terrain: The Transformation of the Workplace in the Twentieth Century.* New York: Basic Books.

Ehrbar, A. F. 1980. "The Upbeat Outlook for Family Incomes." *Fortune* 101: 122–30.

Estey, Marten. 1980. "The State of the Unions." *Executive* 6 (Spring):15–18.

Etzioni, Amitai. 1969. *The Semi-Professions and their Organization.* New York: Free Press.

Expert Committee on Family Budget Revisions. 1980. *New American Family Budget Standards.* Madison and New York: Institute for Research on Poverty, University of Wisconsin and Center for the Social Sciences, Columbia University.

Farley, Reynolds, and Albert Hermalin. 1972. "The 1960's: Decade of Progress for Blacks?" *Demography* 9: 353–70.

Featherman, David L. 1979. "Opportunities Are Expanding." *Society* 13: 4–11. Published by permission of Transaction, Inc. from SOCIETY, Vol. 16, No. 4. Copyright ©, March/April 1979 by Transaction, Inc.

Featherman, David L., and Robert M. Hauser. 1978. *Opportunity and Change.* New York: Academic Press.

Fish, Mary. 1978. *Income Inequality and Employment.* R & D Monograph, U.S. Department of Labor. Washington, D.C.: U.S. Government Printing Office.

Fitch, Robert, and Mary Oppenheimer. 1970. "Who Rules the Corporation: 2 Parts." *Socialist Revolution* 1 (July):73–107 and (September):61–114.

Fitzgerald, F. Scott. 1926. "The Rich

Boy." In *The Stories of F. Scott Fitzgerald* [1980]. New York: Charles Scribners' Sons.

Flanigan, William, and Nancy Zingale. 1975. *Political Behavior of the American Electorate*. 3d ed. Boston: Allyn & Bacon.

Fortune. 1937. "The Industrial War." 14 (November):105–10, 156, 160, 166.

Fox, Thomas, and S. M. Miller. 1966. "Occupational Stratification and Mobility." In *Class, Status, and Power*, edited by Reinhard Bendix and Seymour Martin Lipset. 2d ed. New York: Free Press.

Fraser, Douglas. 1978. "UAW President Fraser Resigns from Labor-Management Group." *Radical History Review* no. 18 (Fall):117–21.

Freeman, Richard B. 1976a. *The Overeducated American*. New York: Academic Press.

———. 1976b. *The Black Elite*. New York: McGraw-Hill.

Fried, Edward R.; Alice M. Rivlin; Charles L. Schultz; and Nancy Teeters. 1973. *Setting National Priorities: The 1974 Budget*. Washington, D.C.: The Brookings Institution.

Galbraith, John Kenneth. 1958. *The Affluent Society*. Boston: Houghton Mifflin.

———. 1967. *The New Industrial State*. Boston: Houghton Mifflin.

Gallup, George. 1972. *The Gallup Poll: Public Opinion 1935–1971*. New York: Random House.

Gans, Herbert. 1962. *The Urban Villagers*. New York: Free Press.

———. 1972. *The Levittowners: Ways of Life and Politics in a New Suburban Community*. New York: Pantheon Books.

Gecas, Viktor. 1979. "The Influence of Social Class on Socialization." In *Contemporary Theories about the Family*, edited by W. R. Burr et al. Vol. I. New York: Free Press.

Giddens, Anthony. 1973. *The Class Structure of the Advanced Societies*. New York: Harper & Row.

Gilbert, Dennis. 1981. "Cognatic Descent Groups in Upper-Class Lima (Peru)." *American Ethnologist* 8:739–57.

Glenn, Norval D. 1975. "The Contribution of White Collars to Occupational Prestige." *Sociological Quarterly* 16: 184–89.

Glenn, Norval D., and Jon P. Alston. 1968. "Cultural Distances Among Occupational Categories." *American Sociological Review* 33:365–82.

Glenn, Norval D., and Sandra L. Albrecht. 1980. "Is the Status Structure in the U.S. Really More Fluid for Women than for Men?" *American Sociological Review* 45:340–44.

Goertzel, Ted G. 1976. *Political Society*. Chicago: Rand McNally.

Gold, David A.; Clarence Y. H. Lo; and Erik Olin Wright. 1975. "Recent Developments in Marxist Theories of the Capitalist State. 2 Parts." *Monthly Review* 27 (October):29–43 and (November):36–51.

Goldstein, Marshall. 1962. "Absentee Ownership and Monolithic Power Structures." In *Trends in Comparative Community Studies*, edited by Bert E. Swanson. Kansas City: Community Studies.

Goldthorpe, John H. 1977. "Class Mobility in Modern Britain: Three Theses Examined." *Sociology* 11: 257–87.

———. 1980. *Social Mobility and Class Structure in Modern Britain*. New York: Oxford University Press.

Goldthorpe, John H., and Keith Hope. 1972. "Occupational Grading and Occupational Prestige." In *The Analysis of Social Mobility: Methods and Approaches*, edited by Keith Hope. Oxford: Clarendon.

Goldthorpe, John H.; David Lockwood; Frank Bechhofer; and Jennifer Platt. 1968. *The Affluent Worker: Industrial Attitudes and Behavior*. Cambridge: Cambridge University Press.

Goode, William J. 1979. *The Celebration of Heroes: Prestige as a Social Control System*. Berkeley: University of California Press.

Gordon, David M. 1972. *Theories of Poverty and Underemployment*. Lexington, Mass.: D. C. Heath.

Green, Mark. 1979. *Who Runs Congress?* 3d ed. New York: Bantom Books.

Greene, Bert. 1978. *Pity the Poor Rich*. Chicago: Contemporary Books.

Greenstone, J. David. 1977. *Labor in American Politics*. Chicago: University of Chicago Press.

Guest, Avery M. 1974. "Class Consciousness and American Political Attitudes." Reprinted from *Social Forces* 52:496–510. Copyright © The University of North Carolina Press.

Hacker, Louis. 1970. *The Course of American Economic Growth and Development*. New York: John Wiley & Sons.

Halberstam, David. 1972. *The Best and the Brightest*. New York: Random House. 1973. Greenwich, Conn.: Fawcett.

Halsey, A. H., et al. 1980. *Origins and Destinations: Family, Class and Education in Modern Britain*. New York: Oxford University Press.

Hamilton, Alexander. 1780. Quoted in Arthur J. Schlesinger, Jr., *The Age of Jackson*. Boston: Little Brown, 1945, p. 10.

Hamilton, Richard. 1966. "The Marginal Middle Class: A Reconsideration." *American Sociological Review* 31: 192–99.

————. 1967. *Affluence and the French Worker*. Princeton, N.J.: Princeton University Press.

————. 1972. *Class and Politics in the United States*. New York: John Wiley & Sons.

————. 1975. *Restraining Myths: Critical Studies of United States' Social Structure and Politics*. Beverly Hills, Calif.: Sage Publications.

Hamilton, Richard, and James Wright. 1975. *New Directions in Political Sociology*. Indianapolis: Bobbs-Merrill.

Harrington, Michael. 1962. *The Other America: Poverty in the United States*. New York: Macmillan.

Harrison, Bennett. 1972. "Public Employment and the Theory of the Dual Economy." In *Public Service Employment*, edited by H. L. Sheppard. Lexington, Mass.: Lexington Books.

Hatt, Paul K. 1950. "Occupation and Social Stratification." *American Journal of Sociology* 55:533–43.

Haug, Marie. 1977. "Measurement in Social Stratification." *Annual Review of Sociology* 3:51–77.

Hauser, Robert M. 1976. "On Boudon's Model of Social Mobility." *American Journal of Sociology* 81:911–29.

Hauser, Robert M., and David L. Featherman. 1977. *The Process of Stratification*. New York: Academic Press.

Hays, Samuel. 1957. *The Response to Industrialism*. Chicago: University of Chicago Press.

Hemingway, Ernest. 1936. "The Snows of Kiliminjaro." *Esquire*, August.

Henle, Peter. 1972. "Exploring the Distribution of Earned Income." *Monthly Labor Review* 95:16–27.

Herman, Edward S. 1981. *Corporate Control, Corporate Power*. Cambridge: Cambridge University Press.

Higham, John. 1963. *Strangers in the Land*. New York: Atheneum.

Hodge, Robert W.; Donald J. Treiman; and Peter H. Rossi. 1966. "A Comparative Study of Occupational Prestige." In *Class, Status and Power*, edited by Reinhard Bendix and Seymour Martin Lipset. 2d ed. New York: Free Press.

Hodge, Robert W., and Donald Treiman. 1968. "Class Identification in the United States." *American Journal of Sociology* 73:535–47.

Hodges, Harold M. 1964. *Social Stratification: Class in America.* Cambridge, Mass.: Schenkman.

Hodgson, Godfrey. 1975. "Do Schools Make a Difference?" In *The Inequality Controversy: Schooling and Distributive Justice,* edited by D. M. Levine and M. J. Bane. New York: Basic Books.

Hollingshead, August B. 1949. *Elmtown's Youth.* New York: John Wiley & Sons.

————. 1950. "Cultural Factors in the Selection of Marriage Mates." *American Sociological Review* 15:619–27.

Hollingshead, August B., and Frederick Redlich. 1958. *Social Class and Mental Illness: A Community Study.* New York: John Wiley & Sons.

Horan, Patrick M. 1978. "Is Status Attainment Research Atheoretical?" *American Sociological Review* 43: 534–41.

Howe, Louise Kapp. 1977. *Pink Collar Workers.* New York: G. P. Putnam's Sons.

Hunter, Floyd. 1953. *Community Power Structure: A Study of Decision Makers.* Copyright 1953, Chapel Hill: University of North Carolina Press. By permission of the publisher.

Hurn, Christopher J. 1978. *The Limits and Possibilities of Schooling.* Boston: Allyn & Bacon.

Inkeles, Alex, and Peter H. Rossi. 1956. "National Comparisons of Occupational Prestige." *American Journal of Sociology* 61:329–39.

Jackman, Mary. 1979. "The Subjective Meaning of Social Class Identification in the United States." *Public Opinion Quarterly* 43:443–62.

Jackson, Elton F., and P. J. Burke. 1965. "Status and Symptoms of Stress: Additive and Interaction Effects." *American Sociological Review* 30:556–64.

Jackson, Elton F., and Richard F. Curtis. 1968. "Conceptualization and Measurement in the Study of Social Stratification." In *Methodology in Social Research,* edited by Herbert M. Blalock, Jr., and Ann B. Blalock. New York: McGraw-Hill.

Jaher, Frederic Cople, ed. 1968. *The Age of Industrialization in America.* New York: Free Press.

Janowitz, Morris. 1971. *The Professional Soldier: A Social and Political Portrait.* 2d ed. New York: Free Press.

————. 1976. *The Social Control of the Welfare State.* New York: Elsevier.

Jefferson, Thomas. 1821. "Autobiography." In *The Life and Selected Writings of Thomas Jefferson,* edited by Adrienne Koch and William Peden. New York: Modern Library, 1944.

Jencks, Christopher. 1980. "Structural versus Individual Explanations of Inequality: Where Do We Go From Here?" *Contemporary Sociology* 9: 762–67.

Jencks, Christopher, et al. 1972. *Inequality: A Reassessment of the Effect of Family and Schooling in America.* © 1972 by Basic Books, Inc. By permission of Basic Books, Inc., Publishers, New York.

————. 1979. *Who Gets Ahead?* New York: Basic Books.

Jones, Alfred W. 1941. *Life, Liberty and Property.* Philadelphia: Lippincott.

Kadushin, Charles. 1966. "Social Class and the Experience of Ill Health." In *Class, Status and Power,* edited by Reinhard Bendix and Seymour Martin Lipset. 2d ed. New York: The Free Press.

366

Kahl, Joseph A. 1953. "Educational and Occupational Aspirations of Common Man Boys." *Harvard Educational Review* 23:186–203.

————. 1957. *The American Class Structure.* 1st ed. New York: Rinehart.

Kahl, Joseph A., and James A. Davis. 1955. "A Comparison of Indexes of Socio-Economic Status." *American Sociological Review* 20:317–25.

Kalleberg, Arne L., and Larry J. Griffin. 1980. "Class, Occupation and Inequality in Job Rewards." *American Journal of Sociology* 85:731–68.

Kanter, Rosabeth Moss. 1977. *Men and Women of the Corporation.* Copyright © 1977 by Rosabeth Moss Kanter. By permission of Basic Books, Inc., Publishers, New York.

Karabel, Jerome, and A. H. Halsey, eds. 1977. *Power and Ideology in Education.* New York: Oxford University Press.

Kassalow, Everett. 1978. "How Some European Nations Avoid U.S. Levels of Industrial Conflict." *Monthly Labor Review* 101 (April):97.

Kaysen, Carl. 1957. "The Social Significance of the Modern Corporation." *American Economic Review* 47: 311–19.

Keller, Suzanne. 1963. *Beyond the Ruling Class.* New York: Random House.

Keniston, Kenneth, et al. 1977. *All our Children: The American Family under Pressure.* New York: Harcourt Brace Jovanovich.

Kerr, Clark, and Abraham Siegel. 1954. "The Interindustry Propensity to Strike—An International Comparison." In *Industrial Conflict,* edited by Arthur Kornhauser et al. New York: McGraw-Hill.

Knoke, David. 1976. *Change and Continuity in American Politics.* Baltimore: Johns Hopkins University Press.

Koenig, Thomas. 1980. "Corporate Support for Political Contribution Disclosure." Unpublished paper presented at the American Sociological Association, New York.

Koenig, Thomas; Robert Gogel; and John Sonquist. 1979. "Models of the Significance of Interlocking Directorates." *American Journal of Economics and Sociology* 38: 173–86.

Kohn, Melvin L. 1959. "Social Class and Parental Values." *American Journal of Sociology* 64:337–51.

————. 1969. *Class and Conformity: A Study in Values.* Homewood, Ill.: Dorsey Press.

————. 1976. "Interaction of Social Class and Other Factors in the Etiology of Schizophrenia." *American Journal of Psychiatry* 133:2:179–80. Copyright, 1976, The American Psychiatric Association.

————. 1977. *Class and Conformity.* 2d ed. Chicago: University of Chicago Press.

Kolko, Gabriel. 1962. *Wealth and Power in America.* New York: Praeger Publishers.

————. 1969. *The Roots of American Foreign Policy.* Boston: Beacon Press.

Komarovsky, Mirra. 1946. "The Voluntary Associations of Urban Dwellers." *American Sociological Review* 11: 689–98.

————. 1962. *Blue Collar Marriage.* New York: Vintage Books.

Kotz, Nick. 1979. *Hunger in America: The Federal Response.* New York: The Field Foundation.

Ladd, Everett C., and Charles D. Hadley. 1978. *Transformations of the American Party System.* 2d ed. New York: W. W. Norton.

Landecker, Werner S. 1981. *Class Crystallization.* New Brunswick, N.J.: Rutgers University Press.

Langerfeld, Steven. 1981. "To Break a Union." *Harpers* 262 (May):16–21.

Laslett, John M., and Seymour Martin Lipset, eds. 1974. *Failure of a Dream?*

Essays in the History of American Socialism. New York: Anchor Books.

Laumann, Edward O. 1966. *Prestige and Association in an Urban Community.* Indianapolis: Bobbs-Merrill.

_____. 1973. *Bonds of Pluralism: The Form and Substance of Urban Social Networks.* New York: John Wiley & Sons.

Lavin, David; Richard Alba; and Richard Silberstein. 1981. *Right vs. Privilege: The Open Admissions Experiment at the City University of New York.* New York: Free Press.

Laws, Judith Long. 1979. *The Second X: Sex Role and Social Role.* New York: Elsevier.

Leggett, John C. 1968. *Class, Race, and Labor: Working-Class Consciousness in Detroit.* New York: Oxford University Press.

LeMasters, E. E. 1975. *Blue-Collar Aristocrats: Life Styles at a Working-Class Tavern.* Madison: University of Wisconsin Press.

Lenski, Gerhard. 1954. "Status Crystallization: A Non-Vertical Dimension of Social Status." *American Sociological Review* 19:405–13.

_____. 1966. *Power and Privilege: A Theory of Social Stratification.* New York: McGraw-Hill.

Levin, Henry M. 1977. "A Decade of Policy Developments in Improving Education and Training." In *A Decade of Federal Antipoverty Programs* edited by Robert H. Haveman. New York: Academic Press.

Levine, Donald M., and Mary Jo Bane, eds. 1975. *The "Inequality" Controversy: Schooling and Distributive Justice.* New York: Basic Books.

Levitan, Sar A. 1980. *Programs in Aid of the Poor for the 1980s.* 4th ed. Baltimore: Johns Hopkins University Press.

Levitan, Sar A.; Garth L. Mangum; and Ray Marshall. 1976. *Human Resources and Labor Markets.* New York: Harper & Row.

Levitan, Sar A., and Robert Taggart. 1976. *The Promise of Greatness.* Cambridge, Mass.: Harvard University Press.

Lewis, Oscar. 1966. "The Culture of Poverty." *Scientific American* 215 4:19–25.

Lewis, Sinclair. 1922. *Babbitt.* New York: Harcourt Brace Jovanovich.

Liebow, Elliot. 1967. *Talley's Corner: A Study of Negro Streetcorner Men.* Boston: Little, Brown.

Link, Arthur S., and William Cotton. 1973. *American Epoch.* Vol. I. 4th ed. New York: Alfred A. Knopf.

Lipset, Seymour Martin. 1960. *Political Man.* New York: Doubleday.

_____. 1981. *Political Man.* Expanded Edition. Baltimore: Johns Hopkins University Press.

Lipset, Seymour Martin, and Reinhard Bendix. 1959. *Social Mobility in Industrial Society.* Berkeley: University of California Press.

Lipsky, David. 1981. *Essentials of Collective Bargaining.* Englewood Cliffs, N.J.: Prentice Hall.

Litwack, Leon, ed. 1962. *The American Labor Movement.* Englewood Cliffs, N.J.: Prentice Hall.

Lord, Walter. 1955. *A Night to Remember.* New York: Henry Holt.

Lorwin, Lewis L. 1933. *The American Federation of Labor.* Washington, D.C.: The Brookings Institution.

Louis, Arthur M. 1968. "America's Centimillionaires." *Fortune* 77 (May): 152–57.

_____. 1973. "The New Rich of the 1970's." *Fortune* 88 (September): 170–75, 230, 232, 236, 238, 242.

_____. 1979. "In Search of the Elusive Big Rich." *Fortune* 99 (February): 92–104.

Lubell, Samuel. 1956. *The Future of Ameri-*

can Politics. 2d ed. Garden City, N.Y.: Doubleday Anchor.

Lundberg, Ferdinand. 1968. *The Rich and the Super-Rich*. New York: Lyle Stuart.

————. 1975. *The Rockefeller Syndrome*. Secaucus, N.J.: Lyle Stuart.

Lynd, Robert S., and Helen Merrell Lynd. 1929. *Middletown*. New York: Harcourt Brace Jovanovich.

————. 1937. *Middletown in Transition*. New York: Harcourt Brace Jovanovich.

Maccoby, Michael. 1976. *The Gamesman*. New York: Simon & Schuster.

Madison, James (with Alexander Hamilton and John Jay). 1787. *The Federalist Papers*. New York: New American Library. 1961.

Malbin, Michael. 1979. "Campaign Financing and the Special Interests." *Public Interest*, no. 56 (Summer):3–42.

Malkiel, Burton, and Judith Malkiel. 1973. "Male/Female Pay Differentials in Professional Employment." *American Economic Review* 63:693–705.

Manis, Jerome G., and Bernard N. Meltzer. 1954. "Attitudes of Textile Workers to Class Structure." *American Journal of Sociology* 60:30–35.

Marquand, John P. 1949. *Point of No Return*. Boston: Little, Brown.

Marx, Karl. 1979. *The Marx-Engels Reader*, edited by Robert C. Tucker. 2d ed. New York: W. W. Norton.

McClendon, McKee J. 1977. "Structural and Exchange Components of Vertical Mobility." *American Sociological Review* 42:56–74.

————. 1980. "The Missing Link in the Process of Getting Ahead." *Contemporary Sociology* 9:758–62.

Miller, Herman P. 1971. *Rich Man, Poor Man*, Rev. ed. New York: Thomas Y. Crowell.

Miller, S. M. 1960. "Comparative Social Mobility." *Current Sociology* 9:1–89.

Miller, S. M., and Frank Reissman. 1961. "The Working Class Sub-Culture. A New View." *Social Problems* 9:86–97.

Mills, C. Wright. 1951. *White Collar*. New York: Oxford University Press.

————. 1956. *The Power Elite*. New York: Oxford University Press.

————. 1968. "Comment on Criticism." In *C. Wright Mills and the Power Elite*, edited by G. William Domhoff and Hoyt B. Ballard. Boston: Beacon Press.

Mincer, J., and S. Polachek. 1974. "Family Investments in Human Capital: Earnings of Women." *Journal of Political Economy* 82:575–608.

Mintz, Beth. 1975. "The President's Cabinet, 1897–1972." *Insurgent Sociologist* 5 (3):131–49.

Mosca, Gaetano. 1939. *The Ruling Class*. New York: McGraw-Hill.

Moses, Stanley, ed. 1975. "Planning for Full Employment." *Annals of American Academy of Political and Social Science* 418: March.

Moynihan, Daniel P., ed. 1969. *On Understanding Poverty: Perspectives from the Social Sciences*. New York: Basic Books.

Moynihan, Daniel P. 1973. *The Politics of a Guaranteed Income: The Nixon Administration and the Family Assistance Plan*. New York: Random House.

Mueller, Charles, et al. 1980. "Symposium on Featherman and Hauser, Opportunity and Change." *Contemporary Sociology* 9:4–16.

Müller, Susan. 1978. "Industrial Structure and Low-Level Earnings: A Re-examination of the Meritocratic Model." Unpublished Ph.D. thesis, Cornell University.

Müller, Walter, and Kurt Mayer, eds. 1973. *Social Stratification and Career Mobility*. The Hague: Mouton.

Nagle, John. 1977. *System and Succession: The Social Bases of Political Elite Recruitment*. Austin: University of Texas Press.

Naples, Michele. 1981. "Industrial Conflict and Its Implications for Productivity Growth." *American Economic Review* 71:36–41.

National Advisory Commission on Civil Disorders. *Report.* (The Kerner Report). 1968. Washington, D.C.: U.S. Government Printing Office.

Neugarten, Bernice. 1949. "The Democracy of Childhood." In *Democracy in Jonesville*, edited by W. Lloyd Warner. New York: Harper & Row.

Nie, Norman H.; Sidney Verba; and John R. Pedrocik. 1976. *The Changing American Voter.* Cambridge, Mass.: Harvard University Press.

Nock, Steven L., and Peter H. Rossi. 1978. "Ascription versus Achievement in the Attribution of Family Social Status." *American Journal of Sociology* 84:565–90.

NORC (National Opinion Research Center). 1953. "Jobs and Occupations: A Popular Evaluation." In *Class, Status, and Power*, edited by Reinhard Bendix and Seymour M. Lipset. 1st ed. Glencoe, Ill.: Free Press.

————. 1978. *General Social Surveys, 1972–1978: Cumulative Codebook.* Chicago: University of Chicago Press.

Oaxaca, Ronald. 1973. "Male-Female Wage Differentials in Urban Labor Markets." *International Economic Review* 14:693–709.

Okun, Arthur M. 1975. *Equality and Efficiency: The Big Tradeoff.* Washington D.C.: The Brookings Institution.

Ornati, Oscar. 1966. *Poverty Amidst Affluence.* New York: Twentieth Century Fund.

Orshansky, Mollie. 1965. "Counting the Poor: Another Look at the Poverty Profile." *Social Security Bulletin V* 28, no. 1.

————. 1974. "How Poverty is Measured." In *The Sociology of American Poverty*, edited by Joan Huber and H. Paul Chalfant. Cambridge, Mass.: Schenkman.

Ossowski, Stanislaw. 1963. *Class Structure in the Social Consciousness.* New York: Free Press.

Paglin, Morton. 1979. "Poverty in the United States." *Policy Review* 8:7–24.

Papanek, Hanna. 1973. "Men, Women and Work: Reflections on the Two-Person Career." *American Journal of Sociology* 78:852–72.

Parenti, Michael. 1968. "Immigration and Political Life." In *The Age of Industrialization in America*, edited by Frederic Cople Jaher. New York: Free Press.

Pareto, Vilfredo. 1935. *Mind and Society.* New York: Harcourt Brace Jovanovich.

Parkin, Frank. 1970. *Class, Inequality and Political Order: Social Stratification in Capitalist and Communist Countries.* New York: Praeger Publishers.

Pechman, Joseph A., ed. 1977. *Setting National Priorities: The 1978 Budget.* Washington, D.C.: The Brookings Institution.

Pechman, Joseph A., and Benjamin A. Okner. 1974. *Who Bears the Tax Burden?* Washington, D.C.: The Brookings Institution.

Pen, Jan. 1971. *Income Distribution.* London: Allen Lane.

Pennings, Johannes. 1980. *Interlocking Directorates.* San Francisco: Jossey-Bass.

Persell, Caroline Hodges. 1977. *Education and Inequality.* New York: Free Press.

Pessen, Edward, ed. 1974. *Three Centuries of Mobility in America.* Lexington, Mass.: D.C. Heath.

Piore, Michael J. 1977. "The Dual Labor Market and Its Implications." In *Problems in Political Economy: An Urban Perspective*, edited by David M. Gordon. 2d ed. Lexington, Mass.: D. C. Heath.

Piven, Frances Fox, and Richard A. Cloward. 1971. *Regulating the Poor: The Functions of Public Welfare.* New York: Pantheon Books, a division of Random House, Inc.

Plotnick, Robert D., and Felicity Skidmore. 1975. *Progress Against Poverty.* New York: Academic Press.

Polsby, Nelson. 1970. "How to Study Community Power: The Pluralist Alternative." In *The Structure of Community Power,* edited by Michael Aiken and Paul E. Mott. New York: Random House.

Pomper, Marlene Michels, ed. 1981. *The Election of 1980.* Chatham, N.Y.: Chatham House.

Projector, Dorothy S., and Gertrude S. Weiss. 1966. *Survey of Financial Characteristics of Consumers.* Washington, D.C.: Federal Reserve System.

Rainwater, Lee. 1965. *Family Design: Marital Sexuality, Family Size, and Contraception.* Chicago: Aldine.

_____. 1970. *Behind Ghetto Walls.* Chicago: Aldine.

_____. 1974. *What Money Buys.* New York: Basic Books.

Redfield, Robert. 1947. "The Folk Society." *American Journal of Sociology* 52:293–308.

Rehberg, Richard A., and Evelyn R. Rosenthal. 1978. *Class and Merit in the American High School.* New York: Longman.

Rein, Martin, and Lee Rainwater. 1977. "The Welfare Class and Welfare Reform." Family Policy Notes No. 4. Cambridge, Mass.: Joint Center for Urban Studies, MIT, Harvard.

_____. 1980. "From Welfare State to Welfare Society." Cambridge, Mass.: Joint Center for Urban Studies, MIT, Harvard.

Reiss, Albert. 1961. *Occupations and Social Status.* Glencoe, Ill.: Free Press.

Reissman, Leonard. 1954. "Class, Leisure and Participation." *American Sociological Review* 19:74–84.

Reynolds, Reid. 1979. "Profiles: A Nation of Paper Pushers." *American Demographics* 1:42.

Rhodes, Albert; Albert J. Reiss, Jr.; and Otis Dudley Duncan. 1965. "Occupational Segregation in a Metropolitan School System." *American Journal of Sociology* 70:682–94.

Riesman, David. 1953. *The Lonely Crowd: A Study of the Changing American Character.* New Haven, Conn.: Yale University Press.

Ritter, Kathleen, and Lowell Hargens. 1975. "Occupational Positions and Class Identifications of Married Women." *American Journal of Sociology* 80:934–48. Reprinted by permission of The University of Chicago Press.

Ritzer, George. 1977. *Working: Conflict and Change.* 2d ed. Englewood Cliffs, N.J.: Prentice Hall.

Roberts, Steven V. 1978. "Social Mobility Found Key to U.S. Views on Class." *New York Times,* April 24.

Rose, Arnold M. 1967. *The Power Structure: Political Process in American Society.* New York: Oxford University Press.

Rose, Richard, ed. 1974. *Electoral Behavior: A Comparative Handbook.* New York: Free Press.

Rose, Stephen, and Dennis Livingston. n.d. "Social Stratification in the U.S." (Wall Chart.) Baltimore: Social Graphics.

Rosenberg, Sam, and Thomas E. Weisskopf. 1981. "A Conflict Theory Approach to Inflation in the Post-War U.S. Economy." *American Economic Review* 81:42–47.

Ross, Howard, 1968. "Economic Growth and Change in the United States Under Laissez-Faire: 1870–1929." In *The Age of Industrialization in America,* edited by Frederic Cople Jaher. New York: Free Press.

Ross, Stanford G. 1979. "Social Security: A Worldwide Issue." *Social Security Bulletin* 42, no. 8 (August):3–10.

Rothman, Stanley, et al. 1976. *European Society and Politics: Britain, France and Germany.* New York: West Publishers.

Rubin, Lillian Breslow. 1976. *Worlds of Pain: Life in the Working-Class Family.* Copyright © 1976 by Lillian Breslow Rubin. By permission of Basic Books, Inc., Publishers, New York.

Rubin, Z. 1968. "Do American Women Marry Up?" *American Sociological Review* 5:750–60.

Ryan, William. 1971. *Blaming the Victim.* New York: Random House.

Salzman, Harold, and G. William Domhoff. 1979. "Corporations, the Civic Sector, and Government: Do they Interlock?" *Insurgent Sociologist* 9 (2–3): 121–35.

Sanota, Gian Singh. 1978. "Theories of Personal Income Distribution: A Survey." *Journal of Economic Literature* 16:1–55.

Sawhill, Isabel. 1973. "The Economics of Discrimination Against Women: Some New Findings." *Journal of Human Resources* 8:386–887.

Schiller, Bradley R. 1980. *The Economics of Poverty and Discrimination.* 3d ed. Englewood Cliffs, N.J.: Prentice-Hall.

Schreiber, E. M., and G. T. Nygreen. 1970. "Subjective Social Class in America: 1945–1968." Reprinted from *Social Forces* 45:348–56. Copyright © The University of North Carolina Press.

Serrin, William. 1981. "Where are the Pickets of Yesteryear?" *New York Times,* May 31.

Sewell, William H., and Robert M. Hauser. 1975. *Education, Occupation and Earnings.* New York: Academic Press.

Sewell, William H.; Robert M. Hauser; and David L. Featherman, eds. 1976. *Schooling and Achievement in American Society.* New York: Academic Press.

Sewell, William H., and Vimal P. Shah. 1977. "Socioeconomic Status, Intelligence, and the Attainment of Higher Education." In *Power and Ideology in Education,* edited by Jerome Karabel and A. H. Halsey. New York: Oxford University Press.

Sheehan, Susan. 1976. *A Welfare Mother.* Boston: Houghton Mifflin.

Simkus, Albert. 1978. "Residential Segregation by Occupation and Race." *American Sociological Review* 43:81–93.

Simmons, Robert G., and Morris Rosenberg. 1971. "Functions of Children's Perceptions of the Stratification System." *American Sociological Review* 36: 235–49.

Smelser, Neil J., and Seymour Martin Lipset, eds. 1966. *Social Structure and Mobility in Economic Development.* Chicago: Aldine.

Smith, James D. 1974. "The Concentration of Wealth, 1969." *Review of Income and Wealth.* Series 20 (June): 143–70.

———. 1975. *The Personal Distribution of Income and Wealth.* New York: Columbia University Press.

Smith, James D., and Stephen D. Franklin. 1974. "New Dimensions of Economic Inequality: The Concentration of Personal Wealth, 1922–1969." *American Economic Review* 64:162–67.

Smith, James, and Finis Welch. 1977. "Black-White Male Wage Ratios: 1969–1970." *American Economic Review* 67:323–38.

Solow, R. M. 1960. "Income Inequality Since the War." In *Post-War Economic Trends in the United States,* edited by R. E. Freeman. New York: Harper & Row.

Sorokin, Pitirim. 1927. *Social Mobility.* New York: Harper & Row.

Spenner, K. I., and D. L. Featherman. 1978. "Achievement Ambitions." *Annual Review of Sociology* 4:373–420.

Srole, Leo, et al. 1962. *Mental Health in the Metropolis: The Midtown Manhattan Study*. Vol. I. New York: McGraw-Hill.

Stack, Carol B. 1974. *All Our Kin*. New York: Harper & Row.

Stendler, Celia Burns. 1949. *Children of Brasstown: Their Awareness of the Symbols of Social Class*. Urbana: University of Illinois Press.

Stolzenberg, Ross M. 1978. "Bringing the Boss Back In: Employer Size, Employee Schooling, and Socioeconomic Achievement." *American Sociological Review* 43:813–28.

Stromberg, Ann H., and Shirley Harkess, eds. 1978. *Women Working*. Palo Alto, Calif.: Mayfield.

Sundquist, James L., ed. 1969. *On Fighting Poverty: Perspectives from Experience*. New York: Basic Books.

Sweezy, Paul. 1968. "Power Elite or Ruling Class?" In *C. Wright Mills and the Power Elite*, edited by G. William Domhoff and Hoyt B. Ballard. Boston: Beacon Press.

Szymanski, Albert. 1978. *The Capitalist State and the Politics of Class*. Cambridge, Mass.: Winthrop.

Taussig, F. W., and C. S. Joslyn. 1932. *American Business Leaders*. New York: Macmillan.

Terkel, Studs. 1974. *Working: People Talk About What They Do All Day and How They Feel About It*. New York: Avon.

Thompson, E. P. 1963. *The Making of the English Working Class*. New York: Vintage.

Thurow, Lester C. 1975. *Generating Inequality*. New York: Basic Books.

————. 1980. *The Zero-Sum Society: Distribution and the Possibilities for Economic Change*. New York: Basic Books.

Thurow, Lester, and Robert Lucas. 1972. *The American Distribution of Income: A Structural Problem*. Washington, D.C.: U.S. Government Printing Office.

Townsend, Peter. 1979. *Poverty in the United Kingdom*. Berkeley: University of California Press.

Treiman, Donald. 1977. *Occupational Prestige in Comparative Perspective*. New York: Academic Press.

Troy, Leo, and Neil Sheflin. 1980. "Survival in the Service Economy." *Executive* 6 (Spring):18–22.

Truman, David. 1971. *The Governmental Process: Political Interests and Public Opinion*. 2d ed. New York: Alfred A. Knopf.

Tuchman, Gaye, ed. 1974. *The TV Establishment: Programming for Power and Profit*. Englewood Cliffs, N.J.: Prentice-Hall.

Tumin, Melvin M. 1955. "Rewards and Task Orientations." *American Sociological Review* 20:419–23.

————. 1966. "Some Principles of Stratification: A Critical Analysis." In *Class, Status, and Power*, edited by Reinhard Bendix and Seymour Martin Lipset. 2d ed. New York: Free Press.

Turner, Jonathan H., and Charles E. Starnes. 1976. *Inequality: Privilege and Poverty in America*. Santa Monica, Calif.: Goodyear.

Tyree, Andrea; Moshe Semyonov; and Robert W. Hodge. 1979. "Gaps and Glissandos: Inequality, Economic Development and Social Mobility." *American Sociological Review* 44: 410–24.

Udry, Richard J. 1967. "Marital Instability by Race and Income, Based on 1960 Census Data." *American Journal of Sociology* 72:673.

U. S. Bureau of the Census. 1975. *Historical Statistics of the United States. Bicentennial Edition. 2 Parts*.

————. 1976a. *Current Population Reports*. Series P-20. No. 295.

————. 1976b. *Current Population Reports*. Series P-60. No. 105.

————. 1976c. *Bicentennial Statistics. Pocket Data Book, U.S.A.*

————. 1977. *Social Indicators, 1976.*

————. 1978. *Statistical Abstract of the United States: 1978.*

————. 1979. *Statistical Abstract of the United States: 1979.*

————. 1980a. *Money Income of Families and Persons in the United States: 1978 Current Population Reports.* P-60, No. 123.

————. 1980b. *Social Indicators, III.*

————. 1980c. *Statistical Abstract of the United States: 1980.*

————. 1980d. *Characteristics of the Population Below the Poverty Level: 1978. Current Population Reports.* Series P-60, No. 124.

U.S. Department of Labor. 1969. *Three Standards of Living for an Urban Family of Four Persons, Spring 1967.* Bulletin 1570-5.

————. 1972. *Three Budgets for an Urban Family of Four Persons, 1969.* Supplement to Bulletin 1570-7.

————. 1977. *Educational Attainment of Workers.* March 1977. Special Labor Force Report 209.

————. 1978. *Employment and Training Report to the President.*

————. 1979. *Monthly Labor Review.* August:29–30.

————. 1981a. *Employment and Earnings.* 28 (January).

————. 1981b. *Educational Attainment of Workers, March 1979.* Special Labor Force Report 240.

U.S. Internal Revenue Service (IRS). 1973. *Statistics of Income, 1969. Personal Wealth Estimated from Tax Returns.*

————. 1981. *Statistics of Income, 1978. Individual Income Tax Returns.*

U.S. Law Enforcement Assistance Administration. 1976. *Criminal Victimization in the United States, 1975.*

U.S. News & World Report. 1980. "Election Tab: A Billion Dollars and Rising." 89:32–33.

U.S. Office of Management and Budget. *Social Indicators, 1973.*

U.S. Public Health Service. 1977. *Health of the Disadvantaged.* Chart Book.

U.S. Senate, 1978. Committee on Finance, Subcommittee on Public Assistance. Hearings on Income-Maintenance Experiments, November 15–17.

Useem, Michael. 1980. "Corporations and the Corporate Elite." *Annual Review of Sociology* 6:41–77.

Uyeki, Eugene S. 1964. "Residential Distribution and Stratification, 1950–1960." *American Journal of Sociology* 69:491–98.

Valentine, Charles A. 1968. *Culture and Poverty: Critique and Counter-Proposals.* Chicago: University of Chicago Press.

Vanfossen, Beth Ensminger. 1977. "Sexual Stratification and Sex-Role Socialization." *Journal of Marriage and the Family* 39:563–74.

Veblen, Thorstein. 1934. *The Theory of the Leisure Class.* New York: Modern Library. (First published 1899.)

Vidich, Arthur, and Joseph Bensman. 1960. *Small Town in Mass Society.* Garden City, N.Y.: Anchor Books.

Wachtel, Howard M., and Charles Betsey. 1972. "Employment at Low Wages." *Review of Economics and Statistics* 44:121–29.

Walton, John. 1970. "A Systematic Survey of Community Power Research." In *The Structure of Community Power*, edited by Michael Aiken and Paul E. Mott. New York: Random House.

Warner, W. L., and J. C. Abegglen. 1955. *Occupational Mobility in American Business and Industry, 1925–1952.* Minneapolis: University of Minnesota Press.

374

Warner, W. Lloyd, and Paul S. Lunt. 1941. *The Social Life of a Modern Community*. New Haven, Conn.: Yale University Press.

Warner, W. Lloyd, et al. 1949a. *Democracy in Jonesville*. New York: Harper & Row.

————. 1949b. *Social Class in America*. Chicago: Science Research Associates.

————. 1963. *Yankee City*. Abridged Edition. New Haven, Conn.: Yale University Press.

Wattenberg, Ben J. 1974. *The Real America*. Garden City. N.Y.: Doubleday.

Weber, Max. 1946. *From Max Weber: Essays in Sociology*, edited by H. H. Gerth and C. Wright Mills. New York: Oxford University Press.

Who's Who in America. 1980. 41st ed. Chicago: Marquis.

Who's Who in American Politics. 1979. 7th ed. New York: Bowker.

Whyte, William Foote. 1943. *Street Corner Society*. Chicago: University of Chicago Press.

Whyte, William H. 1952. *Is Anybody Listening?* New York: Simon & Schuster.

Wilkins, Arthur. 1956. "The Residential Distribution of Occupation Groups in Eight Middle-Sized Cities of the United States in 1950." Unpublished Ph.D. thesis, University of Chicago.

Williams, Robin M., Jr. 1970. *American Society: A Sociological Interpretation*. 3d ed. New York: Alfred A. Knopf.

Wilson, William J. 1980. *The Declining Significance of Race*, 2d ed. Chicago: University of Chicago Press. Reprinted by permission of The University of Chicago Press.

Wolfinger, Raymond E. 1973. *The Politics of Progress*. Englewood Cliffs, N.J.: Prentice-Hall.

Wool, Harold. 1976. *The Labor Supply for Lower-Level Occupations*. New York: Praeger Publshers.

Wright, Erik Olin, and Luca Perrone. 1977. "Marxist Class Categories and Income Inequality." *American Sociological Review* 42:32–55.

Zeitlin, Maurice. 1974. "Corporate Ownership and Control: The Large Corporation and the Capitalist Class." *American Journal of Sociology* 79: 1073–1119.

————. 1977. *American Society, Inc.* 2d ed. Chicago: Rand McNally.

————. 1980. *Classes, Class Conflict and the State*. Cambridge: Winthrop.

Zweigenhaft, Richard. 1975. "Who Represents America?" *Insurgent Sociologist* 5 (3):119–30.

Index of names

Index of subjects

This book has been set VIP in 10 and 9 point Palatino, leaded 2 points. Chapter numbers and chapter titles are set in 36 and 24 point Palatino Bold respectively. The size of the type page is 30 by 47 picas overall.